SUSTAINABLE MARKETING

A HOLISTIC APPROACH

MARK PETERSON

Los Angeles | London | New Delhi
Singapore | Washington DC | Melbourne

Los Angeles | London | New Delhi
Singapore | Washington DC | Melbourne

SAGE Publications Ltd
1 Oliver's Yard
55 City Road
London EC1Y 1SP

SAGE Publications Inc.
2455 Teller Road
Thousand Oaks, California 91320

SAGE Publications India Pvt Ltd
B 1/I 1 Mohan Cooperative Industrial Area
Mathura Road
New Delhi 110 044

SAGE Publications Asia-Pacific Pte Ltd
3 Church Street
#10-04 Samsung Hub
Singapore 049483

Editor: Matthew Waters
Assistant editor: Jasleen Kaur
Assistant editor, digital: Sunita Patel
Production editor: Tanya Szwarnowska
Copyeditor: Martin Noble
Proofreader: Tom Bedford
Indexer: Melanie Gee
Marketing manager: Abigail Sparks
Cover design: Francis Kenney
Typeset by: C&M Digitals (P) Ltd, Chennai, India
Printed in the UK

Library of Congress Control Number: 2021930811

British Library Cataloguing in Publication data

A catalogue record for this book is available from the British Library

ISBN 978-1-5264-9464-1
ISBN 978-1-5264-9463-4 (pbk)

At SAGE we take sustainability seriously. Most of our products are printed in the UK using responsibly sourced papers and boards. When we print overseas we ensure sustainable papers are used as measured by the PREPS grading system. We undertake an annual audit to monitor our sustainability.

To Cindy, my wife, who has always encouraged me in my writing of this book. She inspires me and others each day in her fight against the most aggressive type of brain tumor – glioblastoma.

Brief Contents

Detailed Contents

Author Biography

Dr. Mark Peterson is Professor of Marketing and Sustainable Business Practices at the University of Wyoming where he teaches marketing classes across all levels (undergrad, MBA, and PhD). He received his PhD in marketing from Georgia Tech in 1994 and joined the University of Wyoming faculty in Fall 2007. From 2016 to 2019, Mark served as editor of the *Journal of Macromarketing* – a journal that focuses on how marketing and society influence each other. He is a thought leader for how firms can integrate environmental and social concerns into their business decisions. Mark has lived and worked more than seven years overseas in Germany, South Korea, Turkey, France, and Canada. In the marketing research industry, he has served as a consultant on field-research projects for a variety of clients ranging from Fortune 500 companies to start-ups. His more than 50 refereed-publications have appeared in leading journals in marketing, innovation, and entrepreneurship.

Foreword

It is with great pleasure that I write this forward for the second edition of Sustainable Marketing, authored by Professor Mark Peterson. I recently retired from Virginia Polytechnic Institute & State University (Virginia Tech) in the US as an endowed professor of marketing in the Pamplin College of Business. I now maintain an academic position at North West University in South Africa as Extraordinary Professor in the WorkWell Research Unit of the Faculty of Economic and Management Sciences. Although I am officially retired from Virginia Tech, I maintain an academic position at Virginia Tech through my role as editor-in-chief of the *Journal of Macromarketing*. My predecessor was Professor Mark Peterson, author of this book. He had to step down from this position because of his wife's medical condition. He is one of the most seasoned educators of Macromarketing I have come to know over the years. Professor Peterson is not only a highly respected colleague in the marketing academy but also a scholar who epitomizes the best of human virtues – he is caring, compassionate, generous, and above all wise.

I served as Professor of Marketing at Virginia Tech for the last 41 years. In that role I taught many marketing-related courses. One course I cherished was Marketing and Society. For years I was unhappy with the teaching material available for my students for that course. I taught the course using a set of reading material from academic journals, mostly from the *Journal of Macromarketing*, plus other popular nonacademic books. This was until I discovered Professor Peterson's book on *Sustainable Marketing*. I was impressed with the book when I first examined it. It had topics matching the topics in my course syllabus such as marketing ethics, sustainable marketing, sustainable entrepreneurship, poverty alleviation, the stakeholder (as opposed to the shareholder) concept of business ethics, development of markets in poor countries, regulation of marketing practice through public policy, equity issues in marketing, and other issues of Macromarketing. I adopted Professor Peterson's book as the main textbook for my Marketing & Society course at Virginia Tech. My students loved the book. It was not only highly informative and educational but also entertaining and inspiring. Professor Peterson has a special gift, namely educating his readers at a level that they can all relate to. He speaks the language of college students by translating the academic concepts into layman's language that students easily digest. My students appreciated the many examples, cases, and illustrations throughout the book. I remember one student who, at one point, confessed that the book:

touched my soul. Because of the book and the Marketing & Society class, I now appreciate the big picture of how business should operate in society; that business has an important role to play in enhancing the quality of life of consumers; that government has an important role to play in regulating marketing practice; that business leaders must make enlightened decisions to serve the needs of all the stakeholders, not only the shareholders.

I was truly moved by her 'confession'. I must acknowledge that much of her learning of the important social issues of today's business learned in my Marketing & Society class is credited to Professor Peterson's book. It is truly an exemplary book.

The book is about Macromarketing, a subdiscipline within Marketing that addresses the interface between marketing practice and society. Macromarketing addresses issues related to the effects of marketing practice on society – the good, the bad, and the ugly. Macromarketing also addresses issues concerning how society shapes the development of marketing practice. Although the issues can be highly political, they certainly can be depoliticized by an objective and honest treatment of divergent points of view. Professor Peterson does this exquisitely. He informs, educates, and inspires without being political.

Happy reading. I am sure that you will find this book inspirational as many of my students did.

Joe Sirgy

Preface

I wrote this book to explain how businesses can benefit by taking a more holistic approach to the marketplace. Macromarketing – taking a systems view of the interplay between marketing and society – had a rich history of scholarship, with such accomplished scholars as Shelby Hunt, Terry Pavia, Andy Prothero, Cliff Shultz, and many others contributing meaningfully to understanding the role of marketing in society.

Since 2013, when the first edition of this book appeared as *Sustainable Enterprise: A Macromarketing Approach*, business persons have increasingly developed sustainability-oriented answers for how to approach new complexities of the marketplace that macromarketers have studied over the years. This new edition of the book is intended to help a new generation of business persons tap into the wisdom accrued in macromarketing scholarship over four decades. In this way, the book is about managerial macromarketing – how business can understand macromarketing concepts for application in marketplaces of the world.

In 2009 and 2010, I taught a new marketing and society course to MBA students at the University of Wyoming. Unlike other schools, *all* of the students had to take the course because it was required. This experience proved uniquely valuable, because with all students in the course many doubts and reservations about 'going green' were expressed by students. At the time, no books existed to address this issue of how to operate in the marketplace with a social conscience and achieve profits. I respectfully wrote the first edition of this book, as well as this edition, for those with reservations about sustainable business practices, so they could better understand how businesspersons could better serve as stewards in the world.

I believe most readers will find the contents of this book refreshingly different. Throughout the book, I have woven a theme of entrepreneurship – identifying and developing opportunities, regardless of the resources available. In this way, the book focuses on enterprise, rather than 'business as usual'. Part I presents and explains macromarketing as a valuable frame for understanding what is occurring in marketplaces today. Part II explains factors contributing to market dynamism today, such as empowered consumers, collaborative relationships, and globalization. Part III gives special attention to issues related to the natural environment. Part IV discusses issues related to equity, such as developing markets, and poverty alleviation.

Special new content in *Sustainable Marketing: A Holistic Approach* includes the following: (1) the UN's Sustainable Development Goals – in Chapter 4; (2) Greta Thunberg – profiled at the end of Chapter 8; (3) Black Lives Matter – discussed in the profile of Martin Luther

King, Jr. at the end of Chapter 2; and (4) COVID-19 – discussed in the first part of Chapter 5. Throughout the revision process, I made a special effort to include examples from the UK and the EU, as well as Asia and Africa in this process.

I am excited about new coverage in the book that allows readers to grasp a more complete picture of some market activities that have resulted in negative outcomes for societies. The opening vignette for each chapter titled 'Throwing Shade' features these. 'Throwing shade' is a slang term for casting a subtle but stinging insult. Some targets for shade include: (1) Juul, (2) fast fashion, (3) tax-dodging firms, (4) government corruption, (5) Facebook, (6) greenwashing, (7) Bitcoin's energy consumption, as well as (8) Golden Rice and GMOs. These vignettes allow readers to grasp a human aspect of markets in which some outcomes can be very controversial. Have fun discussing these!

Additionally, new 'Mavericks Who Made It' concluding each chapter now include mavericks from major corporations, as well as the nonprofit world. For example, Paul Polman former CEO of Unilever, and Myriam Sidibe formerly of Unilever and an advocate of hand-washing around the world are two of these mavericks. Some other mavericks from the nonprofit sector in this book include Dr Martin Luther King, Jr., prominent leader of the Civil Rights Movement that inspired the world, and Mother Teresa, founder of the Missionaries of Charity that established homes for caring for the poor in 139 countries of the world.

The 'Throwing Shade' vignettes and the concluding 'Mavericks Who Made It' profiles should lead readers to think more effectively about the content of the chapters and the role businesses and nonprofits have played in social change. Questions follow both the opening vignette and the Mavericks Who Made It profiles.

Because this book addresses timely issues in the environment of the firm, teachers can use it in a variety of courses, including Sustainable Marketing, Marketing and Society, Business and Society, and a forward-looking Marketing Strategy course. This book will match courses that carry 'sustainability' in the title.

Ancillary materials for instructors using this book will be posted at https://study.sagepub.com/peterson2e. These include: (1) PowerPoint slides, (2) instructor's manual, and (3) test bank.

I would like to thank Collin Krueger, my first and only research assistant on this revision. His two months of part-time work in 2020 lifted this book project and informed me about the myriad of sustainable business practices succeeding outside of North America in recent years.

I have also appreciated the encouragement of the College of Business at the University of Wyoming, and my colleagues in the Management and Marketing Department. As well, I give thanks for the thoughtful comments of each of the following who reviewed chapters and helped shape this book to become what it is now.

M. Joseph Sirgy, Virginia Polytechnic Institute & State University, USA

Elaine Thomson, Edinburgh Napier University, UK

Leo Wong, MacEwan University, Canada

I would also like to thank the team at SAGE Publishing UK for helping to make this project come to life. Publisher Matthew Waters encouraged pursuit of this second edition at crucial times in 2018 and 2019. His vision for how this book could boost learning about sustainability comes from his rich experience involved with textbook marketing. As a marketing academic, I salute him and his team for their abilities to change the world through marketing of the written word. Special thanks also go to Assistant Editor Jasleen Kaur and Production Editor Tanya Szwarnowska.

I thank my family for the time and encouraging gestures from my wife Cindy, and daughters Emily, Angela, and Rachel over my years in academia. You have made me sustainable in all my endeavors. That I was able to write this edition as my wife Cindy courageously battled cancer is our family's way of defying cancer. With God's enabling, we have continued to live our lives and to pursue our dreams.

Finally, this book is dedicated to all macromarketers – past, present, and future. Thank you for daring to take a 'big-picture view' of the marketplace and sharing it with others.

Online Resources

Sustainable Marketing, 2nd edition is accompanied by online resources for instructors to help support teaching. These resources are available at: https://study.sagepub.com/peterson2e.

FOR INSTRUCTORS

- Easily **integrate the chapters** into your weekly teaching with the **PowerPoint slides** provided.
- **Test students' understanding** of the content by using the **test bank** compiled by the author.

PART I

Macromarketing for Sustainable Marketing

1
TWENTY-FIRST-CENTURY MICRO AND MACRO ISSUES

Throwing Shade

Source: Photo by Guilherme Stecanella on Unsplash.

The Air in Big Cities

Today, more than half the world's population (55 percent) live in cities (Ritchie and Roser, 2018). By comparison, in 1960, only about one-third of the world's population lived in cities. Researchers studying the mass migration of populations from rural to urban areas predict that two-thirds of the world's populations will live in urban areas by 2050.

(Continued)

People living in cities tend to have higher incomes than those in rural areas, which results in lower levels of poverty (Robison, 2019). However, one of the costs for this benefit is dirtier air breathed by city dwellers.

In an effort to reduce fuel consumption and CO_2 emissions from vehicles in the 1990s after the Kyoto Protocol climate change agreement was signed in 1987, governments in Europe encouraged vehicle manufacturers to produce and sell more vehicles with diesel engines (Sullivan et al., 2004). As a result, Europe embraced the diesel engine. Until the mid 1990s, diesels accounted for less than 10 percent of the car fleet in Europe, but in 2015 they accounted for more than half of the car fleet (Vidal, 2015). Across the EU, there are more than 50 million diesels – compared to 1.6 million in 1998 (Robison, 2019). Only 7 million diesels are registered in the US.

While diesels produce 15 percent less CO_2 than gasoline or petrol engines, they produce 22 times the particulates (which penetrate the lungs, brain and heart). A secondary pollutant – ozone – forms when these pollutants react with sunlight. Diesels also emit four times more nitrogen dioxide (NO_2) which inflames the lungs, heart and brain, and appears to be a contributor to cancer, dementia, as well as respiratory illnesses (McCarthy, 2018).

For years, concerns about climate change overrode the concern about air quality among environmental groups, and government and businesses. Auto manufacturers produced more diesels from the mid-1990s, while governments kept the diesel price below that of petrol. In the UK, France and Germany, owners of autos emitting lower amounts of CO_2 paid lower taxes – thus, these government incentivized citizens to buy more diesels. Diesels comprised 32 percent of new vehicle sales in 2018 in the UK (down from 50 percent in 2014) (Statista, 2020).

In 2015, researchers at West Virginia University in the US conducted independent tests of vehicle emissions and found evidence that diesels made by Volkswagen AG spewed 40 times more NO_2 than in regulatory lab tests. Volkswagen later admitted it had intentionally created software to show its autos met emission standards (McCarthy, 2018). Volkswagen AG has paid $33 billion in fines and settlements. However, in subsequent research, Adac – Europe's largest motoring organization – showed that diesel cars from Renault, Nissan, Hyundai, Citroen, Fiat, and Volvo released more than 10 times the level of NO_2 than shown in tests conducted by the EU (The Guardian, 2015).

Now, the harmful effects of NO_2 and particulates are more evident. Doctors now are confronting the need to educate patients about the dangers of air pollution similar to how they did for smoking cigarettes (Robison, 2019). A study conducted by the research consultancy CE Delft for the European Public Health Alliance in 2018 asserted that diesels accounted for 83 percent of the €66.7 billion costs of air-pollution from traffic (both health and nonhealth) in the EU in 2016 (CE Delft, 2018).

Since 2015 when Volkswagen's rigging of emission tests became known, diesels' share of new car registrations across Europe has dropped markedly from 50 percent to 36 percent (McCarthy, 2018). (By comparison, only 3 percent of cars in the US were diesels in 2015 (Chambers and Schmitt, 2015).)

Twenty-four European cities have adopted diesel bans that will go into effect by 2030 (Behrmann, 2019). For example, diesels will be banned from Paris and Madrid in 2024.

Questions to Consider

- What factors led to having 25 times more diesels in Europe over a 20-year time span from 1998 to 2018?
- Do you think the European leaders who signed the Kyoto Protocol in 1997 to address climate change thought there would be such a surge in the adoption of diesels as there was?
- Are you surprised that there was so much more adoption of diesel cars in Europe than in the US?
- What does this story from Europe say about the effectiveness of government interventions in markets? About consumer preferences in transportation modes? About business' role in auto markets?

CHAPTER OVERVIEW AND LEARNING OBJECTIVES

This chapter will give a historical summary of how we have come to the place where using a macromarketing lens can reduce risk and help identify opportunities for entrepreneurially oriented firms. A macromarketing lens can be useful because it helps us understand the interplay between marketing and society. This chapter will specifically focus on the practice of sustainability and the seven reasons business is more mindful of society today, discuss what marketing and macromarketing are and why they are important, and conclude with a series of examples showing the implications of macromarketing for entrepreneurship.

The chapter concludes with the story of Ray Anderson, founder of Interface, Inc. – a manufacturer of carpet tiles – as a maverick firm that made it. Interface transformed itself in the late twentieth century to become a leader in developing sustainable business practices. After this chapter, you should be able to answer the following questions:

- What are the seven reasons businesses are more mindful of society today?
- What is the definition of markets? Marketing? Society?
- What is macromarketing, and why is it important?
- What is the emerging view of capitalism and its five types of capital (manufactured, financial, natural, human, and social)?
- What role do entrepreneurs play in moving the marketplace toward generating social and environmental gains?
- How can social responsibility be integrated into a sustainable enterprise?

SUSTAINABILITY AND THE TRIPLE BOTTOM LINE

What Is Driving the Turn for Businesses to Be Mindful of Society?

Although theories explaining the roots of Conscious Capitalism are only now emerging, several likely contributing factors can currently be identified (Hollender and Breen, 2010). The seven reasons business is more mindful of society are discussed below.

Reason 1: Technological Improvements

Improvements in technology, especially telecommunications technology, increasingly give power to individual consumers and citizens. In a networked world, accountability is more timely and powerful. Savitz and Weber (2006) call this the 'Age of Accountability'. Accordingly, externalities generated by firms, such as the variety and breath of pollutants produced, no longer go unrecognized. On the other hand, firms that embrace stewardship of the planet and concern for people in their pursuit of profits are more likely to be recognized and rewarded for such an approach to business. Some firms are going beyond separate reports for financial and nonfinancial results (e.g., corporate social responsibility or sustainability reports) and combining these into a single integrated report (Eccles and Krzus, 2010). At the same time, they are using the internet to offer more detailed results to all of their stakeholders and to improve their level of dialogue and engagement with a wider set of stakeholders. Wall Street financial analysts have begun to take note because such integrated reporting adds noticeable value to the company. Contributions to sound business practices and a more sustainable society make enlightened firms more appealing to many stakeholders – including shareholders.

Reason 2: Rising Prosperity and Environmental Values

Second, rising prosperity in countries allows quality-of-life and environmental concerns to move higher in the priorities of consumers and citizens. This is happening all over the world. With higher income, individuals give higher priority to self-expression and to quality of life. There is a strong association between prosperity and environmental values (Inglehart and Welzel, 2005). The increased interest in environmentally friendly products can be seen in the demand for hybrid cars. Toyota anticipated this trend and introduced its Prius hybrid vehicle years before other competing firms (Bonini, Mendonca, and Oppenheim, 2006).

Reason 3: Awareness of Earth's Limits

Rising awareness of the planet's limits suggest that new forms of production and consumption need to be developed. *New York Times* Foreign Affairs columnist and Pulitzer Prize winning author, Thomas L. Friedman (2008) characterizes the Earth as a hot, flat, and crowded planet. Friedman means that the Earth is characterized by (a) a changing global climate, (b) a developing world that is rapidly beginning to use many of the competitive capabilities of the developed world that were once thought to be nonexistent in a developing county, and (c) a developing world with a burgeoning population in urban areas. These all suggest that we are all more vulnerable to volatility and major social, economic, and political change than we previously perceived we were in the twentieth century. The rise of China and India as economic powers suggests that demand for energy will continue to be pressed. As this happens, energy prices will move higher. Many of the sources for fossil fuels, such as Venezuela and Saudi Arabia, seem to be poised for difficult transitions in political leadership in the future. In sum, there is an increasing awareness that a take–make–waste approach within societies needs to be changed.

Reason 4: Firms Can 'Do the Right Thing'

Firms have gained increased ability to 'do the right thing'. The success of the voluntary standards movement in business has given businesses a way to improve process quality in both manufacturing and service businesses. Total Quality Management (TQM) has led to ISO 9000 certification in manufacturing, as well as to ISO 14000 in environmental protection. The ISO 9001:2008 standard provides a tested framework for taking a systematic approach to managing the organization's processes using satisfaction ratings of those inside the firm as well as of customers and partners outside the firm. This is done so the firm and its partners can consistently turn out a product that satisfies customers' expectations. Alternatively, the ISO 14000 family addresses various aspects of environmental management to identify and control the environmental impact of a firm's activities, products, or services, and to improve continually its environmental performance. Using these ISO frameworks for management practice, multinational enterprises have located factories and offices all over the world that can produce at world-class standards. Highly efficient processes have become synonymous with high-quality products and eco-efficiency. The increased power of firms to self-monitor is leading them to pursue eco-effective approaches to business where harm to the environment is avoided.

Reason 5: Intangible Assets

Firms realize the increasing importance of intangible assets. *Fortune* estimates that 75 percent of the total value of the average US corporation can be attributed to the patents, copyrights, employee knowledge, and creativity, as well as customer goodwill they carry. In other words, physical stuff matters much less than what might have been previously thought. In such a world for business, having a purpose beyond earning a profit matters much. It enables a firm to attract the most talented and committed employees who will eventually make a difference in the competitive marketplace for the customers of the firm. It also attracts customers who will use their capabilities to make the firm a success through repeated purchases, involvement in new product development efforts of the firm, as well as word-of-mouth communication about the firm and its offerings.

Reason 6: Nongovernmental Organizations

The rise of nongovernmental organizations (NGOs) bring a voice to those previously unheard in issues related to the citizenship of businesses. This is a powerful and new regulatory force. Those with concerns not adequately addressed by business or government increasingly establish an NGO to focus the attention of individuals, public institutions (local, national, and transnational), businesses, and other NGOs. A web presence also boosts fundraising and marshalling support from NGO constituents. Over the last 15 years, NGOs have proliferated to number in the millions and have grown to become the eighth largest economy in the world with operating budgets totaling more than $1 trillion (Hollender and Breen, 2010). During this time, trust in NGOs has steadily risen, while faith in business has declined as a result of debacles at Enron, WorldCom, and the Economic Meltdown of 2008 (Bonini et al., 2006).

Astute firms these days are working with select NGOs rather than resisting them. For example, global specialty coatings company AkzoNobel (the largest decorative coatings company in the world employing more than 24,000 with annual sales over $6 billion) collaborated with the UK-based NGO Forum for the Future to develop its successful Ecosure paints under the Dulux brand name. These Ecosure paints have a 30 percent lower carbon footprint than regular paints (AkzoNobel, 2011). AkzoNobel was then able to apply its new knowledge for producing lower carbon paints to its other brands of paint.

Reason 7: Branding as a Social Phenomenon

Firms who consider branding to be much more of a phenomenon of society, culture, and politics – rather than one of the individual's mind – are better able to identify opportunities for innovation in branding (Holt and Cameron, 2010). Branding success for diverse firms such as Nike, Starbucks, Patagonia, Vitaminwater, Fat Tire, and the Freelancer's Union suggest that ideological opportunities emerge during major historical changes. Here, the brand can offer a superior cultural expression for consumers.

For example, Nike took the focus off elite athletes succeeding in their chosen athletic domains (the typical advertising approach of its rivals) and put it on the human dimension of competition and life. In the 1970s and 1980s, diminished expectations for US society was widespread as a result of the failure of the Vietnam War, the distrust of government resulting from the Watergate scandal, and the stagflation that plagued the economy for years. In such a milieu of anxiety, Nike articulated an anti-authoritarian theme in advertising by showing Nike athletes in ordinary training scenes showing their tenacious dedication in going it alone and embracing total responsibility for one's success. Nike led the trend for jogging by celebrating ordinary people pursuing their own training. Nike's 'Just Do It' advertising theme developed a cultural mythology about Nike and showed women, people of poverty, and minority athletes succeeding on the level playing field of sport despite the societal discrimination they faced off the field. Here, Nike offered a broader view of competition that suggested that overcoming barriers, such as racism, sexism, and global poverty, is much more impressive than success in sport. This myth used the imperfections of society as a foil to boost Nike's association with those manifesting combative solo will-power and succeeding on their own terms in life.

Table 1.1   Reasons for business turning to be more mindful of society

1. Technological improvements
2. Rising prosperity and environmental values
3. Awareness of Earth's limits
4. Firms can 'do the right thing'
5. Increasing importance of intangible assets
6. Rise of nongovernmental organizations
7. Branding as a social phenomenon

Implications

In sum, society might have been an afterthought for executive teams primarily focused on regulatory compliance in the twentieth century. However, twenty-first-century realities related to the seven reasons businesses have become more mindful of society have brought a heightened sensitivity to societal issues. Today, firms must recognize that society expects more from business; firms that act as if other people matter and protect and restore the ecosystem are more likely to achieve profits in a reliable way into the future (Werbach, 2009). Increasingly, firms are implementing a triple-bottom-line or balanced scorecard that includes firms' economic, environmental, and social results (Savitz and Weber, 2006). Leaders of firms are giving more consideration to society not because these leaders are suddenly more moral in their approach, rather, because they are more pragmatic. If these leaders do not anticipate the changing landscape of societal issues, they will not be able to avoid problems that will damage their firms' reputations, and they will not be able to guide their firms to successful positioning relative to their competitors in the future.

MARKETS
Defining Markets

What comes to mind when you hear the word 'markets?' A shopping center? A bazaar? A financial market like the floor of the New York Stock Exchange? eBay? Monster.com? All of these are examples of markets. A market is a social arena where firms, their suppliers, customers, workers, and governments interact (Fligstein and Dauter, 2007). Sociologists offer valuable perspectives on what are not markets. For example, unstructured, one-shot, anonymous social exchange is not a market. If you sell your laptop to a friend, a market was not part of this transaction. Sociologists give further definition to markets as being social arenas where repeated exchanges occur between buyers and sellers under a set of formal and informal rules. Importantly, markets depend on governments, laws, and social norms about activity in the marketplace.

Because human beings are self-oriented, distortions in the marketplace inevitably occur; often these issues are resolved with the assistance of the government, making it an integral part of the market system. For example, product failure raises problems for market actors. Determining responsibility among the set of suppliers, retailers, and customers can be problematic. Was the product misused by the customer, or was the product inherently flawed in manufacturing or damaged later in storage at the retailing store? The first aspect a sociology of markets (the study of marketing systems) suggests is that market actors will develop social structures to reconcile problems they encounter in exchange, competition, and production. Frequently, laws and government enforcement comprise these social structures, although mediation and arbitration can also be employed. However, if the actors involved cannot reach agreement, then the government must intervene – usually through a court system.

The Role and Influence of Government on Markets

The debate over government's role in the market has long been debated. However, rather than get bogged down in the debate, this section will focus on the effect government has on the market. Specifically, this section will focus on the relationship between government market interaction and monopolies, the idea of the free market, and how changing markets demand a changing government role.

Unfettered Markets and Monopolistic Market Actors

The self-orientation of humans can also lead to distortions in the structure of markets. Monopoly formation (one dominant actor, such as the Standard Oil Company for oil refining in the early 1900s) is an example of a market structure that has been deemed to be deleterious to the proper functioning of markets. The Sherman Anti-Trust Act of 1910 led to the breakup of Standard Oil into smaller competing firms (Peritz, 2008). Additionally, some actors in markets seek to restrain trade as when collusion among sellers in a market occurs. Scottish philosopher Adam Smith observed that in the eighteenth century, whenever rival merchants met, even for sharing a meal together, the interests of their customers were harmed. Higher prices to customers were one way such collusion might be manifested. Economists since Smith have generally agreed with his assertion. Today, governments define acceptable relations between producers or merchants so that competition will drive the activity of markets.

Adam Smith and the Idea of a Free Market

Although buyers and sellers are the most salient actors in markets, history suggests that the self-orientation of humans will inevitably lead to disputes between actors in markets. This implies that in modern societies, governments will need to intervene so that markets can continue to function properly. In the time of Adam Smith, the British government sponsored companies in markets, such as the East India Company. Additionally, laws existed to forbid citizens from changing their jobs. Smith made the case that markets free of such government interventions would thrive and eventually perform a remarkable task for society – increasing the material well-being of society. In other words, if citizens and firms were allowed to own property, if labor were allowed to move freely in the job market, and if the rule of law prevailed, the market-based system for society would efficiently allocate the material resources (land, labor, and capital) (Smith, 2000). Buyers would be able to buy what they desired, while sellers would be able to sell what they desired. Today, China, still ruled by a Communist regime, struggles with the role of the government in markets because of its state-owned enterprises (almost always grossly inefficient entities). Even though the United States does not have China's state-owned enterprise system, US society still struggles with the role of government in markets.

Today, 'free market' is a portmanteau term that means different things to different people. To listen to some commentators in today's media, a free market means a market totally free and clear of any government intervention. No regulation and no taxes. But what about the government's role when market actors encounter problems? Because trust among market actors is so crucial to the proper functioning of markets, when such trust drops, social structures like the government are needed for conflict resolution, as well as for ensuring that safe products and services are provided in markets. So, in effect, a market totally free and clear of government intervention is like a unicorn – easy to draw on paper, but never actually seen walking around anywhere on Earth. No one has found fossil evidence for unicorns, either.

For those who propose strict and powerful regulation of markets, the accompanying increase in laws and licenses required to conduct business might slow market activity and increase the cost of doing business to levels that would render markets ineffective. If the issue is one of regulation of business, imagine if the World Cup soccer matches played every four years used no referees for the matches. It would not take long for the honor system to break down and chaos to reign on the field. On the other hand, if the World Cup organizers misguidedly saw the outcomes of matches as so important that they employed 1,000 referees and put them on the field for each match, it would be likely that the match would not succeed because of the interference of so many referees. An important decision for society is not whether there will or will not be involvement of the government in markets, since there will be government involvement for dispute resolution and for the regulation of safety in goods and services. Rather, the issue is to what degree governments will be involved in markets.

Changing Markets, Changing Government Roles

The variety and dynamism of markets suggests that the role of government must be defined for markets and then redefined over time. For example, new markets are likely to be more fragile than stable established markets. This can be seen in the new markets for renewable energy where government involvement includes incentives (outright subsidies and tax exemptions to producers, as well as the government's support of university research into wind energy production). On the other hand, more established markets such as those for automobiles have attracted different forms of government involvement over the years. In World War II, the US government steered production at auto plants toward the war effort. In the 1960s, the US government imposed requirements for seat belts in cars. In the 1970s and 1980s, protectionist tariffs to protect the US auto industry were endorsed by both the US automakers and unions. Such calls were tempered later but still persist today. In sum, markets change, and the government's role in markets changes, as well. For example, if government regulation and programs cannot keep up with the rapidly changing market, a society will be at greater risk for harmful marketing distortions. More will be said about this in Chapter 2.

MARKETING
Changing Definitions of Marketing

Surprising to some, marketing's definition has changed twice since 1985. The American Marketing Association (AMA), the leading organization for marketers, includes a unit for marketing scholars. The AMA has committed to revisiting the definition of marketing every five years. In 2007, a task force led by Don Lehmann from Columbia University responded to widespread calls across academia to revise the definition of marketing. The 2004 revision had changed the 1985 definition of marketing and had focused exclusively on the firm, even to the extent of excluding the role of middlemen in marketing systems (such as channels of distribution), as well as institutions (such as retailers and wholesalers) (Hunt, 2010). After thorough reworking, Lehmann's task force agreed that the definition of marketing would be more inclusive and explicitly feature (a) the delivery of offerings, (b) institutions, and (c) society-at-large as a beneficiary of marketing. The current definition reads, 'Marketing is the activity, institutions and set of processes for creating, communicating, delivering and exchanging offerings that have value for customers, clients, partners and society-at-large' (AMA Marketing Power, 2007, para. 2).

'Activity' implies that marketing can be done by individuals: entrepreneurs, as well as citizens (Hunt, 2010). 'Institutions' means that manufacturers, wholesalers, retailers, advertising agencies, distributors, and marketing research agencies engage in marketing. Additionally, aggregated systems of institutions in a society participate in marketing, such as channels of distributions, networks, and supply chains. 'Customers' refers to the exchange partners of for-profit firms. 'Clients' refers to the exchange partners of non-profit organizations (such as the American Cancer Society or Civil Air Patrol). 'Partners' refers to those in collaborative networks and alliances that are increasingly evident in contemporary markets. Finally, 'society-at-large' refers to the ultimate beneficiary of

Table 1.2   Defining terms for understanding contemporary markets and marketing approaches

1. **Markets –** social arenas where repeated exchanges occur between buyers and sellers under a set of formal and informal rules.
2. **Marketing –** the activity, institutions, and set of processes for creating, communicating, delivering, and exchanging offerings that have value for customers, clients, partners, and society-at-large.
3. **'Little m' approach –** the tactical aspects of marketing at the firm level, such as product development, promotion, distribution, and pricing.
4. **'Big m' approach –** how tactical marketing for a firm feeds into managerial decision making that affects other realms of the firm, such as operations, human resources, information systems, finance, and accounting.
5. **'Biggest M' approach –** macromarketing – taking a systems view of the interplay between marketing and society. Firms that take such an approach can be characterized as taking a five-capital marketing **approach that articulates** a firm's tactical marketing moves with the other functional areas of the firm in order to achieve triple-bottom-line success.

marketing – society. Marketing benefits society by contributing to increases in productivity and economic growth (Hunt, 2010). Here, society refers to the large-scale community that normally furnishes security and a national identity for its members (Dictionary. com, 2011).

MACROMARKETING
The 'Biggest M'

A marketing management course at most universities strives to impart how firms would consider customers of the firm in their planning. This might be termed the 'little m' approach (dealing with the tactical aspects of marketing, such as product development, promotion, distribution, and pricing).

In the first term at the Harvard Business School, MBA students take their first marketing course. The objectives of the course are to demonstrate the role of marketing in the company and to explore the relationship of marketing to other functions. Harvard marketing professor John Gourville reports that this marketing course takes a bigger view of marketing – how marketing feeds into managerial decision making that affects other realms of the firm, such as operations, human resources, information systems, finance, and accounting. Gourville calls this the 'big m' approach (Datar, Garvin, and Cullen, 2010).

In contrast to limiting the focus of marketing to the firm and its customers, macromarketing has focused on a higher level of aggregation. According to Hunt (2010, p. 14), macromarketing refers to the study of (a) marketing systems, (b) the impact of marketing systems on society, and (c) the impact of society on marketing systems. In other words, macromarketers have taken a systems view of the interplay between marketing and society. In this way, macromarketing can be understood to be the 'biggest M' approach.

Early Macromarketing: Socialism and Capitalism

Macromarketing was the early focus of the marketing discipline in the years 1900–1920 (Wilkie and Moore, 2003). Here, marketing scholars took concern with the value of marketing's distribution activities as these contribute to economic and growth in society. For example, the distribution of harvested corn shows how one product can create a large economy of scale. First, the farmer grows the crop and places it in his grain silo. Next, a truck comes from the grain buyer and unloads the silo. Afterward, the corn could change hands and be processed up to five more times: (a) between the grain buyer and the regional buyer, (b) between the regional buyer and a corn syrup processor, (c) between a processor and the Pepsi-Cola Company, (d) between Pepsi-Cola and a franchised bottler of Pepsi-Cola, and (e) between a bottler and a local convenience store. This total chain of exchanges would comprise the distribution activities for the corn that later became a sweetener in Pepsi sold at a local convenience store. By each actor performing its role in the distribution system, enormous economies of scale are realized with time and money saved by all. Imagine if the farmer had to take his corn and sell it as an ingredient at thousands of convenience stores. The time and expense would exhaust anyone. However, the market system that evolved on its own coordinates and links the efforts of a diverse array of actors. In the end, much is accomplished for relatively little expense.

Although today there is general acceptance of the place for legal and culturally acceptable marketing practices, at the time of marketing's development, it was hard for scholars to understand why middlemen seemed to proliferate as economies grew. At the same time, a parallel effort was underway on the other side of the world to pursue a socialist approach to organizing the production and distribution of society's goods and services. The approach was led by Communists in the Soviet Union, and it proposed no private ownership of the means of production in society and central planning of all public activities in society.

In such a socialist system, independent middlemen were eliminated, and so were field sales people. Independent wholesalers, retailers, advertising agencies, distributors, and marketing research agencies were eliminated as well. These actors in the aggregate marketing systems of a free society such as the United States were the focus of the first marketing scholars who attempted to understand and explain the plusses and minuses of having such intermediaries in the aggregate marketing system.

Today, it is readily understandable that intermediaries do not just handle material goods. They move information about market conditions and possible wants and needs of customers in many directions in their respective marketing systems. In many ways, such information is more valuable than the goods moved today because it can be used to 'create, communicate, deliver and exchange' streams of future offerings that will be valuable to customers. In general, socialism as instituted in the Soviet Union ignored the invisible flows needed to allow an aggregate system of provisioning for a society to work beyond a rudimentary level. For example, prices were not allowed to float in markets (what Friedrich Hayek termed socialism's 'fatal conceit') (Hayek, 1988). Information about consumer demand was not detected, interpreted, organized, and moved to the right places in the system for timely action.

Second-Wave Macromarketing Pioneers

After the first wave of interest in macromarketing in 1900–1920, a second wave of interest began in the 1970s. This was partly a reaction to many scholars' bedazzled interest in firm-centric marketing issues ('little m' for the most part). In the mid-twentieth century, marketing underwent a major refocus on managerial issues for the firm (Nason, 2006). With the success of a neoliberal approach in economics promoting the deregulation of state-regulated indus-tries in the 1970s and 1980s, macromarketing and its concerns about externalities of operating businesses (such as environmental degradation and product safety) were less interesting to mar-keters and marketing scholars taking the firm as the focus of analysis.

Perhaps, as a result of their contrarian ways, a group of independently thinking scholars formed the *Journal of Macromarketing* in 1982 to encourage further research focused on the 'big-gest M'. Over the course of its first 20 years, the *Journal of Macromarketing* adopted an eclectic style that more than anything else offered thinking about marketing set in context. The ele-ments of such context and important questions macromarketing scholars have pursued since then include:

- *Quality of Life*: How does marketing affect material conditions of life, as well as happiness of individuals?
- *Marketing Ethics and Distributive Justice*: Why do marketers behave the way they do? Are the outcomes of marketing just and fair for all in society?
- *Global Policy and the Environment*: What role does marketing have in transnational phenomena, such as environmental degradation, financial crises, water and food shortages, and health problems?
- *Competition and Markets*: What happens in society when firms compete? What is fair competition?
- *Marketing and Development*: What does marketing mean for the current and future state of poor countries?

The traditional dimensions of macromarketing are recast as the acrostic 'QUEENSHIP' in Figure 1.1. This acrostic suggests the versatility and ability to project power that the queen carries on the chess board. In military strategy, the infantry carries a similar designation as 'the queen of battle'. By seeking to understand the interplay of marketing and society (the 'biggest M'), more sustainable approaches to conducting business come into view for the twenty-first-century business.

When reviewing the contextual dimensions listed, these are increasingly influential matters for leaders of firms today. Times have changed. Now and in the future, firms seeking success in the marketplace must go beyond the 'little m' and 'the big m' – the highly controllable aspects of doing business for the firm. Globalization, instantaneous communication in a networked world, the new reality of risk in financial markets, planetary limits, and the imperative of firms to increase profits by marketing to the poorest consumers of the world make it critical for today's CEOs to understand the 'biggest M'.

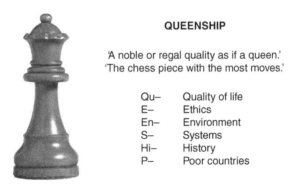

QUEENSHIP

'A noble or regal quality as if a queen.'
'The chess piece with the most moves.'

Qu–	Quality of life
E–	Ethics
En–	Environment
S–	Systems
Hi–	History
P–	Poor countries

Figure 1.1   Traditional dimensions of macromarketing

The 'Biggest M' and Business Acumen

According to Ram Charan, a long-time counselor to CEOs of major corporations around the world, business acumen is linking an insightful assessment of the external business landscape with the keen awareness of how money can be made (Charan, 2006). This managerial skill is the most important for the future success of a firm. If the firm's assessment of the external landscape – how patterns of converging and diverging trends fit together – is not correct, then the firm's competitive positioning will be wrong. In short, if the firm's leaders do not do well in the 'biggest M', the firm could be severely disadvantaged in the future.

A Wide-Angle Lens Is Needed to Perceive and Pursue the 'Biggest M'

Amory Lovins is one of the leading proponents of properly valuing nature and people when doing business. He does not use the word 'sustainability' because he believes it means many things to different people (Hopkins, 2009). Lovins uses a wide lens to view capitalism and does not only see capitalism as the productive use of financial and physical capital (money and goods), but he also sees two additional forms of valuable capital – people and nature. In firms across 30 sectors of the economy, Lovins and his team from the Rocky Mountain Institute (RMI) have seen that firms that use all four kinds of capital 'make more money, do more good, and have more fun'.

Despite some widespread (but dated) thought among business executives that taking an approach to business with the four types of capital in mind would result in higher costs, Lovins' RMI projects with industry (totaling more than $30 billion) for new facilities or for retrofitting of existing facilities typically save approximately 30–60 percent on energy consumption. This significant benefit comes with a two- to three-year payback – one of the highest return, lowest risk investments possible. Pursuing such a green course for a firm means that a firm turns waste into profit. Wastes and emissions are reduced because they are designed out of the systems of the firm. This quickly leads to enormous innovation and competitive advantage. Dow Chemical invested $1 billion to save $9 billion in energy expenses. United Technologies cut its energy intensity 45 percent in five years.

Similar to Lovins' view of capitalism, a five-capital view of capitalism partitions the 'people' dimension in Lovins' view into two kinds of capital – human capital (talents, abilities, and focused interests of people) and social capital (the willingness and capability of people to cooperate with others). Firms pursuing a five-capital approach to capitalism become poised to take advantage of other benefits that increasingly elude firms with a two-capital approach to capitalism. Five-capital firms, which use a triple-bottom-line or a balanced scorecard, are the kind of businesses that people want to do business with because people feel good about supporting such firms. More and more, environmental and social blunders lead to devastating setbacks for firms that are perceived as violating a tacit license agreed upon by the public and the firm (Rousseau's idea of the social contract). According to Lovins, networked activists today scare the leaders of two-capital firms more than regulators do.

Table 1.3 Comparison of the two- and five-capital views of capitalism

Two-capital view of capitalism	Five-capital view of capitalism
Financial capital (money)	Financial capital (money)
Physical capital (goods)	Physical capital (goods)
	Human capital (talents, abilities, and focused interests of people)
	Social capital (willingness and capability of people to cooperate)
	Natural capital (sum total of the ecological systems that support life and cannot be produced by human activity)

In sum, five-capital firms see the landscape of business in a more complete way and are positioned to maneuver across the landscape of business in a more nimble fashion than two-capital firms. Firms that take such an approach can be characterized as taking a five-capital marketing approach that articulates a firm's tactical marketing moves with the other functional areas of the firm in order to achieve triple-bottom-line success. Such success means earning profits while doing the best for the planet and people (and communities). In this way, five-capital firms manifest the broad view of markets and marketing characteristics of macromarketing – the 'biggest M.' Lovins points to the importance of the 'biggest M' in the following way:

> If you are a company that sticks to its knitting, minds its own business and doesn't pay attention to what's happening in the world around you, you're probably riding for a fall and missing some big business opportunities, because in any business I can think of – 30 sectors we've worked in so far – it's the hidden connections between your business and other opportunities that you think are well outside your boundaries that create extraordinary opportunity or risk, depending on the way you handle them. This is another way of saying that you need a really wide-angle lens. You can still have a sharp focus, but you sure need peripheral vision.
>
> (Hopkins, 2009, p. 40)

Implications of the 'Biggest M' for Entrepreneurship

The 'biggest M' influences all areas of marketing – including entrepreneurship. Specifically, the 'biggest M' has influenced entrepreneurs by causing them to focus on more than the two-capital approach, considering factors such as the environment. Through the following examples from both the for-profit and nonprofit sectors, we can see how the 'biggest M' is influencing modern entrepreneurs.

The Major Influencing Factor: A Focus on More than Two Types of Capital

Using a two-capital approach, economists who have dared to consider entrepreneurship have defined entrepreneurship 'as any entity, new or existing, that provides a new product or service or that develops and uses new methods to produce or deliver existing goods and services at lower cost' (Baumol, Litan, and Schramm, 2007, p. 3). As one can see, the focus in such a definition is on financial and physical capital. However, by using a wider lens and a five-capital approach, entrepreneurship can be seen as not just developing (a) new goods and services, or (b) using new methods for providing existing goods and services at lower cost, but also developing goods/services and methods of production and delivery that (c) improve the well-being of the environment or (d) society-at-large. In other words, entrepreneurs pursuing the accumulation of capital beyond the traditional two capitals (manufactured and financial capital) innovate to improve stocks of environmental, human, and social capital, as well as that of manufactured and financial capital.

For decades, Ray Anderson of Interface, Inc. was a two-capital entrepreneur. The story of the mid-course correction at Interface to try becoming an environmentally neutral company is one of primarily becoming a three-capital company (physical, financial, and natural). Along the way, Interface improved the human capital of its employees who worked in cleaner and less toxic industrial settings, as well as developed a transcendent purpose for the firm. This purpose is showing industry and business all over the world how a firm like Interface can transform itself to be a leader in sustainable business practices. In sharing its story and its knowledge with others, Interface accumulates social capital, which is the willingness of others (individuals and institutions) to cooperate with each other in productive endeavors. Interface's efforts also lift society, making individuals and institutions better able and more willing to cooperate in solving sustainability challenges for modern businesses. General Electric's strategic decision in 2003 to pursue opportunities in emerging markets with its more fuel-efficient and low-emission equipment shows signs of two-capital entrepreneurship possibly evolving into a five-capital one. Increasingly, though, new entrepreneurial ventures are emerging that pursue business with a five-capital approach instead of a two-capital one.

Examples of Five-Capital Entrepreneurial Endeavors

For-Profit Ventures

Canadian Tom Szaky dropped out of Princeton University in 2002 to lead TerraCycle, a company he founded to make useful products out of garbage (Szaky, 2009). Szaky remembers an economics class he took at Princeton that taught Milton Friedman's theory that the sole purpose of a firm is to deliver profit to shareholders. 'That just took the wind out of my sails,' Szaky said (Ryan, 2019). 'Yes, you want your company to be profitable so you know it has a future. But I think the purpose of a business is what it does – what service it provides, what product it makes, how it helps people, society, planet. I wanted to create a business that puts those things first.'

TerraCycle began by producing organic fertilizer that was, in fact, worm castings (excrement) packaged in used soda bottles (Szaky, 2009). Called by *Inc.* the 'coolest little start-up in America,' TerraCycle is a privately-owned business headquartered in Trenton, New Jersey that posted $33 million in revenues in 2018 – up from $24 million the previous year (Ryan, 2019).

TerraCycle's purpose is to eliminate the idea of waste. This is done by recycling (turning chip bags into a trash can) or upcycling (turning juice pouches into a pencil case). TerraCycle lists hundreds of products it has made and sold, which range from fashion accessories, like over-the-shoulder bags and backpacks made from juice packs stitched together, to toys, like kites made from Oreo packages. Many of these products are available at major retailers such as Walmart and Whole Foods Market.

Called by some an 'eco-capitalist company' (Szaky, 2009), TerraCycle has created national recycling systems for previously nonrecyclable items. The process starts by offering collect programs (many of them free) to gather waste and then converting the collected waste into a wide range of products and materials. More than 80 million people collect waste in 20 countries for TerraCycle, thereby diverting billions of pieces of waste from landfills.

TerraCycle launched a new program in 2019 called Loop that led major consumer products firms to redesign containers for their products to be more readily recycled (Ryan, 2019). Such firms include Unilever, Procter & Gamble, Clorox, Nestlé, Mars, Coca-Cola, and PepsiCo.

With the exception of countries ruled by dictators, it would be difficult to find any countries today that do not truly desire to see more entrepreneurial activity in their society because of contributions to the economic growth of the country. As a result of the disruption entrepreneurs tend to engender by introducing better ways of doing things, dictators instinctively oppose entrepreneurs and prefer the status quo. In open societies, successful entrepreneurship means more tax money for the government and less pressure to meet the well-being needs of members of society by income redistribution programs resented by many. Fueled by personal computers, mobile phones, and the internet, the democratization of entrepreneurship is well under way in countries around the globe (The Economist, 2009). China and India have certainly awakened to traditional, two-capital entrepreneurship (Khanna, 2007).

Not-for-Profit Ventures

Through mostly not-for-profit and NGOs, social entrepreneurs build or transform institutions to advance solutions to social problems, such as poverty, disease, environmental degradation, illiteracy, human rights abuses, and corruption (Bornstein and Davis, 2010). In these ways, social entrepreneurs pursue a different kind of entrepreneurship that is typically focused on boosting human, social, or natural capital.

Previously known as humanitarians, social entrepreneurs such as Florence Nightingale used an analytical mind with unrelenting persistence to transform the care of wounded British soldiers in the Crimean War of the nineteenth century in Eastern Europe (Bornstein, 2004). She pioneered what would become known as the profession of nursing.

Today, social entrepreneurs like Fábio Rosa of Brazil have helped bring electricity to parts of Brazil that had never experienced life with electricity (Bornstein, 2004). Rosa's 'Project

Light' succeeded in its very first attempt to raise the living standards of low-income rural families by taking cheap electricity to their homes and farms. He did this by using steel wire, which is much cheaper than copper wire. The first experiment took place in Palmares do Sul, a rural community in the southernmost Brazilian state, Rio Grande do Sul. As many as a million rural residents of the state have no electricity, refrigeration, indoor plumbing, water pumps for irrigation, or other common household and farm electric appliances (Ashoka, 2011).

Rosa's pilot project from 1984 to 1988 boosted the living standards for 400 rural families in Palmares and brought results far beyond his expectations. His low-cost electrification not only stopped the flow of rural residents to cities, but also it reversed the flow. A study two years after the project's implementation showed that one in every three beneficiaries was someone who returned from the city to resume living in his former rural area. This was in large part because of the newly affordable electric service (Bornstein, 2004).

'The moment they have better living conditions in their native rural areas, people return from the cities,' Rosa said. These results substantiate Rosa's contention that poor people are not lured to the city because it is better; rather, they are expelled from the countryside because it is unlivable. Given the means to live better, people stay near their rural roots. In the social change realized by Rosa's own engineering innovations related to simple electrification, and his effective work collaborating with government, business, and social institutions in Brazil, Rosa's story manifests some of the best qualities of social entrepreneurs today. As a result of his work, the quality of life for thousands of rural-dwelling Brazilians has improved dramatically.

Rosa has continued his social entrepreneurship by founding the Institute for the Development of Alternative Energy and Self-Sustainability (IDEAAS) which now focuses on solar power for rural communities (Ambientebrasil, 2019). One of the kits IDEAAS sells can supply energy for lighting a home, for recharging cell phones, for powering devices with USB input, and for electrifying a lamp that scares away bats.

More will be said about social entrepreneurs later (see Chapter 12), but what needs to be noted now about social entrepreneurs is (a) that their personal approach to business (which is often an extension of themselves) influences the business world and society's expectations of business, and (b) that an entrepreneur's success in creatively increasing capital stocks is usually ignored by traditional for-profit firms. As corporations increasingly seek profits in more challenging corners of a globalizing world, such as poor communities and those needing infrastructure improvements, they will increasingly learn from social entrepreneurs like Rosa who succeeded in these difficult settings first.

In the stories of their NGOs, social entrepreneurs often achieve a purpose for their endeavors that elude traditional two-capital firms. John Mackey, founder and Co-CEO of Whole Foods Market (one of the most profitable public food retailing business in the United States), looks beyond the accumulation of two capitals in the success of his business. Mackey explains:

I believe that business has a much greater purpose. Business, working through free markets, is possibly the greatest force for good on the planet today. When executed well, business increases prosperity, ends poverty, improves the quality of life, and promotes the health, and longevity of the world population at an unprecedented rate.

(Elkington and Hartigan, 2008, p. 54)

CONCLUSION

Businesses are more mindful of society today because of a changing environment for business. Technology improvements have shifted power to those in a knowledge economy who can harness the groundswell of information available on the internet. As a result, businesses have more forces of accountability for their actions, such as empowered consumers and NGOs. At the same time, society has become more affluent, more brand aware, and more concerned about stewardship of the environment. Additionally, new competitors are emerging from unexpected corners of the planet and increasingly from countries such as China and India. As a result, the macromarketing imperative has emerged in marketing strategy.

Savvy firms of the twenty-first century will need to apply a wide-angle lens to issues outside of the firm, so that the firm's leaders can make sense of these issues in a timely way to navigate the firm successfully into the future. In short, business acumen increasingly means considering macromarketing dimensions. Macromarketing – the biggest M – traditionally has focused on the six QUEENSHIP dimensions of Figure 1.1 (quality of life, ethics, environment, systems, history, and poor countries). When applying a wide-angle lens to issues outside the firm, marketing strategists and entrepreneurs do not have to begin from scratch. Happily, they can draw on the accumulated knowledge of more than 30 years of macromarketing research about these QUEENSHIP dimensions that address marketing systems and the interplay between marketing and society.

Reconceptualizations of capitalism are emerging in this new day for businesses when sustainable business practices are of keen interest to business persons and scholars. One of these new views of capitalism features a five-capital view of business instead of a traditional two-capital view (focused only on manufactured and financial capital). This view proposes that thriving businesses in the future will increasingly be characterized as seeking to accumulate five types of capital – (a) manufactured, (b) financial, (c) natural, (d) human, and (e) social.

QUESTIONS

1. What were surprises you encountered in reading Chapter 1?
2. What are 'little m,' 'big m,' and the 'biggest M?'
3. What is macromarketing?

4. What have been the interests of scholars during the first wave and second wave of macro-marketing?
5. What are the six dimensions of current macromarketing thought?
6. What is business acumen? How does it relate to the 'biggest M?'
7. What is the difference between two-capital firms and five-capital firms?
8. In your opinion, what would it take to reverse business becoming more mindful of society?
9. How have some entrepreneurs integrated the biggest M in their ventures? How have some industrialists?

Mavericks Who Made It

Major Mid-course Correction

Ray Anderson

Source: Interface.com

In many ways, Ray Anderson represented the best of American entrepreneurship and business in 1994. A former football player at Georgia Tech and a veteran of the carpet-manufacturing industry, Anderson launched his own company Interface, Inc. in 1973 to manufacture carpet tile (modular carpet) in LaGrange, Georgia. Just over 20 years later, Interface had become the world leader in carpet tiles with annual revenues exceeding $1 billion.

However, in August 1994, at the age of 60, Anderson found himself in a crisis when the staff from Interface Research Corporation (the research arm of Interface) asked him to talk to them about his environmental vision for the company. Customers of Interface from all over the world had begun asking sales representatives about Interface's environmental position and their efforts to preserve and protect the environment. Leaders within Interface had formed a task force to begin framing a response to these questions; however, these difficult questions could not be answered without the input of the CEO, so Anderson was invited to speak to the task force.

This request distressed Anderson because Interface was so oil-dependent at the time that he later admitted Interface could be thought of as an extension of the petrochemical industry:

> Well, frankly, I didn't have a vision, except 'obey the law, comply, comply, comply,' and I was very reluctant to accept the invitation. The idea that, while in compliance, we might be hurting the environment simply hadn't occurred to me. (Anderson, 1998)

Anderson finally accepted the invitation to address the task force and then embarked on three weeks of reading and soul searching to prepare himself. During this time, Paul Hawken's *The Ecology of Commerce* serendipitously wound up on his desk. In reading Hawken's book, Anderson faced the haunting truth that environments could be ruined by industrial activity – the same industrial activity that Interface had pursued from its inception.

> I read it and it changed my life. It hit me right between the eyes. It was an epiphany. I wasn't halfway through it before I had the vision I was looking for... Hawken's message was a spear in my chest that is still there. (Anderson, 1998)

Hawken, who had founded the highly successful gardening supply store Smith and Hawken, was a business person whose ideas penetrated deeply into Anderson. Hawken departed from many environmentalists by asserting that the only institution on the planet capable of leading humankind out of its current mess and grim future was, in fact, business and industry. Government always seemed to follow, rather than lead. Religious institutions offered only criticism of society's problems, as did colleges and universities. The media also filled itself with criticism rather than solutions.

Anderson's entire outlook on business changed in preparing for the talk he gave about an environmental vision for Interface to representatives from all of Interface's businesses from around the world. He admitted to all in attendance the dire situation that would result from continuing with a traditional approach to business focusing only on the dyad of seller and customer. He called all 7,000 employees to contribute to what very likely would be a painful overhaul of the company and its processes in order to make the company environmentally conscious in all that it did. This internally focused effort would later be termed EcoSense. Anderson challenged Interface's suppliers to do the same. His mission was to first reach sustainability and then go beyond sustainability to convert Interface into a restorative company – one that does not simply not do harm to the environment, but rather puts back more than it takes from the Earth.

For the first year, Anderson persistently urged his employees to catch the vision for Interface becoming a restorative enterprise by reducing, reusing, reclaiming, recycling, and importantly, redesigning. Beyond the core group who first heard Anderson's environmental vision for Interface, Anderson's urgings were barely heeded by the rest of the company, causing changes to be barely perceivable during the first year. However, after that first year, momentum began to gather among the employees, who, one by one, began to advocate for the redesign of the company. Eventually, so many accepted the mission and dedicated themselves to it that not only was the progress made in environmental stewardship remarkable, but also working at Interface became characterized by working not just for profit but for a higher purpose as well. Interface demonstrated to all firms that environmental stewardship could be realized in business and industry – even in what was once an energy-intensive, waste-producing industry.

The shared mission evolved into what is known as Mission Zero. Mission Zero is Interface's promise to eliminate completely the negative impact the company has on the environment by 2020. By the end of 2010, the results were astounding. Greenhouse gas emissions had so far been reduced by 44 percent in absolute terms (94 percent when factoring in offsets). Interface cut

(Continued)

energy consumption by 43 percent, water consumption by 80 percent, and waste sent to landfills by 77 percent (Interface, 2011). Importantly, the culture of the company shifted to a new trajectory in pursuit of innovations for new machines, materials, and manufacturing processes that would help fulfill Mission Zero. During the same period since 1994, the company grew net sales by 32 percent (Anderson, 1998, p. 3; Interface, 2012).

In 2019, eight years after Anderson's death due to cancer, Interface declared Mission Zero accomplished (Corporate Knights, 2020). Importantly, Interface's dramatic turn to embrace sustainability challenged firms across industries to invest in sustainability because of Interface's profitability that could be attributed to Interface's learning about sustainable business practices.

Questions

- What do you make of Interface's redesign?
- What evidence have you seen that other companies around the world have begun to recognize their social and environmental impact?
- How and when did it become important for companies to start thinking about the impact they have on society?

REFERENCES

AkzoNobel. (2011). Coatings. Retrieved from www.akzonobel.com/

AMA Marketing Power. (2007). *Definition of marketing.* Retrieved from www.marketing-power.com/AboutAMA/Pages/DefinitionofMarketing.aspx

Ambientebrasil. (2019). Solar energy kits to be sold in isolated communities in Central Amazonia. *Ambientebrasil,* June 16, 2019. Accessed at https://translate.google.com/translate?hl=enandsl=pt andu=https://noticias.ambientebrasil.com.br/divulgacao/2019/06/16/152483-kits-de-energia-solar-serao-comercializados-em-comunidades-isoladas-da-amazonia-central.html andprev=search andpto=aue

Anderson, R.C. (1998). *Mid-course correction: Toward a sustainable enterprise: The interface model.* White River Junction, VT: Chelsea Green.

Ashoka. (2011). Innovators for the public. Retrieved from www.ashoka.org/node/3291

Baumol, W.J., Litan, R.E., and Schramm, C.J. (2007). *Good capitalism, bad capitalism, and the economics of growth and prosperity.* New Haven, CT: Yale University Press.

Behrmann, E. (2019). A dead end for fossil fuel in Europe's city centers, Bloomberg, July 25, 2019. Accessed at www.bloomberg.com/news/articles/2019-07-26/a-dead-end-for-fossil-fuel-in-europe-s-city-centers

Bishop, M., & Green, M. (2010). *Philanthrocapitalism: How giving can save the world*. New York, NY: Bloomsbury Publishing USA.

Bonini, S.M.J., Mendonca, L.T., and Oppenheim, J.M. (2006). When social issues become strategic. *The McKinsey Quarterly*, 2, 20–32.

Bornstein, D. (2004). *How to change the world: Social entrepreneurs and the power of new ideas*. New York, NY: Oxford University Press.

Bornstein, D., and Davis, S. (2010). *Social entrepreneurship: What everyone needs to know*. New York, NY: Oxford University Press.

CE Delft (2018). Health impacts and costs of diesel emission in the EU. Accessed at https://epha.org/wp-content/uploads/2018/11/embargoed-until-27-november-00-01-am-cet-time-ce-delft-4r30-health-impacts-costs-diesel-emissions-eu-def.pdf

Chambers, M., and Schmitt, R. (2015). Diesel-powered passenger cars and light trucks, Bureau of Transportation Statistics, October 2015. Accessed at www.bts.gov/archive/publications/bts_fact_sheets/oct_2015/entire

Charan, R. (2006). Sharpening your business acumen: A six-step guide for incorporating external trends into your internal strategies. *Strategy and Business*, 42, 48.

Corporate Knights. (2020). Green 50: Top business moves that helped the planet. *Corporate Knights*, April 20, 2020. Accessed at www.corporateknights.com/channels/leadership/green-50-15873659/

Datar, S.M., Garvin, D.A., and Cullen, P.G. (2010). *Rethinking the MBA: Business education at a crossroads*. Boston, MA: Harvard Business Press.

Dictionary.com. (2011). *Society*. Retrieved from http://dictionary.reference.com/browse/society

Eccles, R.G., and Krzus, M.P. (2010). *One report: Integrated reporting for a sustainable strategy*. Hoboken, NJ: Wiley.

The Economist. (2009 March). An idea whose time has come: Entrepreneurialism has become cool. *The Economist*. Retrieved from www.economist.com/node/13216053

Elkington, J., and Hartigan, P. (2008). *The power of unreasonable people: How social entrepreneurs create markets that change the world*. Boston, MA: Harvard Business School.

Fligstein, N., and Dauter, L. (2007). The sociology of markets. *Annual Review of Sociology*, 33, 105–28.

Friedman, T. (2008). *Hot, flat, and crowded: Why we need a green revolution*. New York, NY: Farrar, Straus and Giroux.

The Guardian. (2015). 'Wide range of cars emit more pollution in realistic driving tests, data shows', *The Guardian*, September 30, 2015. Accessed at www.theguardian.com/

environment/2015/sep/30/wide-range-of-cars-emit-more-pollution-in-real-driving-conditions-tests-show

Hayek, F.A. (1988). *The fatal conceit: The errors of socialism*. Chicago, IL: University of Chicago Press.

Hollender, J., and Breen, B. (2010). *The responsibility revolution: How the next generation of businesses will win*. San Francisco, CA: Jossey-Bass/Wiley.

Holt, D., and Cameron, D. (2010). *Cultural strategy: Using innovative ideologies to build breakthrough brands*. New York, NY: Oxford University Press.

Hopkins, M.S. (2009). What executives don't get about sustainability (and further notes on the profit motive). *MIT Sloan Management Review*, 51(1), 35–40.

Hunt, S.D. (2010). *Marketing theory: Foundations, controversy, strategy, resource-advantage theory*. Armonk, NY: M.E. Sharpe.

Inglehart, R.F., and Welzel, C. (2005). *Modernization, cultural change, and democracy: The human development sequence*. New York, NY: Cambridge University Press.

Interface. (2011). March 2012 Investor Report. Retrieved from www.interfaceglobal.com/Investor-Relations/Annual-Reports.aspx, slide37

Interface. (2012). Mission Zero milestones. Retrieved from www.interfaceglobal.com/ZazzSustainabilityAssetts/pdfs/Interface_pdf_summary_report.pdf

Khanna, T. (2007). *Billions of entrepreneurs: How China and India are reshaping their futures and yours*. Boston, MA: Harvard Business School Press.

McCarthy, N. (2018). Diesel pollution costs European taxpayers billions, *Statista*, November 27, 2018. Accessed at www.statista.com/chart/16227/health-non-health-related-costs-of-air-pollution-from-transport-in-europe/

Nason, R.W. (2006). The macromarketing mosaic. *Journal of Macromarketing*, 26(2), 219–23. doi: 10.1177/0276146706291065

Peritz, R. (2008, April 3). *The Sherman anti-trust act of 1890: A more dynamic and open American economic system*. Retrieved from www.america.gov/st/educ-english/2008/April/20080423212813eaifas0.42149.html

Ritchie, H. and Roser, M. (2018). 'Number of people living in urban areas', *Our World in Data*. Accessed at https://ourworldindata.org/urbanization.

Robison, P. (2019). 'The scandal of London's air'. *Bloomberg Businessweek*, October 14, 2019.

Ryan, K.J. (2019). The containers for your most basic household products are about to look a lot different, thanks to this company. *Inc.*, May 27, 2019. Accessed at www.inc.com/kevin-j-ryan/terracycle-loop-reuse-recycle-plastic-containers.html

Savitz, A.W., and Weber, K. (2006). *The triple bottom line: How today's best-run companies are achieving economic, social, and environmental success – and how you can too*. San Francisco, CA: Jossey-Bass/Wiley.

Smith, A. (2000). *The wealth of nations*. New York, NY: The Modern Library Classics.

Statista (2020). Percentage share of new passenger cars in Europe with diesel engines in 2014 and 2018, by country, Statista. Accessed at www.statista.com/statistics/425113/eu-car-sales-share-of-diesel-engines-by-country/

Sullivan, J.L., Baker, R.E., Boyer, B.A., Hammerle, R.H., Kenney, T.E., Muniz, L. and Wallington, T.J., (2004). CO_2 emission benefit of diesel (versus gasoline) powered vehicles. *Environmental Science and Technology*, 38 (12), 3217–23.

Szaky, T. (2009). *Revolution in a bottle*. New York, NY: Penguin.

Vidal, J., (2015). The rise of diesel in Europe: the impact on health and pollution. *The Guardian*, September 22, 2015. *Accessed at* www.theguardian.com/environment/2015/sep/22/the-rise-diesel-in-europe-impact-on-health-pollution

Werbach, A. (2009). *Strategy for sustainability: A business manifesto*. Boston, MA: Harvard Business School.

Wilkie, W.L., and Moore, E.S. (2003). Scholarly research in marketing: Exploring the '4 eras' of thought development. *Journal of Public Policy and Marketing*, 22(2), 116–46.

2
MARKETING AND SOCIETY

Throwing Shade

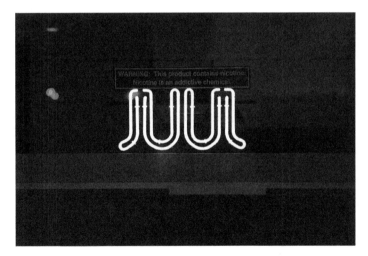

Source: Photo by Jordan Whitfield on Unsplash.

Juul

Juul Labs, Inc. began selling e-cigarettes and flavored nicotine pods in 2015 for the expressed purpose to save millions of lives a year by helping tobacco smokers switch to a less toxic form of consuming nicotine which e-cigarettes offered (Etter, Elgin, and Huet,

(Continued)

2019). Instead of helping veteran smokers, Juul sparked a dramatic increase of nicotine consumption among those who had never smoked – teens.

Researchers at the University of California San Francisco led by Stanton Glantz tracked more than 32,000 smokers and vapers over a three-year period and found that less than 1 percent of smokers switched completely to e-cigarettes (Blakely, 2019). 'E-cigarettes are harmful on their own,' Glantz said. 'For most smokers, they simply add e-cigarettes and become dual users significantly increasing their risk of developing lung disease above just smoking.' In addition to the nicotine taken into the body, the aerosol that users inhale and exhale from e-cigarettes can expose users and bystanders to other harmful substances, such as heavy metals, volatile organic compounds, and ultrafine particles inhaled deeply into the lungs (Cullen et al., 2019).

Despite adding to the risk of lung disease for smokers, Juul quickly became a hit in the marketplace after its introduction in 2015 – but with nonsmokers, such as kids. With slim USB-drive-looking vaporizers and sweet flavors (such as mango, and coco mint), Juul captured the newly addictive consumption of millions. Yet, representatives of the firm defended its marketing. 'We do not want, we do not need and we do not try and get non-nicotine users to use Juul,' a Juul staffer emailed reporters for *Bloomberg Businessweek* (Etter, Elgin, and Huet, 2019). 'More than 70 percent of smokers want to quit. Offering adult smokers a real alternative to cigarettes is a commercial opportunity of historic proportions.'

Despite denials about targeting youth with its sleek vaporizer, with its candy-flavored liquid pods carrying a high dosage of nicotine, and with its social-media presence featuring young models having fun, Juul became the clear leader among e-cigarette brands with 40 percent market share in 2017. Each major cigarette company developed its own e-cigarette brand (R.J. Reynolds created the Vuse in 2013, Altria released MarkTen in 2014), yet Juul became the dominant brand by far – perhaps, because of higher concentrations of nicotine in its pods. (Founder Adam Bowen told *Inc.* magazine that Juul's concentrations of nicotine were 10 times those of rival brands.) Altria, manufacturer of Marlboro, took notice of this market success and snapped up 35 percent of Juul's stock in 2017 which led some to begin talk about Big Tobacco 2.0 (Mukherjee, 2019).

Alarmingly, in the 2017 National Youth Tobacco Survey, 12 percent of high school students and 3 percent of middle school students reported using e-cigarettes in the last 30 days (O'Donnell, 2018). Critics denounced this abrupt jump in youth vaping as an epidemic, such as the US Surgeon General Jerome Adams and the Food and Drug Administration Commissioner Scott Gotlieb.

Despite such outcry, almost 27.5 percent of high schoolers in 2019 reported current e-cigarette use along with 10.5 percent of middle school students in the US. Most youth who are current e-cigarette users reported that Juul is their usual brand which reflects Juul's 75 percent share of the market (Cullen et al., 2019).

Typical of the stories from teens who vape are those who begin casually. However, consumption of Juul can soon escalate to four pods per day. (Each liquid-filled pod contains the same amount of nicotine as a pack of cigarettes.) Whenever such users put away the Juul, stress and negative feelings return. 'I felt kind of trapped,' one teen reported. 'I couldn't stop.'

Juul gradually responded by 'limiting appeal' of its brand (Juul, 2020). Accordingly, Juul cut its flavors from ten to two (Virginia tobacco and menthol), stopped its hip ads with young models, as well as its social media promotions and advertising.

Countries took note of problems associated with vaping and dozens have banned vaping, such as Argentina, Brazil, Mexico, Thailand, and Norway. European countries allow about one-third the nicotine in JUUL pods than in the US. Perhaps related to this lower levels of highly-addictive nicotine, e-cigarette consumption in European countries among teens is much less. In the UK, 3.3 percent of 11 to 18 year-olds report using e-cigarettes 'less than weekly' (Hunt, 2019).

With lawsuits against Juul for its targeting of youth, its economic prospects are not as attractive as they were in its early years. Altria announced that a global crackdown on e-cigarette marketing led it to cut the value of its investment in Juul by $4.1 billion (Dean, 2020). Altria will no longer market the Juul brand or provide retail distribution, but will focus on helping Juul win regulatory approval for its products. Juul has announced it plans to move its headquarters from San Francisco to Washington, DC to repair its relationship with regulators and distance itself from Silicon Valley's 'growth-at-all-costs, culture (Graff, 2020).

Questions to Consider

- How effective was Juul's marketing in its early years?
- How ethical was Juul's marketing in its early years?
- How ethical is Juul's marketing now?
- Why would countries have such different responses to regulating vaping?

CHAPTER OVERVIEW AND LEARNING OBJECTIVES

In this chapter, we will examine marketing's contributions to society. You will learn about flows in the aggregated marketing system, such as flows of physical goods, information, currency, as well as debt.

This chapter initially considers marketing's current contributions to society and then looks at flows of information and debt in the aggregate marketing system. Scholars and business practitioners have suggested that markets are people voting with their money (Dickinson and Hollander, 1991; Forbes and Ames, 2009, p. 14). As a result of such voting, preferences for certain products and services become known. Marketers then see to it that vote-winning products remain in the market. Some of these vote-winning products receive special enhancements and marketing efforts to make them more powerful when receiving votes at the cash register (where consumer votes are cast).

With an absence of marketing capabilities in the aggregate marketing system, innovation and product flows are often restricted. Such limited choice for consumers has characterized socialist systems, such as those of North Korea, or societies ruled by corrupt autocratic regimes, such as Zimbabwe (Legatum Institute, 2012). By comparison, the aggregate marketing system in developed economies can provide almost everything consumers want. However, adverse consequences can come with some consumption practices when consumers enjoy almost unrestricted market choices. Some of these practices include the consumption of tobacco products or attempting to carry heavy debt-loads for consumers. When such consumption practices continue for too long, societal costs emerge. These can emerge in the form of increased healthcare costs for the treatment and care of patients with debilitating illnesses, such as cancer or respiratory illnesses. These can also emerge in the form of macroeconomic problems, such as a sluggish or shrinking economy.

After this chapter, you should be able to answer the following questions:

- What can marketing do for enterprises and society?
- What does an absence or deficiency in marketing do to a society?
- What are the different flows in the aggregate marketing system for a society?
- Why do externalities (consequences for those not part of market exchanges) cause macro-marketing to have a healthy scepticism toward markets?
- What are debt flows in the aggregate marketing system?
- Does a culture of debt prevail in the United States?
- Is it possible for a financial service firm or a bank to be a sustainable enterprise?

MORE ABOUT MARKETING

Marketing is the process by which a firm creates value for its chosen customers (Silk, 2006). In a competitive market with rivals, choosing a segment of customers to give priority is a major decision in a firm's marketing strategy. Such a decision implies positioning a firm's brand relative to competing brands in the mind of the customers of a segment.

For example, an iPhone has a sleek design and possesses sophisticated attributes for many consumers. Voice communication is just one of these attributes and the host of other functions capable by the iPhone positions it strongly relative to other competing brands. Because of the dynamic nature of market competition, Apple Inc. cannot cease to develop the iPhone, but must strive to keep the iPhone ahead of competitors on important attributes to its customers.

In addition to the product features customers seek, the distribution of the iPhone must make it accessible in space and time, the price of the iPhone must be reasonable for customers, and the promotion of the iPhone must create a compelling image and associations for the iPhone brand in the mind of customers. These four dimensions of product, place, price, and promotion of marketing management are referred to as the marketing mix.

A traditional view of marketing would focus on a marketer and a customer being happy with a marketplace exchange. The Chinese character for 'double happiness' captures this well. The left and the right side of the Chinese character are the character for 'happiness'. The double happiness character in Figure 2.1 depicts these two characters side by side, thereby forming 'double happiness'.

Figure 2.1   Chinese character for 'double happiness'

Taking a broader view of marketing, the American Marketing Association has defined marketing in the following way: 'Marketing is the activity, set of institutions, and processes for creating, communicating, delivering, and exchanging offerings that have value for customers, clients, partners, and society at large' (AMA, 2020). Here, the happiness is due to activity and processes across a number of institutions that comprise a firm's upstream supply channel, as well as its downstream distributors that eventually link with the customer. The marketing mix elements can be seen in creating (product), communicating (promotion), delivering (place), and exchanging (price). Those that engage in market transactions include customers, clients of NGOs, partners of firms (both upstream and downstream) and society at large. As can be seen by the number of different undertakings and actors in markets, marketing can be very complex.

Understanding consumer behavior can be complex, too. A research study set in Ireland illustrates some of the challenge for marketers in understanding why consumers do not adopt sustainability-oriented products, such as rooftop solar panels (Claudy, Peterson, and O'Driscoll, 2013). Previous studies about the adoption of sustainability-oriented products disclosed an 'attitude-behavior gap' in which consumers would express favorable attitudes toward sustainability-oriented products – but tended not to actually buy them.

The study in Ireland used Behavioral Reasoning Theory, so the researchers in this study asked not only about reasons for adopting rooftop solar panels, but also about reasons for not adopting them. The reasons for adopting solar panels included (1) economic benefits, (2) environmental benefits, and (3) independence from conventional energy sources. By comparison, the reasons against adoption included (1) initial capital costs, (2) uncertainty regarding the performance of renewable energies, and (3) perceived incompatibility of the solar panels with the existing infrastructure of the home.

Researchers found that the reasons against adopting solar panels were slightly more influential on purchase intentions of consumers than reasons for adopting solar panels were. This enabled researchers to understand why an attitude-behavior gap existed, but it also enabled researchers to identify ways for marketers to close the attitude-behavior gap. Marketers could reduce the influence of reasons for not adopting rooftop solar panels by lowering the price of the solar panels, offering warranties for the performance of the solar panels, and developing new types of solar panels that would fit more roofs on homes in Ireland.

MARKETING AND SOCIETY
World-class Product + No Other Marketing = No Success

At 7:51 a.m. on Friday, January 12, 2007, a 30ish White man wearing a long-sleeved t-shirt and a baseball cap stationed himself against a wall next to a trash basket in Washington, DC's L'Enfant Plaza Metro station (Weingarten, 2007). He opened a violin case at his feet, took out the violin, shrewdly threw a few dollars into the case to cue those passing by to drop their change, and began playing for his audience in the subway station. The acoustics proved to be surprisingly suitable.

After 63 persons had passed by giving no notice to the violinist, a middle-aged man slowed his walk and turned his head but kept moving. Half a minute later, a woman tossed a dollar bill into the violinist's case as she walked past. After six minutes of playing, someone actually stopped against a wall and listened to the violinist. After almost 45 minutes of violin playing for commuters on their way to their government jobs, only seven people stopped and listened.

World renowned violinist Joshua Bell

Source: Image courtesy of Alexduff via Wikimedia Commons. Shared under the CC BY-SA 3.0 license.

The violinist played selections by Bach, Schubert, Massenet, and Ponce – some of the most compelling music written for the solo violin (Bix and Taylor, 2011). In all, almost 1,100 people passed the violinist. No crowd ever formed. By the time he ended, 27 people had thrown money into the violin case. There was no applause at the end. Total revenues for this performance came to $32.17.

As it turns out, a staff writer from *The Washington Post* had arranged the entire musical performance as part of a story on commuting to work (Weingarten, 2007). The violinist was none other than world-renowned violinist Joshua Bell playing a violin valued at $3.5 million – a 1713 Stradivarius. Two days prior to the Metro station performance, Bell had played the same violin before a sold-out concert in Boston where tickets averaged $100 each. At this stage of his career, Bell normally receives $1,000 per minute when he performs. However, Bell and his violin, both world-class products, are not worth $1,000 per minute by themselves:

> Behind every sold-out performance is the work of educators, market researchers and strategists, artistic directors, agents, advertisers, and ticket sellers – in short, all those helping Joshua Bell find and reach that middle-aged couple who is willing to pay $100 per seat at the Boston Symphony. Without them, the man whose talent can command $1,000 a minute walks away with $32 for almost an hour's worth of brilliant performance.

> (Bix and Taylor, 2011, p. 3)

In sum, the musician, who three months later received the Avery Fisher Prize as the best classical musician in America, could not command much of an audience without a complete marketing effort. In marketing management terms, Bell and his Stradivarius comprised only the product dimension of a marketing effort. At L'Enfant Plaza that January morning, the rest of a credible marketing effort (the promotion, the selection of a place for distributing the product, and the price) were either not done or done inappropriately. In the end, Bell remained almost invisible to those who passed him at L'Enfant Plaza. He received less than a thousandth of his normal take for performing. In this way, it is easy to see the impact of a complete and appropriate marketing effort.

Toward the end of his playing, Stacy Furukawa, a demographer at the Commerce Department, stopped her commute and positioned herself 3 meters from the violinist. A huge grin came onto her face. She had been at Bell's free concert at the Library of Congress three weeks previously. She remained until the end of the performance:

> 'It was the most astonishing thing I've ever seen in Washington,' Furukawa said, 'Joshua Bell was standing there playing at rush hour and people were not stopping, and not even looking, and some were flipping quarters at him! Quarters!'

> (Weingarten, 2007)

What Marketing Can Do for Societies

In the aggregate, marketing can be viewed as the provisioning system for a society (Fisk, 1974). In this way, marketing serves an economic function at the interface between supply and demand (Quelch and Jocz, 2007). Marketing adds value to goods and services by making them available to persons who want them, where they are wanted, when they are wanted, and at the price they are wanted. In Joshua Bell's foray into the Washington, DC Metro station, the right persons were not gathered in an appropriate concert hall at 7:30 p.m. at $100 per ticket to hear renditions of the classical masters, such as Bach or Schubert. If marketing had been done more effectively for Joshua Bell, he would have earned significantly more in profits for his performance.

From a societal perspective, marketing meets the consumption needs of those in society. In this way, marketing can be viewed as a social force. Although most marketing done by firms takes a 'little m' approach by tactically applying elements of the marketing mix (product, place, promotion, and price) and does not overtly aim to create value for society, nevertheless, well-done marketing programs cumulatively have a positive impact on society by creating value for consumers.

Despite the social welfare contributions of marketing, not all of marketing's effects can be said to be positive for society. Legal enterprises, such as tobacco marketing, have a deleterious effect on the health of long-time users of tobacco products. Hundreds of years ago, the legal North Atlantic slave trade put millions of Africans into bondage in the United States and the Caribbean, while the Middle Eastern slave trade actually put more into bondage there (Lewis, 1994). Additionally, marketers lapse into deceit and fraud at times, and advertising remains controversial because of its ability to reinforce materialistic tendencies in individuals. In sum, misapplied marketing can reduce the quality of living in a society.

Benefits of Marketing

Marketing provides many benefits to society. Specifically, consumer marketing offers benefits that are very much aligned with those of democracy (Jocz and Quelch, 2008; Quelch and Jocz, 2007).

> *Benefit #1: Marketing facilitates free and fair voluntary transactions that occur as part of exchange.* Normally, both parties benefit as part of market exchanges. A broader view of exchange regards market exchanges as being part of a complex system of exchange between public, government, business, and other social institutions. More will be said about this later in the chapter.

> *Benefit #2: As a result of marketing, consumers have control and choice over offerings presented in the marketplace.* Although an overabundance of choices might drive consumers to use experts to help them make purchases, competitive marketing has driven firms to satisfy smaller segments of consumers with increasingly differentiated products.

Benefit #3: Consumers can actively participate in shaping the marketplace. This can be done by voting in the marketplace for products and services they prefer. Consumers can also participate in formal marketing research programs conducted by firms, as well as co-creating new products with marketers. They also verbally endorse products to other consumers in a positive, negative, or neutral way, which influences potential consumers' decisions. If a product repeatedly gets bad reviews by consumers, demand will drop and the company will cease to make the product. Hence, the consumers shape the market.

Benefit #4: The market facilitates communication between consumers and producers, allowing consumers to provide information to producers about the products they want. Information is essential to a properly functioning market, and it moves buyers and sellers together while reducing uncertainties for both parties in a transaction. Persuasion is also integral to information exchange, as it creates two-way communication between consumers and producers. Through the marketplace, consumers can persuade producers by simply communicating their wants, such as, 'If you the maker of this product would offer a smaller version of it, I would buy it immediately.'

Benefit #5: The market offers nearly universal inclusion. By expanding the number of consumers in the market, marketers benefit through more profit opportunities. Marketing has brought similar brands and consumption experiences to all corners of the globe. In this way, marketing has given the world's cultures more common ground on which to meet.

Benefit #6: Marketing can satisfy the wants and needs of consumers. Marketing has democratized consumption by bringing goods and services to citizen consumers in ways that allow mass consumption. For example, Henry Ford's accomplishment 100 years ago was ingenious as he reduced the cost of production for autos, so that millions of autos could be sold to everyone, not only to the wealthy elite (although only in black). The resulting economic need for parts used in the production process, as well the need for an after-market consisting of car parts and repair services, has boosted employment and subsequently standards of living.

What an Absence of Marketing Can Do to Societies

Some Western economists promised Russia that enormous increases in its standard of living could be realized 'within a few years' once Russia became a 'free-market economy' on January 1, 1992 (Murrell, 1993). Sadly, markets could not be imposed quickly in a top-down fashion. Despite shock therapy and the rapid transfer of the ownership of the means of production in the former Soviet Union, much was missing from the aggregate marketing system when Russia turned away from communism and central planning for the economy.

In the view of institutional economists, institutions comprise 'the rules of the game' in societies (North, 1994). Specifically, institutions are the humanly devised constraints that structure human interaction. These include formal constraints (such as rules, laws, and constitutions), informal constraints (such as norms of behavior, conventions, self-imposed codes of conduct), and the inclination and ability to enforce such constraints. Such rules of the game influence individuals and organizations to pursue actions they perceive likely to fit their mental models of what should work in practice. For example, in 1992, plant managers in Russia had a network of relationships with state bureaucrats and other plant managers that enabled them to survive (Easterly, 2007, p. 62). Rather than execute exchanges in cash that would be subject to government taxation, many of these managers used barter and delivery of goods. In this way, these plant managers continued to produce goods nobody wanted. As a result, the Russian GDP shrank 40 percent in the four-year period from 1992 to 1995 (Holmes, 1997). The share of Russian firms that ran losses actually increased to 40 percent in the years after communism ended (Easterly, 2007).

One example of Russia's situation is the case of the Middle Volga Chemicals Plant in Samara Oblast. This plant found a 'market' for ten tons of toxic chemicals it had produced. First, the plant passed the load of toxic chemicals to the Samara Oblast government, after bribing an official, in lieu of its required payment into the unemployment fund. The government was required to make transfers to relatively poor regional governments, and so it shipped the toxic chemicals to the unemployment compensation fund in the poor republic of Mari-El. No record of what eventually happened to the ten tons of toxic chemicals can be found today.

The invisible institutional framework in Russia in the years after communism continued to destroy value rather than to create it. For example, firm A would produce below-grade steel that was then used as input to firm B for its production of below-grade steel tubing. This weak steel tubing was used by firm C to make cheap bicycle frames soon to rust and break, which were then bartered with firm A as part of firm A's way to pay its employees in goods. All the while, firms A, B, and C used up valuable energy resources. The government authorities at the local and national level went along with such a loop of inferior production because these government officials did not want to confront large-scale unemployment. Without an appropriate conceptualization of what should be accomplished in business transactions, such as the imperative of delivering reliable and quality outputs that are beneficial to society, opportunity seekers in markets will likely become opportunists who benefit at others' expense.

Misperceptions about Markets

In times of economic abundance, markets appear steady, reliable, and durable. While cautioning about the mistake of allowing market success to serve as the metric in the nonmaterial realms of life, author and social critic Paul Stiles (2005) asserts, 'The market economy is the system of choice for providing for the material welfare of mankind, and for good reason: it works' (p. 15).

Markets do not run well on their own. A court system is needed to resolve disputes among buyers and sellers that inevitably will arise. Shocks to markets can also come from outside markets, such as in pandemics when the response to COVID-19 shut down many goods and services markets. An appropriate metaphor for markets is that they exist in earthquake zones. Market busts and shocks to markets are the earthquakes that occasionally impact the effectiveness of markets in abrupt ways. Proper planning in earthquake zones allows them to be inhabitable. Likewise, market actors need to be mindful of how quickly things can change in markets. Markets are dynamic – or at least have the potential to suddenly change.

Regulation and the Free Market

Although free-market ideology may not be dead, it certainly deserves reconsideration in light of its recurring blind spot for asset bubbles as seen in the run up to the Economic Crisis of 2008. Markets need effective regulation to avoid excessive lending that subsequently results in credit crunches in which banks cannot adequately judge the future business prospects for firms applying for loans. When banks cannot evaluate the risks of loans, they do not make loans. The challenge is figuring out the type and intensity of regulation for markets. Some observers note that the patchwork of regulations that evolved over time in the United States proved to be effective in keeping financial markets from calamity from 1940 through 1990 (Sterbenz, personal communication, 2011).

When one returns to economic theory for insight into the nature of financial markets, several important starting assumptions are taken by economists that lead to highly formulaic outcomes. For example, people in markets are viewed essentially as *homo economicus*, rather than as *homo sapiens* (Bishop and Green, 2010). Based on this assumption of a market populated by people behaving as near automatons, economic orthodoxy brought forth the 'efficient market hypothesis' (EMH) for the financial markets. The EMH is also commonly referred to as market efficiency. In the EMH, it is impossible for markets to be wrong because the price of any security represents all the information held by individuals in the market. In the buying and selling of the security by all interested actors in a market, the price of the security is determined by the information about the security available to all of the investors. Bajaj (2006) comments:

> The EMH has proven to be a powerful idea in explaining financial market behavior in good times. However, it is weak or even counter-productive when irrational behavior diffuses through markets leading to bubbles (in which asset prices no longer represent their enduring value), as well as in the inevitable crash that follows a bubble [Cassidy, 2009a]. (p. A1)

In short, the EMH is blind to bubbles and crashes because of its assumptions. In good times of steady growth in the business cycle (a long-term pattern of growth and decline affecting production, inventories, and employment), the EMH seems to work very well.

When the EMH dominates market thinking, three illusions come to life and tend to intensify over time (Cassidy, 2009b) as presented in Table 2.1. First, the market always generates good outcomes. This is the illusion of harmony (among buyers and sellers). Second, the market is sturdy and well grounded. This is the illusion of stability. Third, putting a price on risk through exotic financial products (such as mortgage-backed securities [MBSs], collateralized debt obligations [CDOs], and credit default swaps [CDSs]) and distributing these to those willing to bear such risks appears to greatly reduce the chances of a systemic crisis. This is the illusion of predictability. Played out over a period of months and years, the logic of perfection permeates the talking, reading, and thinking of market actors, regulators, and observers, such as the media. In this way, the culture of financial markets and the broader culture change with few ever recognizing it. Market actors and citizens ignore the susceptibility of markets to sudden change.

Table 2.1 Illusions when the efficient market hypothesis has dominated market thinking

1. The market always generates good outcomes.
2. The market is stable.
3. Markets are predictable.

In the good times, markets work and they seem to work efficiently. At the individual level, the idea of market efficiency becomes the dominant logic. In the later stages of the business cycle, cocky financiers emerge declaring that their losers/winners approach to investing is what makes markets efficient (removing the possibility of arbitrage where assets might be temporarily mispriced). Such unshakable confidence signals that hubris has arrived. Hubris is not part of rational economic behavior.

Challenging the Inherent Stability of Markets

Surprisingly to some, neoclassical economic theory either ignores the contributions of entrepreneurs and marketers or treats them as effervescent phenomena in a market economy that moves inexorably toward equilibrium. With this lens from neoclassical economics, the entrepreneur and marketer take on the role of nuisance factors in the destiny of a market economy.

In 1995, Shelby Hunt and Robert Morgan published their resource-advantage (RA) theory in the *Journal of Marketing* (Peterson, 2011). Hunt is a long-time professor of marketing at Texas Tech University and is regarded as a legendary figure in the realm of marketing academia.

Briefly put, RA theory challenges neoclassical economics' view of general equilibrium and the inherent stability of market economies. While others such as Austrian economists and Keynesian economists have challenged such economic orthodoxy, Hunt and Morgan do this from the vantage point of marketing. As a result, RA theory imparts a dramatically different role to entrepreneurs and marketers as potentially valuable contributors to the life of a society with a sometimes roiling, but never steady market-economy.

RA Theory's Tenets

In presenting RA theory, Hunt and Morgan (1996) use a boxes-and-arrows diagram called 'A Schematic of RA Theory of Competition', that features three boxes representing (a) resources, (b) market position, and (c) financial performance. As shown in Figure 2.2, these three constructs are influenced by societal resources, societal institutions, competitor-suppliers, consumers, and public policy. Here, the important idea is that competition is disequilibrating and ongoing. It is a constant struggle for a comparative advantage in resources that will yield a marketplace position of competitive advantage and, thus, superior financial performance.

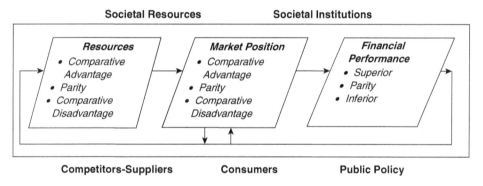

Figure 2.2   Schematic of the resource-advantage theory of competition

A Comparison of RA Theory and Neoclassical Economics

A comparison across the nine premises of RA theory brings some surprising realizations (see Table 2.2). First, neoclassical economics' premise that demand is homogenous in an industry does not square with the consumer segments well known to marketers. Such segments suggest that demand in industries is heterogeneous, as proposed by RA theory. Second, information asymmetries characterized many market transactions because information is not perfectly distributed. Third, if profit maximization was the aim for firms, they would liquidate their assets this year to achieve the most profits this year. Instead, firms pursue superior financial performance and they do this through the use of tangible assets and intangible assets (such as the talents and skills of employees and the relationships the firm nurtures with suppliers and distributors). Finally, markets actors are not passive, but active agents that lead markets to be in constant flux.

Table 2.2   Comparison of foundational premises of neoclassical economic theory and resource-advantage theory (Hunt and Lambe, 2000, p. 35)

	Neoclassical economics	Resource-advantage theory
1.	Homogenous demand in industries.	Demand is heterogeneous across industries, heterogeneous within industries.
2.	Consumer information is perfect and costless.	Consumer information is imperfect and costly.
3.	Profit maximization is the firm's objective.	The firm's objective is superior financial performance.
4.	The firm's resources are capital, labor, and land.	The firm's resources are financial, physical, legal, human, organizational, informational, and relational.
5.	Competition goes to equilibrium resulting in production of commodities.	Competitive dynamics are disequilibrium-provoking, with innovation endogenous (happening as a result of competition).

Source: Adapted from Hunt and Lambe, 2000, p. 35. Copyright Wiley.

THE AGGREGATE MARKETING SYSTEM

Physical Flows in the Aggregate Marketing System

The aggregate marketing system is the collection of all marketing systems in society (Wilkie and Moore, 1999). In the United States, more than 100 million households with more than 300 million consumers comprise the final nodes in the aggregate marketing system. More than 30 million Americans work directly within the AMS with the largest portion being sales persons. To convey some of the enormity of the AMS, William L. Wilkie and Elizabeth S. Moore (2002) focused on one series of exchanges occurring in the aggregate marketing system for a hypothetical consumer named Tiffany to have coffee and pastries one morning in her home. This story about breakfast at Tiffany's illustrates the scope and complexity of marketing and of marketing systems linked around the globe.

AMS Example: Tiffany's Coffee Beans

The coffee beans in Tiffany's breakfast were grown on an eight-acre farm 1,000 meters above sea level in Colombia. The beans went from the farm to a de-pulping mill to separate the inner beans from their shell. They were then spread out to dry for several days in the sun, and then later, they were milled again to remove the parchment sheath covering the green beans. Buyers and the government coffee inspectors tested samples of the beans for grading. The beans were then put in 60-kilogram burlap bags marked with the grower's name and grade of beans. These bags were stored at a warehouse until purchased by a coffee buyer. Then, the beans were transported and later shipped by truck over the mountains to the port city where they were loaded into 20-ton corrugated steel containers for their four-day sea journey to the port of New Orleans in the United States.

Fortunately for those involved with coffee importing to the United States, the Harmonized Tariff Schedule of the United States lists coffee as a free import. After inspection by a team from the US Customs and Border Protection Service, and after testing by the US Department of Agriculture, the beans were driven to the coffee firm's silo facility. Here, the beans were loaded and blended with other similar beans and sent to a roasting plant. At such a plant, the roasted beans were again tested for quality and packaged into containers for consumers. These will then be sold to wholesalers or shipped directly to retailers. Finally, Tiffany made the purchase of the roasted beans, ground them herself in a grinder purchased two years ago at a Target store, and brewed her morning coffee.

BROADLY CONSIDERING MARKET EXCHANGES IN THE AMS

A Closer Look at Macromarketing Systems

Macromarketing scholars traditionally have brought a healthy skepticism when considering market transactions by viewing market exchanges as creating both intended and unintended effects. This is a result of macromarketers' interest in the marketing systems embedded in the AMS, as well as macromarketers' awareness of the complex nature of the AMS as a provisioning system for society.

A macromarketer's systems perspective is a major point of difference between macromarketing ('biggest M') and micromarketing ('little m') (Mittelstaedt, Kilbourne, and Mittelstaedt, 2006). Such a systems perspective leads macromarketers to regard systems as the whole being greater than the aggregation of its parts. To understand the 'system-ness' of a set of elements, it is best to begin by removing elements and then observing the results. For example, if a person's organs are removed one at a time over an extended period, one can observe that digestion occurs in a much degraded way with difficulty, if at all.

Earlier in this chapter, Joshua Bell was removed from the marketing system that gathers the right audience members in a favorable location, at an agreeable time, for the right price.

Outside of this system, Bell's world-class performing talents had no value to those hearing him play (Weingarten, 2007). 'I'm surprised at the number of people who don't pay attention at all, as if I'm invisible,' Bell said, 'Because you know what? I'm making a lot of noise!' (Weingarten, 2007, p. 10). The most awkward times for Bell were the times just after ending his playing of the compositions. The same people who had not noticed him playing did not notice he had finished. No applause. Nothing. Meadows (2008, p. 11) describes a system as 'an interconnected set of elements that is coherently organized in a way that achieves something'. Extracted from his marketing system, Bell achieved little.

Across the Atlantic, the popular mezzo-soprano Katherine Jenkins from Wales who sings a wide variety of songs (from classical, choral, traditional, musical theatre, to pop) replicated Joshua Bell's experience as a subway station performer. Disguising herself in less glamorous clothes and singing in public for the first time without high heels, the 31-year-old Jenkins spent 45 minutes in Leicester Square Station of the London Underground on November 23, 2011 (Bryant, 2011). While enough commuters recognized Jenkins' distinctive voice to draw a small crowd (and some tears from listeners), she only earned about $15 for her performance. By comparison, promoters of Jenkins' concerts operating within a marketing system usually receive more than $150 per ticket for one of her concerts.

Fundamentally, a human system must have (a) elements, (b) interconnections, and (c) a purpose. The elements of a system are often visible and tangible entities. For example, in a shopping center, there are parking lots, buildings recognized as retail stores, back rooms inside the stores full of inventory in boxes, cash registers, and sales people out in the main area of the stores.

The interconnections in the shopping center are the relationships that connect the elements of the shopping center together and enable it to function as a place for commerce and social activity. For example, there are physical flows of goods into the stores (delivered by trucks), as well as physical flows out of the stores (taken away by consumers driving cars). The interconnections of the shopping center system would be harder to detect than the elements of the shopping center. These would include:

1. Regulations and standards that control the flow of electricity into the stores and into the electric signs by the highway leading to the shopping center.
2. Hiring practices that allow a trained set of workers to man the stores effectively.
3. Financial flows from retail outlets to the shopping center owner for renting their space in the shopping center, from the shopping center owner to a consortium of lenders for the mortgage on the shopping center, from the shopping center owner and retail outlets to local, state, and federal governments for tax payments.
4. Information flows that might include flow from the retailers to consumers about prices at the shopping center, promotions and advertisement from retail outlets, and featured brands at the shopping center. Such information flows might also include consumer-to-consumer verbal communication about the temperature of the retail stores during hot summer days, or the presence of teen groups at the shopping center parking lot on Friday nights.

Finally, the function of a nonhuman system or the purpose of a human system may have to be deduced from observation of the system's operation. This least obvious aspect of the system is often the most crucial determinant of the system's behavior. For example, the shopping center brings goods and services to consumers in a convenient and appealing manner. Accordingly, the purpose of the shopping center can be deduced to offering exchange opportunities between retailers and consumers. However, this purpose is likely an intermediate step to an improved quality of life for all who come to the shopping center for trade, employment, or pleasure.

Externalities

Well-performing marketing systems can produce unexpected results for those not actively involved in the exchanges of markets (Mittelstaedt et al., 2006). Externalities are the uncalculated costs and/or benefits of exchange. In terms of macromarketing, these externalities are ways that marketing affects society. For example, when a shopping center becomes so popular that the surrounding road network is overwhelmed by traffic, then those not using the shopping center (but wanting to go someplace else) experience delays as a result of such traffic congestion. Those that drive these roads might become more aggressive in their driving in attempts to make up for lost time in transit because of the slower rates of traffic around the shopping center. Additionally, the extra use of the roads by shoppers, workers, and delivery trucks contributes to the accelerated wearing out of the road network, so that driving these roads might actually become more hazardous as a result of broken asphalt and pot holes. The externalities for the local community are (a) slower travel times and (b) more dangerous driving around the shopping center.

Tobacco Marketing

Although it may be difficult to admit, the marketing of cigarettes might be the most successful marketing ever to occur – at least for the first half of the twentieth century. In 1900, the cigarette was a little-used and stigmatized product in the United States (Brandt, 2007). But with the implementation of machines that could roll, cut, and package cigarettes at extremely cheap cost per unit, cigarette companies marshaled all the best of business practice to distribute effectively now low-priced cigarettes to American consumers. The American Tobacco Company used new forms of advertising and promotion, such as free matchbooks with advertising on the covers to make cigarette smoking appear to be fashionable and chic. As a result, the cigarette deeply penetrated American culture as a symbol of attractiveness, beauty, and power. Tobacco companies sold more than 416 billion cigarettes in their peak year, 1952 (Hilts, 1996). According to Gallup Polls, 45 percent of adults in the United States smoked by 1954 (Blizzard, 2004).

As a result of decades of opposition to cigarette smoking by public health officials, and health agencies, such as the American Cancer Society, cigarette smoking has declined in the United States. In 2018, 13.7 percent of Americans smoked regularly – an estimated 34.2 million adults (CDC, 2018). Nineteen percent smoke in the EU with a high of 27.3 percent in Bulgaria and a low of 8.7 percent in Sweden (Eurostat, 2020). In China, 27.7 percent of adults smoke (52.1 percent of men compared to 2.7 percent of women) (Parascandola and Xiao, 2019). Not surprisingly, China is in the midst of a lung cancer epidemic on an unprecedented scale with 733,000 new lung cancer cases in 2015 and 610,000 deaths.

While the tobacco industry emphasized the individual choice of Americans to smoke in the highly successful Marlboro cigarette ads featuring the American cowboy on the frontier, the enormous health costs to society brought many in the United States to the realization that the externalities created by cigarette smoking were too much to bear. Each year, 435,000 US citizens die from various diseases associated with their addiction to nicotine (Brandt, 2007). Former US Surgeon General C. Everett Koop repeatedly told the public that tobacco deaths equaled three 747 aircraft crashing each day of the year with no survivors. However, smokers typically slowly die in hospitals one at a time, often after extended illnesses and suffering, ashamed they have brought this fate on themselves.

Marketing propelled the initially unpopular cigarette into modern culture

Source: Photo by Mathew MacQuarrie on Unsplash.

With such numbers of Americans entering the healthcare system each year for tobacco-related illnesses, healthcare insurance premiums increased to the point that the majority of Americans who did not smoke were contributing to the healthcare costs incurred by the minority of

Americans who did smoke. In this way, cigarette smoking created negative externalities for nonsmokers, not just through the inhalation of secondary smoke. When the costs of these externalities were better realized, it became clear that the cost of cigarette smoking, like other externalities, was not fully reflected in prices paid in the marketplace for cigarettes (which have increased by an average of 7 percent per year since 1960 compared to a 3.8 percent average increase in the consumer price index (Ryan, 2019)).

Complex Systems

If you have ever wondered why almost no one predicted such Earth-shaking events as the collapse of the Soviet Union, or the economic meltdown of 2008, thinkers are now emerging to explain why experts failed to predict such pivotal events. In *The Age of the Unthinkable*, Joshua Cooper Ramo explains both the hazards and opportunities in an increasingly dynamic world subject to sudden and sometimes radical change (Ramo, 2009). In short, Ramo proposes that complex systems, despite their apparent stability, often become out of balance and become poised for sudden change. Some of these complex systems which Ramo discusses are marketing systems.

Layton's Graphical Depiction of Complex Marketing Systems

In recent years, macromarketers have begun to focus on marketing systems (Layton, 2007, 2010). In this effort, Layton has defined marketing systems as a network of individuals, groups, and/or entities embedded in a social matrix that is focused on economic exchange. Notably, marketing systems are ubiquitous and have the primary role of putting in place assortments of goods, services, experiences, and ideas. Layton's mapping of marketing systems includes such patterns of systems as (a) autarchy/random, (b) emergent, (c) structured, and (d) purposeful (Layton, 2010). Autarchic systems are found in the early stages of market development where individuals or households are largely self-sufficient and use barter for exchange. Emergent marketing systems develop when competition is increasingly substituted for regulated or socially controlled outcomes. Trade within and between communities grows in emergent marketing systems. As corporate entities form from single firms to alliances or networks of firms (cooperating in production, distribution, or innovation), marketing systems become structured marketing systems.

As can be seen in the lower-left corner of Figure 2.3, traditional marketing has focused on the systems within the dotted rectangle, such as single firm offers to a market, distribution channels and vertical marketing systems (VMSs), and supply chains. Finally, purposeful marketing systems develop. These carry the distinguishing characteristic of the use of economic or political power to direct transaction flows toward the goals of the entity exercising such power. Layton maps these across three levels of aggregations: (a) micro (firm, household, or individual, (b) meso (loose aggregations of micro units), and (c) macro (societal in scope, composed of all micro and meso units). In this way, Layton plots 27 marketing systems in this matrix (2010).

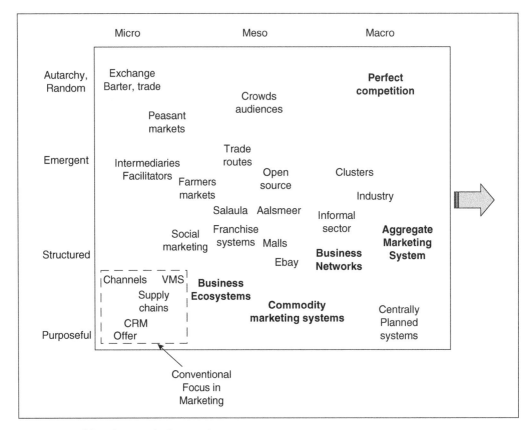

Figure 2.3   Mapping marketing systems

Source: Layton (2010).

Four of these 27 types of marketing systems are considered complex systems: (a) the aggregate marketing system for a country, (b) business networks, (c) commodity marketing systems, and (d) business ecosystems. Business ecosystems are typically composed of many loosely connected participants acting generally as a community and relying on each other for survival and effectiveness through a complex web of relationships. For example, Toyota and its constellation of financiers, suppliers, dealers, and service providers give an example of a business ecosystem. Business ecosystems compete against each other, but they can also simultaneously cooperate with each other in industry trade groups, lobbying efforts, and efforts to benefit both communities and societies in which they operate (Iansiti and Levien, 2004).

Layton plots these complex marketing systems in the meso- and macro-level systems. He also plots and characterizes these systems as being structured or purposeful. However intended, the terms 'structured' and 'purposeful' suggest durability. These terms also imply that an enormous force would be needed to destabilize a system, such as an aggregate marketing system. However, such complex marketing systems might decline or fail as a result of natural disasters, war, famine, blunders, criminal action, or competitive action from rivals. This raises the question of system sustainability. System sustainability depends on the adaptive capabilities of the system. Ramo (2009) notes how some systems manifest resilience in that when they are stressed, they learn and adapt. Accordingly, such resilient systems rebound or reform themselves to be stronger and more effective than they were before they experienced stress.

Ramo views stock markets and ecosystems as complex systems. In his view, such systems have internal dynamics that defy easy description and elude prediction. Change in such complex systems often takes place not in a smooth or gradual way, but as a sequence of fast, catastrophic events. By analogy, sometimes only a light force can induce an avalanche, while in other situations, only a major force can do this.

Consider the major earthquakes in Japan in 2011. In a few minutes, an advanced economy experienced significant and irreversible change. Additionally, these systems are very hard to manage or design from the outside. This is because they resist a Newtonian approach to physics in which the world can be reduced to building blocks that are assembled according to higher order systems built on linear relations.

While not stating it explicitly, Ramo endorses an interpretive approach to improving one's chances to sense that something is about to change in a complex system. In this case, a holistic understanding for complex systems is crucial. In addition, the observer must become extremely empathetic by connecting with the environment around themselves. Only by constantly probing and ceaselessly updating one's worldview can one do better at understanding complex systems. This is much in line with the thoughts of Watkins and Bazerman (2003), who believe firms can improve their ability to predict disasters. According to these authors, becoming more machine-like is not the way to understand the future. Instead, thinking about the future and likely threats in a systematic way should be done using qualitative analysis of information outside the firm, as well as employee inputs. Management must then synthesize what perils might be lurking in the future.

Increasing Importance of Business Ecosystems

Digitization – the process of converting text, pictures or sound into a form that can be processed by a computer – has led to a blurring of boundaries between products and services (Jacobides, 2019). It also has led to consumers' increased dependence on mobile devices and the linking of previously unrelated goods and services. For example, Google began as a search engine for the web, but has branched into phones, tablets, smart watches, televisions, speakers, clocks, thermostats and other devices (Jaffrey, 2020). The Google ecosystem has its own customers, suppliers and complementors (such as application writers).

But the Google ecosystem now encounters competition from rival ecosystems, such as those from Apple, Amazon, Microsoft, and Samsung (even though Samsung manufactures Google Android phones) and these orchestrator firms field their own products and services that compete with Google's. In China, Alibaba (similar to Amazon), Baidu (China's top search engine), and Tencent (known for WeChat that can be used for social networking and digital payments) are all capitalizing on consumer information.

Some observers view ecosystem marketing as the future of competition (Sarkar and Kotler, 2018, Sarkar and Kotler, 2019). Look for new developments in laws related to ecosystems as past laws focused on firms only (Jacobides, 2019). Governance of ecosystems will likely warrant attention from governments and courts. For example, Apple – a smaller ecosystem than Google's – has more than 2 million complementors in the form of app writers. Apple's ecosystem is a managed one in which there are clear criteria for complementors regarding functionality and pricing in the App Store. But it used to be a closed ecosystem in which Apple produced or sourced all of the apps before 2008. And someday, it might become an open ecosystem (like Uber's) where complementors need to meet only certain basic standards to participate.

CONCLUSION

Consumer marketing offers benefits that are very much aligned with those of democracy. Through fair and voluntary exchanges, market participants can specialize their work and receive rewards for meeting the needs of others. The entire undertaking of the marketplace calls for the active participation of all. In this way, markets can be the provisioning system of society delivering what society values and can change the assortment of goods in the marketplace depending on consumer preferences and the information flows in the AMS.

Rather than benefitting a small elite, a fully functioning market can benefit all in society. Marketing can contribute to a better world in ways such as (1) framing consumer choices to facilitate healthier lifestyles, (2) using data analytics for important social causes, and (3) finding ways to regenerate and restore degraded ecosystems (Mohr, 2019).

Despite the successes of markets in provisioning for many societies, externalities (consequences for those not part of market exchanges) have led macromarketing scholars to have a healthy skepticism toward markets. The flow of financial capital is important to the success of the AMS. Debt flows in the AMS, while considered to be a normal part of activity for market actors, carry a degree of risk with them that must be well understood by market actors to avoid economic distress. Credit card balances of US consumers exceed $14 trillion in 2020 (down a bit due to lower consumer spending during the coronavirus pandemic) (New York Fed, 2020). This is part of the continuing story of how markets can allocate scarce resources for society and how risk remains endemic to activity in markets.

QUESTIONS

1. What kinds of things were unexpected for you to learn in Chapter 2?
2. What are your thoughts about marketing being the provisioning system for a society? Could there be better systems?
3. What is the most surprising foundational premise of neoclassical economics from Table 2.1?
4. Do you think markets are in equilibrium or disequilibrium? Explain.
5. Which foundational premise of Resource Advantage Theory would matter the most to business persons adopting a macromarketing approach?
6. Why would it be said by some that cigarette marketing might be the most successful marketing ever done? What are the benefits and costs to society if this is true?
7. How do you see competition emerging between Chinese business ecosystems based on technology (such as Alibaba, Baidu, and Tencent) and ones from the West (such as Google, Apple, Amazon, and Microsoft)?

Mavericks Who Made It

Martin Luther King, Jr.

Source: Photo by Unseen Histories on Unsplash.

Promoters named the event 'The March on Washington for Jobs and Freedom' (History.com, 2019). An estimated 250,000 people gathered in front of the Lincoln Memorial on the Mall in Washington, DC on a hot and humid Wednesday on August 28, 1963. Musicians had performed, such as folk musicians Joan Baez and Bob Dylan, as well as gospel singer Mahalia Jackson. As the world looked on through the relatively new technology of black and white television, Dr. Martin Luther King, Jr. delivered a stirring speech to be known as 'I Have a Dream!'

King made reference immediately to the Emancipation Proclamation that freed slaves in rebellious states 100 years ago in 1863. He called for the end to segregation and racial discrimination which had made African-Americans exiles in their own land.

'Now is the time to make real the promises of democracy,' King said (NPR, 2010). 'Now is the time to rise from the dark and desolate valley of segregation to the sunlit path of racial

(Continued)

justice. Now is the time to lift our nation from the quick sands of racial injustice to the solid rock of brotherhood. Now is the time to make justice a reality for all of God's children.'

King made reference to lines from the Declaration of Independence and the patriotic song 'America' ('My Country Tis of Thee'), as well as the Bible.

'So even though we face the difficulties of today and tomorrow, I still have a dream,' King said (NPR, 2010). 'It is a dream deeply rooted in the American dream. I have a dream that one day this nation will rise up and live out the true meaning of its creed: We hold these truths to be self-evident, that all men are created equal.'

King denounced police brutality, but also told African-Americans they 'must not be guilty of wrongful deeds. Let us not satisfy our thirst for freedom by drinking from the cup of bitterness and hatred' (NPR, 2010).

For those who listen to King's 17-minute speech, King's focus on brotherhood and love cannot be missed. Likewise, the speech was about America realizing its full potential as a racially integrated society. In these ways, the speech addressed all Americans – not just those there in front of the Lincoln Memorial in 1963, and not just African-Americans. As those from other countries listened to the speech, it addressed their concerns about equality and justice in their own societies. In this way, the speech addressed the entire world. The next year, King received the Nobel Peace Prize.

The Civil Rights Movement in the 1960s was the culmination of years of effort by organizers and citizens who ascribed to King's nonviolent approach in political protest and direct action to confront seg-regation and to call for its end (Sonnenfeld, 2018). Some direct action involved boycotting businesses in cities of the American South, such as Birmingham, Alabama. King's close associate Andrew Young (later mayor of Atlanta and US Ambassador to the United Nations) recalled 'So when business slowed down, people decided that they could come together' (Sonnenfeld, 2018). 'And so 100 businessmen in Birmingham, Alabama, in 1963, agreed to desegregate the entire city in spite of George Wallace (the segregationist governor of Alabama then), in spite of the laws of segregation, and nobody ever challenged it. We desegregated Birmingham without an incident over a year before the Congress was able to come up with the Civil Rights Bill.'

Surprising to some today, King received harsh criticism from some African-Americans during the time of the Civil Rights Movement (Haley, 2013). Those advocating Black Nationalism or Black Power felt King's nonviolent approach was not strong enough to succeed in the face of opposition from Whites in the US.

King's objective was integration – not only for African-Americans, but for others marginalized in society as well. A more separatist approach featuring violence (when needed) was endorsed by some like Malcolm X and the Black Panther Party. King viewed such fiery talk of armed resistance as leading to more frustration and bitterness for African-Americans. King opposed black nationalists' rejection of American society as irreparably unjust seeing that such rejection removed 'the one thing that keeps the fire of revolutions burning: the ever-present flame of hope' (King Institute, 2020).

In May 2020, African-American George Floyd died by suffocation while being arrested by Minneapolis police officers for passing counterfeit money at a shop (BBC, 2020). A bystander captured the last painful 8 minutes and 46 seconds of Floyd's life on video. Almost immediately, Black Lives Matter Global Network (BLMGN), a network of activists opposing the wrongful deaths of unarmed African-Americans, led protest marches across the US which attracted hundreds of thousands and continued for weeks. The entire movement referred to as Black Lives Matter includes hundreds of organizations (such as the NAACP Legal Defense and Educational Fund, Color of Change, Reclaim the Block, and Higher Heights) and is not limited to just BLMGN (Goldmacher, 2020). Some rioting and looting occurred in cities, such as Minneapolis, New York, Chicago, Portland, and Seattle.

Protesters demanded an end to police brutality. Additionally, protesters began insisting on defunding the police – and even doing away with the police in order to fund nonpolice social workers who would intervene in communities when needed.

BLMGN had already conducted marches in other countries such as Berlin in 2016 (Perrigo and Godin, 2020). In the aftermath of George Floyd's death in 2020, protesters took to the streets of some cities in Europe, such as Berlin and London (Clothier, 2020). Protesters decried police brutality in the US, but also expressed dissatisfaction with the lack of racial equality where they lived.

Some corporations (such as Airbnb, IBM, Salesforce) and wealthy individuals flooded BLMGN (#BlackLivesMatter) with donations – no doubt in response to the pain felt when watching George Floyd die (Hunter, 2020). But the question arose – how distinct is BLMGN from the Black Lives Matter movement which advocates equal treatment by the police and equal treatment in society?

According to a Black Lives Matter vision document created by BLMGN with other politically active groups in 2016, a Black Lives Matter vision includes communities governing themselves (Dennis and Dennis, 2020). Police would be demilitarized, eventually defunded and then disbanded. Drugs and prostitution would be decriminalized. By divestment in the criminal justice system, communities would be subsidized with education (in the form of free college tuition and forgiveness of college debt), healthcare, housing, and living-wage jobs. School curricula would be revised to remove historical figures with inappropriate behavior (such as owning slaves or tolerating those who participated in imperialistic colonization) as other (to be named later) historical figures from oppressed groups would replace those removed.

Regarding the BLMGN, African-American-Studies scholars Rutledge Dennis and Kimya Dennis wonder about the framing of the Black Lives Matter vision document using language and concepts from anarchist theories, such as separatism and community control, that proved not to be effective in the 1960s during the era of Black Power (Dennis and Dennis, 2020, p. 22). 'How this [BLMGN's Black Lives Matter vision] could be accomplished in the contemporary American social-political-cultural system is the question.'

Referring to the broad Black Lives Matter movement, Harvard Business Professor George Serafeim asserts that it 'has helped create a groundswell of support for strong diversity and fair employment practices' (Serafeim, 2020). But after focusing on ending bad police practices (which is almost universally endorsed in the US and around the world), what will be the priorities of the broad Black Lives Matter movement (made up of many organizations) and how will these differ from the priorities of BLMGN in the future (Cohn and Quealy, 2020)?

(Continued)

Questions

1. What role did business persons play in important moments in the Civil Rights Movement of the 1960s, such as Birmingham in the Spring of 1963? In the broad Black Lives Matter movement of 2020? Did business have a more effective role in 1963 than in 2020?
2. Compare the Civil Rights Movement with the Black Lives Matter movement.
3. Compare the rhetoric of the speech 'I Have a Dream!' with the rhetoric you have heard from the Black Lives Matter movement.
4. Aside from equal treatment by police and the courts, what exactly does BLMGN say that it advocates?
5. What do you think will happen with the BLM movement's relationship with BLMGN?
6. Can you name a country which does not struggle with racial, ethnic, or religious tensions? What does this say about that country or about humans in general?

REFERENCES

AMA. (2020). Definitions of marketing. Accessed at www.ama.org/the-definition-of-marketing-what-is-marketing/

Bajaj, V. (2006, November 7). After Arizona's housing boom, 'For Sale' is a sign of the times. *The New York Times*, p. A1.

BBC. (2020). George Floyd: What happened in the final moments of his life. *BBC News*, July 16, 2020. Accessed at www.bbc.com/news/world-us-canada-52861726

Bishop, M., and Green, M. (2010). *Philanthrocapitalism: How giving can save the world*. New York, NY: Bloomsbury Publishing USA.

Bix, B., and Taylor, O. (2011, March 9). Just what do marketers do, anyway? *MarketingProfs Today*. Retrieved from www.marketingprofs.com/newsletters/marketing/

Blakely, R. (2019). Vaping raises risk of chronic lung disease. *The Times*. December 16, 2019.

Blizzard, R. (2004, October 19). U.S. smoking habits have come a long way, baby. Retrieved from www.galluppoll.com

Brandt, A.M. (2007). *The cigarette century: The rise, fall and deadly persistence of the product that defined America*. New York, NY: Basic Books.

Bryant, M. (2011). Star Katherine Jenkins goes underground as a busker. *London Evening Standard*. Retrieved from www.thisislondon.co.uk/standard/article-24012980-opera-star-katherine-jenkins-goes-busking-on-the-tube.do

Cassidy, J. (2009a, October 5). Rational irrationality. *The New Yorker*. Retrieved from www. newyorker.com/

Cassidy, J. (2009b). *How markets fail: The logic of economic calamities*. New York, NY: Farrar, Straus and Giroux.

CDC. (2018). Current cigarette smoking among adults in the United States. Centers for Disease Control and Prevention. *Smoking and Toabacco Use*. Accessed at www.cdc.gov/ tobacco/data_statistics/fact_sheets/adult_data/cig_smoking/index.htm

Claudy, M.C., Peterson, M., and O'Driscoll, A. (2013). Understanding the attitude-behavior gap for renewable energy systems: Using behavioral reasoning theory. *Journal of Macromarketing* 33(4), 273–87.

Clothier, W. (2020). Black Lives Matter cut through like no other social movement. *The Sunday Times*, Wednesday, July 1, 2020. Accessed at www.thetimes.co.uk/article/black-lives-matter-cut-through-like-no-other-social-movement-8kj8dqwsh

Cohn, N., and Quealy, K. (2020). How public opinion has moved on Black Lives Matter. *The New York Times*, June 10, 2020. Accessed at www.nytimes.com/interactive/2020/06/10/ upshot/black-lives-matter-attitudes.html?action=clickandmodule=RelatedLinks andpgtype=Article

Cullen, K.A., Gentzke, A.S., Sawdey, M.D., Chang, J.T., Anic, G.M., Wang, T.W., Creamer, M.R., Jamal, A., Ambrose, B.K., and King, B.A. (2019). E-cigarette use among youth in the United States, 2019. *Jama*, 322(21), 2095–103.

Dean, J. (2020). Juul vaping investment burns $4bn hole in Altria value. *The Times*, January 31, 2020. Accessed at www.thetimes.co.uk/article/juul-vaping-investment-burns-4bn-hole-in-altria-value-6ddhklktj

Dennis, R., and Dennis, K. (2020). Confrontational Politics: The Black Lives Matter Movement. *The Wiley Blackwell Companion to Race, Ethnicity, and Nationalism*, 11–27.

Dickinson, R., and Hollander, S. (1991). Consumer votes. *Journal of Business Research*, 22, 335–46.

Easterly, R. (2007). *The white man's burden: Why the West's efforts to aid the rest have done so much ill and so little good*. New York, NY: Penguin Press.

Etter, L., Elgin, B., and Huet, E. (2019). Move fast and vape things. *Bloomberg Businessweek*, October 14, 2019, 68–73.

Eurostat. (2020). Tobacco consumption statistics. Eurostat. Accessed at https://appsso.euro-stat.ec.europa.eu/nui/show.do?dataset=hlth_ehis_sk3eandlang=en

Fisk, G. (1974). *Marketing and the ecological crisis*. New York, NY: Harper and Row.

Forbes, S., and Ames, E. (2009). *How capitalism will save us: Why free people and free markets are the best answer in today's economy*. New York, NY: Crown Business.

Goldmacher, S. (2020). Racial justice groups flooded with millions in donations in wake of Floyd death. *The New York Times*, June 14, 2020. Accessed at www.nytimes. com/2020/06/14/us/politics/black-lives-matter-racism-donations.html

Graff, A. (2020). Juul moving headquarters from San Francisco to D.C. *SFGATE*, May 5, 2020. Accessed at www.sfgate.com/bayarea/article/Juul-moving-headquarters-from-San-Francisco-to-15247589.php

Haley, A. (2013). Martin Luther King Jr.: Part 2 of a candid conversation with the civil rights leader. *Playboy*, September 15, 2013. Accessed at https://playboysfw.kinja.com/martin-luther-king-jr-part-2-of-a-candid-conversation-1502358645

Hilts, P. (1996). *Smoke screen: The truth behind the tobacco industry cover-up*. Reading, MA: Addison-Wesley.

History.com. (2019). March on Washington. December 4, 2019. Accessed at www.history.com/topics/black-history/march-on-washington

Holmes, L. (1997). *Post-communism: An introduction*. Durham, NC: Duke University Press.

Hunt, K. (2019). The US and UK see vaping very differently. Here's why. *CNN Health*. Accessed at www.cnn.com/2019/09/17/health/vaping-us-uk-e-cigarette-differences-intl/index.html

Hunt, S., and Morgan, R. (1996). The Resource-Advantage Theory of Competition: Dynamics, Path Dependencies, and Evolutionary Dimensions. *Journal of Marketing*, 60(4), 107–114. doi:10.2307/1251905

Hunt, S., and Lambe, C.J. (2000). Marketing's contribution to business strategy: Market orientation, relationship marketing, and resource-advantage theory. *International Journal of Management Reviews* 2(1), 17–44.

Hunter, T. (2020). These companies took action in support of #blacklivesmatter. *Built In*, August 19, 2020. Accessed at https://builtin.com/diversity-inclusion/companies-that-support-black-lives-matter-social-justice

Iansiti, M., and Levien, R. (2004). *The Keystone advantage: What the new dynamics of business ecosystems mean for strategy, innovation, and sustainability*. Boston, MA: Harvard Business School Press.

Jacobides, M.G. (2019). In the ecosystem economy, what's your strategy? *Harvard Business Review*, 97(5), 128–37.

Jaffrey, D. (2020). Just where is Google's ecosystem up to? *Ausdroid*, July 6, 2020. Accessed at https://ausdroid.net/2020/07/06/just-where-is-googles-ecosystem-up-to/

Jocz, K.E., and Quelch, J.A. (2008). An exploration of marketing's impacts on society: A perspective linked to democracy. *Journal of Public Policy and Marketing*, 27(2), 202–6.

Juul. (2020). Limiting appeal. Accessed at www.JUULlabs.com/combating-underage-use/limiting-appeal/

King Institute. (2020). Black nationalism. Martin Luther King, Jr. Research and Education Institute. Accessed at https://kinginstitute.stanford.edu/encyclopedia/black-nationalism

Layton, R.A. (2007). Marketing systems: A core macromarketing concept. *Journal of Macromarketing*, 27(2), 193–213.

Layton, R.A. (2010). Marketing systems, macromarketing and the quality of life. In P. Maclaren, M. Saren, B. Stern, and M. Tadajewski (Eds.), *The SAGE handbook of marketing theory* (pp. 415–42). Thousand Oaks, CA: Sage.

Legatum Institute. (2012). The Legatum Prosperity Index – Zimbabwe. Retrieved from www.prosperity.com/country.aspx?id=ZW

Lewis, B. (1994). *Race and slavery in the Middle East*. Oxford, UK: Oxford University Press.

Meadows, D.H. (2008). *Thinking in systems*. White River Junction, VT: Chelsea Green.

Mittelstaedt, J.D., Kilbourne, W.E., and Mittelstaedt, R.A. (2006). Macromarketing as agorology: Macromarketing theory and the study of the agora. *Journal of Macromarketing*, 26(2), 131–42.

Mohr, J. (2019). The positives and negatives of marketing. *Marketing News*, June/July 2019. Accessed at www.ama.org/marketing-news/positives-negatives-marketing/

Mukherjee, S. (2019). The fight against Big Tobacco 2.0. *Fortune*, October 2019. 18.

Murrell, P. (1993). What is shock therapy? What did it do in Poland and Russia? *Post Soviet Affairs*, 9(2), 111–140.

New York Fed. (2020). Total household debt decreased in Q2 2020, marketing first decline since 2014. *Federal Reserve Bank of New York*, August 6, 2020. Accessed at www.newyorkfed.org/newsevents/news/research/2020/20200806

North, D.C. (1994, December 19). Economic performance through time. *The American Economic Review*, 84(3), 359–68.

NPR. (2010). 'I Have a Dream' speech, in its entirety. *National Public Radio*, January 18, 2010. Accessed at www.npr.org/2010/01/18/122701268/i-have-a-dream-speech-in-its-entirety

O'Donnell, J. (2018). FDA declares youth vaping an epidemic, announces investigation, new enforcement. *USA Today*, September 12, 2018. Accessed at www.usatoday.com/story/news/politics/2018/09/12/fda-scott-gottlieb-youth-vaping-e-cigarettes-epidemic-enforcement/1266923002/

Parascandola, M., and Xiao, L. (2019). Tobacco and the lung cancer epidemic in China. *Translational Lung Cancer Research*, 8, Supplement 1: s21–s30.

Perrigo, B., and Godin, M. (2020). Racism is surging in Germany. Tens of thousands are taking to the streets to call for justice. *Time*, June 11, 2020. Accessed at https://time.com/5851165/germany-anti-racism-protests/

Peterson, M. (2011). RA theory moves entrepreneurs and marketers to center stage. *Legends of Marketing: Shelby Hunt, Vol. 7: Marketing Management and Strategy*. New Delhi, India: Sage.

Quelch, J.A., and Jocz, K.E. (2007). *Greater good: How good marketing makes for better democracy*. Boston, MA: Harvard Business School Press.

Ramo, J.C. (2009). *The age of the unthinkable*. New York, NY: Little, Brown.

Ryan, C. (2019). Big tobacco is a long way from burning out. *The Wall Street Journal*, December 6, 2019. Accessed at www.wsj.com/articles/big-tobacco-is-a-long-way-from-burning-out-11575628212

Sarkar, C., and Kotler, P. (2018). *Brand activism: From purpose to action*. Idea Bite Press.

Sarkar, C., and Kotler, P. (2019). Ecosystem marketing: The future of competition. *The Marketing Journal*, February 21, 2019. Accessed at www.marketingjournal.org/ecosystem-marketing-the-future-of-competition-christian-sarkar-and-philip-kotler/

Serafeim, G. (2020). Social-impact efforts that create real value. *Harvard Business Review*, 98 (5) September–October, 38–48.

Silk, A.J., 2006. *What is marketing?* Boston, MA: Harvard Business Press.

Sonnenfeld, J. (2018). Former Atlanta Mayor Andrew Young tells CEOs 'I almost have more faith in business than I have in the church'. *Chief Executive*, December 19, 2018. Accessed at https://chiefexecutive.net/andrew-young-ceos-faith-business-church/

Sterbenz, F. (2011). Professor of finance at the University of Wyoming. Personal communication with author.

Stiles, P. (2005). *Is the American dream killing you?: How 'the Market' rules our lives.* New York, NY: Collins.

Watkins, M.D., and Bazerman, M.H. (2003). Predictable surprises: The disasters you should have seen coming. *Harvard Business Review*, 81(3), 72–80.

Weingarten, G. (2007, April 8). Pearls before breakfast. *The Washington Post*. Retrieved from www.washingtonpost.com/wpdyn/content/article/2007/04/04/AR2007040401721.html

Wilkie, W.L., and Moore, E.S. (1999). Marketing's contributions to society. *Journal of Marketing*, 63, 198–218.

Wilkie, W.L., and Moore, E.S. (2002). Marketing's relationship to society. In B. Weitz and R. Wensley (Eds.), *Handbook of marketing*, (pp. 9–38). London: SAGE Publications.

3
STAKEHOLDERS IN MARKETING

Throwing Shade

Source: Photo by Jason Leung on Unsplash.

The Fashion Industry

What happens when billions of trend-seeking fashion consumers around the world meet producers willing to make new clothing for them at cheap prices? The answer is fast fashion (BBC, 2018). In the UK, the impact of fast fashion can be seen in consumers acquiring 26.7 kg of new clothes each year (more than any EU country) while the same

(Continued)

consumers send 235 million items of clothing to landfills. The disposal of clothes even included new and never-worn clothes as British fashion house Burberry's admitted it had destroyed £105 million worth of products from 2013 to 2018 to keep these products from being sold at drastically reduced prices (Kollewe, 2018).

Fast fashion became a phenomenon in the late 1980s as brands such as Spain-based Zara and Sweden-based H & M brought vast amounts of trendy and inexpensive garments into their chain stores around the world. To keep prices low, fast-fashion brands used the cheapest labor available in the world's poorest countries. Such off-shoring of manufacturing began just as globalization intensified. From 1989 to 2019, the fashion industry has almost quintupled from $500 billion to $2.4 trillion (Thomas, 2019).

This eye-popping growth came with costs to society. First, labor in developed countries lost jobs. From 1990 to 2012, the US textile and garment industry lost 1.2 million jobs as firms shifted production to Latin America and Asia. In the 1980s, 1 million worked in the textile industry in the UK, but there were only 100,000 workers in 2019.

Second, human rights in developing countries suffered with low pay (fewer than two percent of workers in these countries earn a living wage), withheld wages, no vacation and unsanitary and unsafe working conditions. One out of six in the world work in the fashion industry – mostly women and kids.

Thirdly, fast fashion has contributed to further degradation of the natural environment. The industry accounts for almost 20 percent of all industrial water pollution each year. It releases 10 percent of the carbon emissions in the atmosphere each year, too. (One kilogram of new clothes generates 23 kilograms of greenhouse gases.) Of the more than 100 billion garments made each year, 20 percent go unsold and are buried, shredded or incinerated (as Burberry admitted – but no longer does).

Stella McCartney, the British fashion designer, wrote an open letter to the fashion industry in the *Sunday Times* newspaper of London calling the industry to take action on critical issues for the industry (Candy, 2019). In her letter, McCartney noted that the fashion industry accounts for more than a third of ocean microplastics while textile dyeing is the second largest polluter of clean water globally. McCartney also decried the lack of creativity in fast fashion as digital technology allows designs put on display at fashion shows to be photographed and sent to overseas factories where these designs are then copied.

McCartney called for the fashion industry to develop alternative sources for materials (such as mycelium-based 'leather' grown in a lab and not from animals). She also proposed that firms choosing to use sustainable materials (such as organic cotton, recycled polyester or other verified inputs) should be rewarded by governments. McCartney also called for firms to pursue circularity in their processes and work with firms such as Italy-based Econyl (www.econyl.com/) which focuses on regenerated nylon made from waste industrial plastic, waste fabric, and discarded fishing nets. McCartney also highlighted Washington-based Evrnu (www.evrnu.com) for textile-to-textile recycling. McCartney declared it unacceptable that less than one percent of textiles are recycled back into textiles each year.

Questions to Consider

- Why do you think sales in the fashion industry have exploded since 1989?
- Would you pay 70 percent more for a pair of pants if they were locally made in your country? [In 2016, 67 percent of respondents in the US said 'no' – even if their annual household-income was more than $100,000.]
- Who would you say is more to blame for the excesses of the fashion industry – fashion producers or fashion consumers? Assign a percentage for the blame you would assign to each. Explain.
- Which of Stella McCartney's criticisms of the fashion industry is the most compelling to you? Explain.

CHAPTER OVERVIEW AND LEARNING OBJECTIVES

The objective of this chapter is to provide readers better understanding for the ethical dimensions of sustainable marketing. Macromarketing (which focuses on how marketing and society influence each other) offers valuable insights about the challenges and possibilities in pursuing sustainability in marketing. Stakeholders are groups that have a stake or interest in the activities that comprise a business. This chapter considers how firms and marketing systems in a society can consider stakeholders. This can be done by choice or by government direction.

Scholars generally define marketing strategy as the marketing behavior of firms when they compete in the markets (Varadarajan, 2011). Marketing strategy scholars have always taken keen interest in the context of competition. Today, major phenomena of interest for such scholars include (a) a changing competitive environment (which features new players – such as Google, Facebook, and state-owned enterprises – and an increased role for government in markets after 2008), (b) digital convergence (which makes industry boundaries more fuzzy – such as those among software, entertainment, research, the internet, and telecom), (c) emerging markets, (d) the marketing of green technologies, and (e) impoverished subsistence marketplaces (such marketplaces account for more than five billion people on the planet) (Srinivasan, 2009). These phenomena are macromarketing in character because they concern the interplay of marketing and society.

In this setting of markets today, stakeholders are increasingly important for firms, as well as for scholars. Although researchers continue to investigate the impact of taking a stakeholder-orientation on firm profits (Bhattacharya, Sen, and Korschun, 2008), scholars increasingly see that firms need to take a broadened and long-term view as part of developing their marketing strategy in the future. In this way, wisdom can be integrated into business decisions. In this chapter, Costco Wholesale serves as an exemplar of a stakeholder-oriented firm.

After this chapter, you should be able to answer the following questions:

- What are three approaches to ethics for sustainability?
- What is the stakeholder concept?
- What are primary stakeholders?
- What are secondary stakeholders?
- What is the special role of government as a stakeholder?
- What are reasons for firms to adopt a stakeholder orientation?

ETHICS, SUSTAINABILITY, AND STAKEHOLDER THEORY

Increasingly, sustainability represents a broader view of marketplace activity for firms to include not only customers and firm owners, but additional stakeholders. Macromarketing has traditionally brought such a broader view to the interplay of marketing and society. Macromarketing resonates with theoretical frameworks for sustainability, such as (1) the triple-bottom-line, (2) five forms of capital, and (3) stakeholder theory.

Global retailer Costco serves as an exemplar of a firm guided by a code of ethics which employs important aspects of a stakeholder approach to business. While the marketplace and academia currently feature innovative firms and universities which eagerly pursue sustainability and research related to sustainability, more can be done to make sustainability a mainstream endeavor for all firms and universities.

Holistic Definition of Sustainability

Examining the topic of sustainability must begin with consideration of the meaning of 'sustainability' because the concept of sustainability can take several forms within and without marketing (Kemper and Ballantine, 2019). Prior to 1987, most persons understood sustainability to mean the maintenance of a rate or level of performance. But in 1987, the UN's Brundtland Commission offered the world a definition of sustainable development (defined as meeting the needs of the present without compromising the ability of future generations to meet their own needs (WCED, 1987, chapt. 2, sect. 4)). In the ensuing decades since 1987, a holistic definition of sustainability has come to mean those concepts and practices of actors in markets (buyers, sellers, and government regulators) that benefit future generations through (1) the reduced negative impact on the resources and systems of the natural environment and/or (2) the positive effect on local communities and society at large (Eagle and Dahl, 2015, p. 5).

For those researching sustainable business practices and their relevance to inter-generational justice, the holistic 'triple bottom line' of people, planet, and profit (Elkington, 1994) is the preferred definition of sustainability. This is so, because of (1) its breadth, (2) its correspondence to the concept of corporate social responsibility (CSR) (Eagle and Dahl, 2015, p. 5), (3) its emerging consensus in use across corporations (Haugh and Talwar, 2010), as well as (4) its alignment with the UN's twenty-first-century effort to boost holistic development in countries around the world through its Sustainable Development Goals (SDGs) (United Nations, 2019). However, researchers of sustainability still might encounter those who (1) use 'sustainability' with a narrow focus on the natural environment, or (2) ignore (naively or intentionally) both the natural environment and the social aspects of market activities and use sustainability to be synonymous with terms such as 'durability' or 'maintaining performance' (Lunde, 2018).

Amory Lovins, founder of the Rocky Mountain Institute based in Boulder, Colorado, is one of the leading proponents of properly valuing nature and people when doing business. He does not use the word 'sustainability' because he believes it means many things to different people (Hopkins, 2009).

So what is one to do when using the term 'sustainability'? Make sure one quickly defines 'sustainability' in order to signal others what view of 'sustainability' is being employed. In this chapter, the holistic, 'triple-bottom-line' version of 'sustainability' for pursuing inter-generational justice will be used.

Ethical Dimensions of Sustainability

Lim (2016) presents three approaches to ethics for sustainability. The first is a consequentialist approach which proposes that the rightness or wrongness of an action is determined by its consequences (good or bad). With a utilitarian view, this means that the rightness (wrongness) of an action depends on how much good (bad) is produced for the greatest number of persons. The second is a deontological approach which proposes that there are distinct moral imperatives (such as rules and duties), so that violation of such imperatives is intrinsically wrong and observance of such imperatives is intrinsically right. The deontological approach depends on how intrinsic value is assigned to different elements in the environment (such as humans, nonhuman living things, and ecological systems). The third is a virtue approach in which correct actions are taken by actors with a virtuous character (wise and honest). The notion of a good life becomes the most fundamental moral question and directing valued behavior to others (charitable or benevolent) manifests the inner qualities of a virtuous person (Hursthouse, 1999). In such a way, sustainable behaviors of a person manifest the virtue of a person.

The consequentialist, deontological, and virtue approaches correspond to the three distinct streams of thought that make up ethics – specifically, (1) outcomes, (2) actions related to principles and rules, as well as (3) agents and their character. Jennings (2010) asserts that a fourth dimension must be part of ethical analysis – an evaluation of the context within which actions take place. Specifically, does the action support or undermine the system or context which makes an action possible and meaningful in the first place? For example, could a person establish a social business that is (1) profitable, (2) legal, and (3) uses its profits to benefit a local community, but despoil the natural environment in such a way as to disrupt entire ecosystems on which life in the local community depends over time? In the Age of the Anthropocene, in which humans represent the most dominant impact on the natural environment, this appears to be happening in local communities as well as at a macro-level of planetary dimensions (Jennings, 2015).

> All four aspects (of ethics) are relevant to sustainability, which is not only about living with constraints, parameters, and limits but also about prescribing some inherently wrong or causally harmful types of action, and about creating the proper kind of sensibility, motivation and moral commitment in people. In sum, virtue, rightness, consequence, and context are all ethically important in navigating sustainability.
>
> (Jennings, 2010, p. 27)

Understanding the multidimensional approach to sustainability ethics brings the importance of the macro or societal-level view. A sustainable society lives within the carrying capacity of its natural and social system (Jennings, 2010). In the realm of business scholarship, macromarketing has taken a systems view of how marketing and society influence each other (Peterson, 2016).

Service-Dominant Logic

Customers' demand for personalized co-created experiences now drives firms to create global networks of suppliers and resource providers to meet the demands of customers. In this world, a new shift in focus for marketers now becomes more apparent. This shift moves the focus of marketing activity from goods to services (Vargo and Lusch, 2017). Here, service is defined as the process of using one's resources for the benefit of another entity. Specifically, service is the application of knowledge and skills (operant resources) to benefit another entity. This new conceptual lens on marketing activity is called service-dominant logic (S-D logic):

> S-D logic is based on an understanding of the interwoven fabric of individuals and organizations, brought together into networks and societies, specializing in and exchanging the application of their competencies for the applied competences they need for their own well being. It is a logic that is philosophically grounded in a commitment to collaborative

processes with customers, partners, and employees; a logic that challenges management at all levels to be of service to all the stakeholders; a logic or perspective that recognizes the firm and its exchange partners who are engaged in the co-creation of value through reciprocal service provision. It is about understanding, internalizing, and acting on this logic better rather than the competition.

(Lusch, Vargo, and O'Brien, 2007, p. 5)

In the early 1900s, marketing was about taking goods and services '*to market*' (Lusch, Vargo, and O'Brien, 2007). The American Marketing Association defined marketing as the set of business activities that direct the flow of goods and services from producers to consumer. Accordingly, much of marketing thought was explaining the activities of middlemen in markets. After World War II, marketing thought in the United States moved to a '*market to*' orientation. Accordingly, customers were researched, segmented, targeted, promoted to, and distributed to.

With this goods-dominant logic from these previous eras of marketing, value creation was done by the producer or by the firm. The consumer, competition, and most other market variables remained independent of value creation. In fact, producers viewed consumers as contaminating or reducing the value they had put into the stuff they made. For example, the day after purchasing an automobile, its resale value dropped noticeably because it was 'used.' However, talented customers can actually increase the value of a car purchased new by installing special features and customization, such as stereo, radio, GPS systems, tinted windows, and custom painting not done at the factory.

In S-D logic, the orientation of marketing becomes '*marketing with*.' Accordingly, the customer is viewed as a collaborative partner who co-creates value with the firm. Service is understood to be the fundamental basis of exchange, whereas goods are viewed as a distribution mechanism for providing service (benefit to another entity). In S-D logic, service is the fundamental basis of exchange. Although often masked by complex combinations of goods, money, and institutions, this service basis of exchange is not always readily apparent. However, the implication of service being the fundamental basis of exchange is that service is always exchanged for service. In this regard, goods derive their value through use – the service they provide. In this vein, long-time Harvard Business School marketing professor Ted Levitt's assertion that 'people want quarter-inch holes, not quarter inch drill bits' (Hunter, 2009, para. 8) makes a lot of sense when applying S-D logic.

Nike Run Club (NRC) is an app that allows runners to track the distance of their runs and play music from curated playlists for jogs, and provides a social network to share one's hard work in training with others (NRC, 2020). The NRC app derives its value through use. Owners of the app can track their runs if they wear the Apple Watch or carry their iPhone or Android mobile phone. The data from running can be uploaded to the internet where more value is created by interacting with the community of runners there to compare and learn about running trends from other users. Here, forces in the external environment for the firm can now be co-created as well, such as the social importance of being part of an online community of runners. In short, Nike used to sell shoes, but it now sells access to camaraderie. In this way, it can be seen that the firm does not create value but makes value propositions (that can be taken up and interactively developed by the customer, the firm, and other entities).

In S-D logic, value is determined by the beneficiary – the one who benefits from the service rendered. Service is defined in terms of customer-determined benefit. As a result, value will be idiosyncratic, experiential, contextual, and meaning laden. Because value creation is interactional, it is inherently relational. NRC illustrates these aspects of S-D logic well as one customer training for a marathon might prefer comparing her preparation for the London Marathon with others preparing for the same race (or who ran it last year). Such value would be different from an employee for IBM who wants to identify jogging trails in London on her next overseas trip there in order to maintain a healthy lifestyle.

With both the iPhone and NRC, Apple, Inc. serves as a resource integrator. But so do others involved in the experience of using the iPhone and NRC. In S-D logic, all social and economic actors are resource integrators – not just firms, but individuals, households, firms, organizations, societies, and nations. In fact, service systems can be said to be any constellation of entities sharing information for the purpose of co-creating value (Vargo and Lusch, 2008, p. 5). These could include cities, city departments, businesses, business departments, nations, and national agencies. The smallest service system would be an individual, whereas the largest service system would be the global economy.

Lusch notes that as the division of labor has increased over the course of human history, another development has occurred – the connectedness of individuals (Lusch, 2006, p. 241). As each person specializes, more dependence and connectedness to others develops. In this way, the importance of the market and marketing can be understood in the way markets and marketing are primary drivers or creators of society. Society cannot exist without the exchange of the most fundamental resources for human existence, such as know-how. Accordingly, society can be understood to involve a complex web of service in both social and economic forms. By recognizing the mutual dependence of individuals in society, the purpose of commerce can be seen in a new light as not making and selling more stuff, but rather as mutually serving each other. In this way, the ethic of the servant leader seems to fit a new era of innovation characterized by networked collaboration.

The Importance of Employing a Stakeholder Orientation

Stakeholder Theory proposes that there are groups or entities beyond the owners of firms to whom a firm has obligations (Freeman et al., 2010). While different lists of stakeholders have emerged in the twentieth century, Peterson (2013) and others have proposed two sets of stakeholders for firms – primary and secondary stakeholders, as can be seen in Figure 3.1. Primary stakeholders include (1) society and local communities, (2) partnering firms,

(3) investor/owners, (4) customers, and (5) employees. Secondary stakeholders include (1) NGOs, (2) competitors, (3) government, (4) the natural environment and future generations, and (5) the media.

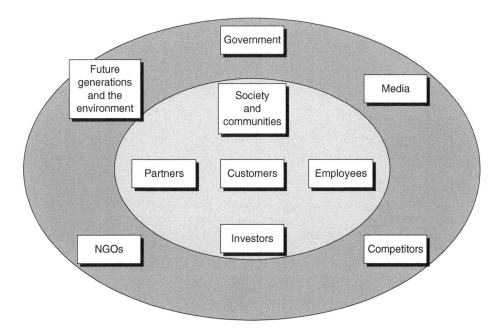

Figure 3.1   Primary stakeholders (inner circle) and secondary stakeholders (outer ring). Primary stakeholder: society and community

A business case for employing a stakeholder orientation is emerging now (Freeman et al., 2019). Scholars in marketing and marketing strategy understand that the reasons for adopting a stakeholder orientation for the firm now go beyond the idea of being the 'good guy'. Firms are increasingly understanding that their focus should not be on transactions in marketplaces, but rather on relationships and the inter-connections among actors in markets (Hillebrand et al., 2015).

In 2019, members of the Business Roundtable, composed of the chief executives of 192 of the largest companies in the US, signed a statement declaring that making profits for shareholders isn't a corporation's sole responsibility (Ignatius, 2019). Instead, firms have a broader mission to serve customers, employees, suppliers and communities, too, according to the statement. This represents what could be viewed in future years as a watershed moment in business history as the leaders of major corporations publicly proclaim that increasing shareholder value should not be the sole focus of a firm (as held by many business thinkers) (Stoll, 2019). Instead, the focus should be broader and should be on multiple stakeholders of the firm (Ferrell et al., 2010).

COSTCO – AN AGENT FOR ITS MEMBERS

Jeff Brotman and Jim Sinegal founded Costco Wholesale in 1983 before the triple bottom line had been conceptualized. But today, Costco offers a glimpse at what a firm might look like if it adopts a service-dominant-logic-approach and views marketing as the advocate for the consumer with *all* resource providers within the networked enterprise, as recommended by Lusch and Webster (2010). A number of Costco's suppliers are featured in this book as examples of unique companies who understand a stakeholder orientation.

Figure 3.2   Costco

Source: Image courtesy of Stu pendousmat at English Wikipedia. Shared under the CC BY-SA 3.0 license.

From its inception, Costco's leadership imparted to its employees an almost fanatical commitment to its customers who pay an annual fee to be members of its network (Crockett, 2019). More than 60 million people comprise Costco's membership (with Business, Gold, and Executive membership levels costing from $50 to $100 per year). As an indicator of customer loyalty, 90 percent of Costco's members renew their membership each year. In 2018, Costco's revenue on its membership fee alone totaled $3.14 billion. When considering that Costco's profits amounted to $3.13 billion in the same year, one can see (a) how low the margins are for Costco customers and (b) how important customer loyalty and membership fees are to Costco's financial well-being.

For its members, Costco serves as a buying agent, preselecting popular products in sizes that offer the best value. Costco operates an international chain of more than 785 membership warehouses (with an average store size of 143,000 square feet) that carry brand-name merchandise (including food and gasoline) at substantially lower prices than typically found at conventional wholesale or retail stores.

According to Craig Jelinek, the company's president, CEO and director:

> Costco is able to offer lower prices and better values by eliminating virtually all the frills and costs historically associated with conventional wholesalers and retailers, including salespeople, fancy buildings, delivery, billing and accounts receivable. We run a tight operation with extremely low overhead which enables us to pass on dramatic savings to our members. (Costco, 2020a)

Headquartered east of Seattle in Issaquah, Washington, Costco ranks number 14 in the Fortune 500 (Fortune, 2019) with revenues of more than $141 billion posting a razor-thin 2.2 percent profit margin. Although Walmart Stores posts the largest revenues in the world atop the Fortune 500 (with $523 billion in sales in 2019), Costco is the leading specialty retailer in the United States (followed by Home Depot, Best Buy, and Lowe's). In 2019, Costco ranked 12th in Fortune's list of the most admired companies in the world which led all retailers (Nickle, 2019).

Costco's mark-ups are capped at 14 percent (by comparison, department-store mark-ups can reach 40 percent), but across the store, the average mark-up is less than 11 percent (Costco, 2020a). What this means for the customer is that when Costco fortuitously comes across an unusual price on goods, the customer receives the benefit. For example, if Reebok manufactures too many running shoes one quarter, it might approach Costco about buying the excess run at a steep discount. If Costco buys this excess run of shoes, it would only add 14 percent on top of the price Costco would pay to Reebok, instead of taking a larger mark-up (putting the shoes on sale at a near normal price) and opportunistically capturing more profit for itself. Another way Costco cares for its customers is by extending them blanket permission for returns up to 90 days after purchase – no receipts, no questions.

Costco offers the best wages and benefits in retailing. As a result, Costco's employee turnover among its 194,000 employees is six percent each year (Hayashi, 2019). More than 60 percent of US employees have at least five years with Costco and 70 percent of store managers began their careers in hourly positions (Costco, 2020b). As a result, Costco enjoys lower training costs for employees because of the low turnover. Another benefit of attracting high-quality employees is minimal inventory shrinkage (as a result of theft and breakage). Costco's inventory shrinkage rate of less than two tenths of 1 percent is well below those of typical discount retail operations (Costco, 2020a).

Figure 3.3 depicts the monthly returns of the share price for Costco (the darker line) compared with the line representing the S&P 500 from 2010 to 2020 (the lighter line). As shown,

Costco's stock performance has exceeded the S&P 500 throughout this period. In any year over this period, investing in Costco proved to be more rewarding than investing in the S&P 500 (a basket of the 500 largest US stocks based on market capitalization representing 80 percent of all US market capitalization (Motley Fool, 2019)).

Figure 3.3   Costco's stock performance, 2010–2020, compared with S&P 500 (Big Charts, 2020)

Source: www.bigcharts.com

Costco's Mission and Code of Ethics

Costco's Mission

The Costco Board of Directors, which has guided Costco to such success in the stock market, has 15 members (Costco, 2020a). These include Charlie Munger, vice chairman of the board of Berkshire Hathaway, a hugely successful investment company chaired by Warren Buffet, as well as Sally Jewell, who has served as CEO of The Nature Conservancy (a global environmental NGO), CEO of REI (an outdoor recreation equipment retailer), and US Secretary of the Interior from 2013 to 2017. The Costco Board meets quarterly. Costco proves to be an attractive entity for some of the best business minds today.

Costco's mission is 'to continually provide our members with quality goods and services at the lowest possible prices' (Costco, 2020c, p. 1). Notably, this succinct statement can be readily understood by employees and stakeholders. 'Our Mission' precedes 'Our Code of Ethics' in a four-page document available on Costco's website for investor relations.

'"We're not doing brain surgery," as Jim Sinegal says,' Costco Senior Vice President for Ecommerce and Publishing Ginnie Roeglin said. (Sinegal co-founded Costco and served as its CEO from 1983 through 2011.) She emphasized that 'trust with our members is extremely important to our success. We're fanatical about the things that go into this. We live and die with the Code of Ethics because there are no short cuts to providing true, honest value' (Roeglin, personal communication, 2011).

Costco's Code of Ethics

Costco's Code of Ethics addresses the primary stakeholder groups of Figure 3.1. The code includes the five points as depicted in Table 3.1.

Table 3.1   The five points of Costco's Code of Ethics

1. Obey the law.
2. Take care of our members.
3. Take care of our employees.
4. Respect our suppliers.
5. Reward our shareholders.

Ethical Code #1: Obey the Law. The first point in the code of ethics, obey the law, is a direct way Costco addresses the stakeholders of society and community. Costco's history plays an important role in shaping its first ethical code. Early inklings of Costco began with Sol Price, who was a pioneer in developing the warehouse club concept with his Fed-Mart in the 1950s (which he sold to a German company in 1975) (Helyar, 2003). He then launched Price Club stores in 1976. Sinegal worked in both operations for Price before launching Costco with current Costco chairman Jeff Brotman in 1983. In 1993, Costco bought Price Club, further reinforcing the imprint of Price on the corporate DNA of Costco's culture.

When Fed-Mart began, competitors put government inspectors on Fed-Mart. As a response, Price and Fed-Mart had to be above reproach. As time went on, Price believed such an approach was good business. Retailers face multiple temptations to give local officials zoning bribes, to allow the retailer's buyers kickbacks from vendors, and to finagle health and safety requirements. None of these actions benefit customers or employees, and they were never tolerated by Price, or later Sinegal.

Another effect of Costco's first ethical code is that community stakeholders are better served when firms obey governmental regulations and laws. One way that Costco serves its community stakeholders is through price competition; 'In fact, our mere presence in a community makes pricing better throughout the area,' Sinegal said, 'Because when you have a tough competitor in the marketplace, prices come down' (Costco, 2009, p. 2). Price competition is helpful not only to consumers and communities themselves, but it also helps maintain a healthy market by encouraging competition and discouraging economic domination. Such domination leads to monopolistic behavior by firms in the form of higher prices to consumers or insensitivity to customer preferences.

> *Ethical Code #2: Take Care of Our Members.* The second point in the code of ethics, take care of our members, could be said by all retailers. However, Price early on came to view his role as a fiduciary for the customer. 'We tried to look at everything from the standpoint of, "Is it really being honest with the customer?"' Price said. He continued, 'If you recognize you're really a fiduciary for the customer, you shouldn't make too much money. If you get something for a lower price, you pass on the savings' (Helyar, 2003, p. 164).

Costco gives an annual 'Salmon Award' to Costco buyers who identify a supplier who improves quality, increases volume, and reduces the price of a product sold in Costco warehouses over time. This happened with a supplier of salmon for Costco who improved quality, saw the sales of salmon increase in Costco stores, and then responded by bringing down the price of salmon with the help of Costco managers. With the Salmon Award, Sinegal wanted to reinforce its buyers in trying to create the next 'salmon story' (Roeglin, personal communication, 2011).

Costco's vigilance for its customers' welfare translates into increased trust, which results in customers being more willing to try new products that appear in the stores. 'With trust, customers know we've done our homework on products,' Roeglin said, 'So they will take a chance on an item' (Roeglin, personal communication, 2011).

One of the elements elaborated in the second point of the code of ethics is 'giving back to our communities'. This is done through employee volunteerism and both employee and corporate contributions to United Way and Children's Hospitals. In response to natural disasters, Costco has used its scope of operations to the advantage of those who have suffered. For example, in the major earthquake of March 11, 2011, in Japan, two people died as a result of the collapse of the parking ramp at the company's Tamasakai warehouse, which sustained significant damage (Costco, 2011). To assist in the relief efforts, all Costco locations around the world began accepting donations at cash registers for the Red Cross/Red Crescent Relief Fund.

> *Ethical Code #3: Take Care of Our Employees.* The third point of the code of ethics, like the first two points, depends on Costco constraining itself to follow rules. Roeglin commented:

> There is an employee agreement or handbook. It says 'here are the rules'. A manager can't just fire a worker. It requires two levels of approval for those who have been with us more than two years. After the 90-day probationary period, they are *our* employees. The result is that

you don't have to watch your back. This fosters a very productive environment without a lot of politics or passive/aggressive stuff. I know a fifteen-year employee who left ten years ago who still says 'we' when referring to Costco.

(Roeglin, personal communication, 2011).

Ethical Code #4: Respect Our Suppliers. The fourth point in the code of ethics strives to find win–win opportunities for suppliers and Costco. 'We want to be top-of-mind to our suppliers,' Roeglin said. 'We want them to send us their best concepts.'

Because a Costco warehouse carries only 4,200 stock-keeping units (SKUs) compared with more than 100,000 for a Walmart supercenter with dry goods and food (RetailingWorks, 2011), or 30,000–50,000 at a grocery store, such as Kroger (Berman, 2011), Costco limits the choice for its customer with its narrow product lines. Each SKU represents a differently packaged product in the store. For example, a 12 oz. shampoo and a 24 oz. size of the same brand represent two separate SKUs. However, the gain for suppliers whose products are sold at Costco's warehouses is dramatic. In 2009, the average sales per SKU at Costco was $18.4 million. By comparison, the average sales per SKU at Kroger was $1.5–$2.6 million (Berman, 2011, p. 68).

Suppliers that sell to Costco must abide by Costco's Supplier Code of Conduct, a six-page document that also is available on the investor relations website. This code addresses issues about the supplier's treatment of employees, compliance with labor and environmental laws, as well as encouraging suppliers to achieve 'Above and Beyond Goals' (Costco, 2020d). Costco reserves the right to conduct audits of suppliers' facilities, its operations, and its books, as well as those of subcontractors the suppliers might use.

As with the other stakeholder relationships detailed in the Costco Code of Ethics, Costco imposes constraints upon itself with suppliers. 'We are mindful of the percentage of business we account for with our suppliers,' Roeglin said. 'We can devastate a supplier if we suddenly walk away. So, we never let that be too large of a percentage' (Roeglin, personal communication, 2011). Compared with the notoriously brusque treatment suppliers receive at Walmart's headquarters in Bentonville, Arkansas, a supporting element for respecting suppliers is to 'treat all suppliers and their representatives as we would expect to be treated if visiting their places of business' (Costco, 2020c).

Ethical Code #5: Reward Our Shareholders. The fifth element in the code of ethics is written as follows: 'If we do these four things throughout our organization, then we will achieve our ultimate goal, which is to reward our shareholders' (Costco, 2020c, p. 1). Costco has a website separate from its main website (www.costco.com) that presents a variety of documents and information to investors, such as earnings, conference call notices, legal settlements, and the annual report.

Costco and Its Secondary Stakeholders

Costco also addresses its secondary stakeholders: the government, the media, competitors, NGOs, as well as future generations and the environment (see Figure 3.1).

> *Secondary Stakeholder #1: The Government.* For the stakeholder of the government, unlike other major corporations, Costco pays taxes. In 2019, Costco's income tax expense was $1.06 billion on income before taxes of $4.76 billion (Costco, 2020a). This amounts to an effective tax rate of 26.9 percent, higher than the US corporate income tax rate of 21 percent.

The relationship between private firms and the public sector can be contentious and complex. Some of the criticisms aimed at Costco originate from Costco's activity in issues involving the public sector, such as the courts or the writing of laws. The Institute for Justice has identified Costco as a corporate beneficiary of eminent-domain takings sites (Berliner, 2011). These occur when local developers use the courts to force land owners to sell their property for public or civic use (highways, utilities, or railroads) or, in some cases, economic development. Costco does not have any registered Washington lobbyists, but it is not averse to petitioning the government for selected interests important to the firm.

> *Secondary Stakeholder #2: The Media.* Regarding media as a stakeholder, Costco puts a wide array of information on its website for investor relations, such as Securities and Exchange Commission filings, audio recordings of CFO Richard Galanti's discussion of earnings reports, results of legal settlements, its Code of Ethics, and its Sustainability Report. Costco publishes its four-color *The Costco Connection* on glossy paper that is distributed to those who are Business or Executive Members. The monthly publication started as a piece for small business owners, but now, it has changed to more of a lifestyle magazine (Roeglin, personal communication, 2011). With a current circulation of more than 14.3 million, *The Costco Connection* has the fourth largest circulation of any magazine in the US (Meyersohn, 2020). Although officers of Costco are quick to point out that their public relations efforts are limited to store openings (Costco, 2020a), with *The Costco Connection* and with its ecommerce presence on www.costco.com, it can be said that Costco actually owns two worldwide media outlets.

> *Secondary Stakeholder #3: Competitors.* Regarding competitors as stakeholders, Costco lists Sam's Club, and BJs Wholesale Club as presenting competing warehouse stores in every major metropolitan area (Costco, 2020a). Among general merchandise retail competitors, Costco lists Wal-Mart, Target, Kohl's, and Amazon.com. Costco also competes against 'category killers', focused on one or a narrow range of merchandise, including Lowe's, Home Depot, Office Depot, PetSmart, Staples, Trader Joe's, Best Buy, and Barnes & Noble.

Costco is willing to join forces with competitors on certain occasions, such as in lobbying Congress on labor reform issues – but such collaborative efforts are rare. Among leaders of retailing companies, there is evidence of respectful rapport at times, as the companies have to learn from the others' successes and failures to keep up in the industry.

One humorous episode illustrating retailers' respect for worthy competitors predates the founding of Costco in 1983. When Price Club opened in the 1970s, Sam Walton, founder of Walmart, came out to investigate (Helyar, 2003). Price commented on Walton's visit, saying:

He came out to look at a Price Club and he was very complimentary. He spent all his time telling me how impressed he'd been with Fed-Mart and how he'd never have all these Wal-marts and be worth $700 million without that model. 'I owe it all to you,' he said. I told him, 'Then don't you think I'm entitled to a finder's fee?' (Helyar, 2003, p. 164)

Secondary Stakeholders #4 and #5: NGOs, Future Generations, and the Environment. Costco encounters a wide array of NGO stakeholders. At the local level, employees give back to their communities not only through ongoing financial contributions through the United Way, but also through countless hours volunteered to local nonprofit agencies (Costco, 2009). Costco fosters a volunteer spirit among its employees by providing organizational help through the Costco Volunteer Center (CVC). The CVC serves as a clearinghouse for identifying local needs and then promoting and tracking volunteer opportunities (Volunteer Screening Blog, 2011). Each month, local charities can present their programs to the group, which finds ways to help.

In addition to boosting the volunteer efforts of its employees, Costco assists Children's Hospitals across North America with financial aid and personal support through the Children's Miracle Network.

In 2006, Costco began a collaborative relationship with the World Wildlife Fund, the world's largest private conservation organization, to identify sustainable fisheries for species designated as being at risk (Costco, 2021e). Costco also works with the Marine Stewardship Council (www.msc.org), the world's leading certification and eco-labeling program for sustainable seafood to identify which species of seafood should be discontinued for sales at Costco as a result of overfishing of the species.

Despite these efforts, the environmental activist organization Greenpeace targeted Costco in 2010 as one of seven food retailers in an effort to make their seafood purchasing and selling practices more sustainable (Lynch, 2010). Greenpeace's 'Oh No Costco!' campaign highlighted Costco's practice of selling 15 out of Greenpeace's 22 red-listed species (destructively farmed seafood) (Schwartz, 2010). Members of Greenpeace picketed the company headquarters in Issaquah, Washington, the day before the appearance of a green blimp that carried the message, 'Costco: wholesale ocean destruction' (Lynch, 2010). Representatives of Costco met with the activists and agreed to take their considerations under review. However, the two groups remained at odds over the definition of 'sustainability' and whether Costco had taken enough steps to address overfishing of the oceans.

Later, Costco stopped sales of some of the species on Greenpeace's list. The 'Oh No Costco!' website then became the 'Oh Costco!' website with the following explanation headlined by 'No Longer Wholesale Ocean Destruction':

> In a stunning win for the oceans, Costco has agreed to remove over half of its red list seafood items, pursue better practices in aquaculture and assume more of a leadership role in the ongoing global effort to develop a more sustainable tuna industry. Over the past eight months, Costco heard from environmental activists around the country – as well as from thousands of its own customers – on how the wholesale giant can and must do better to protect our precious ocean resources.
>
> (Greenpeace, 2011, para. 1)

In response to Greenpeace's concerns, Costco took action and actively worked to help protect the environment. Costco CFO Richard Galanti said:

> Greenpeace gave us a list of species of fish being overharvested. We reviewed the list, and said 'OK, we agree' with these species on the list. So we stopped sales of these species. We are ready to admit it when we don't get it right, and we do it. But unless you are in 100% compliance with their demands, you are the enemy to such groups. You are never going to make the extreme ones happy.
>
> (Galanti, personal communication, 2011)

Secondary Stakeholder #5: Future Generations. Regarding future generations as a stakeholder, Costco deploys sustainability and energy programs and supports education (Costco, 2020a). Because Costco's business model has always emphasized no-frills stores with low overhead costs, Costco did many things in a sustainable way before sustainability was widely pursued by businesses (more will be presented about Costco's green initiatives in later chapters). Costco Director of Corporate Sustainability Karen Raines explained that Costco's business approach has always sought to eliminate needless expenses in operating the warehouses:

> Overhead skylights, reusing boxes at check-out (instead of using plastic bags) were done from the very beginning. Now we are reducing our wastes, such as food waste (after donations to local food banks), by using composting, worm farms, and animal feed farms. A lot of our lighting is on timers and sun sensors. We have solar panels being deployed in pilot programs to reduce our energy consumption and expense.
>
> (Raines, 2011)

Started in 1993, the Costco Backpack Program is a nationwide program (Volunteer Screening Blog, 2011). Each Costco warehouse identifies a local school to 'adopt'. Employees then distribute new backpacks filled with supplies to each student in a chosen grade. Since 2005, more than 225,000 backpacks have been given away in the United States each year by Costco. The Backpack Program is done concurrently with a company-wide Volunteer Reading Program that was launched in 1998. Interested staff members are trained to tutor children who need extra help developing better reading skills. They meet weekly with their students, who range from grade school to high school (Volunteer Screening Blog, 2011).

Lessons from Costco and Its Stakeholder Orientation

Costco serves as a valuable example of a major corporation that manifests characteristics of a stakeholder orientation in many aspects of its operations. Costco offers a valuable case to consider how a large-scale, successful, international enterprise manifests important aspects of a stakeholder orientation. Although not perfect, Costco is importantly a learning organization. 'Jim (Sinegal – co-founder and former Costco CEO) says that 90% of every manager's job is to teach!' (Roeglin, personal communication, 2011) said, 'Everyone is in constant learning or teaching. We're not allowing complacency to settle in.'

Although Roeglin asserts that Costco is not a marketing company, it may be more correct that Costco is not a twentieth-century marketing company (relying on promotion or information asymmetries with customers). Instead, Costco takes a wide-angle view on the marketplace, embraces the 'biggest M', and strives to align the interests of its stakeholders on the way to creating value for customers, as well as other stakeholders in Costco's network of stakeholders.

Membership, in itself, brings accountability to Costco as every customer that walks in a Costco warehouse has a Costco card (and must update the information every year, actually paying to do so). 'Members have a sense of entitlement like a shareholder would,' Roeglin said (personal communication, 2011). 'It's as if they were part owners.' In these ways, Costco offers a valuable view of what more of marketing in the twenty-first century might become – networked value creation among stakeholders.

CONCLUSION

Consideration of others – particularly the stakeholders categorized as future generations and the natural environment – is endemic to sustainable business practices. Such a broader view that aligns with macromarketing offers valuable perspective to scholars in considering the ethicality of sustainability in marketing.

Costco, Inc., a major retailing corporation (ranked 14th in the Fortune 500 list of major corporations (Fortune, 2019), showcases how some important sustainability concepts can be employed by a major corporation. This is important because skeptics of sustainability in marketing in the past have pointed to the enormity and the impossibility of the task for developing any meaningful sustainable business practices in marketing, at all.

Published protocols for implementing and evaluating sustainable business practices contributing to the UN's Sustainable Development Goals (SDG), such as ISO 26000 (ISO, 2019), are now available to firms. Since 1999, Dow Jones has listed the best firms on the environmental, social, and governmental (ESG) dimensions (Dow Jones, 2019). In 2019, Bloomberg teamed with the Sustainability Accounting Standards Board (SASB) to offer financial analysts firm-performance results weighted by a 'responsibility factor' (R-factor) which likely will provide a boost to the performance metrics of firms integrating sustainability into their marketing (Bloomberg, 2019).

Researchers would do well to note such developments for firms to develop their own sustainable business practices and to receive rewards for doing so by financial rating services of the stock and bonds issued by firms. Research is needed on microlevel phenomena. Some of these include (1) factors influencing firms' pursuit (lack of pursuit) of sustainability, (2) decision-maker thinking related to how firms prioritize among the stakeholders of the firm (and at what times in the firm's development), (3) and which elements of the marketing mix for firms (pricing, product, place, and promotion) take precedence in a process of the firm transitioning to sustainability.

Additionally, research of macro-level phenomena of societal sustainability is in order, such as (1) event analysis of the Business Roundtable's 2019 acknowledgement of a firm having more responsibilities than just responsibilities to shareholders, and (2) how the introduction and tracking of new sustainability metrics for firms affects the sustainability of communities, regions, and nations. Likewise, unintended consequences resulting from the pursuit of sustainable business practices (such as job loss in fossil-fuel-dependent industries) and best policy prescriptions for addressing these externalities need to be developed. In this way, researchers will be better able to include the context within which an action takes place in a more complete way – an important aspect of ethical analysis (Jennings, 2015).

QUESTIONS

1. What surprises did you encounter in reading Chapter 3?
2. What does a stakeholder orientation have to do with the pursuit of wisdom in business decisions?
3. In your view, which stakeholder group would be the most challenging for a firm to integrate into its marketing and planning?
4. What factors are contributing to more marketing scholars embracing a marketing and society orientation (the 'biggest M') today?
5. In what ways does Costco manifest a stakeholder orientation?

Mavericks Who Made It

Paul Polman

Source: Image courtesy of Stefan Schäfer, Lich via WikiCommons. Shared under the CC BY-SA 4.0 license.

On January 1, 2009, Paul Polman became CEO of Unilever – an Anglo-Dutch multinational enterprise focused on personal care, food, and home care (Gelles, 2018). Soap brands (Dove and Lifebuoy), ice-cream brands (Ben & Jerry's, Breyer's, and Magnum), a mayonnaise brand (Hellman's), a green-cleaning brand (Seventh Generation), along with tea brands (Lipton's and Tazo) are some of the more than 400 Unilever brands used by 2.5 billion consumers each day across 190 countries (Unilever, 2020a).

Polman went to Catholic school in his home of Enschede, The Netherlands and went to seminary – but not enough students enrolled that year and the seminary closed (Gelles, 2019). Polman turned to the University of Groningen in Holland. He later worked as a maintenance man at an office building at night while he earned an MA in Economics and an MBA at the University of Cincinnati.

Having worked for decades for rival firms Procter & Gamble (P&G) (becoming group president for Europe), and then at Nestlé (as chief financial officer and head of the Americas), he was known for fiscal discipline and international experience (Gelles, 2019). But he took over Unilever in the aftermath of the Economic Crisis of 2008 during the Great Recession.

Polman conducted a strategic review of the firm that looked out to 2020 (Lawrence, Rasche, and Kenny, 2019). His team identified four major influences, such as growth (1) in developing

(Continued)

countries whose consumers need steady income and access to water, (2) in cities of the world that have fragile infrastructures, (3) in stress consumers' environmental conditions (water, sanitation, deforestation, and climate change), and (4) stakeholder empowerment due to communication technology forcing firms to be more transparent.

It became obvious to Polman and his leadership team that old models would not enable Unilever to grow its revenues – especially in emerging markets. The firm needed to develop a business model aimed at contributing to society and the environment instead of taking from them. Accordingly, he pursued sustainability as a strategic vision for Unilever – and at the same time, proposed to double the size of the business and halve the environmental footprint of Unilever.

As an artful leader, Polman recognized that Unilever began as Lever Brothers in 1886 by William Lever, an enlightened capitalist from Britain who packaged small bars of soap and created a model town for his factory workers near Liverpool called Port Sunlight (O'Toole, 2019, p. 55). He called on employees in his firm to re-connect with their founder's values for business to do well and by doing good (Moore, 2020). In order to focus on the long-term objectives, Polman stopped issuing quarterly targets for Unilver to meet – a move that alarmed financial-investment analysts.

In the Great Recession, Unilever's stock price fell 27 percent (Gelles, 2019). When Polman abolished quarterly guidance, shares dropped 8 percent. However, Polman's strategic shift to sustainability captured in Unilever's Sustainable Living Plan to guide the firm from 2010 to 2020 enabled Unilever's stock price to shoot up and more than double during his time as CEO. (This can be seen in Figure 3.4.) To accomplish this, Polman gave managers the ability to make changes that could reduce water use and greenhouse gas emissions, improve health, and create less waste.

Figure 3.4 Unilever's ADR stock performance, 2010–2020 (darker line) compared with FTSE 100 representing the top 100 publicly held firms in the UK (Big Charts, 2020)

'It's not a question in my mind of balancing different or conflicting needs (of stakeholders),' Polman said (George Mason University, 2018). The fact is shareholders – like all stakeholders – can only benefit over the long term if companies are willing to pursue responsible sustainable business models that serve the needs and interest of the societies and environments in which they operate. In fact, I believe that this is the only model in the future that consumers and citizens will give permission to exist.'

Polman encountered internal resistance from some mid-level managers accustomed to doing things with a short-term focus (and little attention to sustainable living), as well as criticism from outsiders who did not like the new multiple-stakeholder model he brought to Unilever. 'It's hard work,' Polman said (Gelles, 2019). 'The road to change has a lot of skeptics and cynics.'

After 10 years at the helm of Unilever, in general, the firm reduced its environmental footprint in manufacturing by half (CO_2 emissions reduced 65 percent, 96 percent reduction of waste sent to landfills), while reductions in upstream sourcing and downstream consumption (waste per consumer use dropped 32 percent) did not drop by half (Unilever, 2020b). The annual revenues of Unilever grew 25.8 percent during Polman's tenure as CEO (Statista, 2020).

In leading Unilever, Polman became one of the most prominent business executives calling for change to the status quo, encouraging corporations to reduce emissions, adopt renewable energy, improve working conditions for employees and produce healthier products (Gelles, 2019). Polman served on a UN panel that created the Sustainable Development Goals – 17 goals for improving the lives of the poor and caring for the planet (more will be presented on these in Chapter 4). He was one of the most outspoken in the corporate world calling world leaders to sign the Paris climate accord.

'There's been no one as clear and focused and all-in as Paul Polman in setting goals for his company, his supply chain and taking his words on the road,' said Mindy Lubber, CEO of Ceres, a nonprofit group advocating for sustainable business. 'His voice has made a difference. He's put his money where his mouth is.'

After retiring from Unilever in 2019, Polman launched a foundation called Imagine with a collection of CEOs who are committed to speeding and scaling up corporate social responsibility and shifting firms to a longer-term view of their performance in the marketplace (Holder, 2019).

'Businesses cannot survive in societies that fail,' Polman said (Moore, 2020). 'So we have a responsibility to be sure that these societies function. Nor do I think we as businesses can be by-standers in a system that gives life to us in the first place. So when that system isn't quite working, we have to take responsibility. It doesn't solve (problems) at all to have more billionaires become (higher-level) billionaires.'

Questions

- How valuable was Polman's experience in cost accounting at P&G, and later as the CFO of Nestlé in charting a new course for Unilever? Explain.
- What other influences likely contributed to Polman taking a new direction in leading Unilever?
- To what degree would you say Polman's approach at Unilever aligned with a macromarketing approach?
- How successful would you say Polman was as CEO of Unilever?

REFERENCES

BBC. (2018). Fast fashion: 'How do you justify selling a £2 T-shirt?' *BBC News*, November 27, 2018. Accessed at www.bbc.com/news/business-46358969

Berliner, D. (2011). Public power, private gain. *Institute for Justice*. Retrieved from www.ij.org/component/content/article/42-liberty/1828-ij-report-documents-10000-plus-eminent-domain-abuses-across-us-

Berman, B. (2011). *Competing in tough times: Business lessons from L.L. Bean, Trader Joe's, Costco, and other world-class retailers*. Upper Saddle River, NJ: FT Press.

Bhattacharya, C. B., Sen, S., and Korschun, D. (2008). Using corporate social responsibility to win the war for talent. *MIT Sloan Management Review*, 49(2), 37–45.

Big Charts. (2020). Chart generated by author at www.bigcharts.com

Bloomberg (2019). Bloomberg SASB ESG Indices. Accessed at www.bloomberg.com/professional/product/indices/sasb/

Candy, L. (2019). Stella McCartney pens an urgent letter to the fashion industry. *The Sunday Times*, September 15, 2019. Accessed at www.thetimes.co.uk/article/stella-mccartney-pens-an-urgent-letter-to-the-fashion-industry-8hnnfdhjw

Costco. (2009). Costco Corporate Sustainability Report. January. Retrieved from http://phx.corporate-ir.net/phoenix.zhtml?c=83830andp=irol-govhighlights

Costco (2011). Costco Wholesale Corporation Comments on Its Operations in Japan Following the Major Earthquake, March 14, 2011. Accessed at https://investor.costco.com/news-releases/news-release-details/costco-wholesale-corporation-comments-its-operations-japan

Costco. (2020a). Costco Wholesale Annual Report 2019. Available at https://investor.costco.com/static-files/05c62fe6-6c09-4e16-8d8b-5e456e5a0f7e

Costco. (2020b). Employees. Accessed at www.costco.com/sustainability-employees.html

Costco. (2020c). Costco Mission Statement and Code of Ethics. Available at https://investor.costco.com/static-files/1a1a8efe-73a8-4079-a8eb-25fcb41316b2

Costco. (2020d). Costco Wholesale Supplier Code of Conduct. Retrieved from https://investor.costco.com/static-files/4563ac77-f3ca-45a8-a9d1-545c56339d92

Costco. (2020e). Costco Statement on Seafood and Sustainability. Retrieved from https://investor.costco.com/static-files/dc1ec625-3656-4b76-b696-4f5b583e2b75

Crockett, Z. (2019). How Costco gained a cult following – by breaking every rule of retail. *The Hustle*, June 30, 2019. Accessed at https://thehustle.co/costco-membership-economics/

Dow Jones (2019). Dow Jones Sustainability Indices Review Results 2019. Accessed at www.robecosam.com/en/media/press-releases/2019/dow-jones-sustainability-indices-review-results-2019.html

Eagle, L., and Dahl, S. (2015). *Marketing ethics and society*. London: SAGE Publications.

Elkington, J. (1994). Towards the sustainable corporation: Win-Win-Win business strategies for sustainable development, *California Management Review*, 36(2), 90–100.

Ferrell, O.C., Gonzalez-Padron, T.L., Hult, T.M., and Maignan, I. (2010). From market orientation to stakeholder orientation. *Journal of Public Policy and Marketing*, 29(1), 93–6.

Fortune. (2019). Fortune 500. Accessed at https://fortune.com/fortune500/2016/costco-wholesale/

Freeman, R.E., Harrison, J.S., Wicks, A.C., Parmar, B.L., and De Colle, S. (2010). *Stakeholder theory: The state of the art*. Cambridge, UK: Cambridge University Press.

Freeman, R.E., Phillips, R., and Sisodia, R. (2019). Tensions in stakeholder theory. *Business and Society*, 59(2), 213–231.

Galanti, R. (2011). Costco CFO, Richard Galanti, personal communication, May 2011.

Gelles, D. (2019). He ran an empire of soap and mayonnaise. Now he wants to reinvent capitalism. *The New York Times*, August 29, 2019. Accessed at www.nytimes.com/2019/08/29/business/paul-polman-unilever-corner-office.html

George Mason University. (2018). Unilever CEO Paul Polman on finding career success and encouraging corporate responsibility. *News at Mason*, May 17, 2018. Accessed at www2.gmu.edu/news/512731

Greenpeace. (2011). Activist ad hoc website opposing Costco's seafood practices. Retrieved from www.oh-no-costco.com/

Haugh, H.M., and Talwar, A. (2010). How do corporations embed sustainability across the organization? *Academy of Management Learning and Education*, 9(3), 384–96.

Hayashi, R. (2019). 8 things retailers can learn from Costco (and one thing NOT to follow). *Payment Depot*, February 19, 2019. Accessed at https://paymentdepot.com/blog/8-things-retailers-can-learn-costco-one-thing-not-follow/

Helyar, J. (2003, November 24). The only company Wal-Mart fears. *Fortune*, 158–66.

Hillebrand, B., Driessen, P.H., and Koll, O. (2015). 'Stakeholder marketing: theoretical foundations and required capabilities.' *Journal of the Academy of Marketing Science*, 43, 4411–28.

Holder, M. (2019). What Paul Polman did next: Former Unilever CEO to lead new sustainability foundation. Businessgreen.com, July 8, 2019. Accessed at www.businessgreen.com/news/3078520/what-paul-polman-did-next-former-unilever-ceo-to-lead-new-sustainability-foundation

Hopkins, M.S. (2009). What executives don't get about sustainability (and further notes on the profit motive). *MIT Sloan Management Review*, 51(1), 35–40.

Hunter, S. (2009, May 18). Customers buy holes not drill bits. *Lotta Guru*. Retrieved from http://lottaguru.com/customers-buy-holes-not-drill-bits/

Hursthouse, R. (1999). *On virtue ethics*. Oxford, UK: Oxford University Press.

Ignatius, D. (2019). Corporate panic about capitalism could be a turning point. *The Washington Post*, August 20, 2019. Accessed at www.washingtonpost.com/opinions/even-the-business-moguls-know-its-time-to-reform-capitalism/2019/08/20/95e4de74-c388-11e9-9986-1fb3e4397be4_story.html

ISO (2019). ISO and Sustainability. Accessed at https://iso26000.info/isosust/

Jennings, B. (2010). Ethical aspects of sustainability. *Minding Nature Journal*, 3(1), 27–8.

Jennings, B. (2015). Ecological political economy and liberty. In Peter Brown and Peter Timmerman (Eds.), *Ecological Economics for the Anthropocene* (pp. 272–318). New York: Columbia University Press..

Kemper, J. A., and Ballantine, P.W. (2019). 'What do we mean by sustainability marketing?.' *Journal of Marketing Management*, 35(3–4), 277–309.

Kollewe, J. (2018). Burberry to stop buring unsold items after green criticism. *The Guardian*, September 6, 2018. Accessed at www.theguardian.com/business/2018/sep/06/burberry-to-stop-burning-unsold-items-fur-after-green-criticism

Lawrence, J., Rasche, A., and Kenny, K. (2019). Sustainability as opportunity: Unilever's sustainable living plan. *Managing Sustainable Business* (pp. 435–55). Dordrecht: Springer.

Lim, W.M. (2016). A blueprint for sustainability marketing: Defining its conceptual boundaries for progress. *Marketing theory*, 16(2), 232–49.

Lunde, M.B. (2018). Sustainability in marketing: A systematic review unifying 20 years of theoretical and substantive contributions (1997–2016). *AMS Review*, 8(3–4), 85–110.

Lusch, R.F. (2006). The small and long view. *Journal of Macromarketing*, 26(2), 240–4.

Lusch, R.F, and Webster, F. (2010). *Marketing's responsibility for the value of the empire* (Report #10 111). Marketing Science Institute Working Paper Series.

Lusch, R.F., Vargo, S.L., and O'Brien, M. (2007). Competing through service: Insights from service-dominant logic. *Journal of Retailing*, 83(1), 5–18.

Lynch, J. (2010, June 30). Green blimp launches Greenpeace campaign against Costco. *Issaquah Reporter*. Retrieved from www.pnwlocalnews.com/east_king/iss/news/97482194.html

Meyersohn, N. (2020). *The Costco Connection is American's fourth biggest magazine. CNN Business*, February 24, 2020. Accessed at www.cnn.com/2020/02/24/business/costco-connection-magazine-retail/index.html#:~:text=The%20Connection%20has%20a%20circulation,grown%20its%20executive%20membership%20program

Moore, M. (2020). Former Unilever CEO Paul Polman wants business leaders to accelerate corporate responsibility efforts. *Fortune*, June 23, 2020. Accessed at https://fortune.com/2020/06/23/csr-paul-polman-unilever-imagine-leadership-next/

Motley Fool. (2019). What is the S&P 500? *The Motley Fool*. Accessed at www.fool.com/knowledge-center/what-is-the-sp-500.aspx

Nickle, A. (2019). Costco, Walmart, Publix on list of most admired companies, The Packer, January 24, 2019. Accessed at www.thepacker.com/article/costco-walmart-publix-list-most-admired-companies

NRC. (2020). Nike Run Club. Accessed at https://apps.apple.com/us/app/nike-runclub/id387771637#?platform=appleWatch

O'Toole, J. (2019). *The enlightened capitalists: Cautionary tales of business pioneers who tried to do well by doing good*. New York, NY: Harper Business.

Peterson, M. (2013). *Sustainable enterprise: A macromarketing approach*. London: Sage Publications.

Peterson, M. (2016). Think Macro! *Journal of Macromarketing*, 36(2), 124–5.

Raines, K. (2011, May 6). Author's interview with Karen Raines, Costco's Director of Corporate Sustainability at Costco headquarters in Issaquah, WA.

RetailingWorks. (2011). Why sell to Wal-Mart and Sam's Club? Retrieved from www.retailing works.com/why.htm.

Roeglin, G. (2011). Author's interview with Ginnie Roeglin, Costco's Senior VP of ECommerce and Publishing at Costco headquarters in Issaquah, WA.

Schwartz, A. (2010). Greenpeace launches aggressive campaign against Costco. *Fast Company*. Retrieved from www.fascompany.com/1665470/greenpeace-launches-aggressive-campaign-against-costco

Srinivasan, M.S. (2009). Business at the Service of the Poor: Perspectives and Possibilities. *Vilakshan: The XIMB Journal of Management*, 6(2), 161–174.

Statista. (2020). Revenue of the Unilever Group worldwide from 20017 to 2019. Accessed at www.statista.com/statistics/269190/global-revenue-of-the-unilever-group-since-2007/

Stoll, J.D. (2019). Shareholders are still king. *The Wall Street Journal*, September 6, 2019. Accessed at www.wsj.com/articles/a-reminder-for-ceos-considering-a-shift-in-focus-shareholders-are-still-king-11567791772

Thomas, D. (2019). *Fashionopolis: The price of fast fashion and the future of clothes*. New York, NY: Penguin Press.

Unilever. (2020a). About Unilever. Accessed at www.unilever.com/about/who-weare/about-Unilever/

Unilever. (2020b). Reducing environmental impact. Accessed at www.unilever.com/sustainable-living/reducing-environmental-impact/

United Nations (2019). Sustainable Development Goals. Accessed at https://sustainable development.un.org/?menu=1300.

Varadarajan, R. (2011). Marketing strategy: discerning the relative influence of product and firm characteristics. *AMS Review*, 1(1), 32–43.

Vargo, S.L., and Lusch, R.F. (2008). Service-dominant logic: Continuing the evolution. *Journal of the Academy of marketing Science*, 36(1), 1–10.

Vargo, S.L., and Lusch, R.F. (2017). Service-dominant logic 2025. *International Journal of Research in Marketing*, 34(1), 46–67.

Volunteer Screening Blog. (2011). Featured Corporate Volunteer Program: Costco. Retrieved from www.volunteerscreeningblog.com/corporate-volunteer-programs/featured-corporate-volunteer-program-costco/

WCED. (1987). *Our common future*. UN World Commission on Environment and Development. Retrieved from www.un-documents.net/ocf-02.htm#I

4
THE ROLE OF BUSINESS IN SOCIETY

Throwing Shade

Source: Photo by William White on Unsplash.

Corporations Paying No Taxes

In *Steve Jobs*, the 2015 biopic film about the founder of Apple, Inc., each scene is set in theaters in the San Francisco Bay Area where important product launches occurred

(Continued)

for firms led by Steve Jobs in 1984, 1988, and 1998 (Lopatto, 2015). While Apple, Inc. is 'based in Cupertino, California', the film *Steve Jobs* had no scenes set in Cork, Ireland where the firm moved its headquarters in the 1980s for more favorable tax treatment (Amaro, 2020). But wait – after a row with the European Commission in 2016 about $15 billion in back taxes due to an unwarranted tax advantage given to Apple by the Irish government, Apple moved its headquarters to the tax haven of the Channel Island of Jersey which has a tax rate of zero for foreign companies (Vega, 2017).

Apple continues to assert that its tax arrangements are all legal (Drucker and Bowers, 2017). The firm won a decision from the EU's general court in 2020 in the $15 billion back-taxes case (Amaro, 2020). (The case could be appealed by the European Commission.) The European Commission had charged Ireland with illegally creating a special tax rate for Apple (which employs more than 6,000 in Ireland) that gave the firm a tax rate as low as 0.005 percent compared with the 12.5 percent corporate tax rate Ireland imposes on other firms (ITEP, 2017). So many firms routed their accounts and intellectual property (such as the Nike logo) through Ireland in 2015 that the gross domestic product (GDP) jumped an astounding 26 percent, instead of the forecasted 7.8 percent increase (Halpin, 2016). Economist Paul Krugman referred to the revised figure for GDP growth as 'leprechaun economics'.

Apple is not the only corporation avoiding taxes. In 2018, retail juggernaut Amazon reported $11 billion of US income, and paid no federal taxes – in fact, claiming a federal income tax rebate of $129 million for research and development incentives (ITEP, 2019). *Fortune* reports that 60 of the *Fortune* 500 companies paid no federal income tax in the US in 2018 (ITEP, 2019).

How do these firms avoid taxes? First, the firms can negotiate tax breaks from host governments (ITEP, 2019). Second, firms can create a subsidiary (or subsidiaries) in countries with low taxes and route their foreign sales to this subsidiary. Apple did both of these. Third, firms can accelerate the depreciation of their capital equipment which reduces their reported profits. Chevron reduced its taxes by $290 million this way. Fourth, firms can offer stock options to executives at a lower price and book the sale at the current value of the stock. Fifth, firms can claim tax credits and subsidies that governments offer to firms, such as Amazon has done.

'We cannot pretend that corporate tax avoidance has no cost,' Matthew Gardner, a senior fellow at the Institute on Taxation and Economic Policy said. 'Corporations zeroing out their tax bills or paying single-digit federal tax rates mean a substantial loss in federal revenue. Calls to cut critical programs and services in the wake of these corporate tax cuts are absolutely connected.'

Questions to Consider

- How clever would you say firms like Apple have been about tax avoidance?
- How ethical would you say firms like Apple have been about tax avoidance?
- The current model for public-sector officials is to toughen the existing tax codes and shame multinational enterprises into paying their fair share of taxes. What does this say about the way some firms regard their role in society? Explain.

- What would you think about scrapping taxes on corporations (treating them as 'pass-through entities') and shifting the tax burden to shareholders of these corporations (after raising the tax rates on dividends and capital gains) and imposing taxes on currently tax-exempt entities holding stock (such as pension funds)?
- Would the proposal in the previous question be more likely to be implemented than intergovernmental harmonization of tax rates?

CHAPTER OVERVIEW AND LEARNING OBJECTIVES

This chapter will examine the role of business in society. Businesses provide employment and income for citizens. Businesses can also do more in society, and increasingly businesses are going beyond a two-capital approach focused on accumulating money and stuff. Still, a debate continues about the appropriateness of taking a five-capital approach that includes the first two types of capital plus human, social, and environmental capital (as discussed in Chapter 1). This chapter will examine emerging business trends, such as how corporate social responsibility has affected the business world. This chapter will also share more about the United Nations (UN) Global Compact (calling on businesses to address human rights, labor rights, and protection of the natural environment). It will also present Wall Street's focus on sustainability, as well as the Conscious Capitalism movement. Clif Bar, Inc.'s founder Gary Erickson is featured as a Maverick Who Made It by going against conventional thinking about selling his venture for millions of dollars and instead developing it as a distinctive nutrition-bar company with 'mojo'. After this chapter, you should be able to answer the following questions:

- Should a CEO regard his or her firm only as a profit-generating unit in an atomized universe of independent and competing businesses?
- Is the business of business simply business?
- How does corporate social responsibility (CSR) relate to taking a stakeholder orientation as presented in Chapter 4?
- What are the Sustainable Development Goals (SDGs)?
- How are firms beginning to disclose nonfinancial reporting?
- What does Conscious Capitalism say about how to integrate concerns about environmental, social, and governance (ESG) into the life of the business?

IS THE BUSINESS OF BUSINESS BUSINESS?

In the agency view of management, the goals of business are predominantly financial, and ethical actions by firms are often perceived as discretionary, if they are not required by law

(Laczniak and Murphy, 2006). Also in the agency view, management acts solely as an agent of the stockholder and is responsible for maximizing investor returns – the supposed primary concern of shareholder groups. Ethics is seen as costly because it frequently requires the expenditure of organizational resources to conform to social norms. The agency view of management was crystallized in the writing of famed economist of the twentieth century Milton Friedman.

Friedman: The Social Responsibility of Business Is to Make Profit

As a libertarian, Milton Friedman championed laissez-faire economics as a professor at the University of Chicago and at the Hoover Institution. As a leading monetarist economist, he opposed the existence of the Federal Reserve Bank. However, he argued that because the Fed did exist, the government should merely increase the money supply by 3 percent each year and only have contact with markets through the courts when businesses needed their civil disputes resolved. Friedman won a Nobel Prize in economics and commanded much intellectual authority before dying in 2006.

In 1970, Friedman wrote a provocative essay that appeared in *The New York Times Magazine* proposing that the social responsibility of business is to increase its profits (Friedman, 1970). It is important to remember that the publication of this piece by Friedman came at a time before either Margaret Thatcher in the United Kingdom or Ronald Reagan in the United States had taken office. These two leaders were proponents of scaling back the role of government in society (through deregulation of the economy and reducing taxes) and of encouraging more of a role for the private sector (through job creation with the accompanying benefits of wealth for citizens). Business education in the United States had not exploded as it did later in the next 20 years with a groundswell in MBA programs. In other words, Friedman was an intellectual leader.

In his essay, Friedman decried any other purpose for business than increasing its profits. However, he did allow the 'hypocritical window-dressing' of a business spending to improve its image in the community by improving amenities in the community or improving the community's government. Through these ways, hiring and retaining employees might be done at lower costs. But Friedman denounced doing such actions as an exercise of 'social responsibility' because doing so only strengthens the too prevalent view that pursuing profits is wicked and immoral. With such a view, the impulse to curb and control business through some external force persists. In this way, talk of social responsibility in business is pure and unadulterated socialism and undermines the basis of a free society:

Once this view is adopted, the external forces that curb the market will not be the social conscience, however highly developed of the pontificating executives; it will be the iron fist of Government bureaucrats. There is one and only one social responsibility of business – to use its resources and engage in activities designed to increase its profits so long as it stays within the rules of the game, which is to say, engages in open and free competition without deception or fraud.

(Friedman, 1970, para. 29)

The Debate Begins: Mackey Challenges Friedman

Thirty-five years after the publication of Friedman's piece, John Mackey, founder and CEO of Whole Foods Market, stepped up to do what other economists feared to do – debate Friedman. The debate focused on the topic of the social responsibility of business in the October 2005 issue of *Reason*. Mackey led the world's largest retailer of natural and organic foods, with stores throughout North America and the United Kingdom. Like Friedman, Mackey identifies himself as a libertarian, but he says his ideas are neither left-wing nor right-wing. Instead, he declares them to be 'up-wing' (Mackey, 2009a).

Figure 4.1   Whole Foods' John Mackey (left) and economist Milton Friedman (right)

Sources: John Mackey image courtesy of Mike Gifford via Flickr. Shared under the CC BY-SA 2.0 license. Milton Friedman image courtesy of Berganus via Wikimedia Commons. Shared under the public domain.

Citing his 27-year-old company's sales of $4.6 billion in the previous year, as well as net profits of more than $160 million, and a market capitalization of more than $8 billion, Mackey asserted that Whole Foods measures success by 'how much value we can create for all six of our most important stakeholders: customers, team members [employees], investors, vendors, communities and the environment' (Mackey, 2005, para. 5). In this way, Mackey adopted a stakeholder perspective (elaborated upon in Chapter 4) to debate Friedman.

Mackey explained that there was no magic formula to calculate how much value each stakeholder should receive from the company. 'It is a dynamic process that evolves with the competitive marketplace,' Mackey said. 'No stakeholder remains satisfied for long. It is the function of the company leadership to develop solutions that continually work for the common good' (Mackey, 2005, para. 6).

Mackey also addressed one of Friedman's criticisms of corporate philanthropy as stealing from investors. He offered more detail about the philanthropy of Whole Foods that continues after 20 years. Five days each year, Whole Foods holds a '5% Day' in which 5 percent of a store's total sales are directed to a nonprofit organization. The stores select the beneficiary groups and tend to focus on groups with large membership lists. Those on the lists receive a phonecall the week of the '5% Day' to shop at the store to support the organization. This usually brings in hundreds of new or lapsed customers. In this way, the '5% Day' benefits a local group, but it is also an excellent marketing technique that has benefitted the investors of Whole Foods immensely over the years.

When Whole Foods drafted its mission statement in 1985, it announced that it would donate 5 percent of the company's net profits to philanthropy. This predated the initial public offering of stock, and no investors have ever raised objections to the policy. Mackey pointedly asks, 'How can Whole Foods' philanthropy be "theft" from the current investors if the original owners of the company unanimously approved the policy and all subsequent investors made their investment after the policy was in effect and well publicized?' (Mackey, 2005, para. 11).

Not stopping there, Mackey asserts that shareholders of a public company own their stock voluntarily and can sell their shares if they do not agree with the philosophy of the business. Alternatively, shareholders can submit a resolution at the annual shareholders meeting to change any policy of the firm (a number of Whole Foods' policies have been changed this way):

Corporate philanthropy is a good thing, but it requires the legitimacy of investor approval. In my experience, most investors understand that it can be beneficial to both the corporation and to the larger society. That doesn't answer the question of *why* we give money to the community stakeholder. For that, you should turn to one of the fathers of free-market economics, Adam Smith. *The Wealth of Nations* was a tremendous achievement, but economists would be well served to read Smith's other great book, *The Theory of Moral Sentiments*. There he explains that human nature isn't just about self-interest. It also includes sympathy, empathy, friendship, love, and the desire for social approval. As motives for human behavior, these are at least as important as self-interest. For many people, they are more important.

(Mackey, 2005, para. 14, emphasis in original)

In reply, Friedman (2005) surprisingly said, 'The differences between John Mackey and me regarding the social responsibility of business are for the most part rhetorical. Strip off the camouflage, and it turns out we are in essential agreement' (para. 2). Friedman (2005) noted the success of Whole Foods in a competitive industry and observed, 'had it devoted any significant fraction of its resources to exercising a social responsibility unrelated to the bottom line, it would be out of business by now or would have been taken over' (para. 2).

Friedman (2005) did assert that corporate philanthropy being a good thing is 'flatly wrong' (para. 8). Friedman declared that outrageous tax laws contribute to this practice making sense because a stockholder can give more to charity if a corporation gives out of pre-tax earnings, rather than the stockholder's earnings, which would be double-taxed (taxes paid by the corporation, and then taxes paid by the stockholder on capital gains on the sale of the stock).

Finally, Friedman (2005) proposed that his statement, 'the social responsibility of business is to increase profits,' and Mackey's statement, 'the enlightened corporation should try to create value for all of its constituencies', are equivalent (para. 15):

Note first that I refer to *social* responsibility, not financial, or accounting, or legal. It is social precisely to allow for the constituencies to which Mackey refers. Maximizing profits is an end from the private point of view; it is a means from the social point of view. A system based on private property and free markets is a sophisticated means of enabling people to cooperate in their economic activities without compulsion; it enables separated knowledge to assure that each resource is used for its most valued use, and is combined with other resources in the most efficient way. Of course, this is abstract and idealized. The world is not ideal. There are all sorts of deviations from the perfect market – many, if not most, I suspect, due to government interventions. But with all its defects, the current largely free-market, private-property world seems to me vastly preferable to a world in which a large fraction of resources is used and distributed by 501c(3)s and their corporate counterparts.

(Friedman, 2005, paras. 15–16, emphasis in original)

In sum, Friedman acknowledges that incorporating stakeholder concerns in the marketing strategy of a business can prove effective in the less-than-perfect world in which business exists. However, he cautions that coercive plays by stakeholders could thwart the social good a business can provide, primarily through profit making. Of course, few stakeholders of a business hold coercive power over a business. Although Mother Nature would ultimately be one such stakeholder (through resource depletion, natural disaster, or pandemic), government would be the likeliest stakeholder to wield coercive power over the business. More will be presented on the role of the state in society in Chapter 5.

Do Markets Need Adult Supervision?

Harvard Business School professor Rebecca Henderson notes a disconnection between Friedman's view of efficient markets and societal challenges, such as environmental degradation and income inequality in an era of billionaires (Henderson, 2020). She asserts that markets require 'adult supervision' to ensure they are truly free and fair – meaning appropriate laws and regulations.

Free markets only work their magic when prices reflect all available information, when there is meaningful freedom of opportunity, and when the rules of the game support genuine competition. In today's world many prices are wildly out of whack, freedom of opportunity is increasingly confined to the well connected, and firms are rewriting the rules of the game in ways that maximize their own profits while simultaneously distorting the market (Henderson, 2020, p. 19).

An example of what Henderson asserts can be seen in the sources of inputs for firms. In a globalized world, a firm can choose to move away from vertical integration (where the firm handles each stage of production) to outsourcing these stages of production to other firms that can be located anywhere in the world. By comparison, workers in one country would incur steep costs as individuals to relocate to another country (selling all and embarking upon language and cultural learning paid by themselves) – if they were allowed to do so. In reality, countries' immigration laws prohibit such moves in almost all cases.

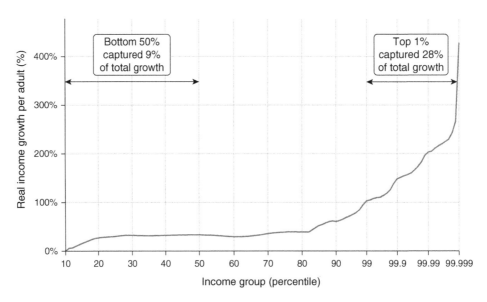

Figure 4.2   Total income growth by percentile in US–Canada and Western Europe, 1980–2016

Source: WID.world (2017, p. 48).

So, manufacturing firms can use markets around the world to diversify their supply chains, but individual workers cannot move into other countries to pursue work in these supply chains. In the service sector, a family in the UK using the internet can have its tax returns prepared by workers in India where wages are lower. This brings more competition to tax preparers who actually live in the UK, thereby putting downward pressure on wages in the UK for tax preparers.

Each of these examples illustrate how lower and middle-class workers in developed countries have seen their wages stagnate. Figure 4.2 depicts how the income groups comprising the bottom 80 percent of those the West had stagnant income from 1980 to 2016 – but those in the top 20 percent of income groups had markedly increased income during this time (WID.world, 2017). More will be shared about globalization and its effect on incomes in Chapter 6.

CORPORATE SOCIAL RESPONSIBILITY
What Does CSR Look Like in Business?

Although many agree that CSR refers to the duties of the firm to society (Smith, 2003), there is little consensus about the nature or scope of the firm's obligations to society (Berger, Cunningham, and Drumwright, 2007). Industry Canada, the department of the Canadian Government with responsibility for regional economic development, investment, and innovation, explains CSR in the following way:

> Corporate Social Responsibility is defined as a company's environmental, social and economic performance and the impacts of the company on its internal and external stakeholders. Some companies use other terms for CSR, such as corporate responsibility, corporate sustainability and 'triple bottom line'. Other companies prefer to treat each CSR item separately, such as environmental management and community or employee relations, etc.

(Industry Canada, 2020)

Pursuing CSR from a desire to do good (the 'normative case'), or from enlightened self-interest (the 'business case'), has characterized firms' responses to societal obligations over time. Philanthropy has long been a mechanism for businesses and business persons to give back (Bishop and Green, 2008). But philanthropy might also allow monopolistic-prone businesses and industrialists to pillage first and then give back later to a few, as a means to forestall societal impatience with the deleterious business practices of monopolistic businesses (Edwards, 2010). Those who have ever experienced frustration with a Microsoft operating system for a PC might wonder whether the good works of the Bill and Melinda Gates Foundation (which address extreme poverty and poor health in developing countries, as well as the failures of America's education system) make up for the lack of choice in operating systems for PCs all consumers experience in a 'competitive marketplace'.

Additionally, 'cause marketing' is increasingly observed despite claims by corporations that their philanthropic efforts are not marketing, per se. Pepsi chose not to spend $20 million on a handful of Super Bowl ads in early 2010, and instead the company pursued a massive social media campaign in which it asked the public to vote online for charities and community groups to receive grants ranging from $5,000 to $250,000 (Campaign US, 2017). This Pepsi Refresh campaign hoped to take advantage of rising consumer interest at the time in social media, such as Facebook, Twitter, and YouTube. The effort proved to be the largest social media initiative on record.

Pepsi Refresh received more than 80 million votes and at its peak 37 percent of those in the US acknowledged awareness of the Refresh Project. Unfortunately, vetting all of the projects receiving votes proved impossible and resulted in persistent fraud allegations. And worse for Pepsi, the lack of a direct connection to the Pepsi product resulted in no real boost to sales.

In July 2010, Pepsi announced it would give $1.3 million in grants to help clear up the Deepwater Horizon spill in states of the US adjacent to the Gulf of Mexico. The firm quietly ended Pepsi Refresh in 2012. The Refresh Project is an example of cause marketing in which firms try to win customers by ostentatiously doing good with products not inherently ethical (such as 'fair trade' goods), but with boosted moral credentials through an association with a cause. It also shows how difficult designing and implementing a successful cause-marketing effort can be.

The Benefits of CSR for Firms

Firms treating CSR issues as tangential to their operations (relegating them to the public relations or corporate affairs departments) miss the opportunity for shifting the focus of the firms' leadership to important new areas of interest. Firms treating CSR as organic to their operations tend to shape public debate on issues relevant for society, and subsequently, to re-direct the firms' R&D efforts to rewarding areas of the future (Porter, 2006). In other words, these social and environmental issues offer opportunities for firms, not just threats or risks (Kanter, 2009). In short, value-creation opportunities come with these social and environmental issues.

Alert businesses can gain advantage over their competitors by identifying and developing effective and efficient ways to meet these needs before anyone else. For example, E.I. du Pont de Nemours and Company (DuPont), a major industrial company, has aligned its research and development efforts to the UN's Sustainable Development Goals related to (1) food, (2) water, (3) energy, and (4) healthcare for the world's population that will increase from 7 billion to 9 billion by 2050. It does this because these goals represent what are the most pressing needs for DuPont's customers (Dembek, 2020). DuPont was a founding member of the World Business Council for Sustainable Development (www.wbcsd.org/) – a CEO-led organization of 200 forward-thinking firms working to accelerate the transition to a sustainable world. Accordingly, it has learned much about successful approaches to sustainability from other like-minded firms since 1995.

Efforts to Develop Standards for CSR

The UN Global Compact

In 2001, DuPont endorsed the UN Global Compact, which is a strategic policy initiative for businesses intended to align their operations and strategies with ten universally accepted principles in the areas of human rights, labor, environment, and anti-corruption (see Table 4.1). The UN realized that meaningful progress on the UN Millennium Development Goals to eradicate poverty and related social ills by 2015 would not be made without the participation of businesses. (The UN's Sustainable Development Goals later superseded its Millennium Development Goals.)

In 1999, former UN Secretary-General of the United Nations Kofi Annan addressed the Davos World Economic Forum. Annan challenged business leaders to provide a human face for globalization by joining a global compact of shared values and principles (UN Global Compact, 2020). The resulting UN Global Compact resulted from principles contained in four existing declarations: (a) the Universal Declaration of Human Rights, (b) the International Labor Organization's Declaration on Fundamental Principles and Rights at Work, (c) the Rio Declaration on Environment and Development, and (d) the United Nations Convention against Corruption.

Although UN Secretary-General Ban Ki-moon reported that almost 6,000 businesses across 130 countries (with about half of these having more than 250 employees) had signed the UN Global Compact by 2010 (Ki-moon, 2010), the majority of businesses in the world still have not signed the UN Global Compact. Because of requirements for businesses to post communications on progress (COPs) each year, more than 1,000 businesses have been de-listed as signatories as a result of lack of communication about their progress on adhering to the principles of the UN Global Compact (UN Global Compact, 2020). Among US businesses, reasons for not signing the UN Global Compact relate to concerns about the implications of labor rights of the Compact, as well as to being involved in a UN endeavor (Williams, 2004).

Table 4.1   The Ten Principles of the UN Global Compact

Human Rights

- Principle 1: Businesses should support and respect the protection of internationally proclaimed human rights; and
- Principle 2: make sure that they are not complicit in human rights abuses.

Labour

- Principle 3: Businesses should uphold the freedom of association and the effective recognition of the right to collective bargaining;
- Principle 4: the elimination of all forms of forced and compulsory labour;
- Principle 5: the effective abolition of child labour; and
- Principle 6: the elimination of discrimination in respect of employment and occupation.

Environment

- Principle 7: Businesses should support a precautionary approach to environmental challenges;
- Principle 8: undertake initiatives to promote greater environmental responsibility; and
- Principle 9: encourage the development and diffusion of environmentally friendly technologies.

Anti-Corruption

- Principle 10: Businesses should work against corruption in all its forms, including extortion and bribery.

Source: UN Global Compact (2020).

Although the principles read as if they were drafted by regulators of business intent on constraining business operations, some nongovernmental organizations (NGOs) have criticized the Compact for lack of accountability for businesses signing the compact. In other words, the UN Global Compact is flawed because it is voluntary. Although these NGOs seek a binding legal framework for the transnational behavior of business in the realms of human rights, environment, and labor, they do recognize the UN Global Compact's intent to define expectations for businesses about their role in society.

United Nations Sustainable Development Goals

In September 2015, all 193 Member States of the United Nations adopted a plan for achieving a better future for all – laying out a path over the next 15 years to end extreme poverty, fight inequality and injustice, and protect our planet (UN, 2020). The 17 Sustainable Development Goals (SDGs) are the focus of the next phase of the UN's work. Many businesses have adopted one or more of these for which to give focus in the coming years. For example, Coca-Cola gives priority to (1) gender equity (SDG 5), (2) clean water and sanitation (SDG 6), (3) decent work and economic growth (SDG 8), (4) responsible consumption and production (SDG 12), (5) life below water (SDG 14), and (6) partnerships for the goals (SDG 17) (Coca-Cola, 2020).

SDGs 1 and 5 represent dignity (Hult et al., 2018). SDGs 2, 3, and 4 represent people. SDGs 6 and 12–15 represent planet. SDGs 7–11 represent prosperity, while SDG 16 represents justice, and SDG 17 represents partnerships needed to achieve SDGs. Figure 4.3 depicts the SDGs while Table 4.2 presents why each matters.

Veteran Unilever staffer Myriam Sibide who worked for 15 years helping the Lifebuoy soap brand of Unilever further public health in countries around the world asserts that brand managers and senior executives could choose any of the SDGs to serve as the social purpose for their brand (Sibide, 2020, p. 13). For example, an automobile manufacturer could target SDG 12 (Responsible consumption and production) as its social purpose. Likewise, a bank could target SDG 17 (Partnerships to achieve the goal) as its social purpose and accordingly sponsoring special efforts to assist NGOs and for-profit firms pursue their SDGs.

Figure 4.3   The United Nations Sustainable Development Goals

Source: United Nations Sustainable Development Goals, https://www.un.org/sustainabledevelopment/. The content of this publication has not been approved by the United Nations and does not reflect the views of the United Nations or its officials or Member States.

Table 4.2   Why each of the UN Sustainable Development Goals (SDGs) matters

SDGs	Why the SDG matters
1. No poverty	700 million live in extreme poverty (10% of world population).
2. Zero hunger	690 million are hungry (almost 9% of world population).
3. Good health and well-being	6.2 million under the age of 15 years died from preventable disease in 2018.
4. Quality education	750 million adults (2/3 of these women) remained illiterate in 2016.

(Continued)

Table 4.2   (Continued)

SDGs	Why the SDG matters
5. Gender equality	200 million girls in 30 countries have undergone female genital mutilation.
6. Clean water and sanitation	At least 892 million people continue to practice open defecation.
7. Affordable and clean energy	3 billion rely on wood, coal, charcoal or animal waste for cooking and heating.
8. Decent work and economic growth	Globally, 61% of all workers were engaged in informal employment in 2016.
9. Industry, innovation and infrastructure	Globally, 16% of population does not have access to mobile broadband.
10. Reduced inequality	Of the 1 billion of persons with a disability, 80% live in developing countries.
11. Sustainable cities and communities	828 million live in slums today (most in Eastern and Southern Asia).
12. Responsible consumption and production	840 million still live without access to electricity.
13. Climate action	From 1880 to 2012, average global temperature increased by 0.85 degrees C.
14. Life below water	More than 3 billion depend on marine and coastal biodiversity for a living.
15. Life on land	Around 1.6 billion depend on forests for their livelihood.
16. Peace, justice and strong institutions	70 million fled war, persecution and conflict in 2018 – highest in 70 years.
17. Partnerships to achieve the Goals	Partnerships needed to share knowledge, technology and financial resources.

Source: United Nations Sustainable Development Goals, https://www.un.org/sustainabledevelopment/. The content of this publication has not been approved by the United Nations and does not reflect the views of the United Nations or its officials or Member States.

In sum, the SDGs allow those interested in sustainability across the public, private and civil sectors to target meaningful ways they can work together. Specifically, they can mobilize efforts to end poverty, address inequalities, and mitigate climate change by 2030.

Principles for Responsible Management Education and Responsible Investment

The SDGs have garnered attention around the world for the role of business in societies. While providing far-reaching aspirations with little implementation guidance, the SDGs have spawned efforts such as the Principles for Responsible Management Education (PRME) in 2008, which now has more than 800 participating business schools agreeing to the principles and reporting on their progress annually (PRME, 2020). Additionally, the SDGs have spawned the Principles for Responsible Investment, which encourages investors and investment groups, such as pension funds, to integrate ESG issues across their investment operations.

Sustainability Reporting

Several voluntary reporting efforts are also enabling more businesses to embrace a stakeholder orientation and report more meaningfully on their ESG initiatives. The Global Reporting Initiative (GRI) is an independent, global organization whose purpose is to make reporting on ESG issues as commonplace as reporting on financial performance – and as important to firm success (Eccles and Krzus, 2010). In 2000, GRI released its first set of guidelines for sustainability reporting. These guidelines are developed in an ongoing way using a multi-stakeholder process. Ninety-three percent of the world's largest 250 firms report on their sustainability performance now (GRI, 2020).

Headquartered in the Netherlands, GRI has regional hubs in Brazil, China, Colombia, India, South Africa, and the US. This suggests the global nature of sustainability reporting today. The UN's SDGs have become a global reference for sustainability reporting policy for countries and firms. The EU's 2014 Directive on the disclosure of nonfinancial and diversity information by large firms has increased the demand for GRI's reporting framework. Europe continues to drive the agenda for ESG as evidenced by the European Commission's issuance of nonbinding guidelines for ESG disclosure (EC, 2017). The development of sustainability reporting continues through the work of GRI, the Sustainability Accounting Standards Board (SASB) based in San Francisco. The Impact Reporting and Investment Standards – an initiative of the Global Impact Investing Network – offers a catalogue of performance metrics that helps guide investor who want to consider the environmental and social impact of their investments (Walker, 2019).

The International Standards Organization: ISO 26000

ISO 26000 is a voluntary guidance standard for integrating businesses' responsibilities toward society into the fundamental expectations of business organizations (Bernhart and Maher, 2011). Emanating from the International Standards Organization based in Switzerland, ISO 26000 was developed by a global, multi-stakeholder group consisting of thousands of contributors and reviewers from more than 90 countries. The International Standards Organization is the same organization that fields voluntary standards for quality processes (ISO 9000), as well as for environmental management (ISO 14001), as previously discussed. The seven core subjects that comprise ISO 26000 are shown in Figure 4.4.

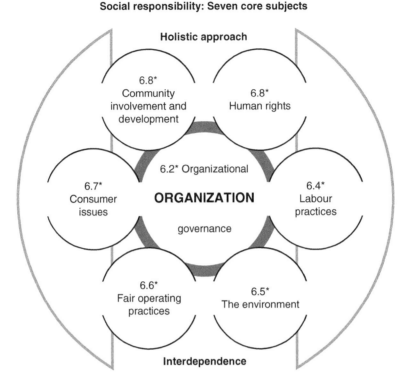

Figure 4.4   The seven core subjects of ISO 26000 for social responsibility

Source: ISO, www.iso.org/files/live/sites/isoorg/files/store/en/PUB100259.pdf

Although the ISO emphatically asserts that ISO 26000 will not lead to certification, these standards will provide a framework for firms to develop and communicate their GSE endeavors to stakeholder groups. These guidance standards became finalized in December 2010, and as more businesses implement ISO 26000 standards, more firms will want to learn about the process of improving their firm's effectiveness in regard to ESG.

In sum, the UN Global Compact has won the attention of important actors in business as well as in civil society to give serious consideration for the role of business in the new economic circumstances of the twentieth century. The successful fielding of voluntary standards, such as GRI's for sustainability reporting and ISO 26000 for integrating social responsibility across the organization, contributes valuably to making a stakeholder orientation a more meaningful approach to conducting business today and in the future.

Lessons from Novo Nordisk

Novo Nordisk, a Danish-based pharmaceutical company, has focused on developing drugs for people with diabetes, hemophilia, and growth hormone deficiency for almost 90 years (Novo Nordisk, 2018). The firm has more than 43,500 employees working in 80 countries, and it markets its products in approximately 170 countries (Novo Nordisk, 2020). In 2001, Novo Nordisk signed the UN Global Compact. Since 2004, Novo Nordisk has reported annually on its ESG performance (Eccles and Krzus, 2010) using GRI's Sustainability Reporting Guidelines. This enables analysts and stakeholders to more readily grasp issues the firm encounters in the ESG realm but also to make comparisons of Novo Nordisk with other firms reporting on their ESG performance.

Although financial reporting is highly regulated, nonfinancial reporting is still in its infancy. For this reason, Novo Nordisk uses AccountAbility's AA1000 Assurance Standard in its ongoing effort to develop its sustainability reporting. The AA1000 Series of Standards is based on the principles of (a) *inclusivity*: people should have a say in the decisions that have an impact on them, (b) *materiality*: decision-makers should identify and be clear about the issues that matter, and (c) *responsiveness*: organizations should be transparent about their actions.

Novo Nordisk has become a leader in sustainability reporting and now integrates financial and nonfinancial reporting. Such reporting is referred to as integrated reporting or One Report and does not necessarily imply a single document but the collection of the material measures of financial and nonfinancial (ESG) performance. In this way, Novo Nordisk offers a glimpse of the future in ESG reporting. Integrated reporting reflects Novo Nordisk's objective to conduct its activities in a financially, environmentally, and socially responsible way.

Novo Nordisk's former CEO Lars Rebien Sørensen explained the firm's deep engagement with social and environmental issues. 'Corporate social responsibility is nothing but maximizing the value of your company over a long period,' Sørensen said (Ignatius and McGinn, 2015). 'In the long term, social and environmental issues become financial issues.'

Figure 4.5 depicts the nonfinancial statement page from Novo Nordisk's 2018 annual report (Novo Nordisk, 2018). Note how this nonfinancial statement features social performance as well as environmental performance. Under social performance, patients, employees, and assurance comprise the three categories of reporting. Under assurance, the ethicality of Novo Nordisk is made more evident to stakeholders with information on (a) survey results focused on the company's reputation with key stakeholders, (b) the percentage of employees trained in ethics, (c) warning letters received and re-inspections required, and (d) audits performed on its suppliers. The company also puts an abundance of other ESG information on its website to allow different stakeholders the ability to create their own report on Novo Nordisk.

Performance highlights

DKK million	2014	2015	2016	2017	2018	2017–2018 Change
Financial performance						
Net sales	88,806	107,927	111,780	111,696	111,831	0%
Sales growth in local currencies[1]	8.3%	8.4%	5.5%	2.3%	4.6%	
Foreign currency impact	(2.0%)	13.1%	(1.9%)	(2.4%)	(4.5%)	
Net sales growth as reported	6.3%	21.5%	3.6%	(0.1%)	0.1%	
Depreciation, amortization and impairment losses	3,435	2,959	3,193	3,182	3,925	23%
Operating profit	34,492	49,444	48,432	48,967	47,248	(4%)
Net financials	(396)	(5,961)	(634)	(287)	367	N/A
Profit before income taxes	34,096	43,483	47,798	48,680	47,615	(2%)
Net profit for the year	26,481	34,860	37,925	38,130	38,628	1%
Total assets	77,062	91,799	97,539	102,355	110,769	8%
Equity	40,294	46,969	45,269	49,815	51,839	4%
Capital expenditure, net (property, plant and equipment)	3,986	5,209	7,061	8,679	9,524	10%
Free cash flow	27,396	34,222	39,991	32,588	32,536	(0%)
Financial ratios[1]						
Percentage of sales	26.2%	26.2%	25.4%	25.4%	26.3%	
Sales and distribution costs	15.5%	12.6%	13.0%	12.5%	13.2%	
Research and development costs	4.0%	3.6%	3.5%	3.4%	3.5%	
Administrative costs						
Gross margin	83.6%	85.0%	84.6%	84.2%	84.2%	
Operating margin	38.8%	45.8%	43.3%	43.8%	42.2%	
Net profit margin	29.8%	32.3%	33.9%	34.1%	34.5%	
Effective tax rate	22.3%	19.8%	20.7%	21.7%	18.9%	
Equity ratio	52.3%	51.2%	46.4%	48.7%	46.8%	
Return on equity	63.9%	79.9%	82.2%	80.2%	76.0%	
Cash to earnings	103.5%	98.2%	105.4%	85.5%	84.2%	
Payout ratio	48.7%	46.6%	50.2%	50.4%	50.6%	

Long-term financial targets[1]						Target[2]
Operating profit growth	9.5%	43.3%	(2.0%)	1.1%	(3.5%)	5%
Operating profit growth adjusted[3]	9.5%	35.2%	3.9%	1.1%	(3.5%)	125%
Operating profit growth in local currencies adjusted[3]	12.7%	12.7%	6.2%	4.8%	2.8%	90%
Operating profit after tax to net operating assets	101.0%	148.7%	150.2%	143.2%	116.7%	
Cash to earnings (three-year average)	93.1%	96.8%	102.4%	96.4%	91.7%	

1. For definitions, see pp. 95–96. 2. Targets effective December 31, 2018. The long-term financial targets were adjusted in February 2019. See '2019 Outlook' p 12. 3. Years 2015 and 2016, adjusted for DKK 2,376 million from the divestment of associated company and DKK 449 million from the income related to the out-licensing of assets for inflammatory disorders respectively.

Social performance						Change
Patients reached with Novo Nordisk diabetes products (estimate in millions)	24.4	26.8	28.0	27.7	29.2	5%
Patients reached with Novo Nordisk products via the Access to Insulin Commitment (estimate in millions)	–	–	–	0.3	0.3	
Donations (DKK million)[4]	84	105	106	103	103	
Employees (total)	41,450[5]	41,122	42,446	42,682	43,202	1%
Employee turnover	9.0%	9.2%	9.7%	11.0%	11.7%	
Gender in management (ratio men: women)	60:40	59:41	59:41	60:40	60:40	
Relevant employees trained in business ethics	98%	98%	99%	99%	99%	
Product recalls	2	2	6	6	3	
Failed inspections	0	0	0	0	0	(50%)
Long-term social targets						Target
Employee engagement[6]	–	–	–	90%	91%	≥ 90
Company reputation (scale 0–100)	79.5	81.1	77.8	79.3	83.3	≥80

(Continued)

Figure 4.5 (Continued)

Environmental performance						Change
Energy consumption (1,000 G)	2,556	2,778	2,935	2,9222	2,890	(1%)
Water consumption (1,000m²)	2,959	3,131	3,293	3,276	3,101	(5%)
CO_2 emissions from production sites and product distribution (1,000 tons)	177	150	130	129	127	(2%)
Waste (1,000 tons)	141	159	153	157	142	(10%)
Long-term environmental targets						Target[7]
Share of renewable power for production	73%	78%	78%	79%	77%	100% by 2020
CO_2 emissions from operations and transportation (1,000 tons)	–	–	–	–	269	0 by 2030
Share performance						**Change**
Basic earning per share/ADR in DKK[1,8]	10.10	13.56	14.99	15.42	15.96	4%
Diluted earning per share/ADR in DKK[1,8]	10.07	13.52	14.96	15.39	15.93	4%
Total number of shares (million), 31 December	2,650	2,600	2,550	2,500	2,450	(2%)
Treasury shares (million), 31 December	57	52	46	56	56	0%
Share capital (DKK million)	530	520	510	500	490	(2%)
Dividend per share in DKK[8]	5.00	6.40	7.60	7.85	8.15[9]	4%
Total divided (DKK million)	12,905	16,230	19,048	19,206	19,547[9]	2%
Share repurchases (DKK million)	14,728	17,229	15,057	16,845	15,567	(8%)
Closing share price (DKK)	260.30	399.90	254.70	334.50	297.90	(11%)

4. Donations to the World Diabetes Foundation and the Novo Nordisk Kaemophilia Foundation. **5.** Includes employees of associated company. **6.** New methodology applied on 2017, hence data between 2014–2016 is not available. **7.** A new long-term environments target was developed in 2018. See p. 17. **8.** Share performance-related key figures have been calculated reflecting a trading unit of DKK 0.20. **9.** Total dividend for the year including interim dividend of DKK 3.00 per share, which was paid in August 2018. The remaining DKK 5.15 per share, corresponding to DKK 12,309 million, will be paid subject to approval at the Annual General Meeting.

Figure 4.5 Financial and nonfinancial reporting in Novo Nordisk's 2018 Annual Report

Source: Novo Nordisk (2018).

The continuing effort to improve corporate transparency can be seen in the story of Novo Nordisk. There are more than 1,750 firms and business associations who have adopted integrated reporting around the world (more than 300 in Japan alone) (GRI, 2020). Regulators in Japan, India, and the UK are taking more interest in integrated reporting as a way to achieve more comprehensive reporting that would promote financial stability. The European Commission has described integrated reporting as 'a step ahead'. Firms such as Unilever, Vodafone, HSBC Financial Services, Mitsubishi, Hyundai, SAP, Coca-Cola, General Electric, Cemex, and South African Airways are a few of the firms that have implemented integrated reporting. Natura, a Brazilian cosmetics company, and Philips (from the Netherlands) are acknowledged as leaders in integrative reporting and have been reporting this way since 2008.

The Effect of ESG and Sustainability Reporting

The picture emerging from these leaders in integrative reporting is an environment of accountability for businesses genuinely interested in ESG reporting. A more complete picture of the firm's operations and risks can be gained for stakeholders outside the firm. This richer flow of information would allow investors – particularly major investors, such as pension funds, mutual funds, and institutional endowment funds – to assess the long-term prospects for the focal company.

Some countries are now making sustainability reporting mandatory. Denmark, Sweden, France, and South Africa have some form of requirement for sustainability reporting (Ioannou and Serafeim, 2011). In a study of 58 countries, researchers found that after the adoption of mandatory sustainability reporting laws and regulations, the social responsibility of business leaders increases. According to the results of this study, sustainable development and employee training become a higher priority for companies when corporate sustainability reporting becomes required by law. Additionally, companies tend to implement more ethical practices, reduce bribery, and corruption. Not surprisingly, management credibility increases in such countries.

In 2019, McKinsey and Company conducted a survey of firm leaders from around the world about ESG programs and found that 57 percent of respondents agree that ESG programs create shareholder value (Delevigne et al., 2020). Institutional investors have increasingly incorporated ESG issues into investment analysis and decision-making. Larry Fink, CEO of BlackRock, Inc. – the world's largest asset manager with more than $7.4 trillion in assets under management at the end of 2019 – sent a headline-grabbing letter to CEOs of the world's largest firms ending in the following way:

> We believe that when a company is not effectively addressing a material issue, its directors should be held accountable. Last year BlackRock voted against or withheld votes from 4,800 directors at 2,700 different companies. Where we feel companies and boards are not producing effective sustainability disclosures or implementing frameworks for managing these issues, we will hold board members accountable. *Given the groundwork we have already laid engaging on disclosure, and the growing investment risks surrounding sustainability, we will be increasingly disposed to vote against management and board directors when companies are not making sufficient progress on sustainability-related disclosures and the business practices and plans underlying them.*
>
> (Fink, 2020a – italics added)

Fink then sent a letter to clients of BlackRock that emphasized the central role sustainability would take in BlackRock's investment decisions in the future because sustainability represented a firm's commitment to long-term value creation, and over the past few years, BlackRock's clients have focused on the impact of sustainability on their portfolios.

> As your fiduciary, BlackRock is committed to helping you navigate this transition and build more resilient portfolios, including striving for more stable and higher long-term returns. Because sustainable investment options have the potential to offer clients better outcomes, we are making sustainability integral to the way BlackRock manages risk, constructs portfolios, designs products, and engages with companies. *We believe that sustainability should be our new standard for investing.*
>
> (Fink, 2020b – italics added)

Fink termed this shift to making sustainability central in investment decisions a fundamental reshaping of finance. Much of this shift is due to concerns about the economic impacts of climate change which are manifesting themselves in the form of higher insurance premiums and in cities having to pay more for bonds. 'Climate change is almost invariably the top issue that clients around the world raise with BlackRock,' Fink said (Fink, 2020a). 'This dynamic will accelerate as the next generation takes the helm of government and business. As trillions of dollars shift to millennials over the next few decades, as they become CEOs and CIOs, as they become the policymakers and heads of state, they will further reshape the world's approach to sustainability.'

CONSCIOUS CAPITALISM
Defining Conscious Capitalism

Roy M. Spence and Haley Rushing (2009) propose that great leaders tend to be great practitioners of the Golden Rule: treating others as these leaders would like to be treated. A leader who has built a firm in a socially responsible manner is a leader who believes in the Golden Rule. This leader has likely viewed the firm from each stakeholder's perspective and has put himself or herself in the place of the stakeholder, asking, 'Is this how I would want to be treated?'

> Increasingly, successful organizations have to look at the whole system in which they operate. They can't just serve one stakeholder (e.g., the customer) and damn all others. In other words, you can't just live the Golden Rule with your customers, but not live by the Golden Rule with your employees or vendors or any other key stakeholder. It's not a pick-and-choose-when-you-want-to-live-by-it kind of principle. Universal principles are tricky that way.
>
> (Spence and Rushing, 2009, p. 141)

Whole Foods Market founder and former Co-CEO John Mackey describes himself as a 'conscious capitalist' (Conscious Capitalism Institute, 2020). The movement he launched – Conscious Capitalism – aims to elevate humanity through business. According to Mackey, he and others joining the Conscious Capitalism movement are unapologetic advocates for free markets, entrepreneurship, competition, freedom to trade, property rights, freedom to contract, and the rule of law. However, unlike much of twentieth-century business thinking that did not grasp the interdependencies of systems (which so often lacks ecological consciousness or a sense of responsibility for other stakeholders than investors), conscious capitalists fundamentally view a business as a community of people working together to create value for other people and all the stakeholders (Mackey, 2009a).

Figure 4.6   Conscious Capitalism, Inc. is an organization that represents a global community of business leaders improving the practice and perception of capitalism to elevate humanity.

Source: Conscious Capitalism, consciouscapitalism.org

Conscious Capitalism at Work: Whole Foods Market

Whole Foods Market's value proposition is to sell organic, natural, and healthy food products to customers who are passionate about food and the environment (Porter, 2006, p. 90). Social issues and environmental issues are fundamental to Whole Foods Market's distinctiveness in retailing. It is also unique for commanding premium prices. The company emphasizes purchasing from local farmers, and its buyers screen out more than 100 common ingredients to food deemed by Whole Foods Market to distort taste or nutrition, such as artificial additives, sweeteners, colorings, and preservatives.

The purposes of Whole Foods Market lie in creating value for all of its major stakeholder groups and in earning profits for its investors (Mackey, 2007). The core values of Whole Foods Market represent a stakeholder orientation and very succinctly express these purposes:

- Selling the highest quality natural and organic products available;
- Satisfying and delighting our customers;
- Supporting team member happiness and excellence;
- Creating wealth through profits and growth;
- Caring about our communities and our environment;
- Creating ongoing win-win partnerships with our suppliers; and
- Promoting the health of our stakeholders through healthy eating education. (Whole Foods Market, 2010, p. 4)

Figure 4.7   Whole Foods Market's mission is to nourish people and the planet

Source: Image courtesy of GEOGOZZ via Wikimedia Commons. Shared under the CC BY-SA 4.0 license.

Over the years, Whole Foods Market has purchased more than 2.8 billion megawatt hours of wind-based renewable energy, earning six Environmental Protection Agency (EPA) Green Power awards from 2005 through 2010. It became the first retailer to offset 100 percent of its energy use with wind energy credits (Benett et al., 2009). Additionally, the company has made a commitment to reduce energy consumption at all stores by 25 percent per square foot by 2015. Stores are constructed using a minimum of virgin raw materials (Whole Foods Market, 2010).

In 2008, Whole Foods Market discontinued the use of disposable plastic grocery bags at the checkouts in all stores. Additionally, Whole Foods Market refunds each customer at least a nickel per reusable bag they use. Most stores participate in a composting program where food waste and compostable paper goods are regenerated into compost.

Factors of Success for Whole Foods Market

An important factor in Whole Foods Market's success is its leadership and conscious culture. Mackey says that conscious leadership at the company is actually servant leadership (Fox, 2011). Here, leaders identify their own flourishing with the flourishing of the organization. In other words, leaders try to serve the organization and its purpose. More will be said about such stewardship in Chapter 8. Mackey emphasizes the importance of a higher purpose for the business because in fulfilling this higher purpose, the business will likely improve its viability in a competitive market. Conscious business is about becoming conscious of the business's higher purpose, which is not about maximizing stakeholder value in the short run. Conscious culture at Whole Foods Market allows the organization to fulfill its higher purpose, implement the stakeholder model, and enable conscious leadership to flourish.

Mackey asserts that it is absolutely essential to trust employees, who are called team members at Whole Foods Market. One way of reinforcing trust among team members is by disclosing information that might cause strife in other organizational contexts. For example, salary information is shared at Whole Foods Market. However, information that would leave Whole Foods Market vulnerable to competitors, such as future plans for developing its stores, is not shared.

Mackey shares salary information because he believes that by making this information public, he will prevent envy among team members. Mackey believes envy is part of human nature and every organization. Every three years, the employees prioritize and vote on the benefits that they most prefer. Teams in Whole Foods Market do their own hiring, work scheduling, and product procurement. Because team members have voted for the company, it has been named by *Fortune* as one of the 100 best companies to work for every year since 1997 (Whole Foods Market, 2010).

The Whole Food Company: The Result of Mackey's Unique Leadership

According to Mackey, he resisted the heroic purpose of the company, trying to change and improve the world, for a long time because he thought the purpose of Whole Foods was to deliver excellent service. But employees of Whole Foods Market consistently told him he was wrong, and that Whole Foods Market's purpose was to impact the world in a positive way. This purpose now animates Mackey personally, as well as the company.

Mackey views his business as a complex adaptive system. In 1982, when Mackey had his first natural food store in Austin, Texas, he saw his dream turn into a nightmare when heavy rains produced floodwaters that came into his store (Sisodia, Sheth, and Wolfe, 2007). As he was beside himself considering the unfolding disaster, customers began flowing in to help him rebuild his store. In this way, Mackey's empathetic regard for his customers was reciprocated to him in this desperate situation.

When Michael Pollan, author of *The Ominvore's Dilemma*, criticized Whole Foods Market for not doing enough to promote local agriculture, or to market grass-fed beef, Mackey engaged him, rather than shunned him.

'When I read his book, of course I wasn't very happy about how Whole Foods was portrayed, and I began a dialogue with him,' Mackey said (Fox, 2011, p. 122). 'We ended up in a debate in Berkeley, California, back in February 2007, and a couple of thousand people showed up. That was a healthy exchange. And to give Michael credit, I think certain parts of his criticism ended up being true. We had put way too much emphasis on organic and not enough on some of these other aspects, and it was good that Michael called us to task. That kind of criticism stings, but there was also an opportunity there. I actually think you should engage your critics and see them, too, as stakeholders who are helping you to improve' (Fox, 2011, p. 122).

Although Mackey has created a viable, competitive, business, the development of this business was not always smooth. In fact, Mackey even made some disastrous mistakes. In February 2007, controversy came to Mackey for writing a blog under an assumed name on a stock message board for seven years. Later that year in November, Mackey wrote a letter to his employees and declared that after limiting his pay to 14 times that of the average team member at Whole Foods Market, he was now taking it down to $1 per year, and having the board donate any future stock options for him to charity:

> The tremendous success of Whole Foods Market has provided me with far more money than I ever dreamed I'd have and far more than is necessary for either my financial security or personal happiness. I am now 53 years old and I have reached a place in my life where I no longer want to work for money, but simply for the joy of the work itself and to better answer the call to service that I feel so clearly in my own heart. Beginning on January 1, 2007, my salary will be reduced to $1, and I will no longer take any other cash compensation. The intention of the board of directors is for Whole Foods Market to donate all of the future stock options I would be eligible to receive to our two company foundations.
>
> (Mackey, 2007, para. 4)

In 2009, Mackey wrote an op-ed piece for *The Wall Street Journal* beginning with a brief statement of opposition to the Obama administration's healthcare entitlement program and then proposing eight alternative steps to reform healthcare (Mackey, 2009b). His opinions brought some protesters at some Whole Foods Markets, but Mackey points out that neither his blogging deception nor his views on healthcare hurt sales (Fox, 2011).

In June 2017, Amazon purchased Whole Foods for $13.4 billion (Wingfield and de la Merced, 2017). Not bad for a business Mackey started himself in Austin, Texas using an approach that would later be termed 'Conscious Capitalism'.

The Benefits of Conscious Capitalism

Jeffrey Hollender and Bill Breen (2010) view conscious capitalists like Mackey as pursuing a better form of capitalism, which is unfolding in a responsibility revolution. In such an age of responsibility, Conscious Capitalism proves to be profitable for two principal reasons. First, a company's most valuable asset, its reputation, provides 'built-in insurance' in a time of general suspicion toward business. For example, 46 percent of respondents in an Edelman Trust Barometer survey in 2010 reported not trusting business to do what is right (Edelman Trust Barometer, 2010). At this time in the history of business, the intangibles of a firm (its patents, trademarks, knowledge, creativity, and consumer relationships) account for 75 percent of the value for the average US firm (Hollender and Breen, 2010). In addition, a firm's reputation is under further scrutiny as a result of the availability of information via the internet. Second, by aligning the interests of all the stakeholders, more harmony is produced, and greater numbers of satisfied stakeholders are willing to assist and contribute to the company. This provides the firm with access to a wider variety of people and their abilities than simply their employees, which in turn increases firm success. In this way, socially and environmentally attuned employees, suppliers, NGOs, reporters, and customers can find ways to boost a purpose-driven company's success. In a global survey of individuals, 52 percent replied that all stakeholder groups are equally important (Edelman Trust Barometer, 2010).

CONCLUSION

This chapter examined the role of business in society. Milton Friedman's voice echoes from 1970 and resonates with many still in his argument that the 'business of business is business'. A debate between Friedman and Whole Foods Market CEO John Mackey, a leader in the Conscious Capitalism movement, sheds light on the legitimacy of some noneconomic aspects of business today. BlackRock's CEO Larry Fink sent a letter to the CEOs of the world's largest firms informing them of BlackRock's intention to disinvest in firms not pursuing sustainability in the future. Fink described it as a fundamental reshaping of finance. Corporate social responsibility (CSR) and a subcategory of CSR, Conscious Capitalism, were presented as approaches drawing heavily on a stakeholder orientation. Although some CSR initiatives of firms are defensive in nature and superficial, Conscious Capitalism proposes an integration of ways to address issues related to ESG into the life of the business.

QUESTIONS

1. What new perspectives about the role of business in society did you gain from reading Chapter 4?
2. Thinking about the exchange between Whole Foods Market's John Mackey and economist Milton Friedman, what are your thoughts about the business of business being business? Had Friedman changed his views since 1970? Were his thoughts misconstrued in 1970? Explain.
3. In your view, how important is the development of standards for CSR to its continued success?
4. In your view, to what degree is Conscious Capitalism a fad? Explain.
5. Would you like to join a firm pursuing Conscious Capitalism as an employee? What aspects of such a firm would make it appealing to you? Unappealing?

Mavericks Who Made It

Raising the Bar at Clif Bar

Gary Erickson

Source: Image courtesy of Mike Mozart via Flickr. Shared under the CC BY 2.0 license.

Two epiphanies define Gary Erickson's entrepreneurial saga in the life of the company he founded in Berkeley, California. The first came on a 175-mile bicycle ride with his buddy Jay (with whom he would cycle one or two thousand miles in Europe every summer) in the San Francisco area in 1990 (Erickson and Lorentzen, 2004). After eating another brand of energy bars all day, Erickson was famished but could not bring himself to eat another bite of the energy bars he was carrying with highly processed ingredients.

'It came to me: "I could make a better bar than this,"' Erickson said. 'I call that moment "the epiphany." Clif Bar exists because I wanted to make a better product for myself and for my friends. Two years later, after countless hours in Mom's kitchen, I had a recipe that worked.'

The second epiphany for Erickson came on April 17, 2000, eight years after founding his company at the age of 33 and naming it after his father Cliff, who is his childhood hero and companion throughout the Sierra Nevada Mountains (Clif Bar, 2020). Clif Bar, Inc., makes portable, convenient, nutritious energy bars for athletes and health-minded people. It had grown from a guy who lived in a garage with his dog, his skis, his climbing gear, bicycle, and two trumpets, to an energized company with $40 million in annual sales (Erickson and Lorentzen, 2004). Clif Bar's success had attracted Quaker Oats, a large retailer who wanted to buy the company from Erickson.

Erickson and his former business partner were minutes from selling their fast-growing nutrition bar company to Quaker Oats for $120 million. At the same time, other ventures were transitioning to corporate ownership. Kraft bought Balance Bar. Nestle had purchased PowerBar. All Erickson had to do was to sign the contract, and he would have netted $60 million. Instead, he went for a walk out in the Clif Bar parking lot.

Attorneys from Clif Bar and Quaker Oats had worked feverishly over the weekend to finalize the details of the sale. The company workforce had also put in extra hours over the previous months to prepare the company for the change in ownership. On his walk late in the morning, Erickson felt nauseated and attributed it to not sleeping well in the stressful weeks leading to the final transaction.

'I told my partner that I needed to walk around the block,' Erickson said. 'Outside, as I started across the parking lot, I began to weep, overwhelmed. "How did I get here? Why am I doing this?" I kept walking. Halfway around the block I stopped dead in my tracks, hit by an epiphany. I felt in my gut, "I'm not done," and then "I don't have to do this." I began to laugh, feeling free, instantly. I turned around, went back to the office and told my partner, "Send them home. I can't sell the company"' (Erickson and Lorentzen, 2004, p. 2).

Immediately, a weight was lifted from Erickson. None of his family or close friends gave him positive feedback about selling the company. Yet, Erickson stuck with his former business partner who feared that Clif Bar could not expand sufficiently without taking on enormous financing from outside the firm. But he realized that the sale of Clif Bar meant the end of his vision.

'I thought I was doing something good with Clif Bar,' Erickson said. 'I never thought of growing the company and selling. Why was that better than owning a company, employing people, creating great products, using the power of the company for philanthropic ends, and possibly making positive changes in the world?' (Erickson and Lorentzen, 2004, p. 23)

(Continued)

When the process of selling the company began, Erickson and his partner had stood before the employees of the company and made a promise not to sell the company to anyone who would not let them continue to run the company. Yet, a few weeks before the contract was to be signed, Quaker Oats let the two entrepreneurs know that their tenure as managers after the sale would be only a matter of months. Clif Bar would move to Quaker Oats headquarters, and the current employees of Clif Bar would be out of their jobs.

Erickson used his 'gut' to make the decision not to sell and never looked back. However, his former business partner did and declared she was finished at Clif Bar and wanted to move on. She walked away with $62 million to be paid over the next five years. It would take Erickson five years to move from owning 67 percent of the shares of Clif Bar to become full owner. Instead of being up by $60 million, Erickson and his wife found their company now owing $62 million to his former business partner – a swing of $122 million!

When Erickson returned to Clif Bar, there were no cheers for him. The employee morale had plummeted over the term leading up to the intended sale of the company. Yet, Erickson set himself to turn around the company and pursue the path in business that would lead to mojo – the magic when he and his team of 65 employees were doing things the way they wanted, sensing the competitors squirm, and hearing the cash registers ring.

With the mojo of being good at what they did and knowing that everybody that mattered knew it, Clif Bar continued to pursue environmental and social goals.

The company set five bottom lines of (a) sustaining our planet, (b) sustaining our brands, (c) sustaining our people, (d) sustaining our community, and (e) sustaining our business. These 'Five Aspirations' are promoted internally and provide a decision-making framework for employees (Choi and Gray, 2011). During annual reviews, employees receive feedback and bonuses based on their contributions to each of the five bottom lines and their abilities to balance their responsibilities.

Clif Bar can boast many successful bottom lines over the years since Erickson's second epiphany. These would include diverting 80 percent of their waste from landfills, providing sabbaticals to employees, expanding its brands to include Clif Shot (energy gel) and Luna (the top selling energy bar for women), paying employees for more than 20 hours of community service each year, and seeing sales move beyond $106 million in 2002. In this year, Erickson bought out his former business partner and became full owner of Clif Bar.

Erickson declared slow growth as a way for Clif Bar to retain its soul as well as mojo in the energy bar segment. Clif Bar had 65 employees when the near sale took place in 2000, but by 2020, it had 1,200 employees (Aziz, 2020). Clif Bar has two bakeries and sells its products across North America, Europe, Australia and New Zealand. Erickson and his wife Kit stepped out of the role of CEO in 2020, but will remain on the firm's Board of Directors.

In June 2010, Clif Bar initiated the Employee Stock Ownership Program (ESOP), which gave 20 percent ownership of the company to its employees, with Erickson and his wife (Kit Crawford) retaining the rest. Upon the announcement of the ESOP, Erickson said, 'by retaining private, employee ownership we will continue to have the freedom and flexibility to build a sustainable business with long-term focus for future generations' (Clif Blog, 2010, para. 3).

Clif Bar continues to reinforce the important dimensions of its unique company culture (being disciplined, entrepreneurial, and playful) in meaningful ways. The company facilities include a gym, rock climbing wall, yoga room, and massage rooms. Employees are allowed to bring their dogs to work, get 2.5 hours of paid exercise each week, and have access to free personal training (Roth, 2010). The firm will pay up to $350 of entry fees for athletic events employees pursue (Clif Bar, 2020). *Outside* magazine has named Clif Bar, Inc. among its Best Places to Work numerous times (Outside, 2010). The firm became climate neutral in 2005 and uses 100 percent green power for electricity in all of its facilities.

'Today, the Business Roundtable is redefining shareholder value, but in the early 2000s, we were already doing it,' Erickson said (Aziz, 2020). 'It was a wild experiment at the time and in fact, we were one of the first – if not the first – corporation in California to embed social and environmental values in our articles of incorporation. I am an athlete as much as a founder and I thrive on competition, so the new challenge of five bottom lines was exhilarating. It was well worth the effort to redefine the game we were playing.'

Questions

- What were Gary Erickson's two epiphanies? How important do you think epiphanies are to leaders of established businesses? To entrepreneurs?
- How important would you say the human dimension of emotion is to the life of established firms? To entrepreneurial firms?
- What is mojo? Why was mojo so important to Gary Erickson?
- What elements of Gary Erickson's story mark him as a maverick?

REFERENCES

Amaro, S. (2020). Apple wins tax battle with EU as court annuls 2016 order to pay $15 billion in taxes. *CNBC*, July 15, 2020. Accessed at www.cnbc.com/2020/07/15/apple-wins-backing-of-eu-court-over-13-billion-euros-in-unpaid-taxes.html

Aziz, A. (2020). The power of purpose: Gary Erickson, founder of Clif Bar, reflects on a life of purpose (Part one). *Forbes*, May 7, 2020. Accessed at www.forbes.com/sites/afdhelaziz/2020/05/07/the-power-of-purpose-gary-erickson-founder-of-clif-bar-reflects-on-a-life-of-purpose-part-one/#5d357ba05071

Benett, A., Gobhai, C., O'Reilly, A., and Welch, G. (2009). *Good for business: The rise of the conscious corporation*. New York, NY: Palgrave Macmillan.

Berger, I.E., Cunningham, P.E., and Drumwright, M.E. (2007, Summer). Mainstreaming corporate social responsibility: Developing markets for virtue. *California Management Review*, 49(4), 132–57.

Bernhart, M.S., and Maher, F.J. (2011). *ISO 26000 in practice: A user guide*. Milwaukee, WI: ASQ Quality Press.

Bishop, M., and Green, M. (2008). *Philanthrocapitalism: How the rich can save the world*. New York, NY: Bloomsbury Press.

Campaign US. (2017). History of advertising: No 185: The Pepsi Refresh Project. *Campaign US*, February 17, 2017. Accessed at www.campaignlive.com/article/history-advertising-no-185-pepsi-refresh-project/1424314

Choi, D.Y., and Gray, E. (2011). *Values-centered entrepreneurs and their companies*. New York, NY: Routledge.

Clif Bar. (2020). Retrieved from www.clifbar.com.

Clif Blog. (2010, June 29). *Clif Bar and Company becomes 20 percent employee owned [Web log post]*.Retrieved from www.clifbar.com

Coca-Cola. (2020). Meeting the SDGs: The greatest global change happens together. *Coca-Cola EU Dialogue*. Accessed at www.coca-cola.eu/news/SDGs-global-change-happens-together/

Conscious Capitalism Institute. (2020). Learn our philosophy. Retrieved from www. consciouscapitalism.org/learn-about-our-philosophy

Delevigne, L., Gründler, A., Kane, S., and Koller, T. (2020). The ESG Premium: New Perspectives on Value and Performance. *McKinsey on Finance*, 73.

Dembek, A. (2020). Our approach to sustainability. DuPont's Chief Technology and Sustainability Officer. Accessed at www.dupont.com/about/science-and-innovation.html

Drucker, J. and Bowers, S. (2017). After a tax crackdown, Apple found a new shelter for its profits. *The New York Times*, November 6, 2017. Accessed at www.nytimes.com/2017/11/06/world/apple-taxes-jersey.html

EC. (2017). Frequently asked questions: Guidelines on disclosure of non-financial information. European Commission. Accessed at https://ec.europa.eu/commission/presscorner/detail/en/MEMO_17_1703

Eccles, R.G., and Krzus, M.P. (2010) *One report: Integrated reporting for a sustainable strategy*. New York, NY: Wiley.

Eccles, R.G., and Serafeim, G. (2011). Leading and lagging countries in contributing to a sustainable society. *Harvard Business School Working Knowledge*. Retrieved from http://hbswk.hbs.edu/item/6716.html

Edelman Trust Barometer. (2010). 2010 Edelman trust barometer. Retrieved from www.edelman.com/trust/2010/

Edwards, M. (2010). *Small change: Why business won't save the world*. San Francisco, CA: Berrett- Koehler.

Erickson, G., and Lorentzen, L. (2004). *Raising the bar: Integrity and passion in life and business*. San Francisco, CA: Jossey-Bass.

Fink, L. (2020a). A fundamental reshaping of finance. Letter to CEOs from BlackRock's CEO. Accessed at www.blackrock.com/corporate/investor-relations/larry-fink-ceo-letter

Fink, L. (2020b). Sustainability as BlackRock's new standard for investing. Letter to BlackRock's clients. Accessed at www.blackrock.com/corporate/investor-relations/blackrock-client-letter

Fox, J. (2011, January/February). What is it that only I can do? *Harvard Business Review*, 89(1/2), 118–23.

Friedman, M. (1970, September 13). The social responsibility of a business is to increase its profits. *The New York Times Magazine*. Retrieved from www.colorado.edu/studentgroups/libertarians/issues/friedman-soc-resp-business.html

Friedman, M. (2005, October). Rethinking the social responsibility of business. *Reason*. Retrieved from http://reason.com/archives/2005/10/01/rethinking-the-social-responsi

Global Reporting Initiative (GRI). (2020). About GRi. Retrieved from www.gri.org

Halpin, P. (2016). 'Leprechaun economics' leaves Irish growth story in limbo. *Reuters*, July 13, 2016. Accessed at www.reuters.com/article/us-ireland-economy/leprechaun-economics-leaves-irish-growth-story-in-limbo-idUSKCN0ZT21K

Henderson, R. (2020). *Reimagining capitalism in a world on fire*. London: Hachette UK.

Hollender, J., and Breen, B. (2010). *The responsibility revolution: How the next generation of businesses will win*. San Francisco, CA: Jossey-Bass.

Hult, G.T.M., Mena, J.A., Gonzalez-Perez, M.A., Lagerström, K., and Hult, D.T. (2018). A ten country-company study of sustainability and product-market performance: Influences of doing good, warm glow, and price fairness. *Journal of Macromarketing*, 38(3), 242–61.

Ignatius, A., and McGinn, D. (2015). Novo Nordisk CEO Lars Sørensen on what propelled him to the top. *Harvard Business Review*, November 2015. Accessed at https://hbr.org/2015/11/novo-nordisk-ceo-on-what-propelled-him-to-the-top

Industry Canada. (2020). Corporate social responsibility. Accessed at www.ic.gc.ca/eic/site/csr-rse.nsf/eng/h_rs00577.html#definition

Ioannou, I., and Serafeim, G. (2011). The consequences of mandatory corporate sustainability reporting. Harvard Business School Working Paper, 11–100.

ITEP. (2017). Fact sheet: Apple and tax avoidance. *Institute on Taxation and Economic Policy*, November 5, 2017. Accessed at https://itep.org/fact-sheet-apple-and-tax-avoidance/

ITEP. (2019). 60 Fortune 500 companies avoided all federal income tax in 2018 under new tax law. *Institute on Taxation and Economic Policy*, April 11, 2019. Accessed at https://itep.org/notadime/

Kanter, R.M. (2009). *Supercorp: How vanguard companies create innovation, profits, growth and social good*. New York, NY: Crown Business.

Ki-moon, B. (2010). Foreword. *United Nations Global Compact Annual Review – Anniversary Edition*. Retrieved from www.unglobalcompact.org/

Laczniak, G.R., and Murphy, P. (2006, December). Normative perspectives of ethical and socially responsible marketing. *Journal of Macromarketing*, 26(2), 154–77.

Lopatto, E. (2015). Finally, a Steve Jobs movie that Steve Wozniak likes. *The Verge*, September 7, 2015. Accessed at www.theverge.com/2015/9/7/9272963/steve-jobs-movie-wozniak-likes-sorkin-boyle-fassbender

Mackey, J. (2005, October). Rethinking the social responsibility of business. *Reason*. Retrieved from http://reason.com/archives/2005/10/01/rethinking-the-social-responsi

Mackey, J. (2007). I no longer want to work for money. *Fast Company.com*. Retrieved from www.fastcompany.com/node/58514/print

Mackey, J. (2009a). Creating a new paradigm for business. In, M. Strong and J. Mackey (Eds.), *Be the solution How entrepreneurs and conscious capitalists can solve all the world's problems* (pp. 73–113). New York, NY: Wiley.

Mackey, J. (2009b, August 11). The Whole Foods alternative to ObamaCare. *The Wall Street Journal*. Retrieved from http://online.wsj.com/article/SB10001424052970204251404574342170072865070.html

Novo Nordisk. (2018). Novo Nordisk annual report 2018: Financial, social and environmental performance. Retrieved from www.novonordisk.com/

Novo Nordisk. (2020). Novo Nordisk Accessed at www.novonordisk.com/

Outside. (2010 October). 50 best places to work in America. *Outside*. Retrieved from http://outsideblog.away.com/blog/2010/04/the-50-best-places-to-work-in-america.html

Porter. (2006, December). Strategy and society. *Harvard Business Review*, 84(12), 78–92.

PRME. (2020). Principles of responsible management education. *The 6 principles*. Retrieved from www.unprme.org/about-prme/the-six-principles.php

Roth, M. (2010, May 12). *Bay area's Clif Bar encourages biking and walking with 2-mile challenge [Web log post]*. Retrieved from http://sf.streetsblog.org/2010/05/12/bay-areas-clifbar-encourages-biking-and-walking-with-2-mile-challenge/

Sibide, M. (2020). *Brands on a mission: How to achieve social impact and business growth through purpose*. London: Routledge.

Sisodia, R., Sheth, J., and Wolfe, D.B. (2007). *Firms of endearment*. Upper Saddle River, NJ: Prentice-Hall.

Smith, N.C. (2003, Summer). Corporate social responsibility: Whether or how? *California Management Review*, 45(4), 52–76.

Spence, R.M., Jr., and Rushing, H. (2009). *It's not what you sell, it's what you stand for: Why every extraordinary business is driven by purpose*. New York, NY: Portfolio.

UN. (2020). About the sustainable development goals. Accessed at www.un.org/sustainabledevelopment/sustainable-development-goals/

UN Global Compact. (2020). United Nations Global Compact. Accessed at www.unglobalcompact.org/

Vega, N. (2017). Apple's offshore move has helped save them billions in taxes. *New York Post*, November 6, 2017. Accessed at https://nypost.com/2017/11/06/apple-avoids-ireland-tax-rate-by-moving-operation-to-island-of-jersey/

Walker, D. (2019). Saving capitalism from itself. *Fast Company*, November 2019. 48–51, 92. Accessed at www.fastcompany.com/90411391/ford-foundations-darren-walker-how-to-save-capitalism-from-itself

Whole Foods Market. (2010). Annual stakeholders report 2010. Retrieved from www.wholefoodsmarket.com/company/investor-relations.php

WID.world. (2017). World inequality report 2018. Accessed at https://wir2018.wid.world/files/download/wir2018-full-report-english.pdf

Williams, O.F. (2004, October). The UN Global Compact: The challenge and the promise. *Leadership and Business Ethics*, 14(4), 755–74.

Wingfield, N., and de la Merced, M.J. (2017). Amazon to buy Whole Foods for $13.4 billion. *The New York Times*, June 16, 2017. Accessed at www.nytimes.com/2017/06/16/business/dealbook/amazon-whole-foods.html#:~:text=Amazon%20agreed%20to%20buy%20the,of%20neighborhoods%20across%20the%20country

5
THE ROLE OF THE STATE IN SOCIETY

Throwing Shade

Source: Photo by BP Miller on Unsplash.

Corruption of Government Officials

Siemens AG is a German-based multinational conglomerate and the largest industrial manu-facturing firm in Europe with branch offices around the world. With 379,000 employees, Siemens' posted revenues of more than $98 billion in 2018 which placed it 70th in the

(Continued)

Fortune 500 (Fortune, 2019). Despite its reputation for manufacturing sophisticated machinery, a colossal corruption scandal exposed in 2008 disclosed that since at least the 1990s Siemens had organized a global system of corruption to boost its market share and increase its prices (Venard, 2018).

Over decades, bribery became the accepted norm at Siemens. Executives used hidden bank accounts and obscure intermediaries (termed agents or consultants). When computing the estimates for a project, Siemens employees used the term 'nutzliche aufwendungen' – a tax-related term meaning 'useful expenditures' which employees understood as bribes. While Siemens had a compliance program for fighting corruption, the program existed only on paper.

Around the world – in countries such as Bangladesh, Vietnam, Russia, Mexico, Greece, Norway, Iraq, and Nigeria – Siemens paid bribes to government officials and civil servants. For example, Eberhard Reichert, the former Technical Manager of the Major Projects division of Siemens Business Service GmbH and Co. – a wholly owned subsidiary of Siemens – pleaded guilty in a US court March 15, 2018 to paying tens of millions of dollars in bribes to Argentinian government officials to win and retain a $1 billion contract to create national identity cards (Dye, 2018). Because most funds wired around the world go through New York-based banks, US prosecutors became involved in the case.

Reichert admitted that for ten years he paid tens of millions of dollars in bribes to Argentine government officials in connection with the national-identity-card project. He and his co-conspirators concealed the illicit payments in various ways, including using shell companies associated with intermediaries to disguise and launder the funds. Reichert used a $27 million contract between a Siemens entity and a company called MFast Consulting AG for consulting services in order to conceal bribes paid to Argentine officials. Siemens pled guilty in 2008 and paid $800 million in US criminal and civil penalties and an $800 million fine to Munich prosecutors.

In 2007, Siemens brought in new CEO Peter Löscher, a former General Electric and Merck executive, as the first outsider to lead the company. In a few months, Löscher replaced 80 percent of the top executives, 70 percent of its second-tier executives, and 40 percent of its third-tier executives (Watson, 2013).

Surprising to many, bribes paid to government officials reduce the amount and quality of goods purchased by the government (Baker, 2005, p. 242). This is because the firms work the bribe payment into the price paid by the government agency. For a $10 million bribery-influenced contract, the government might only receive $9 million of goods. The bribe amount of $1 million goes out of the country to a foreign account. Often, the goods are not the right type or don't work as effectively as a competitor's products would.

Developed countries are not immune from the stain of corrupt officials. Influence peddling might characterize how most dubious government officials in developed countries operate (expecting campaign donations and employment in the private sector after they leave government service) (Kartner and Warner, 2015). Prosecutors in the US have won conviction of more than 50 mayors in the US on corruption charges since 2010 (City Mayors, 2019). These include the mayors of Nashville, Detroit, New Orleans, and Baltimore.

The cost of bribery is borne by the society where the government officials take bribes (Montero, 2018). Global Financial Integrity, an NGO based in Washington, DC, estimates that each year more than $1 trillion intended for developing countries is misdirected to foreign bank accounts controlled by corrupt individuals (Global Financial Integrity, 2020).

When the funds arrive at the bank for the government receiving aid, a large chunk could then be directed to a third-party for some services supposedly rendered. This third-party might be ostensibly a consulting firm fictitiously providing consulting services to the government leaders. The 'consulting firm' was established by the government official or a family member. In another scenario, a firm could submit an inflated invoice to a government agency. If the firm is controlled by a family member of a dishonest government official, then the excess amount received from the dubious transaction could be skimmed off and directed to other shell companies outside of the country.

The funds diverted this way could then be moved to other shell companies across countries in a bewildering set of transactions. The funds become difficult to track this way and then go to a bank account in a country such as Switzerland with restrictive disclosure laws.

Government officials often skew the allocation of resources toward sectors in which graft is more lucrative or less prone to detection, such as from social services to large-scale building or defense projects (D'Souza and Kaufmann, 2013). With reduced effectiveness of government spending (because of diversion of funds and problem-ridden contracts with firms bribing government officials), less money is available to shore up weak institutions in society (investigators, prosecutors, courts, and tax authorities). This is an arrangement preferred by corrupt government officials.

One deterrent for corruption is a free press because an unfettered media tends to expose corrupt government officials (Brunetti and Weder, 2003). Increased transparency in government through online procurement systems, competitive bidding and strengthened audit and investigating are ways to deter corruption in government (D'Souza and Kaufmann, 2013). Deterrence within firms is now exemplified by Siemens which has increased its compliance department from a few workers to more than 400 in 2018. In this way, one can see that the leaders of Siemens want compliance to be a core part of Siemens' business activities, so that participation in corrupt practices to meet sales goals for Siemens' employees becomes alien to the Siemens corporate culture – and extremely difficult to do.

Questions to Consider

- Who do you blame more for corruption – bribe takers or bribe payers?
- How is trust in societies damaged by corruption?

(Continued)

- If you were a sales person selling to a government agency, and someone at the agency told you that the leader of the agency had to be 'taken care of' in the next sales transaction, what would you do?
- What would it take to reduce corruption around the world in the next 10 years?

CHAPTER OVERVIEW AND LEARNING OBJECTIVES

This chapter will examine the role of the state in helping determine the quality of life (QOL) in a society. In addition to guiding a society's response to natural disaster, the governments of modern societies have a broad influence across many realms of life. When government functions well, the quality of life for citizens usually increases. This chapter will review QOL research and recent approaches to measuring QOL across the countries of the world. This chapter will also examine the influence of government in modern societies with a special focus on the influence of government on business. The US government's bailout of auto manufacturers GM and Chrysler will be featured to illustrate some of the challenges of government intervening in a situation with multiple stakeholders. This chapter will also consider the concept of distributive justice and analyze possible reasons for political liberals and political conservatives to think differently when making moral judgments about economic and social issues. After this chapter, you should be able to answer the following questions:

- What are some challenges a society encounters that require the effort of both business and government to overcome?
- How semipermeable are the boundaries between business and government today?
- Is it possible for markets to exist without government?
- For societies embracing democracy and capitalism, what are some distortions that can emerge from government involvement in markets?
- What does recent research about the moral foundations for liberals and conservatives suggest about how citizens might think differently about economic and social issues?

CORONAVIRUS PANDEMIC

The world experienced a global pandemic caused by the coronavirus disease (COVID-19) in 2020 (WHO, 2020). The governments of most countries imposed some form of lockdown. Varying results of government action can be seen in the differing epidemiological statistics across countries. For example, Sweden's government took a lenient approach only closing high schools and universities, while businesses reduced their hours, restaurants reduced their capacities and using masks remained voluntary (Fiore, 2020).

While Anders Tegnell, the chief epidemiologist at the Swedish Public Health Agency and designer of Sweden's coronavirus strategy, declared that the Swedish strategy is working. Twenty-five Swedish academics strongly disagreed with Tegnell asserting that the Swedish government's response led to death, grief, and suffering, while the Swedish economy fared no better than many other countries (25 Swedish doctors and scientists, 2020). The number of coronavirus cases and deaths in Sweden were similar to the United Kingdom, rather than other Scandinavian countries, such as Norway and Finland, as can be seen in Figure 5.1.

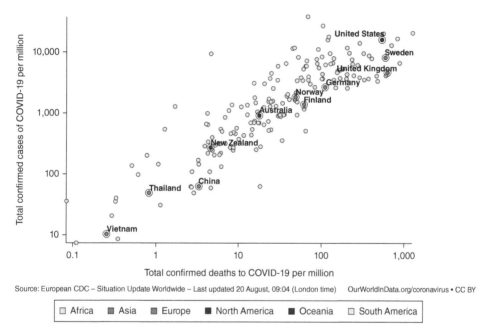

Figure 5.1   Total confirmed COVID-19 cases vs. deaths per million, August 20, 2020

Source: Our World in Data, https://ourworldindata.org/grapher/rate-confirmed-cases-vs-rateconfirmeddeaths?country=SWE-DEU-FIN-NOR-NZL-AUS-VNM-USA-GBR-THA-CHN

The coronavirus pandemic has marked the return of activist governments not seen in peacetime (Crawford, 2020). Countries that took a more activist response to the coronavirus were Vietnam, China, New Zealand, and Germany.

Throughout the pandemic, Germany's government marshalled prevention protocols that facilitated the country's response to the coronavirus (Wieler, Rexroth, and Gottschalk, 2020). Such protocols included (1) early establishment of testing capacities, (2) high levels of testing, (3) an effective containment strategy among older persons, and (4) efficient use of the country's ample hospital capacity, so that intensive care units were not overwhelmed.

Contact tracing also featured prominently in Germany's response that was run by the Gesundheitsämter – composed of 375 tiny public health offices across the country which served as coronavirus intelligence bureaus (Moody, 2020). Whenever someone tested positive for the coronavirus, their doctor alerted the local office, whose staffers phoned the patient to learn who the patient had met over the past two weeks. Along with medical professionals, cobbled-together teams of contact tracers in Germany (comprised of planning inspectors, social workers, police officers, firefighters, army medics, students, and volunteer 'hygiene scouts') spent up to 14 hours each day of the week phoning those who had contact with a person exposed to the coronavirus.

The persons who had contact with the patient were told by the contact tracers to self-isolate for 14 days – sometimes along with everybody else in their household. The contact tracers placed daily calls to these persons who had contact with a coronavirus patient to check for symptoms. Often, these persons had to be cajoled into quarantining themselves and their families against their wills. In some cases, interpreters had to be used by the contact tracers because these persons who had contact with a coronavirus patient did not speak German.

Vietnam leveraged its experience with pandemics (such as SARS in 2003, avian flu in 2010 and large outbreaks of measles and dengue fever in the past) and its one-party state lacking any opposition to enact early prevention protocols (Jones, 2020). By early January before it had any confirmed cases of coronavirus, Vietnam's government initiated drastic action. 'It very, very quickly acted in ways which seemed to be quite extreme at the time, but were subsequently shown to be rather sensible,' Guy Thwaite, Director of Oxford University's Clinical Research Unit in Ho Chi Minh City, said.

Vietnam's government imposed travel restrictions, closely monitored the border with China and increased health checks at borders and other vulnerable places. The government closed schools for the Lunar New Year holiday at the end of January and kept them closed through mid-May. It also launched vast and intensive contact tracing.

Vietnam did not impose a national lockdown. However, it did pursue localized containment in a few communities where coronavirus cases emerged, such as Son Loi, north of Hanoi where more than 10,000 people were sealed off for two weeks.

Being an authoritarian police state, Vietnam employed its communication and propaganda apparatus from the very early stages of the pandemic. The government sent regular text messages to all cell phones telling persons what they could do to protect themselves. Awareness campaigns drew on wartime imagery and rhetoric to unite the public in fighting a common enemy. Using a fun and innovative tactic, pop-star Quang Dang and Vietnam's Health Ministry quickly collaborated to create a video with song and a new dance about virus protection measures on TikTok that became an internet sensation (www.bbc.com/news/world-asia-52628283).

Roughly one of every six adults in Vietnam work for the Communist state security services that include the police, military, paramilitaries, and 'neighborhood guardians' (Ghosh, 2013). Such guardians form a pervasive system of domestic spying that was used to enforce social distancing and quarantines (Jones, 2020). In this way, human rights violations occurred with people being fined or prosecuted for criticizing the government response. 'But not many people will hear about those episodes because of the government's total control of the media,' Phil Robertson of the NGO Human Rights Watch said.

In sum, the coronavirus pandemic brought the role of the government in society into clear view and showed how different government responses could be. Sweden chose a light-touch approach in its response to the coronavirus. Germany implemented early prevention protocols, but had a well-funded healthcare system on which to rely for treating cases. Vietnam had limited healthcare resources, but relied on its learning from past responses to pandemics to implement its emergency plan before a coronavirus case had been reported in the country. It also activated its propaganda capabilities for the purpose of persuading the population to adopt prevention measures. The ever-present and vast security apparatus in Vietnam enforced social distancing and quarantines through neighborhood informants.

How did your country's response compare to Sweden's, Germany's, and Vietnam's?

QUALITY OF LIFE

In describing research in the marketing and society domain, William Wilkie (2001) has observed that such work implicitly rests on the question, 'What type of society do we wish to create and inhabit?' Two subareas of research in this domain have emerged in the last 30 years: social marketing (intending to benefit the target audience directly) and Quality-of-Life (QOL) studies (focused more broadly on how well society or one group of society was faring, or focused on how well one aspect of life, such as work, was faring) (Wilkie and Moore, 1999).

In marketing thought, Philip Kotler (1986) has cited the choices for goods, the cultural environment, and the physical environment as fundamental dimensions of life quality. Joe Sirgy (2001, p. 10) has offered an expanded 'contemporary view of QOL' with a starting set of dimensions for QOL being (a) economic, (b) work, (c) political, (d) leisure, (e) physical (health), (f) environmental, (g) social, (h) family, and (i) spiritual. Here, business can be said to be the dominant force in the first two dimensions, economic well-being and work well-being, while playing a significant role in delivering or providing the material conditions for the others.

The measurement of QOL has involved a broad set of contributors from across the social sciences. Scientific methods of measuring QOL have taken two approaches. The first 'subjective' approach focuses on the measurement of subjective well-being (SWB), or individuals' subjective experience of their lives in terms of life satisfaction or happiness (Cummins, 2000). Subjective well-being refers to affective experiences and cognitive judgments about one's life (Larsen and Eid, 2008). In this vein, quality of life is the product of an overall appraisal of life that includes both good and bad experiences. The second 'objective' approach has focused on social indicators or level of living measures (using quantitative statistics, such as economic output, crime rates, or political freedoms).

Government Services Can Contribute to QOL

The role of the state in modern societies based on democracy and capitalism is broad and extensive (Quelch and Jocz, 2007, pp. 231–2). The civilian employment for the federal government (excluding the US Postal Service) tops 2 million people, making it the largest employer in the country (Bureau of Labor Statistics, 2011). Additionally, about 1 million people serve in the military.

The state establishes the laws and runs the courts, police, fire departments, and military forces. It collects taxes. Central banks in countries around the world contribute directly to the favorability of costs through monetary policy. The fiscal policy of the state also contributes to the cost of living for its citizens. The state runs Social Security and welfare programs, as well as housing programs. State-assisted or state-sponsored schools and institutions of higher learning develop knowledgeable and capable workers who can effectively run businesses, the public sector, and the civil sector, such as nongovernmental organizations (NGOs).

The state initiates public works projects, such as roads, highways, sea ports, airports, canals, as well as water and sewer systems. In many locales, the state provides sanitation services, and in some locales, it provides public utilities. The state operates regulatory agencies (such as the Federal Trade Commission), the Consumer Product Safety Commission, and the US Department of Agriculture that, respectively, ensures fair competition in markets, product safety, and food safety. The state provides records of real estate titles and transactions. It also provides licensing bureaus. The state encourages development of railroad networks and communication networks. It also runs the mail system to link individuals and businesses throughout the country. Developing public policy regarding the cultural heritage of the country and the quality of the physical environment (air quality, water quality, and endangered species) comes under the authority of the state. Additionally, the conservation of natural resources on public lands is another important task of the state that also includes enforcement of public policy.

The government has created markets in the past. For example, in July 1994, the Federal Communication Commission (FCC) gathered leaders of the telecommunications industry at the Omni Shoreham Hotel in Washington, DC, for a week-long auction of licenses to use parts of the electromagnetic spectrum (McMillan, 2002). Previously, the FCC had held hearings to decide which applicants for licenses were to be allocated these licenses for free. The decision of who gets the right to use each piece of spectrum is a difficult one for government. Invariably, the process takes on aspects of a beauty contest where government officials use vague criteria for assigning such licenses. This inefficient process is also prone to favoritism. This was followed briefly by a lottery to allocate licenses that also proved inefficient. So when the first auction was held in 1994, no one knew how much these licenses would be worth in a market for them. As of 2008, the auctions have brought in more than $52 billion to the FCC. In this way, the FCC takes in more revenue than it spends each year. In 2000, the United Kingdom followed with an auction of part the spectrum there and earned $34 billion, while Germany's auction netted $46 billion. In Spain and France, the old beauty contest approach to granting spectrum licenses is still done.

THE SOCIAL RESPONSIBILITY OF GOVERNMENT REGARDING BUSINESS

The US Government Bails Out GM and Chrysler

During the economic crisis of 2008, a series of poor economic decisions made by Wall Street financiers and auto industry executives led to a social decision by the government to bail out firms that were previously thought of as highly sophisticated bankers and auto makers. At this time, the US government quickly introduced the $700 billion Troubled Assets Relief Program (TARP) to bail out banks, insurers, and US automakers (Rattner, 2010). The federal government wound up directing $82 billion to the automakers, their related finance companies, and even some auto industry suppliers. Two of the three major automakers in the United States, GM and Chrysler, accepted funds from TARP as part of a government bailout for these firms.

Shortly after the inauguration of Barack Obama as US president in January 2009, an ad hoc group called the Presidential Task Force on the Auto Industry (comprising 14 US Treasury or temporary government workers and calling itself 'Team Auto') became the government's task force to guide these two automakers through restructuring and/or bankruptcy proceedings. The White House's director of the National Economic Council, Lawrence Summers, and the Secretary of the Treasury, Timothy Geithner, supervised Team Auto under the leadership of former *New York Times* journalist and investment banker Steven Rattner.

Within months, Rattner and his relatively young team of government workers had (a) fired the longtime CEO and Board Chairman of GM Rick Waggoner, (b) appointed replacements for Waggoner, (c) developed a $3 billion Cash for Clunkers Program to boost sales in the auto industry, (d) developed a restructuring plan for GM that included terminating four brands (Pontiac, Saturn, Saab, and Hummer), and (e) served as the mid-wife to a merger of Chrysler into the Italian auto maker Fiat (Rattner, 2010). Over the course of the bailout of GM and Chrysler, these firms used $82 billion dollars in TARP funds (including $1.5 billion for Chrysler Financial, $17.7 billion for GM's financial company General Motors Acceptance Company [GMAC, later renamed Ally], and $400 million for some auto parts suppliers) (Rattner, 2010).

Because of the dire future facing these two auto companies, and because of the flexibility offered to firms in working with their stakeholders in bankruptcy proceedings, much was accomplished in six months. In short, most stakeholders understood that sacrifice needed to be made or these automakers would need to cease operations and liquidate. Numerous stake-holders became apparent during the impending bankruptcy of these two US auto giants. A glimpse of these stakeholders can be seen in the decision of the federal Judge Robert Gerber, who denied the petition of some of GM's bondholders to force a complete (and lengthy) restructuring under the supervision of the court. If such a conventional bankruptcy proce-dure were allowed, the bondholders would have saved a million dollars here and there, while GM would lose $100 million each day (Rattner, 2010). A passage of Judge Gerber's decision included in *Overhaul* by Steven Rattner follows:

> This case involves not just the ability of GM creditors to recover on their claims ... it involves the interest of 225,000 employees, (91,000 in the US alone); an estimated 500,000 retirees; 6,000 dealers and 11,500 suppliers. If GM were to have to liquidate, the injury to the public would be staggering. This case likewise raises the specter of systemic failure throughout the North American auto industry, and grievous damage to all of the communities in which GM operates. If GM goes under, the number of supplier bankruptcies which we already have...is likely to multiply exponentially. If employees lose their paychecks or their healthcare benefits, they will suffer great hardship. And states and municipalities would lose the tax revenues they get from GM and the people employed by GM, and the Government would be paying out more in unemployment insurance and other hardship benefits. Under these circumstances, I find it hardly surprising that the U.S., Canadian, and Ontario governments would not stand idly by and allow those consequences to happen.
>
> (Rattner, 2010, p. 261)

Judge Gerber mentions all of the primary stakeholder groups of Figure 3.1 in Chapter 3 with the exception of GM customers. A lengthy bankruptcy would have harmed consumer confidence in GM regarding (a) the warranties currently in effect on their GM vehicles, (b) the resale value of their vehicles, and (c) the desirability of purchasing the same less-than-competitive vehicles from a company put in limbo by a long bankruptcy. Instead, the expedited bankruptcy of GM allowed its vast systems of stakeholders to begin afresh with $65 billion less debt and the removal of annual structural costs from its North America operations totaling $8 billion (Rattner, 2010). Now, only four GM shareholders remained:

(a) the US government (initially 61 percent owner, reduced through a sale of shares after the initial public offering of stock in the new GM company to 33 percent), (b) the Canadian government, (c) the United Auto Workers retiree healthcare benefits trust, and (d) some of GM's old bondholders (Rattner, 2010).

Tables 5.1a and 5.1b present a snapshot of the GM bailout at the end of 2010. GM's restructuring using a rapid proceeding in section 363 of the US bankruptcy code was enormously complex. These two tables offer an overview of the bankruptcy and emergence of the New GM, which had less in debt and fewer brands.

As shown, shareholders lost their entire investment. With improving performance of the New GM, bondholders have kept doing better, as they make capital gains on the shares of their New GM stock. Although it seems that it lost $17 billion, the US federal government fared well, considering that things could have become worse (Rattner, 2010). The Canadian government and the Ontario government took an 11.7 percent ownership stake in the New GM, as well as receiving a vitality agreement from the New GM to protect jobs remaining in Canada. Although the UAW took job cuts at plants to be closed, the union importantly funded the healthcare for their 500,000 retirees through the establishment of a healthcare trust called the Voluntary Employee Beneficiary Association (VEBA), which took ownership of 17.5 percent of the New GM (Rattner, 2010).

Table 5.1a Summary of some risks and outcomes to selected stakeholders in GM bailout

	GM leaders	GM shareholders	GM bondholders	UAW	UAW retirees	Overseas workers	GM suppliers
Number of stakeholders	30	610 million trading shares	100,000 held 20% of debt	91,000	500,000	134,000	11,500
At risk	survival	total investment	$27 billion	loss of 91,000 fully benefitted jobs paying $28/hr. avg.	health care benefits	55 counties with jobs paying: Mexico – $7/hr. China – $4.5/hr. India - $1/hr.	some of 650000 jobs
Outcome	CEO and Chairman fired, but given $7 million severance	lost it all	$20 billion swapped for 10% stock in New GM	22,500 jobs cut no pay cut	VEBA - a new healthcare trust takes 17.5% stake in New GM	small dip in 2009 sales rebounded in 2010	$450 million taken in federal support
	Board shake-up		$4.9 billion loss	no benefit cut			

Table 5.1b   Summary of some risks and outcomes to selected stakeholders in GM bailout

	Dealers	GM car owners	Federal Gov't	US taxpayers	State Gov't	Local Gov'ts	Canadian Government
Number of stakeholders	6,000	10 million in US with unexpired warranties	Congress plus 30 principals in executive branch	100 million who paid taxes	35 states with facilities	140 cities with facilities	Congress plus 30 principals in executive branch
At risk	survival	warranties lower resale value for cars	$51 billion invested. If GM liquidated $88.5 billion	$50 billion	tax revenues new jobless healthcare	tax revenues (Detroit- $20 mil.)	20 plants 9,000 jobs 700 dealers
Outcome	1,800 dealerships closed	no lapse in warranties	became owner of 61% of New GM	61% owner of New GM (31% in 2012)	mixed results depending on plant closures	mixed results depending on plant closures	gave $9 billion for 11.7% New GM stake
	survivors face less cannibalization	resale value still a market function	loss of $9.6 billion	owe $61.4 per taxpayer for GM bailout		double digit losses on land taxpayer	vitality agreement protects jobs

Although early estimates of the federal government's losses in the bailout of the auto industry came to $40 billion, the decisive and positive moves recommended by Team Auto and approved by President Obama in 2009, along with an upturn in auto sales, led to a revised estimate of $9.6 billion of losses for the federal government (Goolsbee and Krueger, 2015). The US Treasury took a loss of $11.3 billion on its investment in GM, a $0.7 billion loss on its investment in Chrysler and actually realized a $2.4 billion gain on its investment in Ally Financial. In sum, the losses taken by the federal government amounted to each taxpayer in the US in 2008 paying $61.42 for the bailout.

Car sales, rather than car financing, now accounts for GM's profits (Lutz, 2011). In 2010, all three automakers posted annual profits: GM $6.2 billion, Ford (which received no bailout) $6.6 billion, and Chrysler posted a slight profit. In 2019, all three posted profits, as well: GM $90 billion (Investopedia, 2020), Ford $84 million (Isidore, 2020), and Chrysler – now owned by Fiat from Italy – posted record revenues based primarily on sales of its Jeep Gladiator (Barry, 2019).

The Congressional Oversight Panel (COP) noted in January 2011 that the bailout of GM and Chrysler may turn out to be one of the successes of the TARP program (Kroll, 2011).

Given the potential calamity the economy faced by bankruptcies of GM, Ally Financial and Chrysler, the COP's view of the future proved to be right (Goolsbee and Krueger, 2015).

However, the COP asserted that a rescue by the US Treasury of any large US corporation that is considered to be 'too big to fail' creates a moral hazard. As a result of this moral hazard, large corporations will make risky choices or fail to behave in a responsible manner. In such situations, leaders of 'too big to fail' corporations would believe that a bailout from the federal government would eventually arrive. In this way, it can be seen how actions taken by a stakeholder (such as government) today might affect decisions by firms in the future.

IMPERFECTIONS RESULTING FROM GOVERNMENT ACTIVITY IN MARKETS

Setting the Rules of the Game

In setting the rules of the game, regulations and laws established by government to protect citizens might actually give preferential treatment to selected market participants. In some instances, a cartel of privileged sellers might result from imposed government standards and procedures. For example, the Benedictine monks at St. Joseph Abbey in Covington, Louisiana, began making and selling handmade funeral caskets priced between $1,500 and $2,000 to pay for food, healthcare, and the education of the monks at the abbey (Levitz, 2010). The abbey receives about 60 requests per year to make their simple caskets made of cypress.

However, after the Louisiana State Board of Embalmers and Funeral Directors (eight of the nine board members are funeral industry professionals) delivered a cease-and-desist order to the monks in March 2010, and threatened them with fines from $500 to $2,500 per violation of illegal casket sales and jail time up to 180 days, only then did the monks learn that under state law in Louisiana, they needed a license to sell caskets – a high-margin item (no doubt, as a result of lack of competition). As it turns out, the monks would have to become licensed funeral directors to sell funeral merchandise.

The monks tried twice to get the law changed, but the state legislature stalled in its response to their request (First Things, 2010). The Institute for Justice, a public-interest law firm, represented the abbey in its federal lawsuit citing Louisiana's 'casket cartel' in which the Abbey won in a unanimous decision by the US 5th Circuit Court in 2013 (De Rugy, 2013).

'The monks' story is just one example of a national problem in which industry cartels use government power to protect themselves from competition,' Institute for Justice's president Chip Mellor said (Levitz, 2010). A 2008 study by Morris Kleiner, a labor professor at the University of Minnesota, found that 23 percent of workers in the US were required to obtain state licenses compared to 5 percent in 1950 (Simon, 2011). Some states require licenses for florists and interior designers. In Texas, shampoo specialists must take 150 hours of classes – 100 of them on the theory and practice of shampooing.

Playing Umpire

In playing the role of umpire in markets, governments can make choices that are later seen to be incorrect. In the 1857 US Supreme Court ruling known as the Dred Scott decision, the court ruled that slaves were the property of their owners (and could not be taken from their owners without due process) (Fehrenbacher, 2001). Furthermore, the court asserted that the US Congress had no authority to prohibit slavery in territories of the United States. The case was never overturned by the Supreme Court. However, the Civil War and the resulting 14th Amendment to the US Constitution in 1868 established that all persons born or naturalized in the United States are citizens, and that the federal government did not have to reimburse anyone for the emancipation of slaves they once owned.

An important aspect of playing the umpire in markets is the even enforcement of regulations and laws. Because firms have the legal status of individuals in the United States (Mackey, 2009, p. 95), the rule of law must be applied equally to everyone. 'If Whole Foods goes into a city and is told our cheese has to be refrigerated, it's fundamentally unjust if that rule isn't applied to our competitors as well – which, I might add, does sometimes happen in New York City,' CEO of Whole Foods Market John Mackey said (Fox, 2011, p. 120).

Corruption is a challenge in all countries. But in countries without a free press that can criticize government officials and expose corrupt practices, it is much worse. In the past 15 years, the climate opposing corruption has improved in China, but a traditional way of receiving preferential treatment from government officials is to deliver gifts during the Chinese New Year (McGregor, 2005). In the past, cartons of cigarettes or bottles of expensive liquor were typical gifts. Now, laptops, golf clubs, home entertainment centers, and even automobiles might be on someone's holiday gift list. Financial centers such as Beijing and Shanghai are generally clean, said Ty Cobb, a partner at the law firm Hogan Lovells, but 'the further you get away from those centers, the pressure mounts' to pay kickbacks and give gifts (Rubenfeld, 2011, para. 2). Although China might still be lax about even enforcement of anti-bribery statutes, in Russia 'it's hard to tell … whether [an enforcement action is a] political purge or corruption' (Rubenfeld, 2011, para. 5).

Imposing Taxes

Although it is rarely mentioned in the business press, the capability of the government to collect taxes – fiscal capacity – is essential to having an effective government – which contributes enormously to societal QOL. Although this might be taken for granted in developed countries (where 40 percent of GDP is taken in taxes on average), developing countries struggle to collect adequate amounts of tax revenues (where 10 to 20 percent of GDP is taken in taxes on average) (Ricciuti, Savoia, and Sen, 2019). These low rates of tax collections in developing countries come from (1) having a large informal economy in which taxes are eluded, and (2) failing to invest in establishing tax collection capabilities for the government. Political will by lawmakers, the streamlining of laws to remove loopholes for tax evaders, development of a sufficiently paid corps of tax collectors, and the implementation of transparent systems of tax collection (to avoid theft by government officials) are important elements in obtaining sufficient funds for government operations and avoiding excessive debt for governments.

Direct and Indirect Interventions in Markets

Direct Intervention

Intervention in markets by governments can be direct or indirect. In direct and sustained interventions in markets, some governments pursing what is termed 'state capitalism' take ownership of businesses in key sectors (such as energy, transportation, and telecommunications) as well as in the operation of markets themselves. China, Russia, Saudi Arabia, Mexico, Brazil, and India are a few of the countries engaged in twenty-first-century state capitalism where the state is the leading economic actor and uses markets primarily for political gain (Bremmer, 2010).

Before the economic crisis of 2008, global financial institutions, such as major banks and the International Monetary Fund (which aims to keep countries solvent and trading with other nations), pressed developing countries to embrace the 'Washington Consensus'. This set of economic theories espoused (a) fiscal and budgetary discipline; (b) a market economy with property rights, competitive exchange rates, privatization of state-owned enterprises, and deregulation; as well as (c) openness to the global economy through trade liberalization and foreign direct investment. Such policies would be termed 'economically liberal' because they would encourage individuals to control their own lives and make their own mistakes.

After the economic crisis of 2008, enthusiasm in developing countries for the Washington Consensus weakened. The global audience is now increasingly skeptical of minimal involvement of governments in markets. Having a privately owned national champion firm like CEMEX, focused on cement and ready-mix concrete production and distribution, has much appeal in a country like Mexico (Bremmer, 2010). Cemex has close ties to the Mexican government that allows it to protect its position in the market through hostile takeovers of smaller Mexican competitors. CEMEX competes globally and Forbes ranks it at #781 on the Global 2000 in terms of sales ($13.5 billion in 2020) (Forbes, 2020).

State-owned companies operating in global energy markets today include giants PetroChina, Brazil's Petrobras, Mexico's Pemex, and Russia's Rosneft and Gazprom. In 2008, China Mobile had more subscribers than any other cell phone company (with 488 million) (Bremmer, 2010). Importantly, those who run these state-owned companies answer first to those who wield political power in government or in a political party or in a royal family, rather than shareholders or other stakeholders. Those who wield political power want to accomplish political goals, such as solidifying their hold on power, rather than serving the public welfare. In China, the political leadership reserves the right to select the leaders of all major banks and large industrial companies. Would it be easier for a CEO to please shareholders concerned about profits or to please political bosses concerned about employment numbers and material support for other state-owned enterprises?

In India, the Agricultural Produce Marketing Committee (APMC) Act established in the 1950s required farmers to sell their produce in government-owned yards called *mandis* (Khanna et al., 2007). The original purpose of the mandis (meaning literally, markets) was to allow small farmers to avoid having to sell to buyers from higher castes with more money and power. In the mandis, buyers are not allowed to contact the farmers directly and the produce is auctioned. Unfortunately, the mandis did not preclude the exploitation of farmers. The yards are usually gridlocked with trucks unable to enter or leave. In the sun, the unsheltered produce ripens fast and often rots with waste up to 40 percent (Khanna et al., 2007).

At least 95 percent of agricultural produce reaches the end consumer through unorganized marketing channels like mandis, which many times leads to price fluctuations, wastage, and poor quality (Chaudhary, 2011). Farmers often transport produce to markets using carts and tractor trolleys, which not only delays the delivery process but also leads to wastage.

Importantly, information does not flow across the mandis, so inefficient pricing results. Additionally, access to the mandis by any buyer is not always a feature of the mandis. In sum, the mandis are a major hindrance to what the buyers and sellers would like. However, the government operators of the mandis and the political forces desiring the mandis to exist defend the place of the mandis in the Indian economy aggressively.

Indirect Intervention

Although the GM bailout stands as a major intervention of the federal government in markets, intervention in markets can be indirect as well. In qualitative and observational research investigating the origin of materials and then the production, distribution, and recycling of a cotton t-shirt, Rivoli (2005) focuses first on cotton growers in the panhandle of Texas near Lubbock. In the flat, almost lunar landscape, these Texan farmers typically obtain about twice the world market price for their cotton. Although the farmers are entrepreneurial and resourceful, and their local and regional markets work well in matching buyers and sellers of cotton, a very favorable environment results from (a) government subsidies to cotton growers in the United States when world prices remain low, and (b) the government-assisted research programs in the science departments of universities, such as nearby Texas Tech University.

Here, the government subsidies ($3 billion a year to about 20,000 cotton farmers (Amadeo, 2020)) represent direct intervention in markets, whereas the support of scientific research benefitting the US cotton growers represents indirect intervention in markets (Rivoli, 2005). The result of both kinds of intervention is that the cotton farmers in the United States have access to the latest science that allows them to improve their crop yields, and they know how to avoid competing when the risks are too high.

Brazil appealed to the World Trade Organization (WTO) about the subsidies given to US cotton farmers for distorting trade and hurting farmers in developing countries. An Oxfam study found that eliminating these subsidies would boost world prices about 10 percent, which would be especially helpful to the 20,000 subsistence cotton growers in Africa (Grunwald, 2010).

Brazil won a WTO judgment against the United States for its cotton subsidies in March 2010 (Chan, 2010). The WTO gave Brazil permission to impose tariffs and other trade sanctions against US products. The Brazilian sanctions were to include $591 million in tariffs on a wide array of goods, including autos, pharmaceuticals, medical equipment, electronics, textiles, and wheat. However, one day before these sanctions began, negotiators from the Office of the US Trade Representative and the Agriculture Department reached a temporary deal with their Brazilian counterparts, putting the retaliation on hold (Grunwald, 2010). The United States agreed to subsidize Brazilian farmers (with subsidies totaling $300 million) to avoid having Brazil add tariffs to ending subsidies to cars, electronics, and pharmaceuticals imported from the US (Faber, 2017). In 2014, the US reduced cotton subsidies by more than half, due to Brazil charging the US of violating its trade agreement with Brazil (Faber, 2017). The geopolitical dimension of subsidies can be seen here.

Thirty-one percent of farmers in the United States received subsidies in 2017 (EWG, 2020a). From 1995 to 2019, the US government paid $396.9 billion in farm subsidies. The subsidies paid by the US government are highly skewed to the five major commodities: corn, soybeans, wheat, cotton, and rice. (Meat, fruit and vegetables do not receive such price subsidies.)

From 1995 to 2019, Iowa received the highest amount of commodity subsidies – more than $20.4 billion (EWG, 2020b). Remember the Iowa caucuses are the first event in the US presidential elections where farm subsidies are a leading topic and where opposition to such subsidies would likely spoil any presidential candidate's chances for later election. The political dimension of subsidies related to national elections becomes evident here.

In a bailout (such as for the financial services, insurance, and the auto industries), the government would receive much of its money back. With subsidies, there is no repayment. Looking back at the bailout of GM and Chrysler, the US government ended up paying $9.6 billion. In 2018, the US government's commodity subsidies totaled $9.0 billion. There was much hue and cry about the bailout of automakers in 2009, but hardly any discussion in the media about the bailout of farmers when crop prices for corn were not as high as expected in 2017. That is because such payments in the Price Loss Coverage program occur every year and have become culturally accepted in the US.

The US spends more than $20 billion each year on subsidies for farmers (Edwards, 2018). But the EU spends more than triple this amount ($65 billion) each year in farm subsidies (Gebrekidan, Apuzzo, and Novak, 2019). The EU program accounts for 40 percent of the EU's central budget and is one of the largest subsidy programs in the world. Unfortunately, the EU's program has encountered problems with corruption (the Czech Republic prime minister received tens of millions in subsidies in 2018) and mafia involvement in Slovakia and Bulgaria. With this in mind, the US subsidy program appears to be better managed and a better value for US taxpayers than EU taxpayers.

Summary

In summary, government serves as a unique stakeholder for firms and market operations. Unlike other stakeholders, government can (a) set the rules of the game, (b) play umpire, (c) impose taxes, and (d) intervene directly as well as indirectly. Such interventions can be relatively brief as in the bailout of the US auto industry. By comparison, government interventions can be sustained for years as in the farm subsidy programs of the USDA or the indirect interventions in agricultural markets through support for scientific research at universities. Government support for the educational system, in general, makes markets function better with educated buyers, sellers, and other stakeholders. The scale of direct interventions can run into the hundreds of billions of dollars, and the scope of such interventions can extend to supporting market actors in other countries.

Government intervention in markets receives criticism for distorting market prices and outcomes (Grunwald, 2010), but in countries pursuing state capitalism, such as China, such criticism is muted or unheard of because of the harsh political reality that does not allow freedom for the stakeholder of the media. State-owned enterprises, although many times ineffective in global markets as a result of bloated payrolls, enormous debt, and rigid bureaucracies, are increasingly becoming the largest competitors for multinational enterprises (Bremmer, 2010). For example, in 2020, China claimed the second, third and fourth places in Fortune's Global 500 list of the firms with the largest annual revenues in the world (behind number one Walmart with $523 billion in revenues). Sinopec Group (China's state-owned petroleum and chemical giant claimed $407 billion in revenues), State Grid (China's state-owned power company claimed $383 billion), and China National Petroleum (the state-owned parent company of the country's second-largest oil producer, PetroChina, claimed $379 billion) (Fortune, 2020).

Of course, firms and other stakeholders attempt to influence policy makers in government. Amazon and Facebook proved to spend the most on lobbying in 2019 with $12.4 million and $12.3 million (Muskus, 2019). In 2000, Amazon focused its lobbying on issues related to (1) copyright, (2) taxation, (3) computer industry, (4) consumer issues, and (5) law enforcement (Nix, 2019). In 2018, Amazon had dropped law-enforcement-issues lobbying, but had added 14 other policy areas from telecommunications to labor issues, banking and even intelligence. 'It's an arms race,' the nonpartisan Center for Responsive Politics' Massie Ritsch said. 'If your competitors are spending money on professional advocacy to play offense and defense in Washington, you feel you need to do the same' (Schouten, 2009, para. 3).

Government and Distributive Justice

The Development of Distributive Justice

When considering the fair allocation of limited resources, economist Adam Smith strongly opposed mercantilism – the conduct of markets to empower the state – and asserted that society would be much better off if individuals and businesses operated out of their self-interest. The end result would be allocation that would be done as if by 'an invisible hand' and would be much fairer than what currently existed in 1776 when the Scotsman Smith published *The Wealth of Nations*. In recent years, some researchers have suggested that an overapplication of Smith's call to have markets free of government activity resulted in a false separation of the economic and social consequences of decision making of firm leaders and corporate boards in the 1990s (Mintzberg, Simons, and Basu, 2002). The authors further commented:

> As economists like Milton Friedman would have it, business attends to the economic, whereas government takes care of the social. ... Perfectly simple, except for one fatal flaw: Every economist readily recognizes that social decisions have economic consequences, in that they cost resources. So how can any economist or business executive fail to recognize that economic decisions have social consequences, in that they directly impact human beings? (p. 69)

Setbacks in stock markets around the world and subsequent policy mistakes by governments led to the Great Depression of the 1930s (Forbes and Ames, 2009). For example, after the stock market crash of 1929 that was fueled by borrowing to invest in speculative investments, the US government reduced the flow of money in the financial system with high interest rates. Governments around the world invoked protectionist tariffs that further reduced trade and subsequently depressed business activity. Since this time, governments have seen business cycles as endemic to the private-property approach to society's provisioning through markets. As a result, governments have more intentionally addressed distributive justice through social programs as well as through citizens' participation in markets.

The Idea of Distributive Justice and the Size of Government

As a result of the active role the government has taken in addressing issues related to societal QOL (such as employment, inflation, education, healthcare, and pensions), the scale and scope of the government's role in regard to distributive justice continues to be a point for public discussion. This commonly appears in debate over whether a society should have a large government, which would emphasize more redistribution of wealth, or a small government, which would not emphasize distributive justice as heavily. For example, the ideas of Steve Forbes (publisher of *Forbes* business magazine) represent many of those advocating for a smaller role of government interaction in markets. Forbes proposes that government policies should be devoted to ensuring six conditions are present in the economy: (a) the rule of law, (b) respect for property rights, (c) stable money, (d) progrowth tax system, (e) ease in starting a business, and (f) few barriers to doing business.

Brooks (2010) echoes Forbes and calls for a turn away from big government and its expansive social programs, so that citizens can reap the rewards, as well as the consequences, of their own actions. He reports that across multiple studies, an average of 70 percent of those in the United States prefer free enterprise (similar to what Forbes proposes) as the core provisioning system for society to any alternative (that would be characterized by a more dominant role for government) (Brooks, 2010). However, since the outcomes of recent presidential elections in the United States have been fairly evenly split, this would suggest that the issue of big government more evenly divides the voting public. Democrats generally want the government to play a larger role in society, and Republicans generally want the government to play a smaller role in society.

Liberal and Conservative Visions

Constrained and Unconstrained Views

Researchers studying how social values affect political views have recently focused their thinking and research on individuals' political ideologies. Researchers are now studying how individuals who self-identify as liberal or conservative differ in their perspectives on (a) the inherent goodness of humans and (b) the breadth of psychological dimensions used to evaluate social and economic issues (Haidt, Graham, and Joseph, 2009). Regarding the nature of humans, Sowell (2007) has proposed that two visions about the nature of humans have characterized political thought and ideology in Western countries. One vision is the constrained vision, which views the nature of humans darkly and sees humans as being motivated primarily from self-interest. Economic philosophers such as Adam Smith and Hobbes are usually cited as being the leading expressionists for the constrained vision. These thinkers proposed that incentives are the most efficient means to motivate individuals to care and attend to the welfare of others. This is accomplished primarily through markets in modern societies, as individuals have to identify the needs of others and meet them in a competitive marketplace with superior products and services.

Alternatively, the unconstrained vision is more optimistic, and views humans as being willing to care for and attend to the welfare of others. Given the condition of modern societies filled with urban populations, the government is often seen as the institution that is most capable of fairly allocating the resources of society in a manner characteristic of distributive justice.

Making Moral Judgments

Regarding the psychology of making moral judgments, McAdams et al. (2008) has proposed that liberals primarily use two dimensions to make a moral judgment: (a) harm/care (is someone or something being harmed or in need of care?) and (b) fairness/reciprocity (is someone experiencing unfair treatment?). Since the Civil Rights Era in the United States, the focus of liberals has been on alleviating the injustice experienced by minorities and women in a society perceived to have racist and oppressive aspects to such groups (Jacobs, 2009). Ending discrimination became the rallying issue for liberals.

By comparison, conservatives use five dimensions when making their moral assessments about political and social issues (Graham, Haidt, and Nosek, 2009; Haidt, 2012). In addition to the dimensions used by liberals, conservatives use three more: (c) ingroup/loyalty (is the proper allegiance being expressed to the group, tribe, or nation?), (d) authority/respect (are the social order and established hierarchies receiving due respect?), and (e) purity/sanctity (are unclean elements or practices being kept away from the group, tribe, or nation?).

The constrained/unconstrained visions of humans and man-made institutions, along with the two or five dimensions used for making moral assessments, combine in influencing individuals toward liberal or conservative leanings regarding economic freedom and social freedom. This can be seen in Figure 5.2 where Haidt (2008) reports on a large-scale study of the importance of the five moral dimensions across those self-identifying as liberals, moderates, and conservatives. As shown, the liberals emphasize harm and fairness, while the conservatives use these (to a slightly lesser degree), as well as the other three dimensions. Results similar to these have been obtained by researchers in a variety of countries.

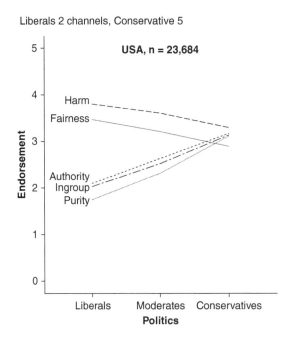

Figure 5.2   Five dimensions of moral psychology for political groups in the United States

Source: Haidt (2008).

Differences between Liberals and Conservatives

Economic freedom would correspond to limited government involvement in markets, while social freedom would correspond to limited reliance on traditional social norms and traditional institutions of society, such as the family, schools, churches, and businesses. In societies, liberals reflect a more atomized society where individuals pursue their own ends as long as they are not harming or being unfair to others. Conservatism reflects a society with more connecting tissue among individuals of the society and where societal structure, in the form of both institutions and social norms, is valued. In sum, liberalism implies more openness to new experiences and a veneration of tolerance and diversity. By comparison, conservatism implies that curbs are needed for human behavior or else excesses will result with sometimes deleterious consequences.

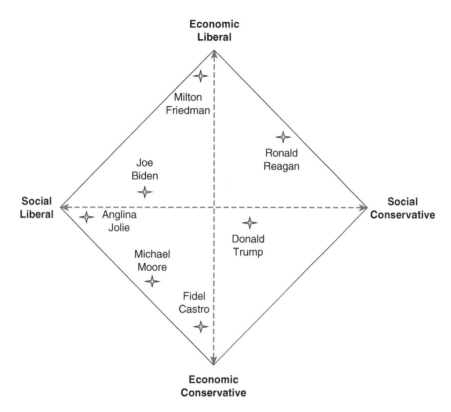

Figure 5.3   Social and economic freedom diamond with positioning of public figures

Source: Inspired by Edelman Trust Barometer, 2010.

Figure 5.3 depicts a four-section diamond with some possible positioning for well-known personalities, some of whom are featured in this book. At the top end would be placed laissez-faire economist Milton Friedman (1970). Opposite to this on the bottom end of the diamond would be Fidel Castro whose brand of communism seeks to restrict or eliminate markets in society. Ronald Reagan, an advocate of lower taxes and a smaller nonmilitary public sector, anchors the upper right of the diamond. Opposite Reagan in the lower left sector of the diamond is documentary film-maker Michael Moore, a long-time critic of capitalism.

Joe Biden occupies a place in the left of the intersection of the dotted lines. This is because of Biden's favor for an activist government and his fondness for globalization norms in trade. Donald Trump takes more socially conservative stands (pro-life and pro-guns), but his preference for managed trade to protect workers in the US and to encourage US-based manufacturing positions him to the right and below the center line. Hollywood's Angelina Jolie, a United Nations (UN) special envoy to refugees around the world occupies a position to the left corner. Although Jolie is willing to participate in the entertainment industry as a highly paid actress, her compassion for the hurting can be seen in her adoption of multiple children.

In sum, the degree of distributive justice that permeates society is a political question in most societies today. Undergirding these ongoing debates about the size of government, the focus of social programs, and the perfectibility of man-made institutions are more assessments made by individuals. Liberals tend to emphasize the freedom of individuals in their decision making about social and economic issues while conservatives value preexisting structure in society, such as traditional institutions and norms.

Trust in Government and Business

The Edelman Trust Barometer manifests the phenomenon of mistrusting the political system (Edelman Trust Barometer, 2019). Figure 5.4a depicts the percentage of citizens across 26 countries of the world who indicated *trust for government* by giving a response of 6 to 9 using a nine-point scale when responding to the following question: 'How much do you trust government to do what is right?' The same question was posed about *trust for business* in the same countries. Figure 5.4b depicts these results.

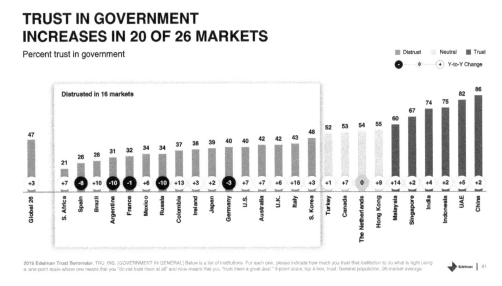

Figure 5.4a   Trust in government across 26 countries of the world

Source: Edelman Trust Barometer (2019).

In sum, there is much room for improvement in citizens' of Western democracies trust in either government or business to do the right thing. Further research remains to be done regarding China, as global business is a relatively new phenomenon there; elections have not taken place since the Communist Party came to power in 1949, making timely information about the outside world difficult to obtain.

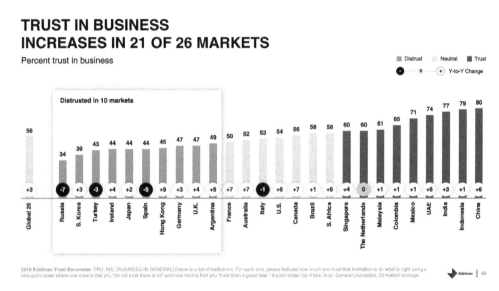

Figure 5.4b   Trust in business across 26 countries of the world

Source: Edelman Trust Barometer (2019).

CONCLUSION

This chapter examined the role of the state in delivering QOL to a society. Quality of life is a primary concern for government and business, but modern government has a broader scope of operation in addressing societal QOL than businesses. The differing degree of government activism can be seen across the countries of Sweden, Germany, and Vietnam in responses to the coronavirus pandemic in 2020. The GM bailout of 2009 suggests how semipermeable the boundaries between business and government can be as the government decided the liquidation of GM and Chrysler would cause too much damage in society. By most accounts, the bailout of GM had many successful outcomes. However, other government activity in markets can have distorting effects on markets and those affected by these markets.

With many social and economic issues facing society, the role of the government in society is resolved through a political process. Distributive justice may be a driving concern for some of those involved in this political process. Research about the moral foundations of political views suggests that liberals and conservatives hold different perspectives about the perfectibility of humans and man-made institutions, with liberals more positive about these. Liberals' moral assessments are more influenced by concerns about harm and fairness, while conservatives use these two dimensions but also are influenced by concerns about the social order. Finally, the story of John Stanford illustrates the potential achievements of one who would choose to spend one's entire working life in government roles as: (1) an officer in the military, (2) county manager in a major metropolitan area, and (3) superintendent of the Seattle Public Schools.

QUESTIONS

1. What new perspectives about the role of the state in society did you gain from reading Chapter 5?

2. Considering everything (such as the number of coronavirus cases and the number of deaths depicted in Figure 5.1, as well as the impositions on human rights by government action/inaction, which country's response would you prefer if it was applied to your country: Sweden's, Germany's or Vietnam's? Explain.

3. In your opinion, to what degree was the GM bailout a success? Explain.

4. Review Tables 5.1a and 5.1b, which present some risks and outcomes for stakeholders in the GM bailout. In your opinion, who lost the least? Who lost the most? Explain why you think this happened.

5. What imperfection that can result from government intervention in markets bothers you the most? Which bothers you the least?

6. Think about what you learned about distributive justice in this chapter. Can it be said that concepts of distributive justice focus on outcomes of the provisioning system of society? How do moral dimensions used in our psychological processing of issues related to distributive justice come into play in the political life of a society?

7. You can access the 'shortest political survey' at www.theadvocates.org. Use this ten-question survey to gain one perspective on your possible political leanings. Which direction do you lean? How would you improve this ten-question survey?

8. Haidt believes that understanding how those with different political views think can lead to increased productivity. For example, if conservatives used terms like 'reciprocity' and 'protecting the weak,' they could more often find common ground with liberals and moderates. What terms or ideas could liberals use to find common ground with conservatives?

Mavericks Who Made It

John Stanford

Source: Photo courtesy of HistoryLink and Seattle Public Schools.

John Stanford's last job before he died of leukemia in 1998 was as Superintendent of the Seattle Public School System. Before that he served four years as Manager of Fulton County, Georgia – the central county in the Greater Atlanta area. Before that, he served 30 years in the US Army, and retired as a Major General (two stars). In the Army, he was a logistician, so he understood supply chains and supporting the endeavors of other unit commanders. He also understood service – using one's abilities to benefit another entity.

But when he was hired to be superintendent of Seattle Public Schools in September 1995, many people in Seattle viewed him as a threat. Not understanding that a core dimension of Army life is learning and training, his initial critics saw that he had no formal experience as an educator. At his first open interview as part of the selection process to be the superintendent, the room was packed and Stanford could hear the murmuring. Many teachers supposed he would be inflexible and abrasive, unable to listen. Many parents feared he would try to bring excessive discipline to the schools that would squelch creativity. Stanford recalled his thoughts as he heard some of the principals of Seattle's schools whisper adamantly 'Don't hire the general!' to the president of the school board as she introduced Stanford to the packed room.

But I also knew how far from the mark that was. Thirty years of leading in the military had taught me that most leaders are the antithesis of those traits. Leading means inspiring, not commanding. Leading means loving the people you lead so they will give you their hearts as well as their minds. It means communicating a vision of where you can go together and inviting them to join. The community was right: a TV general could not have led the public schools. They didn't know me, but their stereotypes were different from my reality. Now I had two hours to change their minds...

(Stanford, 1999, p. xi)

Stanford listened carefully to the concerns expressed in his first interview. He spoke with confidence when he said he would lead the schools to success, but that he could not run the schools alone.

(Continued)

He would need help and would actively invite the participation of parents, businesses, and community groups to help raise the level of achievement in the schools. In this way, he signaled he would take a collaborative approach to the leadership task before him.

Stanford told those gathered for the open interview that despite the daunting problems facing the schools in Seattle, the children of Seattle could be reached and taught if a wide coalition of parents, teachers, staff, business people, and community leaders worked together. At the time, the problems for Seattle were similar to other urban school districts and included aging buildings, declining test scores, an inadequate budget, and racial tensions.

What Stanford did not disclose that first day was that he knew first-hand how students could be reached and put on the path toward excitement about learning and achievement. At the end of his sixth-grade year, his teacher Miss Greenstein visited his parents at their home in Yeadon, Pennsylvania west of Philadelphia one afternoon to tell them that Stanford would have to repeat sixth grade. Stanford felt crushed and humiliated.

Later, Stanford would recall that Miss Greenstein showed courage and love for him because she had the courage to intervene.

'I say courage and love because that's exactly what it took,' Stanford said. 'It took courage and love to look my parents in the eye and tell them – just as it takes courage and love to do the other things a school system must do if it wants to do what's best for its children. It takes courage and love to say to teachers, "You must put aside your adult concerns."' (Stanford, 1999, p. xiii, para. 2)

His parents, neither of whom had completed elementary school, were shocked and disappointed. But Stanford's mother began a program of nightly reading with the young Stanford that eventually led to him becoming energized about learning over a two-year period. In sum, Stanford himself was the embodiment of winning one of the most difficult challenges facing Seattle's Public Schools – reaching 'unreachable' students so that they could lead productive lives.

The Seattle Public Schools took the risk and hired Stanford over two other candidates with superintendent experience and PhDs in education. Stanford took charge of the school district and immediately went out to schools to conduct his own qualitative research by observing, inquiring about teaching practices, and hearing from the community. Surprising to Stanford, capable principals and teachers had much to say about 'adult issues,' such as philosophies of education, or union contracts, but few actually talked about student achievement.

Early in his tenure, Stanford found the 'true North' direction for the school district – student achievement. This became the central theme and the rallying cry for bringing together constituencies from across Seattle. Sub-programs would be developed to emphasize parts of improving student achievement, such as calling all students to read more – a lot more.

Stanford believed that a love of reading wasn't just a schools issue. It was a cultural issue requiring community reinforcement (Stanford, 1999). Parents would need to read to their children every night and make sure their kids did their reading homework. Radio stations would need to broadcast messages encouraging children to read. Local sports celebrities would need to visit schools and talk about the importance of reading. Finally, thousands of volunteers would need to come to schools and tutor children one-on-one and read to them in small groups.

Fun things spiced the community-wide effort to emphasize reading. Students made chains of paper cars and airplanes and strung them through the hallways of the elementary schools as a way to claim the names of every book the kids had read. Principals fulfilled promises by sitting on the school roof for a day in a crazy costume because students at their school read to a certain level. Stanford fulfilled his own promise to be flown in by Army helicopter to one school if the students achieved the school's reading goal.

To Stanford, the pay-off of the reading program was student achievement. Teachers reported gains in reading comprehension and the writing of students improved. Across Seattle, students adopted the superintendent's call to read twenty minutes each day. One mother said she thought she had heard every excuse for her child putting off doing household chores until one night her daughter declined to take out the garbage because she had to do her reading.

Stanford believed the school system would do better in boosting student achievement if it adopted a business approach. He regarded himself as 'CEO of Destiny, Inc.' leading a market-based school system. The school system began listening to its customers by systematically conducting community forums and surveys. Stanford and his team learned much. For example, they learned that parents wanted local schools that challenged students to attain their highest potential. In response, Stanford led an end to school bussing. They also wanted arts and sports programs that were being cut due to budget shortfalls.

To include arts and sports programs, Stanford adopted university-style budgeting in which the city would provide a basic education while donors would contribute so that arts and sports programs and other program enhancements would be included in the curriculum of Seattle Public Schools. He brought in a professional fund-raising partner Alliance for Education. Together, they prepared a business prospectus for each potential donor detailing a comprehensive plan for how requested donations would be invested and what would be the measurable outcomes of each donation. For example, Microsoft would benefit from having a pool of highly literate job applicants in the future.

Businesses and foundations jumped into this first-of-its-kind philanthropy for public education by donating millions of dollars. Stanford and the school board adopted marketing practices too.

> The only way we'd generate the gargantuan amount of support we needed would be to market the schools constantly and deliberately. We'd need to communicate to the community over and over and over again the excitement we were feeling, the amount of change that was taking place, and the quality of what we were doing. We would need to sell the schools the way Nordstrom sells Nordstrom if we wanted to get investors excited enough to give.
>
> (Stanford, 1999, p. 158)

(Continued)

Inside the schools, the biggest change Stanford required of his principals was to become leaders rather than managers of their respective schools. He won a new union contract that would allow principals to hire the best teachers and to hold them accountable for student achievement. Instead of principals dealing with bus schedules and the operational aspects of their buildings and the discipline of students, Stanford wanted them to delegate these tasks to others, so that they could actually lead in their schools. In Stanford's view, the principals needed to set a vision for their school communities, and then inspire their teachers, students, and parents to achieve it.

> They needed to be setting goals for their teachers, helping the teachers set goals for students, and working with the teachers daily to make sure the students reached them. They needed to be observing their teachers, making sure they had the skills to do the job, and seeing that they got the support and training they needed. They needed to be meeting with parents, talking with them about their children and about the parents' role in education. They needed to build teamwork among the teachers, keep them focused on achievement, and rid their schools of the hundreds of other issues that got in the way. They needed to be 'working' their communities, recruiting volunteers and resources for their teachers, getting the community excited about what was happening in their schools. Principals need to stop being the chief disciplinarians of their schools and become their chief education officers.

> (Stanford, 1999, p. 162).

Over a three-year period at the helm of the Seattle Public Schools, test scores for students rose, the performance gap between minority students and white students began closing, incidences of violence declined, and the requirement for student graduation from high school changed from a 0.83 average on a 4.0 scale to a 'C' average of 2.0. But importantly, the city of Seattle mobilized on behalf of children and education. Stanford's philosophy of 'love 'em and lead 'em' connected with many across Seattle.

In 1998, leukemia came upon Stanford and overtook him nine months later. After his death, the entire city mourned for him in public gatherings. He was buried at Arlington National Cemetery. Stanford illustrated transformational leadership in a complex organization and embraced 'the biggest M' in his engagement of stakeholders across Seattle for the transcendent purpose of serving the children of the city. The evidence of his transformational leadership is the changed public schools of Seattle and the improved performances of students, teachers and staff.

Questions

- In your opinion, what parts of Stanford's life story prior to moving to Seattle contributed to his success as a leader of the Seattle Public Schools?
- How important was identifying a transcendent purpose or 'true North' in engaging all sectors of human endeavor in Seattle?

- Point out elements of Stanford's story in Seattle that illustrate the implementation of service-dominant logic and stakeholder theory from Chapter 3.
- What characterized the business approach Stanford employed in running the Seattle Public Schools?
- How many persons of authority in government or business would you say lead by inspiring others, rather than commanding others? What does it take to inspire others?

REFERENCES

25 Swedish doctors and scientists. (2020). Sweden hoped herd immunity would curb COVID-19. Don't do what we did. It's not working. *USA Today*, July 27, 2020. Accessed at www.usatoday.com/story/opinion/2020/07/21/coronavirus-swedish-herd-immunity-drove-up-death-toll-column/5472100002/

Amadeo, K. (2020). Farm subsidies with pros, cons, and impact. *The Balance*, June 29, 2020. Accessed at www.thebalance.com/farm-subsidies-4173885

Baker, R.W. (2005). *Capitalism's Achilles heel*. New York, NY: John Wiley & Sons.

Barry, Co. (2019). Fiat Chrysler profits up on record North America Results. *AP*, July 31, 2019. Accessed at https://apnews.com/1e7dd93f5cd342ffa64e2e53c092157f

Bremmer, I. (2010). *The end of the free market: Who wins the war between states and corporations?* New York, NY: Portfolio.

Brooks, A.C. (2010). *The battle: How the fight between free enterprise and big government will shape America's future*. New York, NY: Basic Books.

Brunetti, A. and Weder, B. (2003). A free press is bad news for corruption. *Journal of Public Economics*, 87(7–8), 1801–24.

Bureau of Labor Statistics. (2011). Retrieved from www.bls.gov/

Chan, S. (2010, April 6). U.S. and Brazil reach agreement on cotton dispute. *New York Times*. Retrieved from www.nytimes.com/2010/04/07/business/07trade.html

Chaudhary, D. (2011, May 4). Produce supplier gets venture capital funding. *The Wall Street Journal*. Retrieved from http://online.wsj.com/article/SB1000142405274870393710457630 2832249875792.html?KEYWORDS=mandis+india

City Mayors. (2019). Corrupt US Mayors. City Mayors Society. *Accessed at* www.citymayors.com/politics/us-corrupt-mayors.html

Crawford, A. (2020). How German is your government? *Bloomberg Businessweek*, April 20, 2020, 8–10.

Cummins, R. (2000). Objective and subjective quality of life: An interactive model. *Social Indicators Research*, 52(1), 55–72.

De Rugy, V. (2013). A victory against state cronyism: St. Joseph Abbey v. Castille. *National Review*, March 21, 2013. Accessed at www.nationalreview.com/corner/victory-against-state-cronyism-st-joseph-abbey-v-castille-veronique-de-rugy/

D'Souza, A., and Kaufmann, D. (2013). Who bribes in public contracting and why: Worldwide evidence from firms. *Economics of Governance*, 14(4), 333–67.

Dye, J. (2018). Former Siemens executive pleads guilty to role in $100 million foreign bribery case. *Financial Times*, March 15, 2018. Accessed at www.ft.com/content/6482c2f2-289c-11e8-b27e-cc62a39d57a0

Edelman Trust Barometer (2010). Edelman Trust Barometer. Accessed at www.edelman.com/sites/g/files/aatuss191/files/2018-10/2010-Edelman-Trust-Barometer_Global_Deck_FINAL.pdf

Edelman Trust Barometer. (2019). 2019 Edelman trust barometer. Retrieved from www.edelman.com/trust-barometer

Edwards, C. (2018). Agricultural subsidies. *Downsizing the Federal Government*, April 16, 2018. Accessed at www.downsizinggovernment.org/agriculture/subsidies.

EWG. (2020a). The United States farm subsidy information. Retrieved from https://farm.ewg.org/region.php?fips=00000andstatename=UnitedStates

EWG. (2020b). Commodity subsidies in the United States totaled $223.5 billion from 1995–2019. Accessed at https://farm.ewg.org/progdetail.php?fips=00000andprogcode=totalfarmandpage=states andregionname=theUnitedStates

Faber, S. (2017). Do cotton framers need more subsidies? *AgMag*, December 20, 2017. Accessed at www.ewg.org/agmag/2017/12/do-cotton-farmers-need-more-subsidies

Fehrenbacher, D.E. (2001). *The Dred Scott case: Its significance in American law and politics*. New York, NY: Oxford University Press.

Fiore, K. (2020). How did Sweden flatten its curve without a lockdown? *Medpage Today*, July 29, 2020. Accessed at www.medpagetoday.com/infectiousdisease/covid19/87812

First Things. (2010, February). While we're at it. *First Things*, 69–70.

Forbes. (2020). CEMEX. Accessed at www.forbes.com/companies/cemex/#51001d6f3512

Forbes, S., and Ames, E. (2009). *How capitalism will save us: Why free people and free markets are the best answer in today's economy*. New York, NY: Crown Business.

Fortune. (2019). Fortune 500. Accessed at https://fortune.com/global500/2019/siemens/

Fortune. (2020). Global 500. Accessed at https://fortune.com/global500/

Fox, J. (2011, January/February). 'What is it that only I can do?' *Harvard Business Review*, 89(1/2), 118–23.

Friedman, M. (1970 September 13). The social responsibility of a business is to increase its profits. *The New York Times Magazine*. Retrieved from www.colorado.edu/studentgroups/libertarians/issues/friedman-soc-resp-business.html

Gebrekidan, S., Apuzzo, M., and Novak, B. (2019). The money farmers: How oligarchs and populists milk the EU for millions. *The New York Times*, November 3, 2019. Accessed at www.nytimes.com/2019/11/03/world/europe/eu-farm-subsidy-hungary.html

Ghosh, P. (2013). A police state where one-in-six works for security forces. *International Business Times*, August 29, 2013. Accessed at www.ibtimes.com/vietnam-police-state-where-one-six-works-security-forces-1401629

Global Financial Integrity. (2020). Global Financial Integrity. Accessed at https://gfinteg rity.org/

Goolsbee, A.D., and Krueger, A.B. (2015). A retrospective look at rescuing and restructuring General Motors and Chrysler. *Journal of Economic Perspectives*, 29(2), 3–24.

Graham, J., Haidt, J., and Nosek, B.A. (2009). Liberals and conservatives relay on different sets of moral foundations. *Journal of Personality and Social Psychology*, 96(5), 1029–46.

Grunwald, M. (2010, April 9). Why the U.S. is also giving Brazilians farm subsidies. *Time*. Retrieved from www.time.com/time/nation/article/0,8599,1978963,00.html#ixzz 1MiuQPxzr

Haidt, J. (2008, March). Jonathan Haidt on the moral roots of liberals and conservatives. *Technology, Entertainment, Design (TED) Conference*. Retrieved from www.ted.com/talks/ jonathan_haidt_on_the_moral_mind.html

Haidt, J. (2012). *The righteous mind: Why good people are divided by politics and religion*. New York, NY: Pantheon.

Haidt, J., Graham, J., and Joseph, C. (2009). Above and below left-right: Ideological narratives and moral foundations. *Psychological Inquiry*, 20(2/3), 110–19.

Investopedia. (2020). The most profitable car companies in 2019. *Investopedia*, January 9, 2020. Accessed at www.investopedia.com/articles/company-insights/091516/most-profit-able-auto-companies-2016-tm-gm.asp

Isidore, C. (2020). Ford's 2019 profits wiped out by a tough fourth quarter. *CNN Business*, February 4, 2020. Accessed at www.cnn.com/2020/02/04/business/ford-earnings/index. html

Jacobs, T. (2009, April). Morals authority. *Miller-McCune*. Retrieved from www.miller-mccune.com

Jones, A. (2020). Coronavirus: How 'overreaction' made Vietnam a virus success. *BBC News*, May 15, 2020. Accessed at www.bbc.com/news/world-asia-52628283

Kartner, J., and Warner, C.M. (2015). Multi-nationals and corruption systems: The case of Siemens. European Research Centre for Anti-corruption and State-Building, Working Paper No. 45. Accessed at www.againstcorruption.eu/publications/multi-nationals-corrup tion-systems-siemens/

Khanna, T., Palepu, H., Knoop, C.I., and Lane, D. (2007). *Metro cash and carry. Harvard Business School Case 9-707-505*. Boston, MA: Harvard Business School.

Kotler, P. (1986). *Principles of marketing* (3rd edn). Englewood Cliffs, NJ: Prentice-Hall.

Kroll, A. (2011, January 13). Auto bailouts: A success story? *Mother Jones*. Retrieved from motherjones.com/mojo/2011/01/auto-bailouts-success-story

Larsen, R., and Eid, M. (2008). Ed Diener and the science of subjective well-being. In M. Eid and R.J. Larsen (Eds.), *The science of subjective well-being* (pp. 1–16). New York, NY: Gilford Press.

Levitz, J. (2010, August 25). Coffins made with brotherly love have undertakers throwing dirt. *The Wall Street Journal*. Retrieved from http://online.wsj.com/article/SB1000142405 2748703846604575448083489852328.html

Lutz, B. (2011). *Car guys vs. bean counters: The battle for the soul of American business*. New York, NY: Portfolio/Penguin.

Mackey, J. (2009). Creating a new paradigm for business. In M. Strong's (Ed.), *Be the solution: How entrepreneurs and conscious capitalists can solve all the world's problems* (pp. 78–113). New York, NY: Wiley.

McAdams, D.P., Albaugh, M., Farber, E., Daniels, J., Logan, R., and Olson, L. (2008). Family metaphors and moral institutions: How conservatives and liberals narrate their lives. *Journal of Personality and Social Psychology*, 95, 978–90.

McGregor, J. (2005). *One billion customers: Lessons from the front lines of doing business in China*. New York, NY: Wall Street Journal Books.

McMillan, J. (2002). *Reinventing the Bazar: A natural history of markets*. New York, NY: W.W. Norton.

Mintzberg, H., Simons, R., and Basu, K. (2002, Fall). Beyond selfishness. *Sloan Management Review*, 44(1), 67–74.

Montero, D. (2018). *Kickback: Exposing the global corporate briber network*. New York: Viking.

Moody, O. (2020). How Germany's coronavirus contact tracers helped to ease its lockdown. *The Times*, May 26, 2020. Accessed at www.thetimes.co.uk/article/the-first-wave-how-germanys-coronavirus-contact-tracers-helped-to-ease-its-lockdown-w7tw5ddjs

Muskus, J. (2019). Amazon's political wipeout. *Bloomberg Businessweek*, November 25, 2019, 20–2.

Nix, N. (2019). Amazon flexes its Washington muscles. *Bloomberg Businessweek*, March 11, 2019, 32–5.

Quelch, J., and Jocz, K. (2007). *Greater good: How good marketing makes for a better democracy*. Boston, MA: Harvard Business Press.

Rattner, S. (2010). *Overhaul: An insider's account of the Obama Administration's emergency rescue of the auto industry*. Boston, MA: Houghton Mifflin Harcourt.

Ricciuti, R., Savoia, A., and Sen, K. (2019). Low tax collection in developing economies has a more devastating impact than we thought. *Quartz Africa*, March 15, 2019. Accessed at https://qz.com/africa/1573957/developing-countries-will-benefit-from-better-tax-collection/

Rivoli, P. (2005). *The travels of a t-shirt in the global economy: An economist examines the markets, power, and politics of world trade*. New York, NY: Wiley.

Rubenfeld, S. (2011, April 1). Panel says provincial China presents compliance challenge. *The Wall Street Journal*. Retrieved from http://blogs.wsj.com/corruption-currents/2011/04/01/panel-says-provincial-china-presents-complianc-challenge/?KEYWORDS=uneven+enforcement

Schouten, F. (2009). Lobbying spending tops $3 billion in '08. *USA Today*. Retrieved from www.usatoday.com/news/washington/2009-01-26-lobbying_N.htm

Simon, S. (2011). A license to shampoo: Jobs needing state approval rise. *Wall Street Journal*, Feb. 7. Accessed at www.wsj.com/articles/SB10001424052748703445904576118030935929752.

Sirgy, M. J. (2001). *Handbook of quality-of-life research: An ethical marketing perspective*. Boston, MA: Kluwer Academic.

Sowell, T. (2007). *A conflict of visions: Ideological origins of political struggles* (revised edition). New York, NY: Basic Books.

Stanford, J. (1999). *Victory in our schools: We CAN give our children excellent public education*. New York: Bantam Books.

Tate, C. (2002). Busing in Seattle: A well-intentioned failure. *HistoryLink.org*, September 7, 2002. Accessed at www.historylink.org/index.cfm?DisplayPage=output.cfmandFile_Id=3939

Venard, B. (2018). Lessons from the massive Siemens corruption scandal one decade later. *The Conversation*, December 13, 2018. Accessed at https://theconversation.com/lessons-from-the-massive-siemens-corruption-scandal-one-decade-later-108694

Watson, B. (2013). Siemens and the battle against bribery and corruption. *The Guardian*, September 18, 2013. Accessed at www.theguardian.com/sustainable-business/siemens-solmssen-bribery-corruption

WHO. (2020). Coronavirus. World Health Organization. Accessed at www.who.int/health-topics/coronavirus#tab=tab_1

Wieler, L., Rexroth, U., and Gottschalk, R. (2020). Emerging COVID-19 success story: Germany's strong enabling environment. *Our World in Data*, June 30, 2020. Accessed at https://ourworldindata.org/covid-exemplar-germany

Wilkie, W.L. (2001). Forward. In P. Bloom and G. Gundlach (Eds.), *Handbook of marketing and society* (pp. vii–xii). Thousand Oaks, CA: Sage.

Wilkie, W.L., and Moore, E.S. (1999). Marketing's contributions to society. *Journal of Marketing*, 63, 198–218.

PART II

Important Factors Affecting Sustainable Marketing

6
GLOBALIZATION AND PROTECTIONISM

Throwing Shade

Source: Photo by Glen Carrie on Unsplash.

Facebook

Launched by Mark Zuckerberg and friends at Harvard University in 2004, Facebook claimed more than 2.6 billion active users in the first quarter of 2020 making it an undeniable global phenomenon (Clement, 2020a). (Facebook also owns three other top-ranked social-media platforms – Instagram, WhatsApp and Facebook Messenger). So what's not to like about Facebook? Set up an account for free and then share photos and messages

(Continued)

with others who connect with you as friends. Haven't seen someone in years? No problem, you can catch up with their lives visually in an instant.

However, Facebook's well-intentioned purpose of giving people the power to build community and bring the world closer together has an ironic character in light of some of the problems Facebook is accused of nurturing (Kettlewell, 2019). 'Basically there are two things wrong with Facebook: how it works and how people use it,' University of Virginia Media Studies Professor Siva Vaidhyanathan said.

Regarding how Facebook works, CEO Zuckerberg continues to remind the world that Facebook does not sell the information of the users of Facebook after years of accusations that it does (Miskus and Ward, 2019). If Facebook did, then it couldn't charge advertisers a premium for exclusive access to its billions of users around the world who use Facebook.

Facebook does sell advertisers the attention of users by tailoring ads to what users' online behavior suggests these users would like (Vaidhyanathan, 2018). The tailoring is done by Facebook's algorithms that track users as they move across the internet on the websites of other firms' websites and apps. Facebook knows more about nonusers than they could ever imagine because Facebook amasses information from public records or from information that can be purchased. It cross-references such information with its own information on individuals (Kettlewell, 2019). In addition, users upload hundreds of millions of photos each day. Ominously, Facebook has not been transparent about what information it collects on individuals, nor how such collection is actually done.

Regarding how people use Facebook, critics charge that Facebook encourages superficial engagement and enables the spread of misleading and inflammatory information – particularly from extremists who might be in hate groups, autocratic regimes, or terrorist organizations (Kettlewell, 2019). Facebook's algorithms promote whatever content receives the most reactions on the site regardless of whether such content is a video of playful kittens or highly charged political rhetoric.

Since its inception, Zuckerberg has asserted that Facebook gives users the opportunity for free expression and speech (Zuckerberg, 2019). However, some advertisers are calling for a monitoring (and editing) of speech on Facebook and are withholding their ad spending on Facebook to make this felt by the leadership of Facebook (Bort, 2020).

Regulators are targeting Facebook for more transparency with consumers about how Facebook combines information on individuals across different pools of information in printed form, as well as on the internet. For example, Germany's Federal Court of Justice upheld a decision of the antitrust watchdog in Germany which would restrict Facebook from combining its Facebook data with information about individuals' activities on other apps and websites without the permission of individuals to do this (Satariano, 2020). If Facebook is not allowed to combine information from other sources on individuals the effectiveness of its ability to target ads will drop markedly – and so will the fees advertisers would be willing to pay for ads on Facebook.

The US Federal Trade Commission imposed a record $5 billion fine on Facebook in 2020, but critics assert that Facebook made billions more than the imposed fine (Coldeway, 2019). Although an otherwise enormous fine, this was like fining someone $50 after they stole and spent $100 – because Facebook booked $56.4 billion in profits from 2012 to 2018 when it began disregarding a 2012 order to guard user information (Clement, 2020b). In a dissenting opinion, FTC Commissioner Rohit Chopra denounced Facebook's behavior-advertising business-model, the divisiveness Facebook brings to society, as well as the $5 billion fine because Facebook benefitted much more from allowing firms to harvest members' personal data by posting small questionnaires within Facebook (Chopra, 2019).

Questions to Consider

- How global would you say are social-media platforms, such as Facebook?
- Have you ever experienced any presentation of ads on the internet that were eerie given your product tastes you don't remember sharing with anyone? If so, what did you think about this and how did you later feel about this?
- On the whole, do social-media platforms like Facebook provide more good than bad? Explain.
- How do you think Facebook could be effectively regulated? Explain.

CHAPTER OVERVIEW AND LEARNING OBJECTIVES

On the frontier of building national media networks with all of the accompanying difficulties involved, MTVNI has had remarkable success. But global brands such as MTV are admired and feared as they build their markets around the world. For example, MTV can bring entertainment to many, but what cultural values in host countries might be undermined by its programming? What does a global brand like MTV give back to society wherever it goes?

Multinational enterprises (MNEs) are said to bring death to distance. Although the principal benefits of globalization to consumers in developed countries might be listed as (a) more choices and (b) lower prices, critics of globalization cite the inequities that often accompany globalization. According to these critics, workers face lower wages, while CEOs take home salaries higher than they have ever been. Additionally, globalization tends to promote diffusion of some negative outcomes of consumer culture, such as overconsumption, as well as criminal trafficking in contraband, such as illegal drugs and human slaves. Again, it seems that transparency is needed to stem the work of such trafficking networks. The story of Peter Eigen, founder of Transparency International, a nongovernmental organization (NGO) devoted to reducing corruption around the world, illustrates how one person can lead an effective movement to attack a malady of the business world said by many to be inevitable.

After this chapter, you should be able to answer the following questions:

- What does a global phenomenon such as industrialized fake news mean to marketers of brands?
- How can globalization be defined?
- What are some benefits of globalization?
- What are some criticisms of globalization?
- What are the seven wars of globalization that societies now wage?
- What group in a society does bribe-paying hurt the most?

A GLOBAL PHENOMENON
Industrialized Fake News

In the 1990s, when journalism scholars talked about 'fake news' they were referring to satires and parodies of journalism seen on television shows, such as *Saturday Night Live* and Jon Stewart's *The Daily Show* (McNair, 2017, p. x). Only a few mentions of 'fake news' occurred in the media until November 2016, and these usually were about hoax artists such as Paul Horner who would fabricate stories (picked up and run by major news media outlets) to bring awareness to problems in society.

Misinformation (defined as incomplete information) and disinformation (defined as false information deliberately disseminated) abound on the internet (Cooke, 2018). However, it is not new because tabloid journalism (or yellow journalism) intent on inflaming the emotions of less critical readers has existed for ages. Spin is a form of misinformation that might have some truthful element to it, but spin intentionally mischaracterizes things through distortion and the ignoring of facts in order to influence others (McIntyre, 2018, p. 9). Counter knowledge is misinformation packaged to look like it is fact that some in the public have begun to believe (Cooke, 2018). Asking questions and evaluating sources are two antidotes for spin and counter knowledge that are both precursors of fake news.

But even critical readers of online information face powerful adversaries that have emerged in recent years from all parts of the globe. According to a *BuzzFeed News* report from June 2018, fake news creators now bring an industrialized approach to the dissemination of fake news (Broderick, 2018). In this report, the founder of Victory Lab (a fake-news creator and disseminator) based in Mexico City, Carlos Merlo, gives a guided tour of one of his 17 fake-news offices. The entire office is located in a single room (six meters square) with a dozen workers (appearing to be in their late teens or twenties) working around eight computer terminals – some with wide viewing-screens.

Merlo explains that the office makes memes – a humorous image, video, or piece of text that is copied (often with slight adjustments) and spread rapidly by users of the internet. To present fake news as more legitimate, Merlo's workers have created 4,000 web 'newspapers'. He buys about 100 sim cards for cell phones each week in convenience stores which require no identification, so that the smart phones of his workers will appear as different smart phones each week (and not the same smart phones involved in circulating fake news from the previous week).

If his fake-news stories came out of the same web newspaper each week, his fake news would not be believed. Instead, Merlo pushes out a fake news story across his network of 'newspapers', in order to keep skeptics of the fake-news story from finding the source of the story. The 'newspapers' run tabloid-like stories, such as one in which actor Paul Walker (featured in the *Fast and Furious* action-movies, but who died in a car crash in 2014) is said to be alive and held in a Mexican jail. More than 6 million online viewers in Mexico engaged with this fake-news story.

Merlo asserts that the way to create fake news on Facebook is to create a webpage (one of his newspapers), insert the fake-news story, and then pay about $50,000. This money is used to pay for Facebook accounts (many from Russia or Asia that are then renamed as if Mexican users had created them) and to have his workers create thousands of bots – with fake Facebook accounts – who 'visit' the webpage and who might leave a comment about the post. He has many of his 4,000 'newspapers' pay to advertise on Facebook alongside the fake-news story. His own 'newspapers' might even receive advertising payments from legitimate businesses that are seeking to place their brands in front of what they believe are human eyeballs viewing these 'newspapers'. Often, the real media will soon be talking about the fake-news story.

To prove how the real media will readily use fake news, Merlo demonstrated what Victory Lab can do using Twitter from his smartphone. He created a hashtag '#GanaConVictorylab' (meaning 'Win with Victory Lab') and then turned over the project to workers in one of his offices. After a two-hour lunch, this hashtag had become the sixth-most tweeted hashtag in Mexico.

One member of a digital-marketing agency in Mexico (who insisted on anonymity), said such digital manipulation has been going on in Mexico for years and that 90 percent of the trending topics in Mexico are fake because they are driven by bots and fake accounts.

So who pays Merlo? While he does not say, one can infer: any entity that wants fake-news circulated, such as political campaigns wanting to create doubt about an opponent or boost their own candidate. When asked if what he does is immoral, Merlo responded that all politics in Mexico is a little immoral (so he feels justified in doing what he does).

Developing countries with few genuine employment opportunities appear to be fertile ground for the growth of fake-news factories. Police in Mexico have cybercrime units which are aware of fake news, but these units have not been able to arrest any fake-news creators in 2018. Because fake-news writers can make thousands of dollars a month in countries like Mexico, it appears that fake news is not going to go away anytime soon and is poised to play a more disruptive role on the internet, if left unchecked.

In North Macedonia, the town of Veles with a population of 55,000 was the registered home of at least 100 pro-Trump websites in late 2016 prior to the US election (Subramanian, 2017). These websites spawned as part of the Google AdSense program in which Google would pay websites in order to have ads displayed on websites based on the content and number of visitors these websites had.

Website developers, such as one 18-year-old man in Veles (with no real affinity for Trump, but rather seeking ad money), made $16,000 off of two politically charged websites from August to November 2016. (The monthly GDP per capita in North Macedonia is $508 (World Bank, 2019).) The North Macedonian man had no real interest in Donald Trump other than that many viewers in the US would read the provocative content he posted about Donald Trump. Google has since taken steps to eliminate such fake-news websites from its Google AdSense program.

BUILDING GLOBAL BRANDS

What the World's Consumers Expect from Global Brands

In 1983, Harvard Business School professor Ted Levitt declared that a global market for uniform products and services had arrived (Levitt, 1983). Many interpreted Levitt's words as a call to standardization across world markets. In this interpretation, marketing practices could be done the same way to achieve success as the world apparently wanted the elements of pop culture in Western markets, such as blue jeans, pop music, and fast food, as well as consumer durables like cars and refrigerators. In time, standardized global brands did not perform as well as predicted by Levitt. In their place, marketers used hybrid approaches to combine the best of global approaches in less visible areas, such as technology, manufacturing, and firm organization, with more local approaches in more visible areas, such as products, distribution, and promotion (Holt, Quelch, and Taylor, 2004). These 'glocal' strategies have strongly influenced marketing ever since.

Toward the end of the twentieth century, an anti-globalization movement became increasingly vociferous. It manifested itself at the annual World Economic Forum in Davos, Switzerland, with window smashing at McDonald's. Later, protests at the November 1999 World Trade Organization meeting in Seattle turned into 'the battle in Seattle'. Many protesters denounced the asymmetrical benefits to developed countries, as well as the externalities of global trade increasingly burdening countries in the developing world, such as exploitative wages, pollution, and cultural imperialism.

As popular culture became global and nations integrated themselves in the global economy, flows of tourists and laborers increasingly crossed borders. Television, movies, and music also flowed across borders. And more recently, the wide diffusion in the use of the internet has further reinforced globalizing forces. (In June 2019, more than 4.5 billion people – 58.8 percent of the world's population – have used the internet. This is more than have flown in a plane, traveled on a train or owned a car (Steenkamp, 2020)). Today, global brands are key symbols in an ongoing conversation people across the world have about what they like and who they are. Increasingly, global brands are viewed as having a powerful impact on people's lives, as well as on the well-being of communities, nations, and the planet.

The Three Dimensions of Global Brands

Research about global brands suggests that people across the world associate three dimensions with global brands and base their purchase decisions on these (Holt, Quelch, and Taylor, 2004, p. 2, para. 5). First, a global brand signals quality. Global brands represent dynamism because many people believe that global brands are always upgrading themselves. By comparison, people perceived that local brands lack dynamism. Second, consumers see global brands as representing a global myth in which consumers can share a global identity with others on the planet. A self-transcendent aspect of this is an accompanying feeling that global brands make consumers feel part of something bigger than themselves or their national market. Global brands make consumers feel like citizens of the world.

Third, people expect global brands to act with social responsibility by addressing problems linked with what they sell and how they conduct business. In the past, there have been dark episodes for global brands, such as oil spills for petroleum giants Exxon and BP, and protests against Nike for not being vigilant in defending workers against abuse by Nike's contract manufacturers in developing countries. Increasingly, consumers will choose not to buy global brands that are perceived as not acting as stewards of the environment, worker rights, and public health. People have become convinced that global brands have a special duty to address social issues relevant to their operations. For example, people expect oil companies to address global warning, but they have much lower expectations for local firms to do so. Also, people across the world do not tend to become upset when local firms mistreat employees, but these same people will not accept global brands mistreating local workers. In effect, global brands are held to a higher standard likely because they are perceived to have extraordinary capabilities and power. An Australian reasoned this way: 'McDonald's pays back locally, but it is their duty. They are making so much money, they should be giving back' (Holt, Quelch, and Taylor, 2004, p. 4, para. 2). To be credible, global brands' social responsibility efforts must demonstrate that the firms have directed their ample resources to benefit society.

A Global Firm with a Global Corporate Culture

United Kingdom-based Reckitt Benckiser (RB) gives a glimpse of what a highly globalized company might look like (Reckitt Benckiser, 2020). Focused on home, health, and personal care products, the firm has 41 manufacturing facilities around the world. Its 'Powerbrands' include the following brands that are among the leaders in worldwide sales in their respective categories: (a) Vanish fabric treatment, (b) Calgon water softener, (c) Lysol multipurpose cleaner, (d) Finish automatic dishwashing detergent, (e) Dettol antiseptic, and (f) Nurofen pain reliever.

RB is one of the FTSE 100 – the top 100 firms based in the United Kingdom as listed by *The Financial Times* and the London Stock Exchange (Sheldon, 2020). In 2019, its revenues were £12.85 billion or $16.83 billion (Reckitt Benckiser, 2020, p. 60). The five-year comparison of the return on RB's share price (darker line) with the return on the FTSE 100 from 2010 to 2020 is depicted in Figure 6.1 (Big Charts, 2020). As can be seen, RB has outperformed the FTSE over this term.

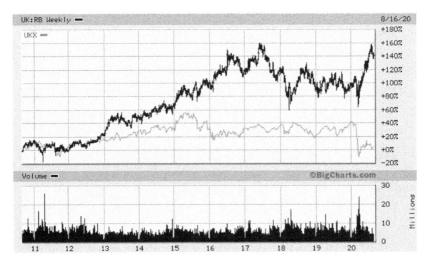

Figure 6.1   Five-year returns of Reckitt Benckiser stock return and FTSE 100 (2010–2020)

Source: www.bigcharts.com

With almost 40,000 employees worldwide, RB has a global workforce with 50 percent in developed countries and 50 percent in developing countries (Reckitt Benckiser, 2020). Most of the top managers in RB regard themselves as being global citizens. Since 1999, RB has deliberately built a corporate culture based on global mobility because the leaders of the firm believe this is one of the best ways to generate new ideas and create global entrepreneurs. Five nationalities are represented on the 12-member board of directors. Such global diversity seems to work for RB.

Former CEO Bart Becht who served as CEO from 1997 to 2011 said:

> It doesn't matter whether I have a Pakistani, a Chinese person, a Brit, or a Turk, man or woman, sitting in the same room, or whether I have people from sales or something else, so long as I have people with different experiences – because the chance for new ideas is much greater when you have people with different backgrounds. The chance for conflict is also higher – and conflict is good per se, as long as it's constructive and gets us to the best idea.

> (Ibarra and Hansen, 2011, p. 72, para. 3)

In addition to national diversity, research on creative industries suggests that collaborations are most productive when firm leaders intentionally bring together both experienced people and newcomers, as well as those who have never worked together previously. More patents, financial returns, and critical praise tend to come from such diverse collaborative groups. Without being put together, people will choose to work with those who have similar backgrounds. Unfortunately, stasis and insularity characterize such groups and innovation usually declines.

NAVIGATING GLOBALIZATION
Globalist Views

Thomas L. Friedman is one of the most influential writers on the topic of globalization. Because his role as a syndicated columnist for *The New York Times* allowed him the scope of operation to travel the world and ponder the changes occurring in the ten years after the Berlin Wall fell in 1989, his book *The Lexus and the Olive Tree* explains the phenomenon of globalization in a holistic way (Friedman, 2000). Friedman saw globalization as the system that replaced the Cold War, and he believed the changes coming to the world would be led by the increased role of business in societies and would be generally positive. Because of this, some refer to his views as representing the most comprehensive, widely read defense of neoliberal globalization (Ritzer, 2009, p. 119).

The title refers to the tension between striving for material gain (represented by the Lexus luxury automobile desired by many the world over) and holding onto cultural traditions that allow individuals to define themselves in a historical narrative (represented by the olive tree). Trade, technology, and finance bring consumers the Lexus, while geopolitics and ethnic and religious traditions nurture the olive tree. When out of balance, either the drive for prosperity or tribal ways have the power to eclipse or even harm the other. For example, the 9/11 attack on the World Trade Center is an example of a tribalistic backlash against the global commerce system. Alternatively, the current migration of millions of rural people to cities in China who are searching for jobs related to the global economy shows how the drive for an improved standard of living can draw people away from places that used to define their cultural identities. Those in the city have access to global amenities, such as fashions, food, and entertainment, in addition to higher-waged jobs.

Friedman defined globalization as 'inexorable integration of markets, nation-states and technologies to a degree never witnessed before' (Friedman, 2000, p. 9, para. 1). Such globalization enables individuals, corporations, and nation-states to extend their reach to places on the world 'farther, faster, deeper and cheaper than ever before' (Friedman, 2000, p. 9, para. 1). According to Friedman, the driving idea behind globalization is free-market capitalism. With communication technology allowing instantaneous transmissions of data and voice signals and the elimination of the Cold War that justified protectionist legislation to restrict trade between countries, governments needed to reduce their interventionist ways in markets in order to allow globalization to provide the most benefits to consumers.

In *The World Is Flat: A Brief History of the Twenty-First Century*, Friedman updates his thinking about globalization by noting that while he was focused on the two-year aftermath of 9/11 to explain anti-American attitudes – particularly in the Middle East – developing countries such as India and China 'caught up' in businesses processes (Friedman, 2006). Specifically, with computers and software now abundant in developing countries, skilled white-collar workers in such locales could now compete in the service economy of the globe. For example, an entrepreneurial businessman Jaithirth 'Jerry' Rao that Friedman met in Bangalore, India, aggressively sought to win Friedman's approval to process Friedman's income taxes for a fee in the coming year. The business man had all of the appropriate forms needed and would fax, e-mail, or mail the completed tax documents to the United States from India. Although Friedman declined Rao's offer, it dawned on Friedman later that his own accounting firm might be outsourcing his own tax preparation to someone like Rao in India. Already hundreds of thousands of US returns are outsourced to India and the number climbs every year (Friedman, 2006, p. 13). In examples similar to this, Friedman makes the argument for the global economic playing field being leveled.

'Flatteners' of the world according to Friedman include (a) the end of the Cold War; (b) the internet-browser company Netscape's highly successful initial public offering (IPO) in 1995 that unleashed $1 trillion investment in fiber optic cable under the oceans in less than five years; (c) new forms of collaboration resulting from software integration; (d) off-shoring of work to China and other developing countries; (e) large firms such as UPS taking over logistics for smaller firms; (f) setting up supply chains among suppliers, retailers, and customers to create value; and (g) Google for informing oneself about information and opportunities from all over the world.

Friedman delineates three great eras of globalization (Friedman, 2006, p. 9). Globalization 1.0 occurred from 1492 to 1820. Here, mercantilist countries and governments conducted globalization through their imperialistic conquests of the New World. The key agent of change was brawn or muscle and how cleverly it could be deployed. Globalization 2.0 occurred from 1820 to 2001. Here, multinational companies conducted globalization. The dynamic forces during this period of industrialization were breakthroughs in hardware, such as steamships and railroads and later telephones and mainframe computers. Globalization 3.0 now is unfolding. Here, individuals and small groups are globalizing themselves. They are collaborating and competing globally being connected through their personal computers that are connected through fiber-optic cable and work-flow software.

Friedman offers compelling descriptions about globalization, and his predictions for increased competition at all levels – especially for individuals – are troubling to some. For example, he asserts that in a future globalized world, everything becomes commoditized – except imagination. Because the software tools and even education are now available to all around the world, what matters now is what one does with those tools and education (Friedman, 2017).

In response to Friedman, some believe globalization has gone too far, while others believe it has not gone far enough. Surprisingly, many 'foreign' cars made in the US have more parts that are made in the US than the cars made by GM, Ford and Chrysler (knowledge@wharton, 2018). The Honda Odyssey made in Lincoln, Alabama has 75 percent of its parts made in the US. However, the Buick Envision crossover vehicle is made in China with only 2 percent of its parts made in the US. In 2017, the largest exporter of US-made cars was not a US firm, but one from Germany – BMW, which had just one plant in the US in Spartanburg, South Carolina. BMW exported almost 3 out of 4 of the 371,000 sport utility vehicles it made in the US. The firm continued its heavy exporting from the US in 2018 and retained its position as the biggest US automotive exporter by value for the fifth consecutive year (Reuters, 2019). In sum, gauging the extent of globalization involved in the manufacturing of complex products, such as cars, is itself a complex undertaking in a world of supply chains that span international borders.

Core-Gap Thesis

Like Friedman, former US defense strategist Thomas P. Barnett believes that globalization has unstoppable momentum and that no one is in charge (Barnett, 2004). However, Barnett believes that globalization must be extended to all countries, but that it currently has far to go in this regard. Barnett believes that globalization is all about connectivity and will result in a peaceful 'mutually-assured dependence'. But globalization is weak in many parts of the world. Although China and India have connected to the globalization system, some regions of the developing world remain poorly integrated. Barnett proposes a Core-Gap Thesis in which countries in the gap that have struggled to plug into globalization and join the functioning core of globalization (the developed countries plus the BRIC countries of Brazil, Russia, India, and China along with a few others). According to this thesis, problems in the Gap countries potentially can flare up and disrupt the ongoing process of economic integration that is dampening flames for violent confrontation. Again, the failed state of Afghanistan is an example of how a disconnected country can harbor extremists intent on disrupting globalization as seen in the terror attacks of 9/11. Figure 6.2 depicts the map of the world with Barnett's Core and Gap regions.

Figure 6.2 Barnett's map of globalization's functioning Core and the Gap (inside dotted line)

Source: http://thomaspmbarnett.com/high-resolution-map/. Shared under the CC BY 3.0 license.

According to Barnett, political and social problems related to underdevelopment in Gap countries pose a threat not to countries in the Core but to the system of globalization. For this reason, the United States and other like-minded countries are in a long war against extremism in Gap countries through their military policing and political skills. Additionally, it is in the best interests of such leading countries in the Core to help Gap countries upgrade their capabilities to conduct business with the outside world. This means a focus on telecoms, banking, business, and investment exchanges, utilities, and border security.

Anti-globalist Views

Counter to the pro-globalization view are those of anti-globalists. Kilbourne (2004) regards globalization as neoliberalism applied to the world. With such neoliberalism, the societal aspects of economic integration receive thin treatment while profit and efficiency become paramount. According to these critics, trade liberalization – the reduction or elimination of tariffs and other trade barriers – should not be the sole response of governments, but so too should promoting equity, employment, and a sensible pace for reforms related to trade (Stiglitz, 2007, p. 17).

In effect, firms' off-shoring or out-sourcing of their manufacturing to lower-wage countries served as a way to outmaneuver workers' unions and governments where firms use to do their manufacturing (Mazzucato, 2018). Such unions and governments previously served as forces of accountability for the societal citizenship of these firms where they were located. With globalization, firms took higher profits (which went to investors) while the rust belts of the American Midwest, northern England and regions of Continental Europe (such as Wallonia in Belgium) encountered wrenching social dislocation.

Often, critics of globalization focus on injustices for those in the developing world resulting from global marketing of consumer products (Witkowski, 2005). First, the marketing of imported products tends to displace cultural goods in developing countries. For example, Coca-Cola leads West Africans to turn away from locally made ginger beer. Second, marketing places the protection of intellectual property for developed country inventions over the needs of local consumers. For example, pharmaceuticals may not be introduced in generic form in developing countries so that pharmaceutical companies from developed countries can seek out profits from the branded versions of these pharmaceuticals. Third, marketing promotes unhealthy dietary patterns from the developed world. Fast food and food containing high-fructose corn syrup are two examples fueling obesity around the world. Food with genetically modified organisms (GMOs), such as soy beans, remains under suspicion by some. Fourth, marketing promotes unsustainable consumption that is bad for the natural environment. As the world's platform for light manufacturing, China further despoils its soil, water, and air each year.

'Global markets undermine national sovereignty and create turmoil,' Former International Society of Marketing and Development President Russ Belk said (Clifford, Rahtz, and Speece, 2003, p. 661). Protectionists in every country fear the flows of products, tourists, immigrants, and contraband because of the perceived threat these pose to society in its current form

(Ritzer, 2009, p. 52). Government leaders of some countries (such as Cuba, North Korea and Venezuela) oppose perceived oppression from developed countries and denounce globalization – especially because they see it as a force benefitting the United States. Because of the imperative for governments to intervene less in markets as globalization continues, social critic Noam Chomsky regards globalization as constraining democratic choice to trivial matters, such as what brands will be consumed. Finally, critics of globalization perceive that the 'have' countries benefit more than the 'have not' countries resulting in a wider gap both between and within countries (Stiglitz, 2007, p. 8).

Some who criticize globalization as a top-down phenomenon benefitting the developed world – particularly multinational enterprises – also see that an alter-globalization or bottom-up version of globalization could one day balance or outweigh the economic emphasis currently carried by globalization. In such a bottom-up globalization, grassroots networks in one country would connect with those in other countries. For example, students in California might financially support and protest on behalf of garment workers in Vietnam, or religious groups in Europe would link to support Chinese artist and dissident Ai Weiwei. In short, globalization could bring greater solidarity for justice and more fully developed democracies around the world (Anderson, Cavanagh, and Lee, 2000, p. x).

Semi-globalist Views

Strategy Professor Pankaj Ghemawat of Barcelona's IESE Business School takes issue with both globalists and anti-globalists for overreaching in making their claims about globalization (Ghemawat, 2017). According to Ghemawat, the true state of the world today is semi-globalization. By 'semi' he means partial as in 10 percent to 25 percent, rather than 50 percent (Ghemawat, 2011a, p. 23, para. 2). Although major multinational enterprises exhibit a high degree of internationalization, most other firms do not (Ghemawat, 2007). Ninety percent of all fixed investment that occurs is domestic (Ghemawat, 2011a, p. 29, para. 3). World Trade Organization director-general Pascal Lamy estimates that global exports account for only 20 percent of all the value produced in the world (GDP) (Ghemawat, 2011a, p. 28, para. 4).

Ghemawat says to ask oneself the following questions: (a) Why are major export deals involving private firms announced at meetings between heads of states? (b) Why do employees of foreign-owned companies often fear their career opportunities will be limited relative to their peers from the firm's home country? (c) Which governments do firms call to represent them at World Trade Organization disputes? (d) Why do foreign-ownership restrictions persist in industries such as media and airlines? (Ghemawat, 2011b).

Not only are firms and their business operations deeply rooted, but also according to Ghemawat, so are the people who staff these companies, invest in them, and buy their products. Ninety percent of the world's people will never travel abroad (Ghemawat, 2011b,

p. 94, para. 8). Two percent of all telephone calls are international ones. In Europe, only 38 percent of news is international, while it is just 21 percent in the United States. Surprisingly, no more than 10 percent of charitable giving crosses national borders and foreign aid for most governments is only one thirty-thousandth of aid to domestic poor. In sum, as distances – geographic, cultural, political, and economic increase – cross-border interactions tend to decrease.

Cosmopolitan Management

In a world requiring adaptation, the composition of the management team is the most critical ingredient. Most management teams are far from cosmopolitan – caring about and being aware of what is happening outside of the immediate region. For example, Ghemawat estimates that Americans comprise 80 percent of the top 200 managers at a global company such as GE (Ghemawat, 2011b, p. 98, para. 4). For firm cosmopolitanism to take hold, a critical threshold of foreign-born managers needs to be working in the company headquarters. Then, skillful leadership needs to be applied in order to allow this cultural diversity to be more of a benefit to the company rather than a detriment. 'For many companies, the greatest challenge may be fostering the human capacity to connect and cooperate across distances and differences, internally and externally,' Ghemawat said (2011a, p. 314, para. 3).

Macromarketing researchers have considered whether firm capabilities and its home-country business ecosystem are the determining factor in firms' involvement in international marketing (Ellis and Pecotich, 2002). An alternative explanation proposed by these researchers was a cosmopolitan explanation for the firm's pursuit of a new market entry overseas. Given a capability and a motivation to go international, an awareness of foreign opportunities would then be the determining factor in pursuing international opportunities. Based on in-depth interviews with international and non-international decision makers at small-to medium-sized firms based in Australia, researchers found support for the cosmopolitan explanation rather than for explanations based on other capabilities of the firm or its country business ecosystem.

Specifically, awareness of opportunities abroad proved to be the critical catalyst in the initiation process of market entry endeavors for the firms in the study. For example, an obstetrician who runs a medical products company, GoMedical, has links with a borderless community of fellow doctors and gives presentations at international conferences. Such appearances have reinforced his relationships with European doctors. Consequently, these apparently 'weak ties' have provided entry points into markets such as Italy, Sweden, and Switzerland. In this regard, the 'strong ties' this medical doctor has in his home country did not contribute to awareness of opportunities in markets of Europe. Although importantly, Australia provided a base for developing GoMedical as a business that could export medical products.

Debate about Globalization

It can be said that the world's most recent globalization surge began after the collapse of the Former Soviet Union in 1991 (Friedman, 2000). But what happened to global income since the Former Soviet Union ended? Figure 6.3 depicts the share of those living in extreme poverty by region. The trends are downward-sloping across all regions – especially in East Asia and the Pacific where China's economic rise has brought hundreds of millions of its population out of extreme poverty. This is good news.

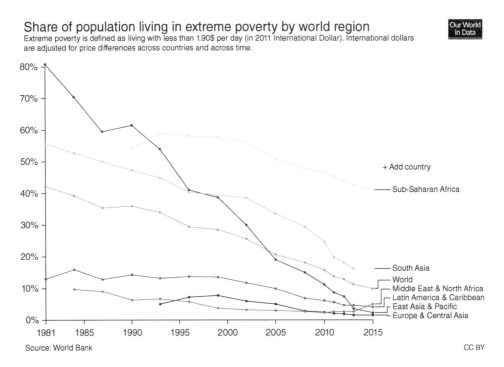

Figure 6.3 Share of population living in extreme poverty by world region

Source: Roser and Ortiz-Ospina (2019). Shared under the CC BY 4.0 license.

Figure 6.4 depicts individual income percentiles across the world from 1980–2016 (Harvard University Press, 2016). This is the result of research by economist Branko Milanovic of the World Bank Research Department. The implication of this chart is that Eastern lower and middle classes benefitted the most in economic terms during the surge in globalization while the middle and lower income groups in Western countries benefitted the least. This relative lack of benefits for the lower and middle income groups in Western countries likely explains why a populist message (focused on how elites have sold out their fellow citizens in order to

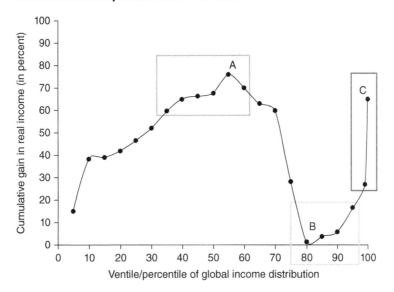

Figure 6.4 Individual income-percentiles and their corresponding income growth, 1980–2016

Source: Harvard University Press (2016).

capture the riches that globalization offers) has connected with many voters in developed countries, such as the US and the UK.

A striking difference exists between developed countries and developing countries regarding the next generation's prospects (Pew Research Center, 2017). When asked 'when children today in our country grow up, they will be (better off or worse off) than their parents', 58 percent in developed countries answered 'worse off', while 56 percent in developing countries answered 'better off'. (In France, 71 percent responded with 'worse off', while in India, 76 percent responded with 'better off.')

In developed countries, resistance to increased globalization has grown in recent years. This is evidenced by a surge in populism which asserts that a corrupt elite (or other) has kept the people of a country from receiving what they deserve (Arditi et al., 2005, p. 2). Populism is now a factor in the developed countries of the world now confronted with some of the economic realities of globalization, such as wage stagnation and increased uncertainty due to immigration and global business competition.

The Wars of Globalization

Globalization entails not just economic flows across national borders, but also flows of every other kind, such as ideas, knowledge, technology, communications, workers, tourists, immigrants, culture, terrorism, pollution, waste, and pandemics, such as the coronavirus. In short, there is good as well as bad coming across national borders. Societies today find themselves afflicted with illegal trafficking in (a) drugs, (b) arms, (c) intellectual property, (d) people, and (e) money to be laundered (Naím, 2003), as well as (f) terrorism, and (g) corruption. To stand against these seven puts societies in seven wars related to globalization.

Transparency International

Gains made in the war against corruption by an NGO called Transparency International may prove instructive for societies in their wars related to undesirable globalized flows. The imperative for national governments to cooperate with each other and for transnational organizations to coordinate the efforts of national governments has never been greater.

Corruption is the abuse of entrusted power for private gain (Transparency International, 2019a). At a minimum, it includes (a) bribery of public officials, (b) embezzlement, (c) trading in influence, (d) abuse of function and illicit enrichment by public officials, and (e) bribery of private sector employees. Bribery distorts market exchanges in favor of those who provide less value and hurts all whose life, livelihood or happiness depends on the integrity of those in authority.

When Peter Eigen from Germany served as the director of the World Bank's office for East Africa in Nairobi, Kenya, he noticed that systematic corruption in Kenya undermined everything his organization tried to do in helping with large infrastructure projects done for the purpose of developing needy countries (Eigen, 2013). When he began work on stopping such corruption, he received a notice from the legal department of the World Bank. He was told he was meddling in the affairs of partner countries, and this was forbidden in the charter of the World Bank.

Things worsened for Eigen as he chaired donor meetings where large corporations from the developed world would review projects proposed for development in Kenya. According to Eigen, the worst projects put forward were the ones approved first (Eigen, 2013). For example, a huge power project costing $300 million in West Kenya – in a beautiful area – would have no clients to buy the electricity, but it would be funded by an unholy alliance between powerful elites in the developing countries and suppliers from the North from such countries as France, United Kingdom, Canada, Japan, and Germany who were bribing these public officials. Eigen and his team knew such a project would destroy the environment as well as the land and streams for a surviving nomadic group of people in the proposed area. But it was not just a useless project. It was going to be an absolutely damaging project for the future of Kenya. It would put a heavy debt on the society of Kenya and would siphon the scarce resources of the society away from much needed schools and hospitals. Transparency International (TI) veterans have concluded that the poor in countries are the ones hurt the most by corruption:

> It was systematically driven by systematic, large-scale corruption with $10 million or $20 million going to Swiss bank accounts or accounts in Lichtenstein for the president and ministers of these countries. I saw not only one project like this during my years in Africa, but hundreds of projects like this. And so I became convinced that it is this systematic corruption that is perverting the economic policy-making in these countries. It is *the* main reason for the misery, for the poverty, for the violence, for the conflicts and for the desperation in these countries. It is why we have more than one billion people below the absolute poverty line. It is why we have more than one billion people without proper drinking water in the world. More than two billion without proper sanitation and the consequent illnesses this brings with 10 million children dying each year before the age of five. The cause of this to a great extent is grand corruption.

> (Eigen, 2013, 5 min, 30 s)

The Early Years of Transparency International

Although stopped by the World Bank from opposing corruption, Eigen departed the World Bank in 1993 and founded TI, an NGO dedicated to playing a leading role in the anti-corruption movement. At the time, only the United States had any strong legislation forbidding employees of US companies from engaging in bribery overseas. The members of the World Bank accepted foreign bribery as just another aspect of the business culture in foreign countries. In Germany, bribery was allowed and was even tax deductible up until 1999.

Over the course of two years, TI convened representatives from major companies and another NGO, the Aspen Institute, and asked them 'what should be done about bribery?' (Eigen, 2013). Initially, the response was 'it is what other cultures demand.' Later, it became 'if we stop it, companies from other countries will gain the business we now have.' But Eigen and his TI team knew that deep down, these major companies detested bribery because it precluded such companies from selling their products made with quality at a low enough price that would benefit foreign societies. TI offered these major corporations an escape route from their dilemma of losing business. TI introduced concepts of collective action. Here, the competitors would go home and petition their respective governments to attend a convention held under the auspices of the Organisation of Economic Co-operation and Development

(34 developed countries) in 1997 and sign a protocol obliging them to criminalize foreign bribery. The competitors did this, and the governments signed the protocol.

TI's actions in standing against corruption provides a valuable model for a three-way partnership among private firms, national governments, and NGOs. Surprising to some, most national governments at that time felt powerless to tell businesses how to conduct their operations outside of their home countries. TI and the Aspen Institute brought together competitors from a wide set of European countries and Japan for collective action. Then, the businesses returned to their home countries urging them to join with other countries to make foreign corruption illegal across these countries.

The Work of Transparency International

Today, TI is a global network including more than 100 locally established national chapters (Transparency International, 2019a). Other chapters continue to form and join this network. These chapters fight domestic corruption in several ways. They convene relevant players from government, civil society, business, and the media to promote transparency across society. For example, they seek increased transparency in elections, in public administration,

Figure 6.5 Transparency International's 2019 Corruption Perceptions Index

Source: Transparency International, www.transparency.org/cpi2019. This work from Transparency International (2020) is licensed under CC BY-ND 4.0.

in procurement, and in business. TI's global network of chapters and contacts also use advocacy campaigns to lobby governments to implement anti-corruption reforms.

TI publishes an annual rating of perceptions for the amount and frequency of public sector corruption in countries around the world called the Corruption Perceptions Index (CPI) (Transparency International, 2019b). The CPI is based on surveys and assessments relating to the bribery of public officials, kickbacks in public procurement, embezzlement of public funds, as well as to the strength and effectiveness of public sector anti-corruption efforts. The results for the CPI in 2019 are depicted in Figure 6.5. As can be seen, Denmark, New Zealand, Singapore, Finland, and Sweden have the lowest perceptions for public sector corruption, while Somalia, South Sudan, Syria, Yemen, and Venezuela have the worst. TI notes that three-quarters of the world's countries have a problem with public-sector corruption.

TI also periodically produces a Bribe Payers Index (BPI) (Transparency International, 2012b). Here, senior executives around the world were asked about the likelihood of foreign firms (among countries with which they have business dealings) to engage in bribery when doing business in the respondent's country. In short, the BPI assesses the supply of bribe money for 22 countries. In the 2008 report, Russia and China had the worst perceptions for paying bribes. They were followed by Mexico and India, respectively.

By doing the needed research on a murky topic, such as corruption, TI shines a light on the darker realms associated with globalization. TI's research and its widespread dissemination through its website (www.transparency.org) is another important ingredient in fueling the anti-corruption movement. TI's approach based on establishing an extensive network of national chapters, imparting collective action concepts to businesses, and working with governments, transnational organizations, and businesses could prove valuable in the other wars related to globalization.

Although these wars have been going on for centuries (Naím, 2005), governments today find themselves unable to adequately budget for them. By comparison, globalization seems to have given more flexibility to drug traffickers, arms dealers, alien smugglers, counterfeiters, money launderers, as well as international terrorists. Without multisector-approaches to counter such traffickers, these wars seem to be tilted in favor of the bad guys and their networks (based on market forces of supply and demand) against an array of weakly connected bureaucracies around the world.

CONCLUSION

This chapter offered a review of issues confronting companies and societies in this time of increased globalization. The global phenomenon of industrialized fake news and the rise of global brands feature prominently in the ongoing story of globalization.

To put globalization in perspective, Ghemawat's four versions of the world from history will be used (Ghemawat, 2011b, p. 95). In the Wild World of World 0.0, no nations existed in the prehistoric times and only local borders mattered. In the Walled World of World 1.0 that emerged in the Age of Enlightenment (about 1700), the nation became the primary method of societal organization and national borders mattered most. In the One World of World 2.0 that emerged in the late twentieth century, global markets and complete global integration seemed to be sweeping the planet. Finally, in the Workable World of World 3.0 that has emerged in the twenty-first century, markets can be seen to have a semi-global character with partial global integration.

Consumers around the world will inevitably decide which World version will predominate the twenty-first century. Research suggests that consumers see global brands (a) as signaling quality, (b) as bringing a myth to consumers of joining a global community defined by consuming common brands, and (c) as being obligated to be socially responsible to the locales where they do business. The social responsibility of multinational enterprises comes under more intense scrutiny when CEOs take enormous pay from their boards of directors representing the shareholders of these firms. With advisory 'say on pay' votes on senior executive compensation now being conducted, attention to CEO pay in the era of increased globalization will continue.

Globalization involves the flows of the material and immaterial across national borders. Three views of globalization included those of (a) globalists carrying neoliberal ideas of restricted governmental action in markets, (b) anti-globalists who oppose neo liberalism and seek more direct government intervention primarily to preclude any lapses in protection of vulnerable populations and the environment, and (c) semi-globalists who see how great distance and differences across societies keep much of business focused on local concerns, but who nevertheless see regulation of markets as important until societies figure out more of the dynamics of closer integration across national borders.

Resistance to increased globalization has grown in recent years. This is evidenced by a surge in populism which asserts that a corrupt elite (or other) has kept the people of a country from receiving what they deserve (Arditi et al. 2005, p. 2). Populism is now a factor in developed countries of the world confronted with some of the economic realities of globalization, such as wage stagnation and increased uncertainty due to immigration and global business competition.

Finally, globalization also means that societies must now wage wars against what criminals increasingly send across national borders, such as drugs, arms, intellectual property, people, and money. Corruption in the form of bribery of foreign officials also crosses borders. Peter Eigen's founding of the Transparency International NGO and its contributions to the anti-corruption movement highlight how a transnational approach to societal problems worsened by increased globalization, such as corruption, can be effectively addressed by a combination of NGOs, businesses, and national governments.

QUESTIONS

- How much influence do you think industrialized fake news has in your country?
- What do you think will be the influence of industrialized fake news five years from now?
- What would appeal to you about joining a global firm like Reckitt Benckiser as a manager? What would scare you a bit?
- In your view, how far has globalization gone – too far, not far enough, or just right? What will the next 20 years bring in terms of global integration of technology, commerce, finance, culture, people, and contraband?
- Is it surprising the US was about 25 years ahead of the other developed countries in criminalizing foreign bribery? Why or why not?

Mavericks Who Made It

Bill Roedy

Source: BillRoedy.com

For many, it might be hard to imagine a career like Bill Roedy's. In 1970, he graduated from the US Military Academy, and then he served as a US Army officer in the northern part of South Vietnam for a year. He received the Bronze Star medal for his service:

(Continued)

The lessons I learned during that time helped shape everything I did after that. I learned the importance of making quick and firm decisions, communicating those decisions clearly to my troops and then doing anything and everything necessary to implement them. I learned the importance of building morale, camaraderie, and a team spirit. I learned how to deal with the chain of command and how to get around it when necessary. And after living on the frontlines for a year, there isn't much that intimidates me.

(Roedy, 2011, p. 11, para. 1)

Roedy later directed all of MTV Networks' global multimedia operations for the MTV brands, including Music Television, Nickelodeon, VH-1, VIVA, TMF: The Music Factory, Game One, Comedy Central, Paramount Comedy, Spike TV, and BET, which includes BET Hip Hop, BET Mobile, and BET.com (Roedy 2011). Roedy was honored as the UN Correspondents' 2009 Global Citizen of the Year for public service initiatives aired on MTV (mostly for HIV/AIDS prevention) that saved lives while building tremendous brand recognition and loyalty throughout the world. 'The bottom line is that for the bottom line, doing good in the world is good for business,' Roedy said. 'I have little doubt that in many countries MTV's proven record of engagement without pushing a political agenda made it a lot easier for us to receive government approval' (Nichols, 2011, p. 1, para. 11).

Wherever he went, Roedy wore sneakers. They became his trademark. He owned them in all colors. The sneakers made his back feel better, but they also encouraged the creative environment he wanted to instill at MTVNI. When he was the first private citizen to address the UN General Assembly, as a result of his work in fighting AIDS, he wore a dark suit and black sneakers. He also wore them to meet the Queen.

Roedy was in Berlin when the Berlin Wall fell in 1989. He believes television played a major role in bringing Eastern Europe to shake off communist rule. 'I'm convinced it wasn't so much about the rock 'n' roll programming,' Roedy said. 'I think it was even more about the commercials. They saw how the other side lived' (Andrews, 2011, p. 1, para. 23).

To build an international business, Bill Roedy did a remarkable amount of traveling. For example, in one month, Roedy visited 20 different countries (Roedy, 2011, p. 98). In another three-month period, he spent fewer than 10 days at home. Based out of London, Roedy went where the most important opportunity existed, which often meant going where problems had to be solved. For example, he traveled to China for 20 years to build relationships that eventually resulted in distribution of MTV in China. He used to joke that there were times he went to China more often than to his office in the United Kingdom – only ten minutes from his home.

In launching MTV in different countries, Roedy discovered that what worked well in one market often had little application to the next market. Accordingly, he was not able to cut down on his travel because building an international business required being there – wherever *there* was. For example, it took nearly five years to put together a patchwork network of local and regional channels that allowed MTV Italy to send 13 hours of daily programming to 11 million households (Roedy, 2011, p. 105). But later, the Italian government's decision to reduce the number of frequencies in Italy forced MTV from the market. Roedy then had to form a joint venture with an Italian Company – Italian Telecom – and lose half of MTV's business in Italy.

Developing distribution agreements meant meeting with small cable operators in distant countries, powerful media moguls, as well as celebrities, such as Bono, Paul McCartney, and Will Smith. Roedy also met with leaders of governments to discuss distribution of MTVNI's programming, such as China's President Jiang Zemin, former Cuban President Fidel Castro, and former South African President Nelson Mandela.

Over the years, MTV became the most distributed brand in the world (Nichols, 2011). However, it adapted its content in every country. 'Everything was sensitized to the local audience and that was really the key factor I think to our success,' Roedy said. We play rap in the Middle East ... but the lyrics are not angry street culture, they're more about, I love my mother' (Nichols, 2011, para. 5). In the Middle East, Pakistan, and Indonesia, MTV airs the Muslim call to prayer five times each day.

Questions

- What did Bill Roedy have going for him when he began his business career in 1979?
- What did Bill Roedy have going against him when he began his business career in 1979?
- Leaving Harvard Business School, Roedy also had a job offer to join NBC – one of the three major broadcast networks – in a finance job overseeing programming. Walking the halls in Rockefeller Center in Manhattan, Roedy said later that it felt 'very corporate'. Instead, Roedy joined the startup cable channel HBO. How do you think Roedy's career would have progressed if he had chosen the conventional job at NBC rather than the unconventional one at HBO?
- How global (one product distributed around the world) was MTV? Explain.

REFERENCES

Anderson, S., Cavanagh, J., and Lee, T. (2000). *Field guide to the global economy*. New York, NY: The New Press.

Andrews, A. (2011, January 29). MTV president Bill Roedy has taken his music channel from the Berlin Wall to SpongeBob SquarePants. *The Telegraph*. Retrieved from www.telegraph.co.uk

Arditi, B., Barros, S., Bowman, G., and Howarth, D. (2005). *Populism and the mirror of democracy*. London: Verso.

Barnett, T.P.M. (2004). *The Pentagon's new map: War and peace in the twenty-first century*. New York, NY: G.P. Putnam's Sons.

Big Charts. (2020). Reckitt Benckiser hare price graph. Retrieved from www.bigcharts.com

Bort, R. (2020). Advertisers are fleeing Facebook over its failure to moderate hate speech. *Rolling Stone*, July 1, 2020. Accessed at www.rollingstone.com/politics/politics-news/face bookadvertisers-fleeing-content-moderation-1023186/

Broderick, R. (2018). URL to IRL: Meet Mexico's king of fake news. *BuzzFeed News*. June 28, 2018. Accessed at www.youtube.com/watch?v=ZZrCeAsjRUI

Chopra, R. (2019). Dissenting statement of Commissioner Rohit Chopra, In re Facebook, Inc. Commission File No. 1823109, July 24, 2019. Accessed at www.ftc.gov/public-statements/2019/07/dissenting-statement-commissioner-rohit-chopra-regarding-matter-facebook

Clement, J. (2020a). Number of monthly active Facebook users worldwide 2008-2020. *Statista*. Accessed at www.statista.com/statistics/264810/number-of-monthly-active-facebook-users-worldwide/#:~:text=How%20many%20users%20does%20Facebook,network%20ever%20to%20do%20so

Clement, J. (2020b). Facebook's revenue and net income from 2007 to 2019. *Statista*, February 3, 2020. Accessed at www.statista.com/statistics/277229/facebooks-annual-revenue-and-net-income/

Clifford J.S. II, Rahtz, D.R., and Speece, M. (Eds.). (2003). *What's wrong with globalism and what's to be done about it?* In Belk, R. (Ed.), Globalization, transformation, and quality of life: The proceedings of the 8th international conference on marketing and development (pp. 661–70). Rijeka, Croatia: Faculty of Economics, University of Rijeka.

Coldeway, D. (2019). 9 reasons the Facebook FTC settlement is a joke. *Tech Crunch*, July 24, 2019. Accessed at https://techcrunch.com/2019/07/24/9-reasons-the-facebook-ftc-settle ment-is-a-joke/

Cooke, N.A. (2018). Fake news and alternative facts: Information literacy in a post-truth era. Chicago, IL: ALA Editions.

Eigen, P. (2013). Peter Eigen: How to expose the corrupt. *TED*, July 25, 2013. Retrieved from www.youtube.com/watch?v=aRRE5TEnfsA

Ellis, P., and Pecotich, A. (2002, June). Macromarketing and international trade: Comparative advantage versus cosmopolitan considerations. *Journal of Macromarketing*, 22(1), 32–56.

Friedman, T.L. (2000). *The Lexus and the olive tree: Understanding globalization*. New York, NY: Anchor Books.

Friedman, T.L. (2006). *The world is flat: A brief history of the twenty-first century, release 2.0*. New York, NY: Farrar, Straus and Giroux.

Friedman, T.L. (2017). *Thank you for being late: An optimist's guide to thriving in the age of accelerations (Version 2.0, with a new afterword)*. New York, NY: Picador/Farrar Straus and Giroux.

Ghemawat, P. (2007, March). Managing differences. *Harvard Business Review*, 85(3), 58–68.

Ghemawat, P. (2011a). *World 3.0: Global prosperity and how to achieve it*. Boston, MA: Harvard Business Press.

Ghemawat, P. (2011b, May). The cosmopolitan corporation. *Harvard Business Review*, 92–9.

Ghemawat, P. (2017). Globalization in the age of Trump. *Harvard Business Review*, 95(4), 112–23.

Harvard University Press (2016). The elephant chart in the EU room. Harvard University Press Blog. Accessed at https://harvardpress.typepad.com/hup_publicity/2016/06/branko-milanovic-elephant-chart-brexit.html

Holt, D.B., Quelch, J.A., and Taylor, E.L. (2004, September). How global brands compete. *Harvard Business Review*, 82(9), 1–8.

Ibarra, H., and Hansen, M.T. (2011, July–August). Are you a collaborative leader? *Harvard Business Review*, 89(7/8), 69–74.

Kettlewell, C. (2019). Dislike: Professor's work paints alarming portrait of Facebook's power. *University of Virginia*, Spring, 26–7.

Kilbourne, W.E. (2004, December). Globalization and development: An expanded macromarketing view. *Journal of Macromarketing*, 24(2), 122–35.

knowledge@wharton. (2018). The auto bailout 10 years later: Was it the right call? *knowledge@wharton*, September 12, 2018. Accessed at https://knowledge.wharton.upenn.edu/article/auto-bailout-ten-years-later-right-call/

Levitt, T. (1983, May/June). Globalization and markets. *Harvard Business Review*, 61(3), 92–103. www.journalism.org/2018/09/10/news-use-across-social-media-platforms-2018/

Matsa K.E., and Shearer, E. (2018). News use across social media platforms 2018. *Pew Research Center*. September 10, 2018. Accessed at www.journalism.org/2018/09/10/news-use-across-social-media-platforms-2018/

Mazzucato, M. (2018). *The value of everything: Making and taking in the global economy*. London: Allen Lane.

McIntyre, L. (2018). *Post-truth*. Cambridge, MA: MIT Press.

McNair, B. (2017). *Fake news: Falsehood, fabrication and fantasy in journalism*. New York, NY: Routledge.

Miskus, J. and Ward. J. (2019). Facebook's real privacy problem is Facebook. *Bloomberg Business-week*, February 11, 2019, 23–4.

Naím, M. (2003, January/February). The five wars of globalization. *Foreign Policy*, pp. 29–36.

Naím, M. (2005). *Illicit: How smugglers, traffickers, and copycats are hijacking the global economy*. New York, NY: Anchor Books.

Nichols, M. (2011, May 12). Bill Roedy reflects on military and MTV in new book. *Reuters*. Retrieved from www.reuters.com

Pew Research Center. (2017). Spring 2017 global attitudes survey. Accessed at pewresearch.org

Reckitt Benckiser. (2020). Annual report 2019. Accessed at www.rb.com/investors/annual-report-2019/

Reuters. (2019). BMW is biggest U.S. automotive exporter by value for fifth year. *Reuters*, March 8, 2019. Accessed at www.autoblog.com/2019/03/08/bmw-biggest-us-automotive-exporter/

Ritzer, G. (2009). *Globalization: A basic text*. Malden, MA: Wiley-Blackwell.

Roedy, B. (2011). *What makes business rock: Building the world's largest global networks*. Hoboken, NJ: Wiley.

Roser, M. and Ortiz-Ospina, E. (2019). Global extreme poverty. Our world in data. Accessed at https://ourworldindata.org/extreme-poverty

Satariano, A. (2020). Facebook loses antitrust decision in Germany over data collection. *The New York Times*, June 23, 2020. Accessed at www.nytimes.com/2020/06/23/technology/facebook-antitrust-germany.html

Sheldon, E. (2020). Is this the perfect FTSE 100 stock to own right now? *The Motley Fool*, July 3, 2020. Accessed at www.msn.com/en-us/money/savingandinvesting/is-thisthe-perfect-ftse-100-stock-to-own-right-now/ar-BB16hPoO

Steenkamp, J.B.E. (2020). Global Brand Building and Management in the Digital Age. *Journal of International Marketing*, 28(1), 13–27.

Stiglitz, J.E. (2007). *Making globalization work*. New York, NY: W. W. Norton.

Subramanian, S. (2017). Inside the North Macedonian fake-news complex. *Wired Magazine*, 15. February 15, 2017. Accessed at www.wired.com/2017/02/veles-NorthMacedonia-fake-news/

Transparency International (2012). Bribe payers index 2011. Retrieved from http://bpi.transparency.org/

Transparency International. (2019a). *About Us*. Retrieved from www.transparency.org/about

Transparency International. (2019b). *Corruption Perceptions Index* 2019. Retrieved from www.transparency.org/cpi2019

Vaidhyanathan, S. (2018). *Anti-social median: How Facebook disconnects us and undermines democracy*. New York, NY: Oxford Press.

Witkowski, T.H. (2005). Antiglobal challenges to marketing in developing countries: Exploring the ideological divide. *Journal of Public Policy and Marketing*, 24(1), 7–23.

World Bank (2019). The World Bank in North Macedonia; Country context. Accessed at www.worldbank.org/en/country/northmacedonia/overview

Zuckerberg, M. (2019). Facebook stands for free expression. *Wall Street Journal*, commentary, October 17, 2019. Accessed at www.wsj.com/articles/facebook-stands-for-free-expression-11571336089

7
CONTEMPORARY CONSUMERS

Throwing Shade

Source: Photo by François DALLAY on Unsplash.

Ups and Downs of Bicycle Commuting

Traffic congestion in cities around the world continues to plague those who live and/or work there (Davies, 2020). In the worst 100 congested cities of the world, an average trip takes 40 percent longer than it would if the streets were clear – with more than a doubling for trip

(Continued)

times during evening rush hours (TomTom, 2020). One long-available option to reduce traffic congestion is bicycle commuting (Claudy and Peterson, 2014).

Bike sharing programs featuring bicycles (that have equipment allowing the bicycles to be rented without reservation) have emerged in many cities of the world. Researchers studied one in Dublin Ireland and found evidence that the bike-share program actually reduced traffic congestion (Bullock, Brereton, and Bailey 2017). Researchers also noted that the Dublin bike-share program boosted the health of participants, reduced auto-accident rates, and allowed participants to access more productive jobs.

But can too much of bike sharing be a bad thing? It can, if tens of thousands of dockless bicycles are brought to a city and then the bike-share company goes bankrupt. That is what has happened when Bluegogo, once the third-largest bike-sharing firm in China, suddenly ceased operation (Bluegogo boasted of 20 million users of its 700,000 bikes) (Campbell, 2018). In Xiamen, Fujian province, China, fields of discarded bicycles grew to three-meters high as city leaders struggled to deal with the crisis Bluegogo's sudden demise triggered (Taylor, 2018).

While the benefits of bicycle commuting are clear for individuals and communities (that can effectively regulate private bike-share firms), the rate of those in urban areas choosing bicycling as their way to commute to work remains at less than 5 percent in the US (McLeod, 2018) and in most cities of Europe (European Cyclists' Federation, 2020). (A few cities in Europe boast of much higher rates of bicycle commuting, such as Copenhagen (49 percent), and Amsterdam (35 percent).

But in the aftermath of the COVID-19 pandemic, bicycle commuting became a way for socially distancing oneself during commutes and the number of bicycle commuters jumped markedly (Beech, 2020). Governments around the world sought to protect their public transport systems, as well as public health, and build on the clean-air gains made during COVID-19 lockdowns. Berlin, Paris, Brussels and Milan are among major European cities that boosted bicycle commuting through establishing cycleways on streets, offering free bicycle repairs and even cycling lessons.

Bicycle manufacturers have rolled out electric bicycles in recent years and consumers have rapidly adopted them. In Germany in 2020, 30 percent of all bicycles sold were e-bicycles (Wrede, 2020). In Paris, bicycle shop owner Stephane Cueff commented on the surge of consumer interest after COVID-19. 'The bicycle has always been a part of France,' Cueff said. 'If there is an upside to the coronavirus, it may be that we are rethinking how we live, and getting back some of what we had lost' (Alderman, 2020).

Questions to Consider

- What factors would you say have reduced bicycle commuting over the years?
- What factors are now boosting bicycle commuting after COVID-19?
- What does this say about consumption behaviour of individuals regarding their commuting choices?
- What role do you see for city governments in sustaining bicycle commuting?

CHAPTER OVERVIEW AND LEARNING OBJECTIVES

This chapter will examine one of the driving factors of market dynamism – changing consumer preferences. Today, consumer behavior increasingly has not only a 'me' dimension (What do I get?), but also a 'we' dimension (What do I get to do with others?). The 'Me' dimension of consumption raises an issue about materialism. Specifically, is more always better? Quality-of-life (QOL) researchers continue to debate at what level an increase in income results in no increase in subjective well-being (happiness). The attitude–behavior gap in which consumers say they intend to buy sustainable products but tend not to do so receives explanation using Behavioral Reasoning Theory. Despite the increased incomes in most countries of the world in recent years, many consumers remain vulnerable when receiving healthcare. Consumers also experience vulnerability as their incomes become uncertain during an economic downturn and as global climate change continues to unfold.

The 'We' dimension of consumption has become more noticeable in the age of Facebook. Communication technology and emerging social media enable individuals and businesses to network themselves like never before. An increasingly networked world means that more than information can be shared more readily in the future. Consequently, collaborative consumption in the form of sharing, lending, renting, reselling, and volunteering all become more sensible. After this chapter, you should be able to answer the following questions:

- What elements compose a dominant social paradigm regarding material acquisition?
- What makes some in society 'vulnerable consumers?'
- What is 'voluntary simplicity?'
- What is it about collaborative consumption that could make it important for success in marketing in the future?
- In the future, could sharing play a prominent role in the economic system?

THE 'ME' IN MARKETS OF TODAY
'Just a Little Bit More'

American industrialist John D. Rockefeller, whose overwhelming success in the oil refining industry led to his Standard Oil Company monopoly being broken up by the US Supreme Court in 1910, was asked, 'How much money is enough? 'Rockefeller, whose fortune exceeded $1.2 billion (one of the first billionaires ever), smiled at his questioner, leaned forward, and said, 'Just a little bit more' (Kessel, 2008).

In his book, *Is the American Dream Killing You?: How the Market Rules Our Lives*, social critic Paul Stiles proposes that 'the Market' is more than just an economic means of distribution, but it now constitutes a belief system in itself. According to Stiles, both the materialistic ethos of the Market (characterized by the assumption that 'more is better') and the Market are actually innately opposed to the traditional foundation of American life that values opportunity and access for all citizens.

Stiles skewers baser pursuits in corporate life ('if it sells, it must be OK'), but he also does the same for baser pursuits in the lives of individuals. For example, he not only criticizes the production of vacuous or harmful media content, but also he criticizes the choices individuals make in consuming such media on a repetitive basis. In the end, Stiles' willingness to consider macromarketing phenomena broadly, and his incisive ability to identify the role of individuals who comprise society in accepting or contributing to each of these macro phenomena, make his criticisms more powerful.

Additionally, the arguments in *Is the American Dream Killing You?* gain power through the comparisons Stiles sees possible when looking at phenomena with a broad lens. For example, in discussing The Market vs. the Nuclear Family, Stiles notes that the qualities the Market rewards, such as (a) the ability to look out for oneself and (b) opportunism, are deadly when applied in intimate relationships because such qualities are fundamentally based on a lack of trust. Stiles goes on to declare that love is not a market principle.

Stiles perceives a duality regarding the Market. According to Stiles, it carries aspects of Jekyll and Hyde. If the Market is surrounded with the right values, it is a good physician. However, if it is not, it is likely to become a predator. Stiles is clear about how the right moral sensibilities are developed outside the market. He is bold in pointing to the spiritual lives of humans as providing the source of such right values. Without these values, individuals can degrade themselves and their environment through their consumption.

In Stiles' view, this scenario is currently being played out. More and more individuals unthinkingly accept the market as the principal arbiter of life's decisions. To Stiles, society's hold on the right values is dangerously weakening. Stiles asserts that a deadly metaphysical conflict is under way driven by the Market's adoption of pure materialism, which regards the soul as nonexistent or irrelevant.

In many ways, Stiles' ideas resonate with macromarketing scholarship. For example, he applies systems theory to understand that the Market is not synonymous with society. In Stiles' view, the Market is a part of society. Stiles recognizes this as a critical distinction and then goes on to assert that the economy has two levels: individuals and the Market. Each influences the other as individuals engage in exchange, and prices inform individuals in markets about how goods and services are currently being valued. However, Stiles makes sure to mention that:

> While a human being is defined by his ability to distinguish between good and evil, to the Market good and evil are nothing but profit and loss – a very different standard. The Market may represent one side of human life – the collective judgment of people acting as traders – but it is not the voice of mankind.

(Stiles, 2005, p. 27)

Is 'More Is Better' Correct?

Stiles' ideas also resonate with macromarketing scholarship about the Dominant Social Paradigm (DSP) (Kilbourne, McDonagh, and Prothero, 1997). The DSP is society's belief structure that organizes how people perceive and interpret the functioning of the world around them (Milbrath, 1989, p. 116). Similar to a worldview (which provides a model of the world and guides adherents in the world), the DSP of Western democracies after World War I became a materially focused ideology encouraging increased consumption for individuals (Bennett and O'Reilly, 2010, p. 6). In short, 'more is better' became the driving ethos of society's members.

Governments have encouraged shopping and consuming beyond one's needs for a modest lifestyle. US President Herbert Hoover articulated the notion that producing and consuming should be the great driving force of national life. In 1928, he told an audience of advertisers and public relations men, 'You have taken over the job of creating desire and have transformed people into constantly moving happiness machines, machines which have become the key to economic progress' (Bennett and O'Reilly, 2010, p. 6).

The role of aspiration and the desire for incremental luxuries – things wanted, but not necessarily needed – is indispensable for productivity in the economic life of a society (Ariely, 2011). However, sociologists such as Max Weber and Daniel Bell have expressed concern that the foundations of thrift and modesty on which capitalism rests are undermined by mass consumer pursuits, acquisitiveness, and widespread indebtedness in society (Kaufman, 2011).

For decades, researchers have grappled with the question of whether money can buy happiness. The Easterlin Paradox, which has been widely researched, suggests that there is no correlation between income and life satisfaction or between income and happiness over a threshold value of about $10,000 per year (Easterlin, 1974). Many researchers believed that once basic needs were covered, money did not buy happiness.

But recently, new large-scale studies have been conducted that suggest there is a positive relationship between income and life satisfaction, as well as between income and happiness. The income threshold for happiness saturation seems to be more like $75,000 per year (Kahneman and Deaton, 2010).

Figure 7.1 depicts the results of the 2017 World Bank study of Life Satisfaction and Country GDP (World Bank, 2019). Here each circle is a country, with a diameter proportional to population. The center of the circle marks the average life satisfaction and gross domestic product (GDP) for that country. Figure 7.1 suggests that life satisfaction is higher in countries with higher GDP per head. Notably, the slope is steepest among the poorest countries, where income gains are associated with the largest increases in life satisfaction, but it remains positive and substantial even among the rich countries.

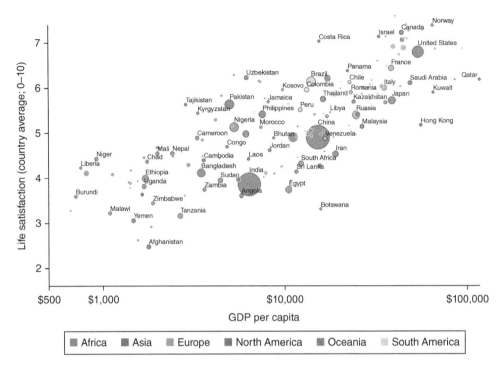

Figure 7.1 Country GDP and mean life satisfaction in 2017

Source: 'Self-reported Life Satisfaction vs GDP per capita, 2017', World Happiness Report 2019, World Bank. Helliwell, J., Layard, R., & Sachs, J. (2019). World Happiness Report 2019, New York: Sustainable Development Solutions Network.

Is 'More Is Better' the Complete Story?

The Gallup World Poll also studied social-psychological factors, which were measured using five standards: Did the respondent

- feel respected on the previous day?
- have family or friends that could be counted on in an emergency?
- learn something new yesterday?
- do what he/she does best yesterday?
- chose how his or her time was spent yesterday?

These five items representing social-psychological wealth accounted for 20 percent of the variance in positive feelings experienced on the previous day (Deaton, 2008).

In sum, it seems that comforts increase life evaluations, whereas pleasures increase reports of positive feelings. In this way, money might have more to do with people having what they want, and social-psychological prosperity has more to do with feelings they like.

Putting this together, both kinds of wealth – monetary and psychosocial wealth – likely contribute to lives characterized by fulfillment and happiness. Figure 7.1 depicts a general linear relationship between country GDP and the country's mean rating of its citizens on life satisfaction.

When examining relationships between income and measures of subjective well-being, researchers found that having low amounts of money led to reports of pain and unhappiness, but that the happiness saturation level was $75,000 per year (Rubin, 2011). With every doubling of income, respondents tended to report that they were more and more satisfied with their lives for household incomes well beyond $120,000. But when asked to assess the experienced happiness of the previous day (enjoyment, laughter, smiling, anger, stress, or worry), money mattered only up to about $75,000. After that, increased income did not buy more or less happiness. Notably, the average household income in the United States was $71,500 with about one third of households above this level.

Interpreting these results, veteran QOL researcher Ed Diener said, 'If you want to enjoy life, focus on relationships and health once you make more than $70,000 a year. If you are poor, it makes a great deal of sense to be concerned about higher income' (Diener et al., 2010).

Research on these QOL issues are complex and will continue (Tierney, 2011). For example, researchers continue to reflect on the stability of subjective well-being in the United States over the last 50 years, despite rising income levels (Bok, 2010, pp. 13–14). Also, those that attach much importance to achieving wealth tend to suffer above-average unhappiness and disappointment. This is likely due to driven individuals neglecting human relationships, and later finding that financial success leads to fleeting happiness gains as adaptation occurs and satisfaction evaporates. Brooks (2010) argues that what is crucial in well-being is not how happy one feels, or how much money is made, but rather the meaning found in life and one's sense of 'earned success,' the belief you have created value in your life or others' lives.

The Attitude–Behavior Gap

Environmentally friendly products have become more numerous in recent years. This development in business highlights the way marketers are catering to consumers' increased concern for the natural environment – an attractive expression of green lifestyle choices (Prothero et al., 2011). But despite the heightened preference for sustainability, consumers' ecological values and attitudes often fail to materialize in actual purchases of green products (Shaw, McMaster, and Newholm, 2016). The disconnect between consumers' expressed preferences for sustainable-product alternatives and their actual (un-)willingness to purchase is referred to by researchers as the *attitude–behavior gap* (e.g. Peattie, 2001; Prothero et al., 2011).

One of the unique features of Behavioral Reasoning Theory (BRT) (introduced this century in psychology) is the inclusion of reasons – both reasons for taking an action, as well as reasons against taking an action – in models of human decision-making. Without incorporating concepts of BRT, research focused on energy conservation has addressed factors that explain renewable energy adoption, while reasons against adopting renewables have not been included (e.g. Bang et al., 2000; Hansla et al., 2008; Kalafatis et al., 1999; Paladino and Baggiere, 2007; Steg, Dreijerink, and Abrahamse, 2005).

Researchers have offered more complete explanations for the attitude-behavior gap for sustainability behaviors using Behavioral Reasoning Theory (Westaby, 2005). As can be seen in Figure 7.2, BRT includes both reasons for performing a behavior, as well as reasons against performing such a behavior. BRT allows understanding for how consumers' reasoning affects the relationship between values, attitudes and adoption intentions towards sustainability behaviors (e.g. Westaby, 2005; Westaby, Probst, and Lee, 2010).

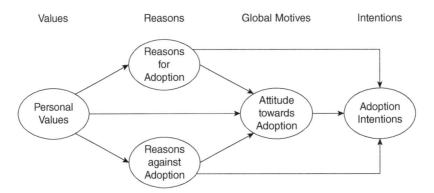

Figure 7.2 Behavioral reasoning theory – values, then reasons, then attitudes, then intentions

Source: Westaby (2005). Adapted from *Organizational Behavior and Human Decision Processes*, 98(2), Westaby, 'Behavioral reasoning theory: Identifying new linkages underlying intentions and behavior', 97–120 (2005), with permission from Elsevier.

One field study of consumers in Ireland employed BRT successfully and focused on the adoption of rooftop solar panels in Claudy, Peterson, and O'Driscoll (2013). The reasons for adopting solar panels included (1) economic benefits, (2) environmental benefits, and (3) independence from conventional energy sources. By comparison, the reasons against adoption included (1) initial capital costs, (2) uncertainty regarding the performance of renewable energies, and (3) perceived incompatibility of the solar panels with the existing infrastructure of the home.

Importantly, reasons against adoption had a bit more of a negative influence on intentions to adopt rooftop solar panels than the reasons for adoption. In this way, one can understand how an attitude-behavior gap would be manifested, because the negative influence of reasons against adoption negate the positive influence of reasons for adoption. If researchers had only asked about reasons for adoption, they would later see that consumers expressed positive attitudes toward adoption, but for some reason did not adopt. When reasons against adoption are included in the statistical modeling of adoption intentions consumers' thinking becomes more readily evident.

The implication for marketers is that obstacles and resistance toward adopting high-involvement purchases, such as solar panels, need to be fully understood. In this way, marketers can change the marketing mix variable (product, place, price, promotion) in order to win more sales and more satisfied customers.

VULNERABLE CONSUMERS

Although recent QOL research sheds light on some important questions regarding income and measures of subjective well-being, such research has consistently identified traps or troughs for individuals' QOL. For example, divorce, unemployment, disease, chronic pain, and being alone all contribute to reductions in life satisfaction and experienced happiness (Bok, 2010, p. 205). With lack of money, these setbacks in life have a more pronounced negative impact on subjective well-being. In other words, it is much worse to experience a life setback if one is poor than if one is not poor.

In research on consumer vulnerability, physical, psychological, and environmental factors contribute to consumers perceiving themselves at a power disadvantage in the marketplace (Baker, Gentry, and Rittenburg, 2005). For example, addiction, age, disability, gender, race/ethnicity, and cognitive deficiencies have all been cited as biophysical factors in degraded marketing exchanges. Likewise, fear of being victimized, social isolation, and socioeconomic status have been identified by researchers as psychological factors contributing to restricted access to the marketplace. Environmental factors include social upheaval or violence, the access to quality goods and services, the distribution of resources for trade, as well as transient states for individuals, such as grief or divorce.

The way markets are set up in societies might exclude many from full participation in some markets. Lack of access to goods and services offered in these markets would mean that significant portions of those living in a country would experience being 'vulnerable consumers'.

Vulnerable Consumers: Healthcare

Healthcare is a service attracting much attention as costs continue to rise worldwide (Davis et al., 2007). Access to healthcare is a contentious issue, as many countries have healthcare resources, but access remains difficult for some. This issue is emerging at a time when lifestyle changes related to more sedentary work and to the overconsumption of food afflicts almost all countries. Ominously, the incidence for diabetes has risen 70 percent in the United States since 1990, but it is estimated that one-third of those with diabetes do not know that they have it (Commonwealth Fund, 2020). In such ways, more people are becoming vulnerable healthcare consumers because they cannot access necessary medical services and diagnosis.

A Reuters poll of respondents across 22 countries conducted by Ipsos reports a near even split between respondents about access to quality and affordable healthcare being easy (48 percent) or difficult (52 percent) (Reuters/Ipsos, 2010). The United States places in the middle of the group of 22 countries with 52 percent of respondents reporting that access to quality and affordable healthcare would be easy to obtain. Sweden places first with 75 percent reporting that such access would be easy, while Japan reports the worst outlook with only 15 percent of respondents reporting that it would be easy to obtain access to quality healthcare.

Figure 7.3 reports on a 2017 study across eleven developed countries regarding the quality, access, efficiency, and equity of the healthcare systems of these countries (Commonwealth Fund, 2020). As can be seen, the US spends the highest percentage of country GDP on healthcare, but posts the lowest performance among the eleven countries. These results also underline how money may not purchase the best when it comes to healthcare for societies. What puts the US in such a position?

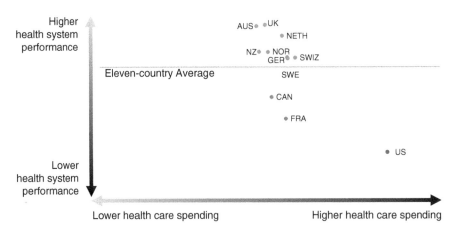

Note: Health care spending as a percent of GDP.
Sources: Spending data are from OECD for the year 2014, and exclude spending on capital formation of health care providers; Commonwealth Fund analysis.

Figure 7.3   Comparison of eleven country healthcare systems

Source: Commonwealth Fund (2020). Accessed at https://interactives.commonwealthfund.org/2017/july/mirror-mirror/

Economists evaluate healthcare in terms of the dollars spent on healthcare and the number of healthcare transactions made by individuals (Peterson and Burton, 2007). Notably, the United States has fewer doctor visits per person than other OECD countries and a similar length of hospital stays. However, the intensity of service delivery at hospitals is greater in the United States as a result of the use of new medical technologies and the greater frequency of invasive procedures performed (such as coronary bypass and angioplasties). Other factors also contribute to higher spending per capita on healthcare in the United States. The United States has the highest incidence of cancer and has the highest incidence of obesity among the OECD countries.

With respect to price, US prices for medical care commodities and services are significantly higher than in other countries. This serves as a key determinant of higher overall healthcare spending. In assessing what drives the difference between US healthcare spending and the rest of the world, some leading health economists have responded this way: 'It's the prices, stupid' (Anderson, et al., 2003, p. 103).

In short, many of the same items and services cost more in the US healthcare system than in other OECD countries. Part of this can be attributed to the United States using newer technology and the latest drugs in its hospitals, but at the final analysis, price is a function of market activity. It seems simply that the healthcare market in the United States is not as efficient as in other similar countries.

Lack of competition among suppliers is one of the reasons for these high prices. For example, the US had 2.9 physicians per 1,000 inhabitants in 2018, while Germany had 4.3, and China (with almost four times as many people) had 2.0 physicians per 1,000 inhabitants (McCarthy, 2020).

Another reason for high prices might be government policy. For example, the pharmaceutical industry receives $32 billion each year in innovation grants from the US' National Institutes of Health without conditions (Unger, 2019). The drugs that result from these grants are then priced at exorbitant rates that the public healthcare programs (such as Medicare and the National Health Service in the UK) have to subsidize. So the taxpayer pays at least twice or three times. If conditions for the grants included reduced prices later for the US' national healthcare program (or if the US and UK coordinated their grants and later conditions), taxpayers would not be paying multiple times for these new drugs. A precedent exists for such policy in the realm of telecommunications. Here, the US government forced AT & T to create Bell Labs in 1925 (where many new technologies developed) as a condition of retaining a monopoly in phone service that continued in effect until 1982.

Figure 7.4 depicts life expectancy in OECD countries (34 democratically governed industrialized countries of the world) as a function of per-capita spending on healthcare using 2018 data (Peter G. Peterson Foundation, 2019). As can be seen, the United States far outspends other OECD countries, but most of the others post better results on an important outcome: life expectancy.

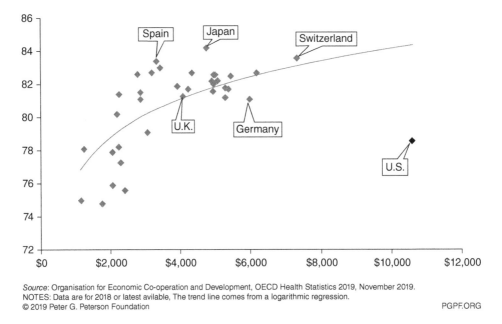

Source: Organisation for Economic Co-operation and Development, OECD Health Statistics 2019, November 2019.
NOTES: Data are for 2018 or latest avilable, The trend line comes from a logarithmic regression.
© 2019 Peter G. Peterson Foundation   PGPF.ORG

Figure 7.4   Life expectancy at birth (in years) and per-capita spending on healthcare (in US$) for OECD countries

Source: The Peter G. Peterson Foundation (2019).

All actors in healthcare systems around the world could do better to reduce the vulnerability of consumers in the healthcare marketplace. First, consumers can take better care of themselves by eating better and exercising more. Most of the diseases that kill people (heart disease, cancer, stroke, diabetes, and obesity) account for 70 percent of healthcare spending, but they are preventable through eating properly, exercising, choosing not to smoke, and minimizing alcohol consumption. The bad news is that two-thirds of those in the United States are now overweight and one-third are obese – meaning they have a body/mass index (BMI) of 30 or more (OECD, 2019). One in five are obese in France, one in four in Germany, and one in three in the UK, Mexico, and Australia. (A BMI calculator can be accessed at www.cdc.gov/healthyweight/assessing/bmi/adult_bmi/english_bmi_calculator/bmi_calculator.html.)

Second, with an aging population burdened by chronic diseases (many resulting from lifestyle choices), it seems that demand for medical services will only go up in the future in developed countries, which will affect third-party payers. Some third-party payers are insurance companies and the government, and they will struggle with rising costs while pharmaceutical companies, medical institutions, and medical professionals pass on higher invoices than in other OECD countries. Changes need to be made in the healthcare market-place or consumer vulnerability will only increase in the future.

Government-run healthcare would provide more access to healthcare in the United States. But how rising costs will be addressed is a question remaining to be answered. Several unhealthy behaviors common in the US (such as a sedentary lifestyle and eating too much for such inactivity) are rooted in cultural norms (Freedman, 2019). A key motivator for healthy behavior is feeling integrated in a community where that behavior (proper diet and exercise) is commonplace, according to Somava Saha, a Boston-area physician and vice-president at Institute for Healthcare Improvement. 'We tend to see health as something that policy mak-ing or healthcare systems ought to do for us,' Saha said.

Researchers estimate that 74 percent of the variation in life expectancy across countries is explained by health-related lifestyle factors (such as inactivity and smoking) and by condi-tions associated with them (such as obesity and diabetes). By comparison, most of the rest of variation (10 to 25 percent) is explained by what healthcare providers do. In sum, what patients do seems to matter much more.

Many firms now offer financial incentives for employees to engage in wellness programs (Beaton, 2018). Paying for gym memberships is one way this can be done. Offering non-smokers a lower monthly rate for health insurance is another way to incentivise wellness for employees. More will be said about employees in sustainable firms in Chapter 8.

More Consumers Become Vulnerable in an Economic Downturn

An economic downturn also stresses consumers. John Quelch and Katherine Jocz (2009) prioritize products and services into four types: (a) essentials (food, shelter, clothing, trans-portation, and healthcare, (b) treats (indulgences whose immediate purchase is considered justifiable), (c) postponables (needed or desired items whose purchase can be reasonably put off), and (d) expendables (perceived as unnecessary or unjustifiable). The assignment of particular goods and services to the categories other than essentials is highly variable. During a recession, consumers can shift products and services, such as travel or entertain-ment, from treats to expendables. Cooking at home (an essential) becomes swapped for dining out (a treat). Most consumers become more price sensitive and less brand loyal dur-ing recessions. This might mean choosing cheaper private labels or switching from organic to nonorganic foods.

Marketers, too, tend to downshift during recessions. Where firms might have adver-tised using television, they might now choose cheaper radio campaigns. To economize, promotional campaigns might be extended and run longer. In terms of product, firms may choose to introduce low-cost versions of their more popular brands termed 'fighter brands'. Anheuser-Busch did this when it introduced Natural Pilsner in the early 1980s downturn. After the downturn, the fighter brand can be withdrawn or continued as a value brand in the overall product line. However, for many worried consumers, trusted brands mean much during tough economic times. Dell has sought to reassure different segments with appeals such as 'Out of the box, within your means', 'Depend on Dell for simple solutions in tough times', 'The ideal laptop works anywhere, in any economy', and 'Weak economy, powerful you' (Quelch and Jocz, 2009, p. 60).

More Consumers Become Vulnerable When Mother Nature Moves

Researchers who have studied marketing in economic recessions note that consumers seem to return to their 'normal' ways of consuming within two years of the recession's end (Quelch and Jocz, 2009). But what if a different way of consumption had to be undertaken by everyone worldwide?

The COVID-19 coronavirus pandemic of 2020 changed consumption for just about everyone on planet Earth in a matter of a few weeks and became 'a real-time experiment in downsizing the consumer economy' (Cohen, 2020). Public gatherings in restaurants, bars, sports arenas, libraries, schools, places of work, and elsewhere became off limits by government decree. Such drastic measures were intended to limit the number of COVID-19 infections that posed a risk for swamping the healthcare systems of countries around the world. All of this due to an invisible-to-the-naked-eye virus organism with a potential for rapid multiplication and exponential-rate of spreading through populations.

While the COVID-19 pandemic shows how the world's economy and life for humans can be disrupted in a compressed timeframe of weeks, many environmentalists warn a similar disruption could be looming for many countries due to global climate change. According to environmentalist-entrepreneur Paul Gilding (2011), the modern world has caused the Earth to exceed its capacity of people, industry, and growth.

With regards to use of water resources, freshwater consumption continues to climb around the world. The agriculture sector accounts for 70 percent of total freshwater withdrawals and in many drier countries, it accounts for more than 90 percent of total withdrawals (Ritchie and Roser, 2018). (In countries such as the Netherlands and Germany, agriculture takes less than one percent of total withdrawals.) In 2014, India topped the world's countries in annual water use for agriculture with 760 billion cubic meters, followed by China at just over 600 billion m^3 and the US at 485 billion m^3. Thirty-five percent of agricultural land receives irrigation in India.

In the agricultural heartland of India's northern plains (which grows almost one-third of India's food), farmers generally pay little or nothing for groundwater they use (Spindler, 2019). Some observers predict 40 percent of India's population could lack drinking water by 2030.

According to Gilding, overconsumption leads to such environmental problems as those occurring in India. 'If you cut down more trees than you grow, you run out of trees,' Gilding said. 'If you put additional nitrogen into a water system, you change the type and quantity of life that water can support. If you thicken the earth's CO_2 blanket, the earth gets warmer. If you do all these and many more things at once, you change the way the whole system of planet Earth behaves, with social, economic, and life support impacts. This is not speculation, this is high school science' (Gilding, 2011, p. 2).

Voluntary Simplicity or Minimalism

Rather than wait for top-down solutions to the current commons problem, Gilding recommends widespread action be taken by individuals. In this way, the political landscape will change and government leaders will understand the imperative for legal and regulatory change. Toward this end, voluntary simplicity or minimalism is an intentional movement to reduce individual consumption to free resources, particularly money and time, so that life satisfaction can be sought through nonmaterial aspects of life (Huneke, 2005; Millburn and Nicodemus, 2015).

There are different approaches to voluntary simplicity. Intending to improve the quality of their own lives, 'Downshifters' seek less stressful ways of living and step out of the 'earn and spend' cycle of living. High-paying, high-stress jobs are exchanged for lower paying jobs with more intrinsic value to the work and with more control given to pursue hobbies and relationships. By comparison, 'Ethical simplifiers' move to simpler lifestyles for environmental and social justice reasons. They seek to minimize their part in environmental degradation and the exploitation of the poor around the world. Regardless of being motivated for self-centered reasons or social reasons, those pursuing voluntary simplicity seek to 'shop less and live more'.

Table 7.1 presents the results of Huneke's (2005) survey of 119 US respondents who had chosen voluntary simplicity in their lifestyles. Like previous surveys of simplifiers, more than 75 percent of the respondents were female. Here a list of 21 practices derived from a search of the literature and prior studies was presented to respondents. The top-12 rated practices are presented in descending order of their mean importance. As shown, there are a variety of ways to pursue voluntary simplicity with the most important being avoiding impulse purchases, recycling, and eliminating clutter.

Table 7.1 Twelve most important voluntary-simplicity-practices (rated on a 9-point scale)

Avoiding impulse purchases	8.1
Recycling	7.6
Eliminating clutter	7.3
Working at a satisfying job	6.9
Buying locally grown produce	6.8
Limiting exposure to ads	6.8
Buying environmentally friendly products	6.7
Limiting car use	6.6
Buying from socially responsible producers	6.5
Buying from local merchants	6.5
Limiting/eliminating TV	6.4
Limiting wage-earning work	6.4

Source: Huneke, M.E. (2005, July). The face of the un-consumer: An empirical examination of the practice of voluntary simplicity in the United States. *Psychology and Marketing*, 22(7), 527–50. Copyright Wiley.

Since its founding in 1997, the Center for a New American Dream has raised awareness about the negative impact of a hyper-consumer culture (Center for a New American Dream, 2020). In addition to helping define conscious consuming and green living, the Center has focused on helping individuals downshift and find balance in life – pursuing more of what matters, rather than just more material possessions. The Center celebrates nonmaterial values and is an example of a new kind of environmentalism that puts people in the foreground, rather than animals challenged by the economic activity of humans. Andrew Kirk, environmental history professor at the University of Nevada – Las Vegas said, 'That's the thing about this current wave of environmentalism. It's not about, how do we protect some abstract pristine space? It's what can real people do in their home or office or whatever. It's also very urban. It's a critical twist in the old wilderness adage: Leave only footprints, take only photographs' (Green, 2007, para 11).

The turn to voluntary simplicity has brought out some high-profile endeavors to lead a different lifestyle. Colin Beavan became known as the 'No Impact Man' when he embarked on a yearlong experiment to live with no impact on the environment. Unlike philosopher and social critic Henry David Thoreau who moved to Walden Pond in 1854 to live two years in a woodland cabin near Concord, Massachusetts, Beavan stayed in Manhattan and sought to scale down his consumption radically.

For an entire year, Beavan, his wife, and small daughter unplugged from the electrical grid, produced no trash, traveled only by self-propelled means, and bought only food that was grown within 250 miles (No Impact Project, 2011). By the end, Beavan and his family reported that not only was the 'no impact' approach to living beneficial to the environment, but also it made them unexpectedly healthier, happier, and richer in ways they had not imagined.

THE 'WE' IN MARKETS OF TODAY
Others as Enablers for the Consumer

In a networked world, due to the internet and social media, linkages bring a new potential for markedly different consumption experiences for all. Such linkages might be characterized as being (1) consumer-to-consumer, (2) consumer-to-business, and (3) business-to-business. Information sharing is the potential root for markedly different consumption experiences. For example, consumer-to-consumer linkages undergird what Pearson (2011a) calls 'pre-commerce'. In 'pre-commerce', online consumers share ideas and product knowledge, as well as provide solutions for each other (Pearson, 2011b). To illustrate, consumers interested in the music of singer/guitarist Jack Johnson might go to www.jackjohnsonmusic.com, click on 'community', join the discussion, trade tickets for an upcoming concert with others, arrange carpooling to the concert, and even leave suggestions for another children's CD. If Johnson ever delivered a disappointing live performance, this would be a place for fans to offer a critique. In a similar way, reading product reviews of Jack Johnson's latest CD at Amazon.com would help a consumer decide whether to make the purchase.

According to Nielson – a leading research firm, 92 percent of online consumers trust recommendations from people they know more than advertising, but importantly 88 percent trust reviews written by other consumers as much as they trust recommendations from personal contacts (Warren, 2020). For someone interested in purchasing an iPhone, she could go online to a consumer product-review site, such as *Consumer Reports* (www.consumerreports.org), and examine product reviews for iPhones. If she liked the one of the iPhones, she could go to a site for price comparisons, such as Google Shopping (shopping.google.com).

YouTube product reviews are another valuable reference for consumers now. These reviews can be accessed at www.youtube.com/ and entering the product name and 'reviews' as a search term.

Price comparison websites are now available to assist consumers, too. Table 7.2 presents *Shopify Blog's* 10 favorite price-comparison websites (Hayes, 2019).

Table 7.2   Shopify blog's top 10 price comparison websites

---
1. Google Shopping
2. PriceGrabber
3. Shopping.com
4. Shopzilla
5. Become
6. Bing Shopping Campaigns
7. Pronto
8. Bizrate
9. Amazon Sponsored Products
10. Camelcamelcamel

Source: (Hayes, 2019).

This example for online research and price-comparison for an iphone illustrates the power consumers today have at their fingertips. Buycotting also illustrates consumer power when it is organized for group action.

Buycotting

Rather than boycotting (avoiding interaction with a disfavored entity, such as an environmentally irresponsible business), buycotting focuses on purchasing and promoting entities viewed as 'doing the right thing'. Global public relations firm Weber Shandwick conducted a survey of 2,000 US and British consumers who had taken at least one of nine actions in response to something that a firm or brand did (McGregor, 2018). Fifty-nine percent of these more activists-minded consumers reported it was more important than ever to participate in consumer boycotts, while far more – 83 percent – reported it was more important to support firms who behave well and make purchases from them.

Buycotting is not restricted to one type of political activism. In 2018, actress Alyssa Milano tweeted a call for a one-day boycott of Amazon, Apple TV, and Fed Ex for the purpose of pressuring these firms to sever ties with the US' National Rifle Association. In immediate response, political commentator Michelle Malkin tweeted a boycott for gun owners to increase purchasing from these same firms.

Brent Schulkin organized a boycott he called a 'carrotmob' on March 29, 2008, after Schulkin had approached 23 stores in his neighborhood of San Francisco and solicited bids for promising to spend revenues from Carrotmob patrons on energy-efficient improvements (Caplan, 2009). A small convenience store K&D Market won the auction with a promise to plow 22 percent of the day's revenue into greener lighting. During the Carrotmobbing, hundreds of green-minded customers descended on K and D Market lining up down the block outside at times and spending more than $9,200. Owner David Lee was delighted with the results and spent more than $2,000 on improved seals for refrigerators and energy-efficient lighting for the store.

Although Schulkin has moved Carrotmob into an inactive status, the website www.carrotmob.com remains live in order to inspire and guide other organizers in how to develop buycotts. Initially, observers thought that Carrotmobbing was a San Francisco phenomenon, but it didn't take long for Carrotmob buycotts to become a global phenomenon in countries such as Canada, Germany, France, Australia, and New Zealand. In 2018, an impactful Carrotmob occurred in Argentina at a Buenos Aires farmers market that can be viewed on YouTube at www.youtube.com/watch?v=JP3RPHsX7Ig.

Reconsidering Ownership

Although buycotting suggests the power available to consumers who organize other like-minded consumers to lead businesses toward greener and more socially responsible practices, technology and peer communities have given new meaning to sharing. *Time* calls 'sharing' one of the 'ten ideas that will change the world' (Walsh, 2011). Gansky (2010) notes that there are changing attitudes of consumers to ownership, particularly toward high-dollar products that are only necessary a few times a year. Networked-enabled sharing is now being done on the 'Mesh' of mobile, location-based capabilities, as well as the Web and social networks. Finally, Rachel Botsman and Roo Rogers (2010) consider sharing more broadly in what they term 'collaborative consumption,' which includes sharing, bartering, lending, trading, renting, gifting, and swapping.

'We are relearning how to create value out of shared and open resources in ways that balance personal self-interest with the good of the larger community,' *What's Mine is Yours* co-author Rachel Botsman said. 'For the first time in history, the age of networks and mobile devices has created the efficiency and social glue to create innovative solutions, enabling the sharing and exchange of assets from cars, to bikes, to skills to spare space' (Rowan, 2011, para 5).

The story of Airbnb highlights the dizzying potential in what some term the 'access economy,' which goes against much of the logic of the 'ownership economy'. Airbnb founders Joe Gebbia and Brian Chesky knew each other from the Rhode Island School of Design and had moved to the South of Market or SoMa area of San Francisco where they were working as designers (Botsman and Rogers, 2010). When the annual industrial design conference came to San Francisco in October 2007, hotel rooms sold out. Gebbia and Chesky asked themselves why they shouldn't rent out their extra room by advertising it on the conference website. They did this and earned close to $1,000 in one week.

Their guests included a male designer from India who saw renting from Gebbia and Chesky as a great way to meet new people, a 35-year-old woman from Boston who wanted relief from a long commute and/or a high price for a hotel room, and a 45-year-old father of five from Utah.

'It completely blew away our assumptions,' Gebbia said. Surprisingly, Gebbia and Chesky did not feel like they were hosting strangers in their home. 'They are strangers until you have a conversation with them,' Chesky explained (Botsman and Rogers, 2010, p. ix).

The pair recruited another friend Nathan Blecharczyk as a Web developer, and built a simple website in early 2008. The name Airbnb began as 'air beds for conferences', but it now represents the idea that with the internet and a spare room, just about anyone could become an innkeeper. By April 2010, Airbnb.com had 85,000 registered users and more than 12,000 properties in 3,234 cities across 126 countries of the world. But it has not stopped at conferences. 'When we started, I never thought people would be renting out tree houses, igloos, boats, villas and designer apartments,' Chesky said (Botsman and Rogers, 2010, p. xi). Castles in England rent for about $3,000 per night on Airbnb.com.

Travelers can search Airbnb listings and examine the profile of hosts along with the ratings given by past travelers, as well as photos of the room in which they would stay. The only fixed rules on Airbnb is that travelers must be able to ask questions of hosts prior to booking, and rooms cannot be a commodity, such as hotel or motel rooms. Both travelers and hosts rate each other after the stay, and these results accumulate to establish someone's reputation on Airbnb. Through secure financial intermediaries, such as PayPal or credit card companies, the pre-payment made by a traveler does not become final until after the first 24 hours of a traveler's stay. The aspect of payment increases trust and puts both parties on their best behavior, making the entire process more reliable, but so does the online profile of host and traveler on Airbnb, which some refer to as 'a trail of digital bread crumbs that makes it harder to pull off a scam' (Wortham, 2010, para. 30). Airbnb takes a standard 3 percent service fee from hosts, and a 6 percent to 12 percent service fee depending on the reservation price. The average New York City host with Airbnb makes $1,600 per month.

Endless Possibilities for Collaborative Consumption

Consumer Adoption of Transportation Sharing

While originating in Switzerland and Germany in the 1980s, it has only been since the turn of this century that car sharing has made significant inroads into mainstream markets (Schuessler, Axhausen, and Ciari, 2013). The number of car sharing users worldwide has increased from 350,000 in 2006 to 4.94 million in 2014 (ACEA, 2018). Today, car-sharing services exist in over 1,100 cities, in 27 countries on five continents (Shaheen and Cohen, 2013). Moreover, the global car sharing market size is set to record impressive double-digit year-over-year growth (34.8 percent) between 2017 and 2024, with projected revenues of more than $16.5 billion by 2024, according to a recent research report by Global Market Insights, Inc. (markets.businessinsider.com, 2017).

As a result of advances in smartphone technology and social networks, transportation sharing has rapidly moved from a highly localized niche service to one that is widely accepted in metropolitan areas around the globe (Kockelman and Zhou, 2011; Shaheen and Cohen, 2013). The limited empirical evidence on car sharing seems to suggest that consumers' motivation to adopt car sharing is primarily driven by self-interest and usefulness (Bardhi and Eckhardt, 2012; Lamberton and Rose, 2012). The same can be said for any quick and cheap ways to get around urban areas, such as peer-to-peer ridesharing (Uber and Lyft), electric scooter rental (Lime, Bird, Scoot, as well as Skip) (Irfan, 2018), or bike sharing (dock-based or dockless systems) (Johnson, 2018).

Focusing now on car sharing, consumers also have reasons not to engage in car sharing. Many of these reasons result from the rival nature of access-based solutions (Peterson and Simkins, 2019). If too many other consumers rent the cars to be shared, this can lead to unavailability for a consumer when the car is needed at a certain location. Likewise, consumers may associate search costs with car-sharing solutions that ultimately prevent them from adopting.

Other studies found that consumers adopt car sharing not only because of functional benefits but also because of self-image and social reasons, such as being identified as pro-environment actions. In this way, car sharing can become conspicuous consumption (Catulli et al., 2013; Kockelman and Zhou, 2011).

Peer-to-peer car sharing entails consumers making their cars available for rental to other consumers similar to how Airbnb works (Holley, 2018). Turo and Getaround are two such peer-to-peer car-sharing firms. Turo allows its hundreds of thousands of members who own cars to post their cars online and rent them out for as little as $10 a day – or by the hour.

For Getaround, all the cars are connected so customers can unlock them from the company's app, according to Getaround's website, and all trips are covered with insurance and 24/7 roadside assistance (Azevedo, 2019). Getaround's services are available in more than 300 cities around the world – 140 US cities and 170 cities in Europe, such as Barcelona, Berlin, and London. The firm prides itself in giving people a way to make extra money while also making a positive impact on the environment by helping have fewer cars on the road. The variety offered to renters is another advantage of peer-to-peer car sharing. 'Today's a BMW day – or is it a Volvo day?' the ZipCar website asks (Rowan, 2011, para. 4). Avis acquired ZipCar in 2013.

Other Forms of Sharing

Fueled by the connectivity of the internet and custom apps, the ways to share appear to be limitless. JustPark (originally known as Parkatmyhouse) allows consumers in the UK to rent their driveways. SnapGoods lets users in a local setting share and rent physical products from mountain bikes to household tools. Zopa facilitates peer-to-peer money-lending, and so far the default rate is less than 1 percent. Kickstarter allows people to invest small sums in creative ventures. Bag Borrow or Steal applies the Netflix film-rental idea to expensive handbags, so that women can avoid the 'emotional and financial sacrifices involved in the endless search for the "right" accessory' (Bag Borrow or Steal, 2020). Rent-That-Toy facilitates rental of toys by brands. Searching by age category expedites shopping. The Sharing Economy also includes freelancing (TaskRabbit, for dog walking, handymen, and personal assistants; Care.com, for caregivers; and Upwork, for traditional freelance work, such as writers, graphic designers, and coders).

Noncommercial forms of sharing are also abounding on the internet now. Couchsurfing links people who have a spare sofa with travelers who would like to sleep on it (The Economist, 2010). Reciprocity is the key here as couchsurfers must do the same for someone else in the network someday in the future. For exchanging children's clothes, there is thredUp. Freecycle facilitates giving things away so that one's stuff does not end up in a landfill. Hey, Neighbor! facilitates a network in a user's neighborhood where updates can be shared with other neighbors, such as 'Felt the baby kick today,' as well as requests for small favors like moving a couch or picking up mail while one is away (www.heyneighbor.com).

Consumers are setting up and executing their own 'swishes' which are clothes swapping events (Smithers, 2020). Research suggests that 83 percent of those living in the UK have at least six items of clothing not worn in the last year. Most were purchased for a special event, such as a wedding or party and owners do not plan to wear them again.

Originally, 'swish' meant 'impressively smart and fashionable' in the UK. Now, weekly swishes are underway in Cornwall, United Kingdom. An average of 35 attendees gather in unused corridors of commercial buildings for the exchanges. Entrance fees are charged consumers and points awarded for making exchanges. 'Many women treat swishing like a clothes library,' Cornwall swish-organizer Anna Dalziel said. 'You sometimes see the same items rotating week to week. Some people come before they go on holiday just to stock up and I know some women who have swapped around 500 items over the past year. Facebook has been brilliant for us. I just announce to everyone who has signed up when the next event is and it goes from there' (Hickman, 2011, para. 18).

Fashion resale apps, (such as The RealReal, ThredUp, Depop, StockX, Poshmark and GOAT) lead the secondhand market (Sorokanich, 2019). Those born after 1980 comprise more than half of the shoppers using these resale apps, but Depop reports that those under 26 years of age comprise 90 percent of its active users. The retail analytics firm GlobalData reports the sector accounts for $24 billion in sales and forecasts much growth. Given that textile production accounted for 1.3 billion tons of CO_2 in 2015 (more than all international flights and maritime shipping combined), the environmental impact of consumers buying fewer new clothes in the secondhand fashion market is enormous.

CONCLUSION

This chapter offered a macromarketing perspective on a sacred cow of American culture – consumption. Social critic Paul Stiles' work in *Is the American Dream Killing You?* proposed that the economic system in which people exist works so well that hyper-consumption now threatens society. Other voices have echoed Stiles' views including macromarketing scholars who have asserted that the DSP holds powerful sway in society. This DSP is characterized by widespread acceptance of a 'more is better' ethos characterized by material acquisitiveness for consumers and dominance of the natural environment by society. Business practitioners, such as Andrew Bennett and Ann O'Reilly, have reported that a majority in developed markets are concerned about a consumption-obsessed society. Consumption has always had limits to vulnerable consumers because of their lack of access to markets (Baker, Gentry, and Rittenburg, 2005) and to consumers in depressed times of business cycles (Quelch and Jocz, 2009). However, environmental degradation (Gilding's *The Great Disruption*) looms as a possible disruption to consumer culture and might force many to adopt lifestyles of less consumption. Taking a defiant stance toward mindless consumption, the voluntary simplicity movement encourages individuals to consume less to enjoy more.

Rising consumer choice in marketplaces helps firms realize that satisfying consumers increasingly is more difficult. A networked world implies the need for more market intelligence and more social capital. Collaboration becomes necessary as well. Firms adopting a service-dominant (S-D) logic will work with other firms, as well as consumers, to co-create products and services. A networked world also implies that consumers are increasingly obtaining what they want from other consumers, rather than from firms. With the rise of sharing, the role of community has come into focus. Sharing goes against a primary ethos of the market – competition. Nevertheless, forms of sharing are becoming more visible in exchange, such as fashion resale apps facilitating the secondhand market for clothes and shoes. Efforts to nurture the commons of society, and volunteering, are now becoming understood to be part of how society will care for its resources and people in the future. The implications of social media along with the rise of online communities suggest that preserving communities can be more valuable than short-term profits to both individuals and businesses.

QUESTIONS

- What aspects of the 'me' dimension of markets had you not considered before reading Chapter 7?
- What aspects of the 'we' dimension of markets had you not considered before reading Chapter 7?

- To what degree do you agree with Paul Stiles' assessment that 'the Market' actually poses a threat to the well-being of individuals, families, and other institutions in American society? How do you see evidence of hyper-consumption today?

- In what ways do you see consumers with limited access to fair or good exchanges in the marketplace today? At what times have you felt like a vulnerable consumer?

- What power do consumers have in markets today that they did not have 50 years ago? Five years ago?

- What practices of voluntary simplicity appeal to you in Table 7.1? Which do not appeal to you? Explain.

- In your opinion, what are the prospects for buycotting in the future? What would it take for you to participate in a buycott? If you had a business, would you want to be buycotted?

- What forms of collaborative consumption appeal most to you after reading Chapter 7? Which ones do you think will be around ten years from now?

Mavericks Who Made It

Mother Teresa

Source: catwalker/Shutterstock.com

The image on the left is of Australia's Mother Teresa stamp. But dozens of other countries across all of the world's continents have honored Mother Teresa by putting her image on a postal stamp, including Muslim-majority countries in Africa (such as Chad, Mali, and Senegal), as well as the atheistic and Communist country Cuba. Sweden, Austria, Germany, and the US have also issued Mother Teresa postal stamps.

Mother Teresa won the Nobel Peace Prize in 1979 for her humanitarian work with the poor (Rosenberg, 2017). Most persons around the world probably associate Mother Teresa with her work with the dying and forgotten on the streets of Kolkata (formerly Calcutta), India with the Roman Catholic order she founded in 1948 – the Missionaries of Charity. However, by the time she died in 1997, her Missionaries of Charity had expanded to nearly 4,000 nuns operating 610 foundations in 123 countries around the world.

Global aspects of Mother Teresa's life are remarkable. She was born in 1910 in the Ottoman Empire into an Albanian family in what is now Macedonia. At 18, she joined the Sisters of Loreto Abbey in Ireland to learn English with the view of becoming a teacher in India where English was the language of instruction. During her life, she spoke five languages: Albanian, Serbo-Croat, English, Bengali, and Hindi.

Arriving in 1929, she taught in Darjeeling in the lower Himalayas, as well as in Calcutta. During her time as a teacher, Calcutta experienced the Bengal famine of 1943 in which more than 2 million people died of starvation, malaria, and other diseases related to malnutrition, unsanitary conditions, and lack of health care. Massive riots occurred in July 1946 in Calcutta pitting Hindus against Muslims leaving more than 4,000 dead and 100,000 homeless in less than 72 hours. In short, mounting human suffering surrounded Mother Teresa's school.

On a train ride from Calcutta to Darjeeling in 1946, Mother Teresa experienced what she later described as her call to help the poor in a new way. She left her convent and lived among the poor. With no income, she had to beg for food and supplies. She also experienced doubts and loneliness and temptation to return to her convent. But she endured and was able to lay the foundation of a new religious community to help the poorest among the poor. Her Missionaries of Charity would care for the 'the hungry, the naked, the homeless, the crippled, the blind, the lepers, all those people who feel unwanted, unloved, uncared for throughout society, people that have become a burden to the society and are shunned by everyone' (Associated Press, 1997).

Hospices became a first priority in the work of the Missionaries of Charity. This was done to provide a beautiful death 'for people who lived like animals to die like angels – loved and wanted', Mother Teresa said (Spink, 1997). Other efforts followed focused on orphanages, leper hospices, AIDS hospices. Additionally, charity centers for refugees, the blind, disabled, aged, alcoholics, the homeless, and victims of natural disasters and epidemics followed. In 2016, Pope Francis canonized her as Saint Teresa of Calcutta (Povoledo, 2016).

In many ways, Mother Teresa's life contradicts commonly held tenets of consumption-based living in the modern world. Instead of focusing on herself, she focused on others – especially the neediest. Current calls for voluntary simplicity or minimalist living in developed countries (Millburn and Nicodemus, 2015), don't include the service ethic so evident in Mother Teresa's life, because they are still linked to materialist pursuits – albeit low-level materialistic pursuits. Because the life she led would be so physically, mentally and emotionally demanding for others, her admirers infer she had a divine source of power that others without her spiritual understanding do not.

Not only did Mother Teresa love the neediest on the streets of Kolkata, but she learned to appreciate the exchange that characterized her work with those in extreme poverty. 'The poor give us much more than we give them,' Mother Teresa said (Associated Press, 1997). 'They're such strong people, living day to day with no food. And they never curse, never complain. We don't have to give them pity or sympathy. We have so much to learn from them.'

In her Nobel lecture, she disclosed that she found aspects of life in developed countries to present more formidable challenges than what she encounters in developing countries.

(Continued)

Around the world, not only in the poor countries, but I found the poverty of the West so much more difficult to remove. When I pick up a person from the street, hungry, I give him a plate of rice, a piece of bread, I have satisfied. I have removed that hunger. But a person that is shut out, that feels unwanted, unloved, terrified, the person that has been thrown out from society – that poverty is so hurtable [*sic*] and so much, and I find that very difficult.

(Mother Teresa, 1979)

Questions

- Why do you think such a diverse set of countries all over the world have honoured Mother Teresa by featuring her image on a postal stamp for the country?
- Mother Teresa stood only about 1.5 meters high (5 foot), but she accomplished so much in her life. Have you known others who are physically different, but whose lives are marked by high achievement and/or by a high QOL?
- Were you surprised that in Mother Teresa's Nobel Lecture she noted that the poverty of developed countries is harder to remove than the poverty of developing countries?
- Do you agree or disagree with her? Explain.

REFERENCES

ACEA. (2018). Number of car sharing users worldwide from 2006 to 2014 (in millions). Accessed January 8, 2018 at www.statista.com/statistics/415636/car-sharing-number-of-users-worldwide/

Alderman, L. (2020). 'Corona cycleways' become the new post-confinement commute. *The New York Times*, June 12, 2020. Accessed at www.nytimes.com/2020/06/12/business/paris-bicycles-commute-coronavirus.html

Anderson, G.F., Reinhardt, U.W., Hussey, P.S., and Petrosyan, V. (May/June 2003). It's the prices, Stupid: Why the United States is so different from other countries. *Health Affairs*, 22(3), 89–105. Retrieved from http://content.healthaffairs.org/cgi/reprint/22/3/89.pdf

Ariely, D. (2011, May). The upside of useless stuff. *Harvard Business Review*. Retrieved from http://hbr.org/2011/05/column-the-upside-of-useless-stuff/ar/1

Associated Press (1997). Mother Teresa – in her own words. Washingtonpost.com, September 5, 1997. Accessed at www.washingtonpost.com/wp-srv/inatl/longterm/teresa/stories/words.htm

Azevedo, M.A. (2019). Carsharing startup getaround reportedly raising $200M at $1.7B Valuation, *Crunchbase News*, September 6, 2019. Accessed at https://news.crunchbase.com/news/carsharing-startup-getaround-reportedly-raising-200m-at-1-7b-valuation/

Bag Borrow or Steal. (2020). About Us. Available at www.bagborroworsteal.com/aboutus

Baker, S.M., Gentry, J.W., and Rittenburg, T.L. (2005, December). Building understanding of the domain of consumer vulnerability. *Journal of Macromarketing*, 25, 128–39.

Bang, H.K., Ellinger, A.E., Hadjimarcou, J., and Traichal, P.A. (2000). Consumer concern, knowledge, belief, and attitude toward renewable energy: An application of the reasoned action theory. *Psychology and Marketing*, 17(6), 449–68.

Bardhi F, and Eckhardt, G.M. (2012). Access-based consumption: The case of car sharing. *Journal of Consumer Research*, 39(4, 881–98.

Beaton, T. (2018). 86% of employers use financial incentives in wellness programs. *Health Payer Intelligence*, May 7, 2018. Accessed at https://healthpayerintelligence.com/news/86-of-employers-use-financial-incentives-in-wellness-programs

Beech, P. (2020). Could the pandemic usher in a golden age of cycling? *World Economic Forum*, May 13, 2020. Accessed at www.weforum.org/agenda/2020/05/covid-19-usher-golden-age-cycling-coronavirus-pandemic-bike-cycle/

Bennett, A., and O'Reilly, A. (2010) *Consumed rethinking business in the era of mindful spending*. New York, NY: Palgrave Macmillan.

Bok, D. (2010). *The politics of happiness: What government can learn from the new research on well-being*. Princeton, NJ: Princeton University Press.

Botsman, R., and Rogers, R. (2010). *What's mine is yours: The rise of collaborative consumption*. New York, NY: HarperCollins.

Brooks, A.C. (2010). *The battle: How the fight between free enterprise and big government will shape America's future*. New York, NY: Basic Books.

Bullock, C., Brereton, F., and Bailey, S. (2017). The economic contribution of public bike-share to the sustainability and efficient functioning of cities. *Sustainable Cities and Society*, 28, 76–87. doi:10.1016/j.scs.2016.08.024

Campbell, C. (2018). The trouble with sharing: China's bike fever has reached saturation point. *Time*, April 2, 2018. Accessed at http://time.com/5218323/china-bicycles-sharing-economy/

Caplan, J. (2009, May 15). Shoppers, unite! Carrotmobs are cooler than boycotts. *Time*. Retrieved from www.time.com.

Catulli, M., Lindley, J.K., Reed, N.B., Green, A., Hyseni, H., and Kiri, S. (2013). What is mine is not yours: Further insight on what access-Based consumption says about consumers. In R.W. Belkm L. Price, and L. Peñaloza (Eds.), *Consumer culture theory*. Research in Consumer Behavior, Volume 15 (pp. 185–208). Bingley, UK: Emerald Group Publishing Limited.

Center for a New American Dream. (2020). About. Retrieved from https://newdream.org/about-us.

Claudy, M.C., and Peterson, M. (2014). Understanding the underutilization of urban bicycle commuting: A behavioral reasoning perspective. *Journal of Public Policy and Marketing*, 33(2), 173–87.

Claudy, M.C., Peterson, M., and O'Driscoll, A. (2013). Understanding the attitude-behavior gap for renewable energy systems: Using behavioral reasoning theory. *Journal of Macromarketing*, 33(4), 273–87.

Cohen, M. J. (2020). Does the COVID-19 outbreak mark the onset of a sustainable consumption transition? *Sustainability: Science, Practice and Policy*, 16(1), 1–3, doi: 10.1080/15487733.2020.1740472

Commonwealth Fund. (2020). Mirror, Mirror 2017: International Comparison Reflects Flaws and Opportunities for Better U.S. Healthcare. *The Commonwealth Fund*. Accessed at https://interactives.commonwealthfund.org/2017/july/mirror-mirror/

Davies, A. (2020). The world's most traffic-choked cities, ranked. *Wired*, January 28, 2020. Accessed at www.wired.com/story/worlds-most-traffic-choked-cities-ranked/

Davis, K., Schoen, C., Schoenbaum, S.C., Dory, M.M., Holmgren, A.L., Kriss, J.L., and Shea, K.K. (2007). *Mirror, mirror on the wall: An international update on the comparative performance of American health care*. New York, NY: The Commonwealth Fund.

Deaton, A. (2008, April 1). Income, health and wellbeing around the world: Evidence from the Gallup World Poll. *Journal of Economic Perspectives*, 22(2), 53–72.

Diener, E., Ng, W., Harter, J., and Arora, R. (2010). Wealth and happiness across the world: Material prosperity predicts life evaluation, whereas psychosocial prosperity predicts positive feeling. *Journal of Personality and Social Psychology*, 9(1), 52–61.

Easterlin, R.A. (1974). Does economic growth improve the human lot?: Some empirical evidence. In P.A. David and W.R. Levin (Eds.), *Nations and households in economic growth Stanford* (pp. 98–135). Stanford, CA: Stanford University Press.

The Economist. (2010, October 14). The better business of sharing. What to do when you are green, broke and connected. You share. *The Economist*. Retrieved from www.economist.com/node/17249322

European Cyclists' Federation. (2020). Capital cities. Accessed at https://ecf.com/resources/cycling-facts-and-figures/capital-cities.

Freedman, D.H. (2019). The worst patients in the world. *The Atlantic*, July 2019, 28–30.

Gansky, L. (2010). *The mesh: Why the future of business is sharing*. New York, NY: Portfolio.

Gilding, P. (2011). *The great disruption: Why the climate crisis will bring on the end of shopping and the birth of a new world*. New York, NY: Bloomsbury Press.

Green, P. (2007, March 22). The year without toilet paper. *The New York Times*. Retrieved from www.nytimes.com

Hansla, A., Gamble, A., Juliusson, A., and Gärling, T. (2008). Psychological determinants of attitude towards and willingness to pay for green electricity. *Energy policy*, 36(2), 768–74.

Hayes, M. (2019). 17 best price comparison engines to increase ecommerce sales. *Shopify Blog*, November 1, 2019. Accessed at www.shopify.com/blog/7068398-10-best-comparison-shopping-engines-to-increase-ecommerce-sales#googleshopping

Hickman, L. (2011, June 14). The end of consumerism. *The Guardian*. Retrieved from http://guardian.co.uk

Holley, P. (2018). Airbnb for cars is here. And the rental car giants are not happy. *The Washington Post*, March 30, 2018. Accessed at www.washingtonpost.com/news/innovations/wp/2018/03/30/airbnb-for-cars-is-here-and-the-rental-car-giants-are-not-happy/

Huneke, M.E. (2005, July). The face of the un-consumer: An empirical examination of the practice of voluntary simplicity in the United States. *Psychology and Marketing*, 22(7), 527–50.

Irfan, U. (2018). Electric scooters' sudden invasion of American cities, explained. *Vox*, September 7, 2018. Accessed at www.vox.com/2018/8/27/17676670/electric-scooter-rental-bird-lime-skip-spin-cities

Johnson, D. (2018). Bike-share companies are transforming US cities – and they're just getting started. *The Conversation*, April 19, 2018. Accessed at http://theconversation.com/bike-share-companies-are-transforming-us-cities-and-theyre-just-getting-started-95267

Kahneman, D., and Deaton, A. (2010 September 21). High income improves evaluation of life but not emotional well-being. *Proceedings of the National Academy of Sciences of the United States of America (PNAS)*, 107(38), 16489–16493. Retrieved from www.pnas.org/content/early/2010/08/27/1011492107.full.pdf+html

Kalafatis, S.P., Pollard, M., East, R., and Tsogas, M.H. (1999). Green marketing and Ajzen's Theory of planned behaviour: A cross-market examination. *Journal of consumer marketing*, 16(5), 441–60.

Kaufman, M.T. (2011, January 26). Daniel Bell, ardent appraiser of politics, economics and culture, dies. *The New York Times*, p. A21.

Kessel, B. (2008). How much money is enough? *MSN.com*. Retrieved from http://articles.moneycentral.msn.com/Investing/StockInvestingTrading/HowMuchMoneyIsEnough.aspx

Kilbourne, W., McDonagh, P., and Prothero, A. (1997). Sustainable consumption and the quality of life: A macromarketing challenge to the dominant social paradigm. *Journal of Macromarketing*, 17(1), 4–24.

Kockelman, K., and Zhou, B. (2011). Opportunities for and impacts of carsharing: A survey of the Austin, Texas market. *International Journal of Sustainable Transportation,* 5(3), 135–52.

Lamberton, C.P., and Rose, R.L. (2012). When is ours better than mine? A framework for understanding and altering participation in commercial sharing systems. *Journal of Marketing*, 76(4), 109–25.

markets.businessinsider.com. (2017). Carsharing market to witness a massive 34%+ growth over 2016-2024. http://markets.businessinsider.com/news/stocks/Carsharing-Market-to-witness-a-massive-34-growth-over-2016-2024-1002207831

McCarthy, N. (2020). The countries with the highest density of doctors. *Statista*, March 19, 2020. Accessed at www.statista.com/chart/21168/doctors-per-1000-inhabitants-in-selected-countries/

McGregor, J. (2018). Why 'buycotts' could overtake boycotts among consumer activists. *The Washington Post*, February 29, 2018. Accessed at www.washingtonpost.com/news/on-leadership/wp/2018/02/28/why-buycotts-could-overtake-boycotts-among-consumer-activists/

McLeod, K. (2018). New data on bike commuting. *News from the League*, September 13, 2018. Accessed at https://bikeleague.org/content/new-data-bike-commuting

Milbrath, L. (1989). *Envisioning a sustainable society*. Albany, NY: State University of New York Press.

Millburn, J.F., and Nicodemus, R. (2015). *Minimalism: Live a meaningful life*. Asymmetrical Press.

Mother Teresa. (1979). Nobel Prize Lecture, December 11, 1979. Accessed at www.nobelprize.org/prizes/peace/1979/teresa/lecture/

No Impact Project (2011). No Impact Project. Accessed at www.sustainable.org/living/responsible-buying-a-consumption/1298-no-impact-project.

OECD. (2019). *The heavy burden of obesity: The economics of prevention*. OECD Health Policy Studies. Accessed at www.oecd.org/health/the-heavy-burden-of-obesity-67450d67-en.htm

Paladino, A. and Baggiere, J. (2007). Are We 'Green'? an Empirical Investigation of Renewable Electricity Consumption". In S. Borghini, M.A. McGrath, and C. Otnes (Eds.), *E - European Advances in Consumer Research* Volume 8, (340–341). Duluth, MN: Association for Consumer Research.

Pearson, B. (2011a). *Pre-commerce: How companies and customers are transforming business together*. San Francisco, CA: Jossey-Bass.

Pearson, B. (2011b May 31). Why pre-commerce is a game-changer. Retrieved from www.pre-commerce.com

Peattie, K. (2001). Towards sustainability: The third age of green marketing. *The Marketing Review*, 2(2), 129–46.

Peter G. Peterson Foundation (2019). US life expectancy is lower than other developed countries. December 18, 2019. Accessed at www.pgpf.org/Chart-Archive/0201_us_lifeexpectancy_low_despite_cost

Peterson, C.L., and Burton, R. (2007, September 17). U.S. health care spending: Comparison with other OECD countries. *CSR Report for Congress* (Order code RL34175). Washington, DC: Congressional Research Service.

Peterson, M., and Simkins, T. (2019). Consumers' processing of mindful commercial car sharing. *Business Strategy and the Environment*, 28(3), 457–65.

Phila Mirror. (2015). Indian theme on foreign stamps: Australia will issue stamp on Mother Teresa. *Phila Mirror*, September 14, 2015. Accessed at https://philamirror.info/2015/09/14/indian-theme-on-foreign-stampsaustralia-will-issue-stamp-on-mother-teresa/

Povoledo, E. (2016). Mother Teresa is made a saint by Pole Francis. *The New York Times*, September 3, 2016. Accessed at www.nytimes.com/2016/09/05/world/europe/mother-teresa-named-saint-by-pope-francis.html

Prothero, A., Dobscha, S., Freund, J., Kilbourne, W.E., Luchs, M.G., Ozanne, L.K., and Thøgersen, J. (2011). Sustainable consumption: Opportunities for consumer research and public policy. *Journal of Public Policy and Marketing*, 30(1), 31–8.

Quelch, J., and Jocz, K. (2009, April). How to market in a downturn. *Harvard Business Review*. Retrieved from http://web.ebscohost.com/ehost/pdfviewer/pdfviewer?vid=3andhid=108andsid=23ed06ec-40b1-4f25-9ea8-67171dac23a8%40sessionmgr110

Reuters/Ipsos (2010, April 17). Half (52%) of global citizens would find it difficult for a very ill family member to get quality, affordable healthcare. Retrieved from www.ipsos-na.com

Ritchie, H., and Roser, M. (2018). Water use and stress. *Our World in Data*, July 2018. Accessed at https://ourworldindata.org/water-use-stress

Rosenberg, S. (2017). October 17, 1979: Mother Teresa won the Nobel Peace Prize. *Lifetime*, October 17, 2017. Accessed at www.mylifetime.com/she-did-that/october-17-1979-mother-teresa-won-the-nobel-peace-prize

Rowan, D. (2011, February 11). Rentalship is the new ownership in the networked age. *Wired*. Retrieved from www.wired.com

Rubin, C. (2011, September 7). At what price happiness? *Inc*. Retrieved from www.inc.com

Schuessler, N., Axhausen, K., and Ciari, F. (2013). Estimation of carsharing demand using an activity-based microsimulation approach: Model discussion and some results. *International Journal of Sustainable Transportation*, 7(1), 70–84.

Shaheen, S.A., and Cohen, A.P. (2013). Innovative mobility carsharing outlook: Carsharing market overview, analysis, and trends – Summer Edition. *Transportation Sustainability Research Center*, University of California, Berkeley.

Shaw, D., McMaster, R., and Newholm, T. (2016). Care and commitment in ethical consumption: An exploration of the 'attitude–behaviour gap'. *Journal of Business Ethics*, 136(2), 251–65.

Smithers, R. (2020). Swap till you drop? Call to 'swish' little-used clothes to cut waste. *The Guardian*, January 2, 2020. Accessed at www.theguardian.com/money/2020/jan/02/swap-till-you-drop-call-to-swish-little-used-clothes-to-cut-waste

Sorokanich, L. (2019). By 2023, the secondhand clothes market will double to $51 billion. Here's why. *Fast Company*, December 17, 2019. Accessed at www.fastcompany.com/90430079/by-2023-the-secondhand-clothes-market-will-double-to-51-billion-heres-why

Spindler, B. (2019). 'We can't waste a drop.' India is running out of water. *The Wall Street Journal*, August 19, 2019. Accessed at www.wsj.com/articles/we-cant-waste-a-drop-india-is-running-out-of-water-11566224878

Spink. (1997). *Mother Teresa: A complete authorized biography*. New York, NY:. HarperCollins.

Steg, L., Dreijerink, L., and Abrahamse, W. (2005), 'Factors influencing the acceptability of energy policies: A test of VBN theory,' *Journal of Environmental Psychology*, 25(4), 415–25.

Stiles, P. (2005). *Is the American dream killing you?: How 'the market' rules our lives*. New York, NY: Collins.

Taylor, A. (2018). The bike-share oversupply in China: Huge piles of abandoned and broken bicycles. *The Atlantic*, March 22, 2018. Accessed at www.theatlantic.com/photo/2018/03/bike-share-oversupply-in-china-huge-piles-of-abandoned-and-broken-bicycles/556268/

Tierney, J. (2011, May 16). A new gauge to see what's beyond happiness. *The New York Times*. Retrieved from www.nytimes.com

TomTom. (2020). Traffic index 2019. Accessed at www.tomtom.com/en_gb/traffic-index/ranking/

Unger, D. (2019). Mission critical. *strategy+business*, April 24, 2019. Accessed at www.strategy-business.com/article/Mission-critical

Walsh, B. (2011, March 17). Today's smart choice: Don't own. Share. *Time*. Retrieved from www.time.com

Warren, M. (2020). Word of mouth marketing in 2020: How to create a strategy for social media buzz and skyrocket referral sales. *Big Commerce*. Accessed at www.bigcommerce.com/blog/word-of-mouth-marketing/#word-of-mouth-marketing-statistics

Westaby, J.D. (2005). Behavioral reasoning theory: Identifying new linkages underlying intentions and behavior. *Organizational Behavior and Human Decision Processes*, 98, 97–120.

Westaby, J.D, Probst, T.M., and Lee, B.C. (2010). 'Leadership decision-making: A behavioral reasoning theory analysis,' *The Leadership Quarterly*, 21(3), 481–95.

World Bank (2019). World Happiness Report (2019). Report accessed at https://world-happiness.report/ed/2019/, Image accessed at https://ourworldindata.org/grapher/gdp-vs-happiness

Wortham, J. (2010, August 28). Neighborly borrowing, over the online fence. *New York Times*. Retrieved from www.nytimes.com/2010/08/29/business/29ping.html

Wrede, I. (2020). COVID-19 causes 'bike explosion' as Germans long for a ride. *DW*, June 24, 2020. Accessed at www.dw.com/en/covid-19-causes-bike-explosion-as-germans-long-for-a-ride/a-53905967

PART III

Sustainable Marketing for the Environment

8
THE ENVIRONMENTAL IMPERATIVE

Throwing Shade

Source: Photo by uomo libero on Unsplash.

Greenwashing

Greenwashing occurs when a firm presents itself as being green (mindful of the environment) but actually performs poorly on environmental measures (Delmas and Burbano, 2011). Often such greenwashing occurs because a firm initiates a public relations effort to silence environmental critics without changing things for the environment (Mendez, 2020).

(Continued)

Brands need to present real evidence to validate their claims to be environmentally friendly. Brands that provide no such evidence, but use vague terms about their environmental commitment might be guilty of greenwashing. Such vague terms might include 'sustainable, 'socially responsible', 'eco-friendly', 'bioplastic', or 'recycled content', 'natural', or 'green'. In the US, the Federal Trade Commission has developed Green Guides to provide guidance on what firms should do when making green claims (FTC, 2020). In this way, the FTC regards greenwashing as an issue related to truth in advertising.

In 2020, the watchdog NGO Truth in Advertising presented a short list of firms accused of greenwashing (Truth in Advertising, 2020). These included the following: (1) VW, BMW, Chevy, Ford, and Mercedes-Benz for marketing 'clean diesel' autos (when their diesels release nitrogen oxides more than 65 times what the Environmental Protection Agency allows), (2) Procter & Gamble's Charmin Freshmates for marketing the product as 'flushable' because they are safe for sewer and septic systems (when only well-maintained plumbing systems can handle these wipes when flushed), and (3) Reynolds American's Natural American Spirit cigarettes as an eco-friendly cigarette (when cigarette smoke contains hundreds of toxic chemicals and at least 69 that cause cancer).

Ben & Jerry's might be regarded by many as a 'woke' or socially aware business. It sources Fair Trade ingredients in order to improve the lives of farmers in developing countries and it has long supported climate action, as well as racial justice (Ben & Jerry's, 2020). But its critics note that Ben & Jerry's product is an unhealthy one (Holman and Buckley, 2020). A half pint of chocolate chip cookie dough ice cream at Ben & Jerry's delivers 25 grams of sugars and 16 grams of fat with its 280 calories (Fatsecret, 2020). Currently, glucose is increasingly regarded as the new tobacco and some ethnic minority groups (such as Black Americans) are more likely to contract Type 2 diabetes than Whites.

The Organic Consumers Association (OCA) has sued Ben & Jerry's in a consumer deception lawsuit asserting that Ben & Jerry's marketing claims about 'happy cows' and 'caring dairies' are not based on fact (Regeneration Vermont, 2020a). In other words, many consumers believe Ben & Jerry's uses grass-fed organic milk due to its marketing, but it does not. According to Regeneration Vermont, the nonprofit group advocating for a return to sustainable and regenerative agriculture in Vermont, Ben & Jerry's sources its milk from concentrated animal feeding operations (CAFOs) in which cows remain in confinement on concrete – not grass – for their entire lives (Regeneration Vermont, 2020b). Additionally, independent testing by the OCA discovered traces of glyphosate (the weed killer Round Up developed by Monsanto) in 10 of 11 Ben & Jerry's ice cream flavors. Michael Colby, a co-founder of Regeneration Vermont says that after meeting with Ben & Jerry's for a year in hopes that Ben & Jerry's would source organically, he was told by Ben & Jerry's founder Ben Cohen that Ben & Jerry's would not transition to organic because it wouldn't allow them to 'maximize profits' as a wholly owned subsidiary of Unilever.

> **Questions to Consider**
>
> - How do you feel when you learn that greenwashing happens in markets today?
> - What does this say about firms' wishes to be perceived as being aligned with environmental concerns close to the hearts of consumers?
> - Can you think of some brands that you might need to scrutinize now regarding their claims to be environmentally friendly? Which ones would these be?
> - Should there be closer oversight of firms making green claims or is the current arrangement where NGOs and the media call out greenwashing firms sufficient?

CHAPTER OVERVIEW AND LEARNING OBJECTIVES

This chapter will discuss what Philip Kotler – a leading thinker in marketing – calls 'the environmental imperative' (Kotler, 2011a). Macromarketing scholars have long focused on environmental degradation as an externality of marketing. In fact, 'environment' is the third of the six core dimensions in macromarketing's QuEEnSHiP acronym presented in Chapter 1. The question emerging from such research was, 'can anything be done about this externality?' Now, managerially oriented scholars like Kotler are suggesting that the some of the assumptions of marketing practice, such as limitless resources of the Earth and unconstrained carrying capacity for waste on the planet, are wrong. At this juncture when such fundamental assumptions of marketing are being rethought, macromarketing offers valuable insights into crucial societal issues regarding the environment. Many of these issues have already received treatment over the years by two schools within macromarketing – the developmental school and the critical school of thought.

This chapter also presents the importance of the ethical concepts of citizenship (being responsible to society at large) and stewardship (being responsible to another stakeholder) in responding to the environmental imperative. For firms pursuing environmental stewardship, employees will lead this effort. In this pursuit, the values and principles of employees help firms discover new products, new markets, and new internal processes for conducting operations.

Not surprisingly, firms that treat the physical environment with respect tend to do the same with other stakeholders, beginning with their own employees. In other words, stewardship is not limited to environmental stewardship. Stewardship of resources also applies to human resources – within the firm first, and then outside the firm. Transparency is a core dimension of firms marked by stewardship ethics. This can be extended to an 'open books' atmosphere where just about all information in the company is made available to employees in the firm.

Firms responding to the environmental imperative are likely to find a receptive audience to their actions. Notably, many environmentalists who took an adversarial stance toward business are now seeking to work with businesses because of the recognition of the importance of jobs and employment to society (Nordhaus and Shellenberger, 2007). Here, a recognition that profits must be made by businesses is an important aspect of this revised way of regarding business persons and their endeavors.

Values-driven firms, such as New Belgium Brewing Company based in Fort Collins, Colorado, pursue profits and draw on a more humanistic approach to stakeholders to obtain these profits. The results of taking a triple-bottom-line approach can be seen in the firm being able to make its Belgium-style brown ale more distinctive and appealing to a wider set of customers. New Belgium accomplished this by using its community of pastoral amateurs to call consumers to this movement that pursued a less materialistic but higher quality of life.

After this chapter, you should be able to answer the following questions:

- What is the environmental imperative?
- How did the developmental school and the critical school differ in their views regarding the role of marketing systems in environmental stewardship?
- How are citizenship and stewardship similar? Different?
- Why are employees endemic to success in shifting to sustainable business practices?
- How can sustainable enterprises choose to identify and reinforce their values and principles for a far-flung workforce?
- What advantages do values-driven companies gain regarding branding?
- How can sustainable enterprises reinforce a high-involvement culture of the firm?
- How can sustainable enterprises reinforce sustainable suppliers around the world?

FROM BAD BUSINESS TO GOOD BUSINESS
Commerce in the Age of Transparency
Urgency Regarding Environmental Degradation

Pope Francis issued *Laudato Si'* – a 70-page encyclical on the environment in 2015 (Pope Francis, 2015). In his provocative encyclical, he called for urgent action to stop climate change and proposed that caring for the natural environment be added to traditional Christian works of mercy, such as feeding the hungry and visiting the sick (McKenna, 2016). The Pope did not mince words in describing man's destruction of the environment as a sin and accusing mankind of leaving coming generations 'debris, desolation and filth' (Pope Francis, 2015, p. 47). He also called the climate a common good meant for all and decried the asymmetrical burden climate change imposes on poor countries. He also denounced profit maximization.

Laudato Si' resonates with many macromarketing concepts as evidenced by Pope Francis' use of the word 'systems' 58 times.

Northwestern University's Philip Kotler is one of the most respected scholars of marketing and his ideas about marketing and society are macromarketing ones, too. His popular textbooks have influenced business culture around the world to the point that terms in his book (such as consumer orientation, segmentation, targeting, and positioning) are known by those who have never studied marketing formally (Hackley, 2009, p. 2).

Philip Kotler of Northwestern University's Kellogg School of Management

Source: Photo used with permission of Philip Kotler and featured on the cover of Philip Kotler, *My Adventures in Marketing* (Idea Bite Press, 2017).

Today, Kotler cites not one, but a set of environmental challenges that compose an environmental imperative for society, such as (a) climate change, (b) depletion of the ozone layer that protects the Earth from ultraviolet radiation, (c) soil degradation and increased desertification, (d) increased air and water pollution, (e) reduction in the availability of fresh water, and (f) increasing depletion of physical and natural resources, such as oil, copper, timber, and ocean fisheries. Kotler sees that companies now need to make drastic changes in their product development, manufacturing, financial, and marketing practices if sustainability is to be achieved. This is the environmental imperative.

In this era of the environmental imperative, firms will not want to appear indifferent to larger economic, social, and environmental concerns (Kotler, 2011a). With consumers e-mailing, blogging, and tweeting both the good and bad aspects of firms and their activities, firms are now 'swimming in a highly transparent fishbowl' (Kotler, 2011a, p. 134). As a result, accountability has increased markedly for firms in society in what some have termed the Age of Transparency (Meyer and Kirby, 2010).

The Influence of the Internet

When asked if there would be a widespread conversation in society about a 'green economy' if the internet did not exist, *The New York Times* Environment Correspondent Felicity Barringer, said, 'No' (Barringer, 2008, personal communication). With the internet, entrepreneurs with green innovations can keep these in front of possible consumers and investors much longer as a result of new communication technologies. Using social media, corporate-sized nongovernmental organizations (NGOs), such as the Environmental Defense Fund and the Natural Resources Defense Council (1.3 million supporters), can mobilize its supporters on legal and scientific issues regarding the environment (NRDC, 2011). Online communities, such as SustainLane – billing itself as a people-powered green guide – serve as a way people interested in living healthy lives on a green planet can discuss local green news and share information and tips (SustainLane.com, n.d.). The members of SustainLane.com have written reviews on more than 30,000 green products and businesses across the country.

By going to www.scorecard.org, one can quickly find the largest polluters where one lives or works. Figure 8.1 depicts one of the results from entering the zip code for Hollywood in Los Angeles County in Southern California. As shown, Los Angeles County is one of the worst/dirtiest counties in the United States.

Even pollution from far away can be traced back to its source. For example, the North American Commission for Environmental Cooperation released a study showing that three-quarters of the dioxin in the breast milk of Inuit women in Nunavut, Canada's northernmost territory, came from municipal waste incinerators in the Midwest and Eastern parts of the United States (Weaver-Zercher, 2010).

In April 2006, a dense cloud of soot, toxic chemicals, and gases from smokestacks of coal-burning plants in northern China along with dust and desert left China and swept over Seoul, Korea. A US satellite spotted the cloud as it came across the Pacific. As a result of such weather-born exports from the developing world, air filters in places such as Lake Tahoe and eastern California become dark (Bradsher and Barboza, 2006). Particles of sulfur, carbon, and other compounds can work their way deep into the lungs contributing to respiratory damage, heart disease, and cancer. A conservative estimate of deaths from air pollution alone in the United States each year is 130,000 (Diamond, 2005, p. 492). In China, sulfur dioxide from burning coal results in 400,000 premature deaths each year (Bradsher and Barboza, 2006, p. 1). In sum, as scientific measurements have become more sophisticated, the global aspect of air pollution has become undeniable. China's problems are now the world's problems. Much of the particulate pollution in Los Angeles originates in China according the *Journal of Geophysical Research* (Kahn and Yardley, 2007, p. 1).

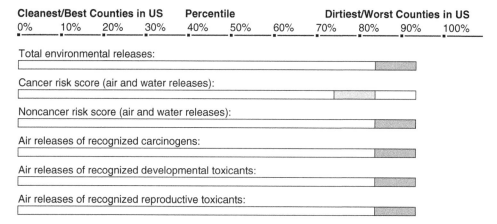

Figure 8.1   Results from Scorecard.org suggest pollution is the unglamorous side of Hollywood

Source: Scorecard, http://scorecard.goodguide.com/env-releases/county.tcl?fips_county_code=06037#major_chemical_releases

Can Marketing Be Reinvented?

However, air pollution is just one of the maladies afflicting countries today – especially in the developing world. The long list of other environmental problems include the following: biodiversity losses, cropland losses, desertification, disappearing wetlands, grassland degradation, invasive species, overgrazing, river flow cessation, salinization, soil erosion, trash accumulation, water pollution, and shortages (Diamond, 2005, p. 358).

Despite decades of disseminating marketing principles and techniques focused on finding out what customers want and giving it to them (the 'little m'), Kotler now emphasizes a new turn for marketing in which marketers need to replace a narrow view of meeting one need for the customer with a more complete view of the customer (similar to the 'biggest M'):

> People today have a lot of concerns about the future. They hear about water shortages, air pollution, fat in their diet, rising healthcare costs. Most manufacturers don't address these concerns. Each focuses on a slice of the customer's life. A toothpaste manufacturer only thinks of the person's teeth and a washing machine manufacturer only thinks of a person's need to clean clothes. Marketers need to replace their vertical perspective of a customer with a horizontal perspective where they see the customer's full humanity. Companies need to show that they share the same concerns as customers and that they are acting on these concerns.

> (Kotler, 2011b, p. 34, para. 5)

Kotler singles out companies that care about the planet as those likely to win larger followings in the future. This is because largely unexamined assumptions of marketers about marketing are now being reconsidered. Kotler predicts that the environmental agenda emerging from this reconsideration of marketing's fundamental assumptions will have a profound effect on marketing theory and practice (Kotler, 2011a, p. 132).

Macromarketing Perspectives on Sustainability

Sustainable development refers to 'meeting the needs of the present without compromising the ability of future generations to meet their own needs' according to the UN's Brundtland Commission formerly known as the UN's World Commission on Environment and Development (WCED, 1987, chapt. 2, sect. 4). An emerging consensus is that the three pillars of sustainability are social, environmental, and economic sustainability (Haugh and Talwar, 2010, p. 385). These correspond to the 'triple bottom line' of people, planet, and profit discussed in Chapter 1.

Schools of Macromarketing Sustainability Thought

Among macromarketing scholars, two schools of thought have emerged about sustainability – the developmental school and the critical school (Prothero and McDonagh, 2020). The developmental school views markets as the most efficient provisioning mechanism for economic growth, human development, and quality of life. Accordingly, questions about sustainability would focus on how existing marketing systems can be improved to provide sustainability to societies. The critical school offers a critique of marketing and what it sees as marketing's inherent dependence on neo liberal ideas of competition in markets as allocating society's resources. Those in the critical school regard exchange as being based too much on the materialism and status needs of consumers. In sum, the developmental school sees markets and marketing as part of the solution for moving toward sustainability, while the critical school sees markets and marketing as part of the problem – moving societies away from sustainability.

The developmental school views marketing systems as improving people's lives. Sustainable consumption can be initiated by consumers because consumers vote with their money in markets. Consequently, the favored versions of their products succeed in markets. This means that producers change their behavior to survive. Also, governments can intervene in markets to provide incentives that would advance the interests of consumers, such as providing tax breaks for renewable energy companies, or corporate average fuel economy targets (CAFÉ) standards for automobile emissions. If the developmental school had a theme song written by the Beatles, it would be 'We Can Work It Out' because this school believes that marketing systems can change and evolve.

By comparison, the critical school views marketing systems as inherently unstable. According to the critical school, markets are inherently unstable because an underlying Dominant Social Paradigm (DSP) influenced the development of marketing systems. In short, the DSP can be characterized by a materialism of 'more is good,' as well as a pragmatic stance toward competitive markets that 'if it works, it must be good'. If the critical school had a theme song written by the Beatles, it would be 'Revolution' because this school believes that nothing short of a radical overhaul of the DSP and its implied goal of wealth accumulation would be needed to change the course of societies.

Currently, consumers in developed countries consume resources well beyond their real needs as part of the materialistic lifestyle, and consumers in lesser developed countries aspire to consume beyond their needs (Ger and Belk, 1996). Longtime macromarketing scholar George Fisk was known to repeat the following question to stir reflection on the implications of the materialistic lifestyle being passed to those in developing countries: 'What are we going to do in twenty years when 500 million Chinese start their cars in the morning to drive to work?' (Fisk, 1997, personal communication).

Fisk's rhetorical question implies an endorsement of the critical school's indictment of the ideology that the meaning of life is to be found in buying things – which undergirds the DSP (Ger, 1997; Kilbourne, McDonagh, and Prothero, 1997). If the DSP does not radically change, marketing systems will ruin the environment. Fisk's forecast for China adopting Western consumption habits proved to be true, in general. After two decades of exponential growth, China had more than 300 million vehicles registered in 2017 (Zheng, 2017). Ten of the 25 most-congested cities in the world are now in China.

Kotler envisions stakeholders will have to accept many difficult changes if companies are to attain sustainability. Environmental sustainability considers the impact of business on (a) the quality and quantity of natural resources, (b) the environment, (c) global warming, (d) ecological concerns, (e) waste management, (f) lowering energy and resource use, (g) renewable energy production, and (h) improved pollution and emissions management (Townsend, 2008). Kotler envisions CEO and senior executive compensation packages as having to change. For example, senior executives must not only have to show economic success but also success in achieving predetermined goals for the company in the eight areas of environmental sustainability.

Can the DSP Be Changed?

The critical school asserts that a radical change needs to be made in the DSP. Although this suggests that a catastrophic climate event might be the precipitating event leading to such a de-valuing of wealth accumulation (Gilding, 2011), another way could be less sudden and more gradual over time. Prothero is one scholar from the critical school who sees the way forward as marketing environmental stewardship as a commodity (Prothero and Fitchett, 2000). In other words, can green become 'cool?' This would imply deemphasizing consumption while emphasizing citizenship (Prothero, McDonagh, and Dobscha, 2010).

The existence of a consumer segment termed 'lifestyles of health and sustainability' (LOHAS, for short) implies that there is a chance that the DSP could be radically changed over time. One estimate of the LOHAS segment suggests that 25 percent of adults in the United States fall into this category or the 'cultural creatives' category (those whose consumption is strongly influenced by values related to environmental concern). Current distinctive consumption for this segment includes (1) organic foods, (2) energy-efficient appliances, (3) alternative medicines, (4) eco-tourism, and (5) 'slow fashion' made with natural and durable materials allowing clothes to last longer (Sung and Woo, 2019).

Recent research suggests that a sustainability discourse in the marketplace and in the media might be moving many toward a more holistic and global perspective (Prothero et al., 2010). In light of the fragility of the world exposed by the coronavirus pandemic in 2020, consumers in the US report they are more likely to buy environmentally friendly products (Dahlhoff, 2020). In a global consumer survey conducted by the Conference Board in 2020, two-thirds of respondents reported buying brands because of the brands' environmental practices, and more than half reported stopping their purchases of brands because of the brands' lack of fair labor conditions. Additionally, the concept of buying local to avoid the carbon emissions incurred in long-distance transportation has begun to be part of consumer thinking. It now is even green and chic to many.

Production for self-use – or prosumption – is increasingly common in places like Australia (Perera, Hewege, and Mai, 2020). Some prosumption activities include: (1) generating free energy from the sun and selling the excess, (2) recycling water and waste to reap financial benefits, (3) sharing mobility, and (4) accessing shared data networks.

Such moves to prosumption give hope that a consumption ideology may emerge that includes carbon neutrality as a focus (Prothero and McDonagh, 2020). However, business could do more to ensure consumption practices do not threaten future generations by supporting innovation and creativity for sustainability. Eliminating the planned obsolescence of products (seen in products that wear out too soon requiring replacement) and switching from a carbon-based economy to a bio-circular one.

The rise of these elements as part of a green commodity discourse suggests that social marketing of an idea, cause, or behavior, might prove to weaken the current DSP and possibly shift cultural norms to a sustainability mindset (Kotler, 2011a, p. 135). In this way, a convergence of the views of the developmental and critical schools of macromarketing might occur. The positive aspect of marketing (the social marketing of environmental stewardship and the demarketing of overconsumption) might save marketing from destroying the very foundation on which it exists, for 'without a habitable natural environment, there will be no quality of life' (Kilbourne et al., 1997, p. 19).

The Two Phases of Business Sustainability

Andrew J. Hoffman is an accomplished scholar at the University of Michigan who holds a joint appointment in Michigan's Ross Business School and the School of Environment and Sustainability. He asserts that there have been two phases of business sustainability (Hoffman, 2018).

Sustainable Business 1.0

The first phase could be called Sustainable Business 1.0 and ran from the 1970s (when government imposed environmental regulations) to about 2018 when Hoffman published his article in the *Stanford Social Innovation Review*. Integrating sustainability practices in firms characterized this phase. In many ways, reducing unsustainability was the focus.

In Sustainable Business 1.0, things changed so that eventually a market shift occurred. In part, this shift came from a change in consumers' increased regard for green products, but also from firms marketing green products that were more appealing and effective. However, these two influences are among many that shifted market conditions.

When a market shifts, asking questions such as 'Will it pay to be green?' becomes irrelevant (Hoffman, 2019). Hoffman asserts that such a question is similar to asking 'does it pay to innovate'. The answer is not simple because it depends on who innovates, what they innovate, when they innovate, and how they do it. Answers to these questions require hard work, along with keen analysis and astute judgement about strategy for the firm. Instead, business leaders would do better to ask (1) what is driving change in the marketplace, and (2) how can I frame the issue so that members of my organization can readily use their skills and abilities to effectively respond to needed change?

Hoffman characterizes four types of drivers that led business to focus on reducing unsustainability during this first phase of business sustainability. Table 8.1 presents the four types of drivers that have moved markets to shift because of pressures to do so: (1) market drivers, (2) resource drivers, (3) social drivers, and (4) coercive drivers. Table 8.1 also features sources of external influence for each of the drivers, as well as how firm leaders could frame the issue using the language of business. For example, market-driven change might be occurring because of consumers. Accordingly, leaders of the firm could frame the issue as related to consumer demand or the need for product development. In another example, resource-driven change might be occurring because of suppliers and buyers. Accordingly, leaders of the firm could frame the issue as related to the need to design a better process. In the case of a firm with child-labor problems among overseas suppliers, members of the firm could design inspection procedures and hire outside inspectors for making unannounced visits in the factories of overseas suppliers. Table 8.1 could be used in a similar manner for analyzing other situations facing firms wanting to integrate more sustainable business practices.

Table 8.1   Drivers, sources of external influence and framing of issue internally for the firm

Driver type	Source of external influence	Framing of issue internally
Market	consumers competitors trade associations consultants	consumer demand, product development strategic direction market growth operational efficiency
Resource	suppliers and buyers banks shareholders and investors insurance firms	process design capital acquisition capital investment risk management
Social	environmental NGOs the press religion academia communities	operational efficiency corporate reputation human resource management
Coercive	courts domestic regulation international regulation	operational efficiency regulatory compliance

Source: Hoffman (2019).

Sustainable Business 2.0

Sustainable Business 2.0 – now, in effect – will be characterized by businesses pursuing innovative ways for transforming markets using innovation across the spectrum of functions business conducts. For example, not only will there be more electric vehicles, but enabling such EVs to power homes when they are parked outside during electrical grid outages will be possible. Alternatively, if one is allowed to recharge one's EV at work for free (or a reduced rate), bidirectional charging vehicles, such as the Nissan Leaf, owners could routinely power their homes from their vehicle (Schmidt, 2019).

Additionally, the possibility of driverless cars, robots, and increased digitization of the analog world holds the promise of bringing sustainability into reality in ways never conceived in the past (Hoffman, 2018). For example, blockchain technology – a distributed ledger system run on the internet – holds the potential to introduce transparency into opaque supply chains that cross international borders. Potentially, blockchain would allow one to see each transaction in a series of transactions in a complex supply chain. In this way, consumers and business could be empowered to conduct more rigorous audits of supply chains to police against labor abuses. Such technology also holds the opportunity to evaluate the mark-up in the price of goods across the supply chain. This could lead to a welcome focus on actual value added by members of a supply chain in negotiations among members of a supply chain in the future. In such ways, Sustainable Business 2.0 will bring about market transformation.

Doing the Right Thing

While Kotler wonders about how sustainability can be made to boost the business prospects for firms, individual actors continue to 'do the right thing' regardless of the short-term economic consequences. No doubt, the emerging discourse favoring environmental stewardship reinforces individual decision-makers to behave more like citizens, rather than like traders of goods and services when confronting environmental issues for the firm. For example, Jay and Jacki Givens have owned Givens Collision Repair Center in Frederick, Maryland, since 1998 (van Schagen, 2011). From the beginning, the Givenses have always been as green as possible, reusing everything they could. They installed special equipment to spray Waterborne products (high-quality, water-based paints that release half the toxins of solvent-based paint products), but they knew they could do more. They recently built a new facility, and eco-minded upgrades, such as strategically placing windows and skylights, and installing high-efficiency heat pumps and insulation, led to remarkable savings.

However, the Givenses were not just motivated by savings of greening their new building. They installed a BaySaver filtration system underground to clean and filter any groundwater leaving their property before it reached the Chesapeake Bay. It was a $185,000 undertaking that will never see a monetary return for the Givens (van Schagen, 2011, p. 66).

'There has definitely been a lot of good that has come out of it that I don't think we'll ever be able to put a dollar figure on,' Jacki said. 'But you've got to lay your head down at night and know that you're doing things the right way – that means a lot to us' (van Schagen, 2011, p. 66).

One of their employees, manager Rex Ransom, explained what installing the water filtration system means to the workers this way: 'I think it's pretty neat … to know that they care enough to make sure that the water that's getting down to the water treatment plant isn't going to affect my kids,' Ransom said. 'They're responsible for 18 people and 18 people's families, and they really take that seriously' (van Schagen, 2011, p. 66).

'We're proud of what we're doing,' Jacki said, 'and we're going to continue to do what we can – not just for us, but for our kids and our grandkids – to move not just our facility but our industry into a greener and cleaner arena' (van Schagen, 2011, p. 66). In their advertising, the Givens now promote their 17,000 square foot state-of-the-art 'Green' facility as the 'shop of choice' to those concerned about the environment (Autobody Alliance, 2020).

The Givens' approach to their business illustrates the three ethical norms in the American Marketing Association's (AMA's) statement of ethics (AMA, 2011). First, Givens Collision and Repair Center seeks to do no harm. In this they deliberately choose to avoid harmful actions, such as releasing unfiltered groundwater leaving their property. This 'beyond compliance' ethic is similar to other firms that have dedicated themselves to stewardship and citizenship. Second, the Givens foster trust in the marketing system. Toward this end, the firm strives for fair dealing and the avoidance of deception in the delivery of the services the firm provides. The savings realized through green processes of their business and the green aspects of their new building relieve the firm from financial pressure that might lead to opportunistic behavior with stakeholders. Finally, the Givens embrace ethical values that nurture relationships with their employees as well as other stakeholders. The six ethical values highlighted in the AMA Statement of Ethics and Norms include (a) honesty, (b) responsibility, (c) fairness, (d) respect, (e) transparency, and (f) citizenship. These are presented in Table 8.2. Such values can serve as a ready starting point for firms' intent on identifying dimensions of their approach to business.

Table 8.2   Ethical values for marketers from the AMA statement of ethics

Honesty	– to be forthright in dealings with customers and stakeholders.
Responsibility	– to accept the consequences of our marketing decisions and strategies.
Fairness	– to balance justly the needs of the buyer with the interests of the seller.
Respect	– to acknowledge the basic human dignity of all stakeholders.
Transparency	– to create a spirit of openness in marketing operations.
Citizenship	– to fulfill the economic, legal, philanthropic, and societal responsibilities that serve stakeholders.

Source: AMA (2011).

Importantly, codes of ethics can become meaningless if the leaders of the firm treat such codes and their underlying ethical values as mere ornaments for a ruthless culture focused on the material success of the firm. Enron, based in Houston, Texas, began as an energy-trading and services firm that rapidly rose to post sales of more than $101 billion in 2000 (McLean and Elkind, 2004). It was cited by *Fortune* as America's Most Innovative Company six times. However, it collapsed and declared bankruptcy in late 2001 because it engaged in purposeful and systematic accounting fraud. More than 20,000 employees lost their jobs. Those employees who had focused their 401k retirement plans on Enron stock lost their retirement savings, too.

The ethical values of Enron displayed in its code of ethics were 'respect, integrity, communication, and excellence'. Although such values are admirable to readers outside the firm, many inside the firm likely interpreted these values to be applicable only for how the employees should treat each other and not necessarily applicable for how the employees should treat those not in the firm. The Enron leadership reinforced a shallow approach to business by posting up-to-the-minute updates of the Enron stock price not only in the lobby of Enron's headquarters but also in the elevators. Such cues made the point that raising the stock price of Enron was to be the unswerving pursuit of all employees in the firm. In the end, the firm's 'profit uber alles' culture – the understanding that profit was more important than anything else – led firm leaders and some Enron employees to commit crimes for the purpose of attaining more success in the marketplace than what Enron had rightfully earned (Wee, 2002).

Citizenship and Stewardship

Several action steps accompany each value in the AMA Statement of Ethics. The first point for action listed under the citizenship value is 'to protect the ecological environment in the execution of marketing campaigns' (AMA, 2011, p. 2, para. 4). Citizenship in this regard is similar to the principle of stewardship as part of enlightened marketing (Laczniak and Murphy, 2006). While citizens have rights, they also have obligations to the wider society (Prothero et al., 2010, p. 153). Stewardship embraces a duty to the common good and responsibility to act for the betterment of the host environment and community. Such duty and responsibility obligates marketers not to impose external costs on society and future generations – especially the physical environment – that would result from marketing operations. McDonald's decision in the early 1990s to eliminate nonbiodegradable polystyrene containers and return to more ecologically friendly – but more expensive – paper packaging is one example of citizenship and stewardship.

The word 'steward' comes from the old English word 'stigweard', which means 'guardian of the house and more specifically, of the farm animals' (Audebrand, 2010, p. 420). The traditional responsibility of the steward to an owner is important, but so are wider obligations to the general public, to future generations, to other species, and to all of the natural world. Stewardship involves not only carefully tending the environment, but guarding and protecting it from harm. Phrases such as 'looking after something', 'being accountable for something', and 'doing something on behalf of someone', are all heard when people discuss stewardship. Stewardship does not imply ownership or final authority regarding what is guarded and protected. In this way, stewards recognize they are embedded in a system and are responsible to someone, to some others, or to something else.

In a notable study of firms committed to triple-bottom-line achievement, the citizenship and stewardship aspects of stakeholder marketing became apparent (Mish and Scammon, 2010). These private firms in the United States have a commitment to simultaneous social, environmental, and economic objectives. Each of these firms have operated for at least two bottom lines (profit and either planet or people) for 15 years and at least three bottom lines for at least 5 years (profit, planet, and people). Eight of the nine firms claimed membership in the Green Business Network (http://greenbusinessnetwork.org), a network of more than 5,000 US businesses that are 'green' in the sense of operating to solve – rather than to cause – social and environmental problems (Green Business Network, 2011). In short, these firms had operated as stewards for many years, so they give a valuable perspective on stewardship.

The leaders of these firms viewed the marketplace as unified in the sense that all actors in the marketplace are interconnected peers. Additionally, these leaders interpret the actions of their firms in relation to all players throughout the entire system. These firms carried a moral stance that their actions should in no way harm the weakest-link stakeholders in the market system, such as the environment or future generations.

Although each firm regarded itself as doing marketing differently from others (such as unilaterally disclosing all nontoxic ingredients on product labels rather than hiding them as 'trade secrets'), each firm committed itself to the interconnectedness of the market system in order to help transform industries and institutional norms. The perception about the interconnectedness of the actors in the market system allowed these firms to generate intelligence about all stakeholders and diffuse this intelligence through the organizational structure of these firms. By viewing their stakeholders as partners or potential partners, these stakeholders became sources of value for the customers of these firms. With this view, stakeholder needs hold implications for system well-being, as well as for the well-being of each actor in the system.

Other research calls firms to recognize that the same stakeholder might be represented in multiple stakeholder groups for the firm (Smith, Drumwright, and Gentile, 2010). For example, a customer might also be a citizen, parent, employee, community member, or person who may one day be healed of a major illness because of a treatment derived from a rare plant in an endangered forest. To avoid a myopic view of the marketplace where only customers or competitors would be in focus (and other stakeholders perceived only in a fuzzy way), firms must move from a market orientation to a stakeholder orientation (Ferrell, et al. 2010). This research suggests that marketers must first map the stakeholders of their firms. Although this can be more difficult than it first appears, stakeholders must be identified beyond generic categories as real people with names and faces. The importance of these stakeholders must be rated, as well as their interconnections.

The Role of Employees

'Sustainability is really about transformation,' IESE (Madrid) Professor Pascual Berrone said (Geller, 2018). 'To truly become green, you'll need organization-wide commitment to change. If you want your sustainability effort to be honest and genuine and to create a positive impact on the environment, then it has to be company-wide, and the commitment has to come from the top.'

The easiest stakeholders to list with names and faces should be the employees of the firm.

For firms pursuing environmental stewardship, the employees' values and principles are like a compass that enables these firms to find their way to new products, new markets, and new internal processes for conducting operations. In a McKinsey survey, CEOs rated employees as the group that has the greatest impact on the way companies manage their societal expectations (Bielak, Bonini, and Oppenheim, 2007). These employees represent an enormous reservoir of talent and energy for building a firm with stewardship ethics of caring for the social, environmental, and economic outcomes of business operations (Yankelovich, 2006).

In most firms that view the environment and future generations as stakeholders, employees are the ones who prove to be instrumental in the process of changing organizational culture. In Chapter 1, Interface, Inc.'s employees asked Ray Anderson to address them on his environmental vision for the company. At that time, Anderson had no vision at all. But the encounter with his employees set him on a course of deep reflection that eventually led to Anderson's 'mid-course correction' to join his employees in leading his company to climb 'Mt. Sustainability' (Anderson, 2009).

Values typically become more important for the firm in uncertain times because they orient employees on all levels to the firm's abiding priorities, such as its social purpose. Research on small firms in the technology sector suggests that when uncertainty in the external environment increases, owner-managers increase their engagement with employees. This, in turn, results in improved performance (Sawyerr, McGee, and Peterson, 2003). Notably, this study found no such role for external networking as it did for internal networking of the owner-managers of these firms.

New Belgium Brewing Company's Employees

Values-centered entrepreneurs who embrace a mission of being socially responsible in the manner of Conscious Capitalism (discussed in Chapter 4), tend to work with employees in a more egalitarian way than traditional firms. For example, New Belgium Brewery, which makes Fat Tire Beer, practices open-book management and trains all employees in financial literacy so that they can read the firm's financial books in a more meaningful manner (Choi and Gray, 2011).

Although salary information for employees is aggregated so individuals' salaries cannot be directly known, all other financial information can be accessed by any employee through the accounting department. New Belgium also includes all of its employees in strategy development, budgeting, and departmental planning. It takes time, but integration of employees in the management life of the company results in a high-involvement culture.

New Belgium first came to life in the basement of founders Jeff Lebesch and Kim Jordan in 1991 (Bradley, 2019). In 2001, Jordan – then the remaining CEO after Lebesch departed earlier, sold the firm to its employees through an employee stock ownership plan (ESOP). This led to employees taking responsibility for suggesting cost reductions, such as those of Doug Miller who runs the loading dock at the Fort Collins brewery. When Miller encounters an overnight shipment being sent out from the loading docks, he will find the employee sending the shipment and convince this person to use a less expensive form of delivery. 'Dude, this is $100 to get it there tomorrow,' Miller said. 'Or it's there a few days later, and it's $8.' At New Belgium, employees like Miller think like an owner of the firm – because they are.

New Belgium brewery employees in Fort Collins, Colorado

Source: Furnari (2016).

Citing environmental activist Guy Dauncey (www.earthfuture.com), the leaders of the firm believe that 'if it's not fun, it's not sustainable' (Moses, 2011, p. 1). New Belgium's original Belgian-type beer is called Fat Tire, which refers to a wide-tired bicycle used by Lebesch when he traveled through Belgium to research beer formulas. Bonding between the firm and its employees is reinforced by the firm presenting each employee with a cruiser bicycle after one year of service. After five years of service, employees celebrate with a company-funded trip to Belgium. In these ways, New Belgium provides meaningful ways to connect emotionally with New Belgium as the core element of a brand community (Sartain and Schumann, 2006).

The firm cites its organizational culture as the most important and transferrable tool to drive sustainability. 'We have tried to make our relationship with our co-workers – in terms of running the business – very transparent,' co-founder and CEO Kim Jordan said. 'I think that's a foundational piece of who we are' (Choi and Gray, 2011, p. 74). To Jordan, transparency means shining a light on the firm's successes as well as on its shortcomings, so that stakeholders can be the judge of New Belgium's authenticity – how its actions match the things the firm says about itself (Jordan, 2007). In its 2007 Sustainability Report, New Belgium's sustainability director admitted that an aggrieved ex-employee rightly accused the firm of incorrectly using the phrase '100 percent wind-powered' when natural gas provided over half the energy needed to make beer at the firm (Orgolini, 2007).

New Belgium's transparency is also evident in the four-page Annual Summary of New Belgium's Sustainable Business Story made publicly available on the firm's website (New Belgium, 2010). This summary presents (a) New Belgium's values-driven commerce, (b) its high-involvement culture, (c) its philanthropy, (d) its environmental impact, and (e) its recent accomplishments in sustainability. Although including technical detail (similar to the nonfinancial reporting of other sustainability-oriented firms, such as Denmark-based healthcare company Novo Nordisk), the summary is made 'fun' by the graphic design and tone of the writing. The founders of New Belgium sought to make profits not despite their triple-bottom-line approach (people, planet, and profits), but because of it. Integrating servant leadership concepts into the conduct of operations at 'the Mothership' – the employees' term for the brewery in Fort Collins, Colorado – managers strive to empower employees to make the very best product.

Together, everyone 'figures out the future' (New Belgium, 2007). However, there are limits to open-book management and a degree of hierarchy is needed in any business (Bradley, 2019). CEO Jordan had to pound her fist on a conference room table to force the brewers at New Belgium to make an IPA beer. There had been resistance to doing this because an IPA is not a Belgian beer.

The firm captures waste methane from its process water treatment plant and burns this to generate electricity for running its brewery and offices, resulting in saving $60,000 in electricity expenses in 2009 (New Belgium, 2010). This closed-loop approach is one aspect of New Belgium's operation. Using this approach, the firm pursues a 'cradle-to-cradle' route to eco-effectiveness by designing things intelligently so they are not useless at the end of their lives (McDonough and Braungart, 2002). Their products and their components can be used again and again with zero waste.

New Belgium offers a rich example of a values-driven enterprise that celebrates the community aspect of working for a common purpose in business (Yankelovich, 2006). With its high-involvement culture, New Belgium attracts employees that do not want to be hired from the neck down. Such employees become 'highly empowered and resourceful operatives: HEROs for short' (Bernoff and Schadler, 2010, p. 10). In other words, such employees are ready to join a collaborative community according the highest value to people who look beyond their specific roles to make marginal contributions that boost the common purpose of the firm (Adler, Heckscher, and Prusak, 2011). At New Belgium, Don Rich and Marc Finer figured out that the cardboard dividers between bottles were not needed in 12-unit packages of Fat Tire beer. The triple-bottom-line savings were (a) more than $280,000 for the cost of the dividers, (b) 150 tons of paperboard for the dividers, and (c) eliminating the leading cause of downtime in packing the product – the dividers. In the Annual Summary of New Belgium's Sustainable Business Story, it was noted that 'Marc and Don got at least a few high fives in the hallway for this one' (New Belgium, 2010, p. 1).

Today, jobs at any firm require increasingly higher levels of discretionary effort. Such effort takes an extra degree of initiative, and this depends on employee commitment. Before World War II, only 18 percent of jobs could be classified as high-discretion jobs (Yankelovich, 2006, p. 112). The rest were characterized by routine. By 1982, discretionary jobs accounted for 43 percent of jobs, and in 2000 they accounted for 62 percent of jobs. For jobs that cannot be outsourced or automated, many of the remaining jobs call for high levels of commitment. Values-driven firms such as New Belgium position themselves well for the future. In 2008, a *National Geographic* survey of more than 80 percent of US workers polled agreed that it was important to work for a company or organization that makes the environment a top priority (Kaufield, Malhotra, and Higgins, 2009).

Branding New Belgium from the Inside Out

In *Cultural Strategy: Using Innovative Ideologies to Build Breakthrough Brands*, authors Douglas Holt and Douglas Cameron featured New Belgium as a case study in how brands are more of a phenomenom of society and culture than they are of the mind's conception of tangible and emotional benefits (Holt and Cameron, 2010). Holt and Cameron served as consultants to the firm during the development of the firm's first (and probably last, according to the authors) television advertising campaign.

After spending an enormous time at the brewery, the pair of consultants noted that few of the brewery employees were active participants in the mountain outdoor adventure subculture, even though *Outdoor* magazine had included New Belgium as one of the best places to work in 2010 (Roberts, 2010). New Belgium's founders were both professionals (Jeff an electrical engineer and Kim a social worker) who had given up their careers to pursue an avocation they loved regardless of where it took them (Holt and Cameron, 2010). To Jeff and Kim, much fun came from experimenting with beer styles and improvising beer equipment. Very few of the staff were trained professionally for their jobs, and the founders liked it this way. For example, the COO joined the company as a graduate student in philosophy. In sum, the cultural assets of the company were (a) a company of creative amateurs, (b) pastoral organization of a family, and (c) the single-speed cruiser that represented human-scaled technology that had not been overpowered by other technology.

Kim Jordan, one of New Belgium's founders and current CEO, describes her experience with the firm in the following way:

> What could be greater than a job where you get to think about and talk about and co-create a brand with people? And for me, brand is absolutely everything we are. It's the people here. It's how we interact with one another. And then there's the other piece of that creativity, obviously – designing beers. Not only do I get to play with scissors and crayons, but I get to sit with a group of incredibly creative people and talk about what kind of beers do we want to make that please us and will please our customers.
>
> (Jordan, 2010)

Holt and Cameron steered New Belgium's advertising campaign toward presenting the essence of New Belgium – amateurs who brewed beer for the joy of doing it. Such amateurs worked in a place where new things happened most days and everyone was encouraged to create some fun during the day. For example, the firm has a mountain biking course on site and employees are encouraged to use it before and after work, as well as during lunchtime. By comparison, the target group for the advertising campaign were beer drinkers on the West Coast whose work lives were typical of many working in office cubicles where the technology of e-mail and voice mail had intensified the pace of the day and kept them from what they yearned to do – constructing the self through creative acts:

> Our creative challenge was to devise a pastoral call to arms, calling out to [trapped white collar workers] in Seattle, Silicon Valley, Santa Monica, San Diego, and points beyond, allowing them to dream a bit that they too might someday have a chance to give it all for their avocation rather than their 8-to-8 job.
>
> (Holt and Cameron, 2010, p. 237)

In the end, Holt and Cameron came up with a call-to-arms declaration of 'Follow Your Folly: Ours Is Beer.' In this way, the campaign proposed that the community of New Belgium were part of a movement of fellow travelers who were enjoying a quality of life very appealing to what David Brooks terms 'Bourgeois Bohemians' (or Bobos – the knowledge workers of today's educated class) (Brooks, 2000). The two ads focused on an engineer who dropped out of the rat race to make single-speed bicycles by hand in a mountain town.

In this way, the downshifting to a higher quality of life became the crucial association for New Belgium beer. The ad campaign was run for 14 weeks as an experiment in five markets of the Western United States where sales results were later compared with five markets where the ad campaign did not run. Sales increased 37 percent where the ad campaign ran compared with 2 percent where it did not (Holt and Cameron, 2010, p. 242). In short, the campaign inspired by the organizational culture of New Belgium proved to be a major success as a result of customers who wanted an accessible way to connect with the cultural expression represented by the New Belgium brand.

In the end, New Belgium's story represents a firm push away from the materialistic, 'more-growth' ideology of the DSP. 'What is wealth?' New Belgium sustainability specialist Katie Wallace said. 'Is it bling or is it being outdoors in a clear environment, organic food from farmers you know and having lower obesity in schools? We are not just here for more cash and bigger houses. We are here for quality of life' (Wallace, 2009).

The End of Employee-Ownership at New Belgium

After co-founding New Belgium in 1991, Jordan sold the firm to its employees in 2001 through an employee stock ownership plan (ESOP) and stayed as CEO. The median salary of New Belgium workers in 2019 was $65,000 and the ratio of CEO pay to that of the average employee was less than 10:1 (compared to other firms where the ratio averages 400:1) (Bradley, 2019).

The ESOP served as a vehicle to function as a retirement account for employees, in essence. With growing firms, the shares of ownership increase in value along with the rise in the value of the firm.

However, the New Belgium Brewery employees voted on December 17, 2019 to accept Japanese beverage-giant Kirin's sales offer (Ferrier, 2019a). Accordingly, New Belgium will no longer be an employee-owned firm.

In the short term, this means a windfall for more than 300 employees who will receive '$100,000 of retirement money, with some receiving significantly greater amounts' according to New Belgium co-founder and former CEO Kim Jordan. New Belgium employs about 700 in Fort Collins, Colorado and Asheville, North Carolina.

The sale eased financial stress for New Belgium due to its establishment of a brewing facility in North Carolina in 2015 at the end of a 217 percent surge in the number of craft

New Belgium Brewery co-founder and former CEO Kim Jordan

Source: New Belgium Brewery.

breweries across the US from 2005 to 2015 (Carley and Yahng, 2018). Other factors contributing to a lack of growth for New Belgium included consumers in larger numbers choosing hard seltzers and ultrapremium beers (Bradley, 2019). In short, the current value of the firm and the shares of stock in the firm owned by employees had stalled. The employees voted to cash in their stock through the sale to Kirin.

However, the whimsy of New Belgium's branding now becomes tinged by the associations of Kirin – owner of a stake in Myanmar Brewing along with co-owner Myanmar Economic Holdings Limited (MEHL). MEHL is a military conglomerate led by commander-in-chief Min Aung Hlaing of Myanmar who is accused of leading a military-backed genocide and ethnic cleansing against Rohingya Muslims on the west side of Myanmar (pushing them into neighboring Bangladesh). Human Rights groups in the US – Karen Community of North Carolina and Karen Organization of America (both representing the Karen ethnic minority from Myanmar in the US) – wrote a letter to New Belgium employees asking them to 'stand for human rights and justice' and vote against the sale of New Belgium to Kirin because of the rape and murder involved in the pogrom against Rohingya Muslims (Ferrier, 2019b).

The sale means that control of New Belgium will no longer be local. While Jordan insists that the brand and its employees stand for quality in beer, nevertheless, decisions about New Belgium's direction and corporate priorities will now be the responsibility of Lion Little

World Beverage based in Australia – a subsidiary of Kirin. Whereas in the past, competitive strategy and staffing decisions for New Belgium originated and were made in Fort Collins, now approval needs to be given from Australia (and eventually Japan). In a positive sense, Lion Little management and Kirin might provide market and operational knowledge that New Belgium did not have before the sale.

Corporate takeovers typically involve some negative effects for local communities including (1) loss of civic leadership, (2) reduction in local philanthropy, (3) fewer jobs, and (4) diversion of investment to other locales (Brunell, 2006). Time will tell how the sale affects New Belgium's culture (for example, its past priority given to sustainable business practices), as well as its competitiveness.

Questions

- What consumer phenomenon is driving the growth of craft breweries?
- Do you think the sale of New Belgium Brewery is a good thing? For which stakeholders? Be specific – for example, which employees?
- Do you think the sale of New Belgium Brewery is a bad thing? For which stakeholders? Be specific – for example, the local community of Fort Collins or Asheville, North Carolina?
- How would a sustained human rights campaign protesting Kirin's involvement in Myanmar affect a sustainability-oriented brand, such as New Belgium?

CONCLUSION

This chapter discussed some of the major issues related to the environmental imperative for societies. Because of an absorption with 'little m' issues regarding more profitable marketing practices for the firm without regard to externalities, marketing scholars are just now beginning to give attention to the profoundly important topic of the environmental imperative. Pope Francis has already shared his thoughts about environmental degradation and he is not pleased about it. 'Whatever is fragile, like the environment, is defenseless before the interest of a deified market, which becomes the only rule,' Pope Francis said (Pope Francis, 2015, p. 17). 'By itself, the market cannot guarantee integral human development and social inclusion' (Pope Francis, 2015, p. 32).

Two schools in macromarketing have debated important questions related to the environmental imperative over the years. Those in the developmental school of macromarketing believed marketing systems could be changed. Opposing this view were scholars in the critical school who believed the culture of consumption must be radically altered if environmental degradation were to cease. A crucial question of this dialectic of opposing schools of thought is as follows: 'Can societies shift to a less materialistic and less status-seeking foundation and accept less consumption?' This question persists today, although there are signs that the culture of consumption can be changed by none other than marketing itself – in the form of social marketing and the desirability of 'going green'.

In the course of business operations, decisions must be made that have ethical aspects. In fact, ethical issues dominate board meetings, but most of them come back to the notion of corporate culture (Mendonca and Miller, 2007). Although the firm might meet legal compliance on an issue, those in the firm must answer whether the courses of action being considered are honorable and whether they serve the public good. Ethics of citizenship and stewardship orient those in the firm to consider obligations to others and to society that go beyond self-interest. In this way, enlightened self-interest can be pursued.

Employees form the fabric from which the firm is woven. Engaged employees who bring their best to the enterprise and commit themselves to solve the problems entailed in 'figuring out the future' are increasingly indispensable to success. Values-driven firms pursing a triple-bottom-line not only attract talented workers but also can become committed employees to the purpose of these firms. New Belgium Brewing Company's story highlights how branding can be done from the inside with employees defining the organizational culture and then the values of this culture infusing advertising for the brand. However, market forces have led New Belgium to sell the firm to Japan's Kirin Holdings Co.

QUESTIONS

- Explain what is meant by 'the Age of Transparency'.
- Go to www.scorecard.org and find out how two places you have lived rate on air and water quality. Who are the major polluters for these places?
- Regarding marketing systems and the environment, do you tend to agree more with the developmental school of macromarketing or the critical school? Explain.
- To what extent do you believe companies, firms, and consumer/citizens can voluntarily downshift from a highly materialistic quantity-of-life approach to living to one focused more on quality of life?
- What would it take to see a noticeable shift?
- What aspects of New Belgium's story appeal to you? What aspects of working for New Belgium would you want to know more about before going to work there?
- In your own life, if you really 'followed your folly' as suggested by New Belgium's advertising, what would you do? What would it take to continue pursuing this as your long-term vocation or avocation?

Mavericks Who Made It

Greta Thunberg

Source: Image courtesy of Anders Hellberg via WikiCommons. Shared under the CC BY-SA 4.0 license.

In August 2018, at the age of 15, Greta Thunberg began spending her school days protesting inaction on climate change outside the Swedish parliament building in Stockholm. This came after two years of trying to persuade her parents to reduce the family's carbon footprint with mixed results. Her mother, Melena Ernman, an internationally known opera singer, did stop flying to reduce her carbon footprint – thereby giving up her career (Crouch, 2018).

'Greta forced us to change our lives,' says her father Svante. 'I didn't have a clue about the climate. We started looking into it, reading all the books – she has read them too. She is supposed to be in school, we cannot support her action. But we respect that she wants to make a stand. She can either sit at home and be really unhappy, or protest and be happy.'

Greta has Asperger's syndrome – a form of autism. However, she views her condition not as a disability but as a gift – what she calls her superpower – which has helped her realize the urgency of the climate crisis. Each day, Thunberg would sit quietly on the sidewalk outside the parliament in the middle of Stockholm. She would hand out leaflets asserting 'I am doing this because you adults are shitting on my future.'

'The best thing about my protest has been to see how more and more people have been coming and getting involved,' Thunberg said.

Did they ever. In the following months, her School Strike for Climate (also known as Fridays for Future, Youth for Climate, Climate Strike or Youth Strike for Climate) was taken up by other like-minded students around the world. (See https://globalclimatestrike.net/.) Thunberg shifted to taking every Friday as a strike day and coined the term 'Friday for Future' which inspired other school students around the world to join her. In May 2019, organizers executed around 2,200 strikes in 125 countries. In September 2019, there were 4,500 strikes across 150 countries – with more than four million protesters in Germany, 1 million in Italy and several hundred thousand in Canada (Barclay and Resnick, 2019). More than four million joined the global climate strike on September 20, 2019 (Alter, Haynes and Worland, 2019).

'We can't just continue living as if there was no tomorrow, because there is a tomorrow,' Thunberg said. 'That is all we are saying.'

By the end of 2019, Thunberg had addressed heads of state at the UN, met the Pope, and had been named *Time's* Person of the Year for 2019 (meaning she represented a momentous turn in the world's thinking that year). Some have likened her to Joan of Arc, the fifteenth-century peasant girl who reported seeing visions of saints who instructed her to join and inspire the French armies attempting to evict the English from France (Pernoud and Clin, 1999). Joan became canonized as a saint – but only after being betrayed and burned at the stake by some traitorous leaders of the French.

Thunberg doesn't like crowds and speaks in a direct manner (Alter, Haynes, and Worland, 2019). She is not distracted by the celebrity of herself or others, and she cannot be flattered. She also looks much younger than her age with her two braided pigtails standing about 1.5 meters (5 feet). But these features of Thunberg have helped vault her to become a global sensation.

'I want you to panic,' she told CEOs and world leaders at the World Economic Forum in Davos, Switzerland in January 2019. 'I want you to feel the fear I feel every day. And then I want you to act.'

The next year at the 2020 World Economic Forum, she called for an immediate end to investments in oil and gas extraction and move to zero emissions – not in 2030 or 2050, but right now (Carmichael, 2020). Because she condemns nuclear power, and because energy consumption goes with economic development, she appears to be calling for a no-growth future for the economies of the world – much like the Critical Marketing School.

'People are suffering,' Thunberg said angrily at the UN Climate Summit in September 2019 (YouTube, 2019). 'People are dying. Entire ecosystems are collapsing. We are in the beginning of a mass extinction and all you can talk about is money and fairy tales of eternal economic growth.'

Michael Shellenberger, a self-proclaimed environmental humanist as opposed to an environmental alarmist, responded later to Thunberg's scolding (Shellenberger, 2020). 'And yet it was economic growth that lifted Thunberg's ancestors out of agrarian poverty, raised life expectancy from 40 to 70 years, and liberated women and girls from feudal patriarchy. Without Sweden's economic growth and the fossil fuels upon which it depended, the person who is Greta Thunberg would not exist.'

Questions

- How do you explain the sudden fame of Greta Thunberg?
- Thunberg's views align with those of macromarketing's Critical Marketers discussed in the chapter with opposition to continued economic growth. How does her story help you better understand critical marketing? Explain.
- Thunberg has served as a speaker at rallies sponsored by the UK's Extinction Rebellion (XR) which advocates painful disruption to the flow of everyday living (by setting up roadblocks and damaging property) in order to focus attention on XR's no-growth proposals. Is this a good thing for Thunberg?
- What do you predict for Thunberg's future in the next 10 years?

REFERENCES

Adler, P., Heckscher, C., and Prusak, L. (2011, July–August). Building a collaborative enterprise. *Harvard Business Review*, 95–101.

Alter, C., Haynes, S., and Worland, J. (2019). Time 2019 Person of the year – Greta Thunberg, *Time*, December 23, 2019. Accessed at https://time.com/person-of-the-year-2019-greta-thunberg/

American Marketing Association (AMA). (2011). Statement of ethics. Retrieved from www.marketingpower.com

Anderson, R.C. (2009). *Confessions of a radical industrialist: Profits, people, purpose – doing business by respecting the earth.* New York, NY: St. Martin's Press.

Audebrand, L.K. (2010). Sustainability in strategic management education: The quest for new root metaphors. *Academy of Management Learning and Business*, 9(5), 413–28.

Autobody Alliance. (2020). Givens Collision Repair Center. Accessed at www.autobodyalliance.com/shop/givens-collision-repair-center/

Barclay, E., and Resnick, B. (2019). How big was the global climate strike? 4 million people, activists estimate. *Vox*, September 22, 2019. Accessed at www.vox.com/energy-and-environment/2019/9/20/20876143/climate-strike-2019-september-20-crowd-estimate

Barringer, F. (2008). Personal communication with author during visit to the University of Wyoming.

Ben & Jerry's. (2020). Our history. Accessed at www.benjerry.com/values/issues-we-care-about

Bernoff, J., and Schadler, T. (2010). *Empowered: Unleash your employees, energize your customers and transform your business.* Boston, MA: Harvard Business School Press.

Bielak, D., Bonini, S.M.J., and Oppenheim, J.M. (2007, October). CEOs on strategy and social issues. *The McKinsey Quarterly*, 1–8.

Bradley, R. (2019). New Belgium Brewery's employees think like owners. Because they are. *Fast Company*, October 18, 2019. Accessed at www.fastcompany.com/90411668/new-belgium-brewerys-employees-think-like-owners-because-they-are

Bradsher, K., and Barboza, D. (2006, June 6). Pollution from Chinese coal casts a global shadow. *The New York Times*. Retrieved from www.nytimes.com

Brooks, D. (2000). *Bobos in paradise: The new upper class and how they got there.* New York, NY: Simon & Schuster Paperbacks.

Brunell, R.M. (2006). The social costs of mergers: Restoring local control as a factor in merger policy. *NCL Review.*, 85, 149.

Carley, S., and Yahng, L. (2018). Willingness-to-pay for sustainable beer. *PloS one*, 13(10), doi: 10.1371/journal.pone.0204917.

Carmichael, B. (2020). Greta Thunberg is a bigger threat to the world with her ill-informed climate change ideology than Donald Trump – Bill Carmichael. *The Yorkshire Post*,

January 24, 2020. Accessed at www.yorkshirepost.co.uk/news/opinion/columnists/greta-thunberg-bigger-threat-world-her-ill-informed-climate-change-ideology-donald-trump-bill-carmichael-1743766

Choi, D.Y., and Gray, E.R. (2011). *Values-centered entrepreneurs and their companies*. New York, NY: Routledge.

Conick, H. (2018). Philip Kotler, the father of modern marketing, will never retire, American Marketing Association. Accessed at www.ama.org/marketing-news/philip-kotler-the-father-of-modern-marketing-will-never-retire/

Crouch, D. (2018). The Swedish 15-year-old who's cutting class to fight the climate crisis. *The Guardian*, September 1, 2018. Accessed at www.theguardian.com/science/2018/sep/01/swedish-15-year-old-cutting-class-to-fight-the-climate-crisis.

Dahlhoff, D. (2020). Companies will have to get creative to advance sustainability amid crisis. *strategy+business*, May 19, 2020. Accessed at www.strategy-business.com/blog/Companies-will-have-to-get-creative-to-advance-sustainability-amid-crisis?gko=88f92

Delmas, M.A., and Burbano, V.C. (2011). The drivers of greenwashing. *California Management Review*, 54(1), 64–87.

Diamond, J. (2005). *Collapse: How societies choose to fail or succeed*. New York, NY: Penguin Books.

Fatsecret. (2020). Ben & Jerry's chocolate chip cookie dough ice cream. Fatsecret. Accessed at www.fatsecret.com/calories-nutrition/ben-and-jerrys/chocolate-chip-cookie-dough-icecream

Ferrell, O.C., Gonzalez-Padron, T.L., Hult, T.M., and Maignan, I. (2010). From market orientation to stakeholder orientation. *Journal of Public Policy and Marketing*, 29(1), 93–6.

Ferrier, P. (2019a). End of an era: New Belgium employees OK brewery's sale to international conglomerate. *Fort Collins Coloradan*, December 17, 2019. Accessed at www.coloradoan.com/story/money/2019/12/17/new-belgium-kirin-sale-gets-approved-employee-vote/2668575001/

Ferrier, P. (2019b). Human rights groups tell New Belgium to reject sale to Kirin, citing Myanmar genocide links. *Fort Collins Coloradan*, December 13, 2019. Accessed at www.coloradoan.com/story/money/2019/12/13/new-belgium-sale-kirin-raises-questions-link-myanmar-genocide/4386027002/

FTC. (2020). Green Guides. Federal Trade Commission. Accessed at www.ftc.gov/news-events/media-resources/truth-advertising/green-guides

Fisk, G. (1997). Personal communication with the author during visit to the University of Texas at Arlington.

Furnari, C. (2016). New Belgium Founder Vows to Remain Independent Amide Rumors of Sale. *Brewbound*. August 3, 2016. Accessed at www.brewbound.com/news/new-belgium-founder-vows-remain-independent-amid-rumors-sale

Geller, L.W. (2018). Getting beyond greenwashing. *sustainability+business*, September 24, 2018. Accessed at www.strategy-business.com/article/Getting-Beyond-Greenwashing?gko=22d3a

Ger, G. (1997). Human development and humane consumption: Well-being beyond the 'good life'. *Journal of Public Policy and Marketing*, 16(1), 110–25.

Ger, G., and Belk, R.W. (1996). Cross-cultural differences in materialism. *Journal of Economic Psychology*, 17(1), 55–77.

Gilding, P. (2011). *The great disruption: Why the climate crisis will bring on the end of shopping and the birth of a new world*. New York, NY: Bloomsbury Press.

Green Business Network. (2011). Green Business Network. Retrieved from http://greenbusinessnetwork.org/

Hackley, C. (2009). *Marketing: A critical introduction*. Thousand Oaks, CA: Sage.

Haugh, H.M., and Talwar, A. (2010). How do corporations embed sustainability across the organization? *Academy of Management Learning and Education*, 9(3), 384–96.

Hoffman, A.J. (2018). The next phase of business sustainability. *Stanford Social Innovation Review*, 16(2), 34–9.

Hoffman, A.J. (2019). Note on business sustainability as a market shift. WDI Publishing, William Davidson Institute (WDI) at the University of Michigan. Conceptual note 2–501–315.

Holman, J. and Buckley, T. (2020). I scream, you scream, we all scream for social, economic, and environmental justice. *Bloomberg Businessweek*, July 27, 2020, 34–39.

Holt, D., and Cameron, D. (2010). *Cultural strategy: Using innovative ideologies to build breakthrough brands*. Oxford, UK: Oxford University Press.

Jordan, K. (2007). Letter from the CEO. *New Belgium Brewing Company 2007 Sustainability Report*. Retrieved from www.newbelgium.com

Jordan, K. (2010). Our joy ride – Kim (video). Retrieved from www.newbelgium.com/culture/jobs.aspx

Kahn, J., and Yardley, J. (2007, August 26). As China roars, pollution reaches deadly extremes. *The New York Times*. Retrieved from www.nytimes.com

Kaufield, R., Malhotra, A., and Higgins, S. (2009, December 21). Green is a strategy. *strategy+business*. Retrieved from www.strategy-business.com

Kilbourne, W., McDonagh, P., and Prothero, A. (1997, Spring). Sustainable consumption and the quality of life: A macromarketing challenge to the dominant social paradigm. *Journal of Macromarketing*, 4–24.

Kotler, P. (2011a). Reinventing marketing to manage the environmental imperative. *Journal of Marketing*, 75, 132–5.

Kotler, P. (2011b, April 30). How I do it. *Marketing News*, 34.

Laczniak, G., and Murphy, P. (2006). Normative perspectives for ethical and socially responsible marketing. *Journal of Macromarketing*, 26(2), 154–177.

McDonough, W., and Braungart, M. (2002). *Cradle to cradle: Remaking the way we make things*. New York, NY: North Point Press.

McKenna, J. (2016). Pope Francis says destroying the environment is a sin. *The Guardian*, September 1, 2016. Accessed at www.theguardian.com/world/2016/sep/01/pope-francis-calls-on-christians-to-embrace-green-agenda

McLean, B., and Elkind, P. (2004). *The smartest guys in the room: The amazing rise and scandalous fall of Enron*. New York, NY: Portfolio Trade.

Mendez, L. (2020). Greenwashing is real – here's how to avoid it. *Architectural Digest*, May 7, 2020. Accessed at www.architecturaldigest.com/story/greenwashing-and-sustainable-brands.

Mendonca, L.T., and Miller, M. (2007). Exploring business's social contract: An interview with Daniel Yankelovich, *The McKinsey Quarterly*. Retrieved from www.mckinsey-quarterly.com

Meyer, C., and Kirby, J. (2010, April). Leadership in the age of transparency. *Harvard Business Review*, 38–46.

Mish, J., and Scammon, D.L. (2010). Principle-based stakeholder marketing: Insights from private triple-bottom-line firms. *Journal of Public Policy and Marketing*, 29(1), 12–26.

Moses, S. (2011). New Belgium Brewery: If it's not fun, it's not sustainable. *Commute by Bike*. Retrieved from www.commutebybike.com/2011/07/15/new-belgium-brewery-if-its-not-fun-its-not-sustainable/

New Belgium. (2007). 2007 Sustainability Report: New Belgium Brewing Company. Retrieved from www.newbelgium.com

New Belgium. (2010). Annual summary of New Belgium's sustainable business story. Retrieved from www.newbelgium.com

Nordhaus, T., and Shellenberger, M. (2007). *Breakthrough: From the death of environmentalism to the politics of possibility*. Boston, MA: Houghton Mifflin.

NRDC. (2011). Natural Resources Defense Council. Retrieved from www.nrdc.org

Orgolini, J. (2007). Letter from the sustainability director. New Belgium Brewing Company 2007 Sustainability Report. Retrieved from www.newbelgium.com

Perera, C.R., Hewege, C.R., and Mai, C.V. (2020). Theorising the emerging green prosumer culture and profiling green prosumers in the green commodities market. *Journal of Consumer Behaviour*, 19(4), doi: 10.1002/cb.1807.

Pernoud, R., and Clin, N.V. (1999). *Joan of Arc: Her Story*. Palgrave Macmillan.

Pope Francis. (2015). Encyclical letter Laudato Si' of the Holy Father Francis on care for our common home. Accessed at www.vatican.va/content/francesco/en/encyclicals/documents/papa-francesco_20150524_enciclica-laudato-si.html

Prothero, A., and Fitchett, J.A. (2000). Greening capitalism: Opportunities for a green community. *Journal of Macromarketing*, 20(1), 46–55.

Prothero, A., and McDonagh, P. (2020). Ambiguity of purpose and the politics of failure: Sustainability as macromarketing's compelling political calling. *Journal of Macromarketing*.

Prothero, A., McDonagh, P., and Dobscha, S. (2010). Is green the new black? Reflections on a green commodity discourse. *Journal of Macromarketing*, 30(2), 147–59.

Regeneration Vermont. (2020a). Ben & Jerry's legal bedfellows: From big tobacco to Monsanto. May 2, 2020. Accessed at https://regenerationvermont.org/ben-jerrys-legal-bedfellows-from-big-tobacco-to-monsanto/

Regeneration Vermont. (2020b). Ben & Jerry's – 20 years of greenwashing. Accessed at https://regenerationvermont.org/20-years-of-greenwashing/

Roberts, M. (2010). Outdoor's 2010 best places to work. Retrieved from www.outsidetelevision.com/shows/outside-today/new-belgium-brewing

Sartain, L., and Schumann, M. (2006). *Brand from the inside: Eight essentials to emotionally connect your employees to your business*. San Francisco, CA: Jossey-Bass.

Sawyerr, O., McGee, J., and Peterson, M. (2003). Perceived uncertainty and firm performance in SMEs: The role of personal networking activities. *International Small Business Journal*, 21(3), 269–90.

Schmidt, B. (2019). Nissan sees Leaf as home energy source, says Tesla big battery 'waste of resources'. *The Driven*, July 11, 2019. Accessed at https://thedriven.io/2019/07/11/nissan-sees-leaf-as-home-energy-source-says-tesla-big-battery-waste-of-resources/

Shellenberger, M. (2020). New documentary film, 'Juice,' challenges elitism of anti-growth environmentalism. *Forbes*, August 7, 2020. Accessed at www.forbes.com/sites/michaelshellenberger/2020/08/07/new-documentary-film-juice-challenges-elitism-of-anti-growth-environmentalism/#459890ea5669

Smith, N.C., Drumwright, M.E., and Gentile, M.C. (2010, Spring). The new marketing myopia. *Journal of Public Policy and Marketing*, 29(1), 4–11.

Sung, J., and Woo, H. (2019). Investigating male consumers' lifestyle of health and sustainability (LOHAS) and perception toward slow fashion. *Journal of Retailing and Consumer Services*, 49, 120–8.

SustainLane.com. (n.d.). Home Page. Retrieved from www.sustainlane.com/

Townsend, C.R. (2008). *Ecological applications: Towards a sustainable world*. Oxford, UK: Blackwell.

Truth in Advertising. (2020). Earth day 2020: Companies accused of greenwashing. *Truth in Advertising*, April 17, 2020. Accessed at www.truthinadvertising.org/six-companies-accused-greenwashing/

van Schagen, S. (2011, April). Driving change: Family-owned collision repair shop going green. *The Costco Connection*, 66.

Wallace, K. (2009, April 9). Presentation at Sustainable Business Practices Forum. University of Wyoming.

WCED. (1987). *Our common future*. UN Commission on Environment and Development. Retrieved from www.un-documents.net/ocf-02.htm#I

Weaver-Zercher, V. (2010, January). The afterlife of trash. *Sojourners*, 30–2.

Wee, H. (2002, April 11). Corporate ethics: Right makes might. *BusinessWeek*. Retrieved from http://www.businessweek.com

Yankelovich, D. (2006). *Profit with honor: The next stage of market capitalism*. New Haven, CT: Yale University Press.

YouTube. (2019). Emotional Greta Thunberg attacks world leaders: 'How dare you?' Accessed at www.youtube.com/watch?v=xVlRompc1yE

Zheng, S. (2017). China now has over 300 million vehicles...that's almost American's total population. *South China Morning Post*, April 19, 2017. Accessed at www.scmp.com/news/china/economy/article/2088876/chinas-more-300-million-vehicles-drive-pollution-congestion

9
ENVIRONMENTALLY ORIENTED BUSINESS

Throwing Shade

Source: Photo by zhang kaiyv on Unsplash.

China and Climate Change

In many respects, China is the greenest country in the world. It has more wind and solar power in place than any other country (Hook, 2019). Yet, China is also the leading builder of new coal plants, and accounted for 27 percent of global CO_2 emissions in 2017 – more than the

(Continued)

combined percentages of the US (15 percent) and the EU countries (9.8 percent) combined (Ritchie and Roser, 2020).

While China is the largest clean energy market in the world, wind and solar accounted for 5.2 percent and 2.5 percent of the power generated in China in 2018 (Slav, 2019). But lack of efficient use of solar panels plagues China. For example, a major issue for China is curtailment – the amount of solar energy that is generated but is not purchased because it cannot be absorbed by the electricity grid (Standaert, 2019). In 2016, 17 percent of solar energy generated could not be used. In 2018, seven percent could not be used.

The air quality in many places in China is so bad that solar energy production is reduced from 15 to 11 percent (Locker, 2019). In 2018, 59 percent of China's energy came from coal (ChinaPower, 2020) compared to about 18 percent for the EU (Eurostat, 2020). One half of the world's coal that is burned every year is burned in China (EDF, 2020). From 2011 to 2020, China consumed more coal than the rest of the world combined (Temple-West, 2020).

In 2017, China launched its national carbon market that covered the power sector which includes more than 1,700 (mostly state-owned) companies responsible for about one-third of China's carbon emissions. This would make China's carbon market the world's largest. Plans call for this national carbon market to gradually take in about 7,000 Chinese firms across eight industrial sectors, such as (1) power, (2) petrochemical, (3) chemical, (4) building materials, (5) iron and steel, (6) nonferrous metals, (7) paper production, and (8) aviation. These firms would account for more than 9 percent of 2017 global emissions. However, China's carbon market has struggled to take off because of the difficulties in establishing a comprehensive data collection system that would enable policymakers to set targets and allocate carbon credits based on these targets (Temple-West, 2020).

Despite this ambitious effort to use the market-based incentives of a carbon market to reduce carbon emissions (in which firms would be assigned limits on carbon emissions and those cutting their emissions would sell the amounts they don't emit to other firms emitting more), the general momentum on climate and environmental issues has declined since 2014 when the Chinese economy grew strongly (Hook, 2019). With slow economic growth, the top political priority for China's leaders becomes stabilizing the economy.

Despite concerns of China's leaders about the country's prospects for economic growth, China claims the largest share of global manufacturing output with 28.4 percent in 2018 (Richter, 2020). The combined shares of the next three countries amounts to 29.6 percent (US 16.6 percent, Japan 7.2 percent and Germany 5.8 percent). China is a manufacturing superpower – which means its role in carbon reduction and climate change mitigation will remain a crucial one for the world.

In sum, the size of China's economy and its economic growth enable it to play a key role in reducing environmental degradation in the future. But whether China is a net benefactor of the global environment or a net detractor of the global environment remains to be seen.

While China has bolted to the forefront of renewable energy deployment, it continues to build coal-fired electricity-generation plants – not only in China, but around the world through its Belt and Road Initiative (E360 Digest, 2019). This initiative is a multi-trillion-dollar investment strategy aimed at building infrastructure in 126 countries around the world through Chinese investment. In a 2019 report by researchers in China, the US, and the UK, researchers estimate that if development continues as planned, the carbon emissions from these countries would more than double by 2050 resulting in a 2.7 degree rise in warming of the planet.

Questions to Consider

- How would you say things are going in China regarding energy efficiency?
- How would you say things are going in China regarding climate change?
- Who would you say has a more important role in addressing climate change: China, the US, or the EU? Explain.
- What would it take for China to drastically reduce its use of coal? Explain.

CHAPTER OVERVIEW AND LEARNING OBJECTIVES

Through a presentation of exemplars, this chapter will showcase some of today's most important topics in environmentally oriented business. Among these are (a) the background for environmentally oriented business, and (b) the roles of government, big business, and entrepreneurial ventures in greening the marketplace. The Patagonia story suggests how a firm might emphasize environmental activism in its endeavors. Firms such as Patagonia are on a mission to make money, serve humanity, and help the planet (Lovins, 2010). These are triple-bottom-line firms who meaningfully integrate people, planet, and profits into their marketing and operations.

Conservation is a foundational concept of environmental stewardship, which is embraced by companies such as outdoor retailer REI, Inc. Today, conservation of the atmosphere's ability to regulate our climate is emerging as an important issue. National governments continue to debate what can be done while the provincial government of British Columbia has enacted a carbon tax in order to reduce greenhouse gas emissions that are harmful to the atmosphere. In 2005, Walmart changed course and declared itself as pursuing an environmental orientation. By 2009, Walmart's CEO had appeared twice before Congressional committees asking for limits on greenhouse gas emissions.

Finally, this chapter will look at Neiman Enterprises CEO Jim Neiman, who explains what it took to transform his business into one that is more environmentally oriented. This forest-products company based in Northeast Wyoming took 10 years to obtain certification from the Sustainable Forest Institute because Neiman wanted his employees to understand the value of adopting sustainable business practices rather than have them imposed on them by his decision. Neiman will be featured as a Maverick Who Made It.

After this chapter, you should be able to answer the following questions:

- What does it mean to become an environmentally oriented business?
- How important is the concept of conservation to environmental stewardship?
- What are the six natural-resource systems the Environmental Protection Agency (EPA) has proposed to be the focus of environmental stewardship?
- How do common goods differ from public goods?
- Is the atmosphere surrounding our planet a public good or a common good?
- If the natural infrastructure that supports civilization becomes degraded and incapable of reliably performing services to humans, can national governments be expected to work together to repair this natural infrastructure?
- What role is the US government now taking to reduce greenhouse gas emissions?
- What other actors are taking action to reduce greenhouse gas emissions in the US?

PATAGONIA AND THE ENVIRONMENT

When told he could pursue an initial public offering (IPO) to sell shares in his privately owned company, Yvon Chouinard (pronounced 'shun ARD'), owner of Patagonia (a designer, marketer, and distributor of high-performance outdoor wear based in Ventura, California), shook his head. 'That would be the end of everything I've wanted to do,' Chouinard said. 'It would destroy everything that I believe in' (Casey, 2007, para. 39).

In 2019, Patagonia's fleece vests had become the fashion trend in Wall Street firms who had their firm's logo stitched on the front of the vest (on the other side of the vest from the Patagonia label) (Otani, 2019). To the chagrin of the finance workers who might regard themselves as future tycoons, Patagonia announced it was keeping new orders of its torso-hugging vests for 'mission-driven companies that prioritize the planet'. In the future, private-equity firms, banks, oil companies, mining companies and start-ups must persuade Patagonia they are helping America turn green. 'They're trying to protect their brand from being taken hostage by this image of Wall Street bankers,' said Patrick Curtis, chief executive of financial careers website Wall Street Oasis.

Chouinard is a successful entrepreneur whose story inspires his devoted contrarian employees (where 900 apply for every job opening) (Casey, 2007). Today, leaders of other businesses, such as Walmart, seek Chouinard's counsel in seeking solutions to what Chouinard describes as the environmental crisis.

Chouinard readily expresses irreverence for traditional business and a reverence for nature. In the introduction to his book *Let My People Go Surfing: The Education of a Reluctant Businessman* (2005), Chouinard begins with brutal honesty:

I've been a businessman for almost fifty years. It's as difficult for me to say those words as it is for someone to admit being an alcoholic or a lawyer. I've never respected the profession. It's business that has to take the majority of the blame for being the enemy of nature, for destroying native cultures, for taking from the poor and giving to the rich, and for poisoning the earth with the effluent from its factories.

Yet business can produce food, cure disease, control population, employ people, and generally enrich our lives. And it can do these good things and make a profit without losing its soul. (p. 3)

Chouinard describes Patagonia (www.patagonia.com) as an experiment to challenge conventional wisdom and present a new style of responsible business (Chouinard, 2005, p. 5). In this way, Chouinard intends to present an alternative to the endless growth implied by capitalism that deserves the blame for the destruction of nature. He declares that he and his employees have the means and the will to prove that doing the right thing leads to a good and profitable business.

Today, Patagonia is organized around environmental activism (Beer, 2019). In 1996, the firm articulated its statement of purpose that sets the firm on a course to 'build the best product, do no unnecessary harm, use business to inspire and implement solutions to the environmental crisis' (Patagonia, 2011).

Almost 70 percent of its product line now comes from recycled materials (Corporate Knights, 2020). For example, Patagonia's Frozen Range parka is part of the Shell, Yeah! line of waterproof jackets that uses 100 percent recycled goose and duck down (reclaimed from cushions, bedding, and other used items that can't be resold) (Pettway, 2019). The two-layer Gore-Tex shell is made with polyester derived from recycled plastic bottles. Sixty-nine percent of Patagonia's garments include recycled materials. The firm aims to use only recycled materials or renewable materials by 2025 – the year the firm intends to become carbon neutral (Corporate Knights, 2020).

Patagonia and Philanthropy

The third part of Patagonia's mission statement is to 'use business to inspire and implement solutions to the environmental crisis' (Patagonia, 2011). Through philanthropy, Patagonia has created organizations that allow other firms to direct their philanthropy to environmental causes. For example, the firm co-founded the Conservation Alliance in 1989 with other outdoor companies, such as REI, The North Face, and Kelty (Conservation Alliance, 2020).

In 2001, Yvon Chouinard also founded 1 Percent for the Planet with Craig Mathews, owner of Blue Ribbon Flies outfitter and guide service for fly fishing based in West Yellowstone, Montana (1 Percent for the Planet, 2011). Chouinard and Mathews hatched a plan to encourage more businesses to donate 1 percent of sales to environmental groups. Chouinard called it an 'Earth Tax'. Mathews suggested that it be named '1 Percent for the Planet.' Mathews' idea eventually won over Chouinard.

Every member company of 1 Percent for the Planet has the opportunity to engage in a dialogue with the rest of the 1 Percent for the Planet membership to foster new business relationships and to connect for sharing ideas and resources. 'Companies like Clif Bar, and New Belgium are members of 1 Percent for the Planet,' Lisa Myers Patagonia's Director of Environmental Grants said. 'These more than 1,200 members of One Percent for the Planet are our peers' (Myers, 2011, personal communication).

Patagonia's Environmental Wisdom

Much of Patagonia's environmental wisdom came in costly ways. In 1991, the firm was growing at 50 percent a year but became derailed during the savings-and-loan crisis (Corporate Knights, 2020). 'The bank reduced our credit line twice in several months and the company ended up borrowing from friends to meet payroll and laying off 20% of its workforce on July 31,' Chouinard recalled. 'That's a day I still refer to as Black Wednesday' (Chouinard, 2010, p. 5).

'We had become dependent, like the world economy, on growth we could not sustain,' Chouinard said. 'If I hadn't stayed in business, I never would have realized – the hard way – the parallel between Patagonia's unsustainable push for growth and that of our whole industrial economy' (Chouinard, 2010, p. 5).

Chouinard believes he learned the hard way to stop growing at an unsustainable rate and still stay in business. He and his team at Patagonia admit they do not have all the answers, but they take confidence when realizing that they have been asking the questions longer than anyone else. Today, Patagonia is a thriving firm posting more than $1 billion a year in sales (Mittica, 2019). The firm also has become a B Corp which requires it to consider its environmental and social impacts and could prioritize these ahead of profits (Patagonia, 2018).

Questioning Leads to Learning and Transparency

After this near-death experience for his firm in 1991, Chouinard and those who remained over-hauled the company mission statement and began asking questions. Growth for the firm was questioned. Soon, the employees of the firm were asking about the environmental harm caused by manufacturing and distributing clothes. 'That's the problem with questions,' Chouinard said. 'Once you start, you can't stop' (Chouinard, 2010, p. 5).

After opening a brand new store in Boston, almost everyone who worked there had a headache. It turned out that the clothing shipped to the store – made of cotton – was finished using too much formaldehyde. Fixing the ventilation at the new store would not fix this problem. Accordingly, Patagonia's employees asked how cotton is grown. After getting answers, the firm switched over to organically grown cotton for its clothes made of cotton.

Afterward, questions came about conditions inside factories where Patagonia's clothes were stitched together. Many of these were in the Far East. What goes into dyes and finishes on clothing that would make them more water repellant? How about shipping and carbon footprints? 'It was expensive, time-consuming and deeply complex,' Chouinard recalled. 'As I said recently at Patagonia's Tools for Grassroots Activists Conference, a gathering of environmental activists at a camp in the Sierra Nevada, 'Leading the examined life is a pain in the ass. But it's worth it' (Chouinard, 2010, p. 5).

Patagonia's leaders are not shy about disclosing the damage their own company does to the natural environment. The firm's spirit of total disclosure can be seen in their launching of *The Footprint Chronicles*, an interactive minisite on its website, which details what the company makes and how it makes it in minute detail.

In recent years, Patagonia has moved into film production by making documentaries with messages about protecting the environment (Beer, 2019). These include *180 Degrees South* (released in 2010, retracing Chouinard's 1968 sea journey to Patagonia, Chile), *DamNation* (released in 2014, depicting the damage dams can do to ecosystems), and *Public Trust* (released in 2020, presenting the fight for America's public lands).

'We recognize that people make decisions based on emotion, and the best way to elicit emotion is through film,' Chouinard said. 'It's not through books or catalogs or speeches. So we're in the film business. We're working on ten films at a time these days. Some of them don't make a cent. But that's not the purpose.'

BACKGROUND FOR ENVIRONMENTALLY ORIENTED BUSINESS

Conservation

REI is a national outdoor retail co-op, based in Seattle, Washington, that began as a way for 21 mountain climbing buddies to obtain the outdoor gear they needed (REI, 2020a). In 2020, REI boasted more than 19 million members who pay a one-time $20 fee and most years received a REI dividend of 10 percent on purchases made. In this way, REI uses a co-operative (co-op) structure. In 2019, REI posted sales of $3.12 billion and invested 70 percent of its profits in the future of the outdoors. REI offers its own line of award-winning gear and apparel, in addition to products from the top brands for camping, climbing, cycling, fitness, hiking, paddling, snow sports, and travel. These other brands include Patagonia, The North Face, and Columbia.

REI declares itself to be passionate about the outdoors and committed to promoting environmental stewardship. For example, REI stays closed on Black Friday (the day after Thanksgiving in the US) as a way to deemphasize overconsumption, and instead encourages its member and employees to enjoy the outdoors with family and friends on this day (REI, 2020b). IT also offers rentals and the sale of lightly used REI goods in what it calls 're-commerce' (in-store 'Garage Sales' and online through the Used Gear Program). Those who take responsibility for how their actions affect environmental quality can be called environmental stewards (EPA, 2005).

Environmental stewardship is not new. Influenced by naturalists such as John Muir who petitioned the US Congress to pass the National Parks bill passed in 1899, Republican Teddy Roosevelt championed conservation during his US presidency from 1901 to 1909 (Gingrich and Maple, 2007, p. 28). It has been said that perhaps Roosevelt's greatest and most enduring contribution as president was instilling an ethos of natural resource conservation in Americans (Lallanilla, 2011). He also preserved some 230 million acres – about the size of *two* Californias and one Ohio – as national parks, national forests, game preserves, national monuments, and other federal reservations. He created the Forest Service and appointed renowned conservationist Gifford Pinchot as its head. On the way to these accomplishments, he showed future presidents and environmentalists how to achieve legislative success.

'The conservation of natural resources is the fundamental problem,' Roosevelt once said. 'Unless we solve that problem it will avail us little to solve all others' (Lallanilla, 2011, p. 1).

Conservatives, such as Paul Weyrich (founder of the Heritage Foundation think-tank), William Lind (an expert on military affairs), as well as former US Speaker of the House Newt Gingrich, give ringing endorsement to conserving natural resources. 'As conservatives,' Weyrich and Lind said:

> We believe in conserving many things: traditions, morals and culture, but also clean air and water, farms and countryside, energy [much of which must now be imported] and the soil itself, on which we all depend for our daily bread. Conservatives do not like waste. Reckless, frivolous, thoughtless consumption was never a conservative virtue. A society's real strength comes from production, saving and investment, not consumption. Earlier generations of Americans understood this and lived accordingly.
>
> (Weyrich and Lind, 2009, pp. 50–1)

Renowned Harvard biologist E.O. Wilson theorized that an innate bond exists between humanity and nature. He termed this love of life or living systems as biophilia (Gingrich and Maple, 2007, p. 26). With this in mind, the move to preserve nature from human use or to conserve nature (so that it can be used wisely for future availability or productivity) can be seen to be part of environmental stewardship. In other words, a moral imperative to protect and manage nature based on love for it is shared by many today across the entire political spectrum (Gingrich and Maple, 2007).

Natural Infrastructure – Could It Break Down?

The EPA believes that environmental stewardship is indispensable for becoming a more sustainable society (EPA, 2005). Toward this end, the EPA proposes that environmental stewardship can focus on the following natural resource systems: (a) air, (b) ecosystems, (c) energy, (d) land, (e) materials, and (f) water. Increasingly, however, the capability of humans to control environmental systems seems to be in question. For example, although plants and animals comprise part of nature, the atmosphere and weather systems are another part of nature. With increased awareness about global climate change (recorded temperatures across the Earth have increased 1 degree Fahrenheit over the last century), it seems that the planet might be on the verge of shifting to a new equilibrium with a higher overall temperature (Thorne, Ferrell, and Ferrell, 2008, p. 320). The propensity for this shift is likely being exacerbated by the greenhouse gases pumped into the atmosphere each day by humans and animals. Concentrations of carbon dioxide – an otherwise harmless gas that plants use in photosynthesis – are growing at a rate that plant life cannot adequately process. As a result, the blanket of greenhouse gases in the atmosphere is thickening with the effect that temperatures and weather are changing.

The specter of global climate change puts Teddy Roosevelt's words about the depletion of natural resources as the fundamental problem in a new light. Rather than caring for nature for aesthetic or moral reasons that may be optional to humans, the environment must be cared for because it actually serves as infrastructure for human civilization. Natural resource systems such as the six serving as the focus for environmental stewardship according to the EPA can be damaged beyond repair or degraded in their ability to provide service to humankind.

Stewart Brand, the founder and editor of the *Whole Earth Catalog* and an ecologist, calls himself an 'ecopragmatist' (Brand, 2009). Brand asserts that civilization requires a tranquil climate to prosper. In this way, the climate provides ecosystem services to humans. Brand makes the observation that modern humans are trained to overlook infrastructure. Humans seem to notice infrastructure only when it does not work. Brand states:

> There are some exceptions. People like the romanticism of railroads and admire bridges and ships. Small towns decorate their water towers. But working mines, containership ports, power plants, power lines, cell-phone towers, refineries, dumps, sewerage – all bear one sign: KEEP OUT. Those places are left to the workers, who are low-status. One might say exactly the same about ecosystem infrastructure, such as watersheds, wetlands, fisheries, soil, and climate. (p. 16)

Brand proposes that a deep bow of thanks is due to environmentalists who have been drawing attention to dangerous breakdowns of natural infrastructure and setting about the protection and restoration of it:

A bridge is infrastructure, and so is the river under it. Both support our life, and both require maintenance, which has to be paid for somehow. Radio spectrum is infrastructure, and so is an intact ozone layer. Both support our life, and both require international agreements to avert a 'tragedy of the commons.' (p. 16).

Common Goods Dilemma

A common dilemma occurs when a shared resource is degraded or consumed for short-term gain by those sharing the resource, rather than managing the resource for the long-term benefit of all. Elinor Ostrom, the first woman to win the Nobel Prize in economics (in 2009) for her research about cooperative ownership, points out that a 'common' actually means that agreements or institutions are in place for the successful sharing of a common good. For example, farmers in some Swiss villages share a communal meadow to graze cows. No overgrazing occurs because there is a common agreement among villagers that no one is allowed to graze more cows than they can care for over the winter – a rule in effect since 1517 (Walljasper, 2010).

According to Ostrom, 'the commons' more accurately refers to the wide and diverse set of common-pool resources or common goods (such as forests, grazing lands, irrigation waters, and fisheries) and public goods (such as knowledge and national defense). So, what many refer to as a 'commons dilemma' would be better termed a 'common goods dilemma'.

Figure 9.1 depicts a typology of goods based on the excludability and rivalrousness of the goods (Varian, 1992). Excludability refers to whether some people can be excluded from using the good. The rivalrousness of goods is based on the degree to which the consumption of the good by one person reduces the availability of the good to others for similar consumption.

	Excludable	Nonexcludable
Rivalrous	**Private goods** food, clothes, autos, iPods	**Common goods (Common-pool resources)** grazing lands, forests, irrigation waters, fisheries
Nonrivalrous	**Club goods** movie theaters, private parks, satellite television	**Public goods** air, broadcast television, national defense

Figure 9.1   A typology of goods based on excludability and rivalrousness

Source: Varian (1992).

As shown in the upper-left quadrant of Figure 9.1, food for one person is a private good because it is excludable and rivalrous. It can be owned by one person, and when a person eats a lunch, it cannot be eaten by others. Common goods can be found in the upper-right quadrant of the matrix. Here, irrigation waters are shared by many farmers (making them nonexcludable), but they are rivalrous (because the consumption of any portion of the irrigation waters renders that portion unusable by other farmers). In the lower-left quadrant, club goods are those that are excludable and nonrivalrous. For example, tickets can be sold to a cinema screening of a movie (making the movie screening excludable), and many patrons can view the movie simultaneously without reducing the movie consumption of others (making the movie screening nonrivalrous). Finally, in the lower-right quadrant, public goods are those that are nonexcludable and nonrivalrous. The air we breathe is an example. The air is shared by all (making it nonexcludable), and one person's breathing does not reduce the amount another person can breathe (making it nonrivalrous).

Although the air we breathe is a public good, the atmosphere surrounding the Earth turns out to be a common good whose overuse by all humans can degrade the services it provides humankind. Specifically, the production of greenhouse gases by humans is increasing the heat-insulating property of the atmosphere. In this way, a dilemma concerning an important common-pool resource – the atmosphere – is now emerging because the infrastructure service of a tranquil climate provided by the atmosphere seems to be at risk of degradation (Cohen and Winn, 2007).

A Challenge Unprecedented in Scale and Scope

Because no country controls the atmosphere surrounding the planet, addressing global climate change effectively seems to be a challenge on a scale that humankind has never before faced. The Kyoto Protocol, signed by 192 countries in 1997, set binding limits for developed countries to reduce their greenhouse gas emissions (Friedman, 2008). According to the Kyoto Protocol, these developed countries (excluding the United States and Australia who did not sign the protocol) would reduce their overall CO_2 emissions from 2008 to 2012 by 20 percent (Lomborg, 2007). Carbon dioxide accounts for 80 percent of the world's emissions of global warming gases from human-made sources (Bradsher, 2006). Other gases from industrial processes, plus methane from landfills and coal mines, account for the rest of these emissions.

Although Kyoto's backers hailed it as a small first step, it is widely seen as mostly symbolic because the impact on rising global temperatures (even if the United States and Australia had signed the protocol and adhered to it) would be only slight in the face of surging development in Third World countries such as China and India.

Who has contributed most to global CO₂ emissions?

Cumulative carbon dioxide (CO₂) emissions over the period from 1751 to 2017. Figures are based on production-based emissions which measure CO₂ produced domestically from fossil fuel combustion and cement, and do not correct for emissions embedded in trade (i.e. consumption-based). Emissions from international travel are not included.

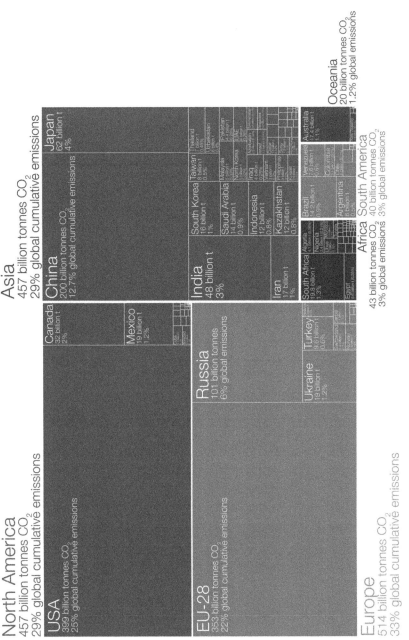

Figure 9.2 Cumulative CO₂ emissions since 1751

Source: Hannah Ritchie and Max Roser (2017) - 'CO₂ and Greenhouse Gas Emissions'. Published online at OurWorldInData.org. Retrieved from: https://ourworldindata.org/co2-and-other-greenhouse-gas-emissions

In 2006, when confronted with the forecast that China would overtake the United States in carbon emissions by 2009, the Chinese government's response was to blame the developed countries for their leading role in greenhouse gas emissions during the history of the Industrial Age. 'You cannot tell people who are struggling to earn enough to eat that they need to reduce their emissions,' said Lu Xuedu, the deputy director general of Chinese Office of Global Environmental Affairs (Bradsher, 2006). Xuedu's remark points to cumulative emissions since the beginning of the Industrial Age. As can be seen in Figure 9.2, the US has emitted the most over this period, followed by the EU and then by China.

The Paris Agreement

The Paris Agreement (launched in 2016) is an agreement within the United Nations Framework convention on Climate Change as a global response to climate change. The goal for the Paris Agreement is to keep global temperatures from rising above 2 degrees Celsius – and if possible, below a 1.5 degree rise in temperature (UNFCC, 2020).

By February 2020, 189 of the 196 nations of the UN had become party to the Paris Agreement. In June 2017, US President Donald Trump announced that the US would withdraw from the agreement in November 2020 (BBC News, 2017). Despite this setback (reversed by the Biden administration in January 2021) to the collaborative effort of almost all of the world's countries, the Paris Agreement represents a milestone in global cooperation. While critics point out that the Paris Agreement has no binding enforcement mechanism and that major industrialized nations were not implementing policies to meet their pledged targets for emission reduction (Friedman, 2019), it represents a beginning for coordinated action across the world. In other words, the preliminary phase is over, so meaningful action can now become the focus of the world's countries.

The Trump Administration's announcement to withdraw the US from the Paris Agreement received special response from a number of US cities, states, businesses and universities. These entities in the US reaffirmed their commitment to helping the US reach its Paris Agreement goals despite President Trump's decision (America's Pledge, 2020). Twenty-four states formed the United States Climate Alliance to continue pursuit of goals related to the Paris Agreement (www.usclimatealliance.org/) (US Climate Alliance, 2020).

Figure 9.3 depicts the annual total carbon dioxide emissions by world region since 1751. As can be seen, CO_2 emissions began noticeably rising after 1950 until now. Europe and the US industrialized first among regions, so these regions became the leading emitters. However, with globalization's transfer of many factories to China, this country is now the leading emitter in the world. This trend is readily perceived by examining Figure 9.4 which depicts world fossil-based emissions since 1970. Here, China and other countries in Asia now rise to the lead positions in the graph for annual CO_2 emissions.

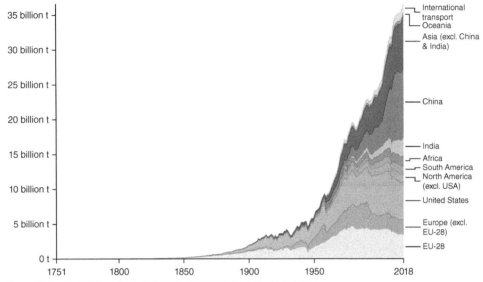

Figure 9.3 Annual total CO_2 emissions, by world region since 1751

Source: Hannah Ritchie and Max Roser (2017) - 'CO_2 and Greenhouse Gas Emissions'. Published online at OurWorldInData.org. Retrieved from: https://ourworldindata.org/co2-and-other-greenhouse-gas-emissions

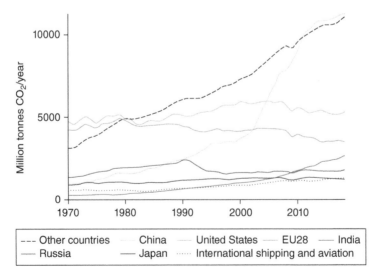

Figure 9.4 World fossil CO_2 emissions, 1970–2018

Source: Figure courtesy of Tomastvivlaren via Wikicommons. Shared under the CC BY-SA 4.0 license.

In sum, Figure 9.4 shows that the world now emits more than 35 billion tons of CO_2 into the atmosphere each year than in 1950. Industrialization accounts for much CO_2. Not surprisingly, countries in the EU and the US have seen their CO_2 emissions decline this century as their economies became service economies, while developing country giants with increased industrialization, such as China and India, have seen their CO_2 emissions climb. Figure 9.4 shows the only lines trending upwards are for Other Countries, China, and India).

In sum, the atmosphere could be regarded as a common good with rules for protecting its climate regulating properties, but because of the slow movement among governments to take action on this, a dilemma regarding this common-pool resource exists. The global average temperature in 2019 was 1.1 degrees Celsius above the long-term average (Carrington, 2020). In 2018, the UN's Intergovernmental Panel on Climate Change (IPCC) issued a report and press release stating that in order to have a good chance of limiting warming to 1.5 degrees Celsius from pre-industrial times, carbon emissions would need to decline 45 percent by 2030 (Shellenberger, 2020). 'The IPCC did not say the world would end, nor that civilization would collapse, if temperatures rose above 1.5 degrees Celsius,' environmentalist and opponent of climate alarmism Michael Shellenberger said (p. 4).

While the coronavirus lockdown imposed by many governments around the world resulted in a 25 percent drop in CO_2 emissions in April 2020, and a 30 percent drop in nitrous oxide (NO_2), researchers see that such a short-term reduction in greenhouse gas emissions would only result in global warming declining by just .01 degree Celsius by 2030. Instead, economy-wide changes across countries around the world would be needed for a zero-emissions economy. Such an economy could be realized by transitioning to vehicles and buildings that emit much less carbon by using renewable energy or hydrogen as fuels.

In a massive effort by more than 200 scientists named Project Drawdown to find the most impactful steps to reduce carbon emissions, refrigeration was decided on as the most impactful step (Hawken, 2017). This is because of hydrochlorofluorocarbons (HFCs) used as a refrigerant in many air-conditioning units. In terms of warming the atmosphere, HFCs have a warming effect 1,000 to 9,000 times that of CO_2. HFC substitutes are available (such as propane and ammonia), but with air-conditioning adoption soaring in developing countries, much work will need to be done for transitioning air-conditioning units being installed, as well as taking air-conditioning units out of service at the end of their lives. Ninety percent of refrigerant emissions happen at the end of the life of air-conditioning units.

Two of the top ten steps to reduce carbon emissions had to do with slowing population growth (which would result in less consumption). Educating girls and family planning were steps ranked sixth and seventh, respectively. The difference between a woman with no years of schooling and one with 12 years of schooling is more than four children (Hawken, 2017, p. 81). The investment in educating girls in developing countries is highly competitive with other carbon reduction steps – and has the potential for an incalculable return on investment beyond carbon reduction.

Also, capturing and burying CO_2 using methods of carbon sequestration might contribute to meaningful reductions in emissions. However, such methods still need further development.

Public Sector Entrepreneurship to Reduce CO_2 Emissions

Carbon capture and storage (CCS) is an emerging technology that might allow the vast coal reserves of the planet to be used while reducing carbon dioxide emissions that would protect the climate (Pew Center on Global Climate Change, 2011). CCS involves separating the CO_2 from other gases emitted in the process of burning coal and liquefying the resulting gas. The liquefied CO_2 can be transported for several hundred miles and then injected deep underground, miles below the surface of the Earth, in suitable geological formations, deep underground saline aquifers, or disused oil fields (Jha, 2008). The last method is often used in a process called 'enhanced oil recovery', where CO_2 is pumped into an oil field to force out the remaining pockets of oil that would otherwise prove difficult to extract. The United States has the capacity for underground storage of current levels of domestic CO_2 emissions from its coal-fired electricity-generation plants for more than 300 years (Pew Center on Global Climate Change, 2011).

The US government's CCS efforts took an important step in April 2017 when the government's first industrial-scale CCS project in Decatur, Illinois (that received $141 million in government funds and $66.5 million from the private sector) began operations (Energy.gov, 2020). The CCS facility will capture and store 1 million tons of CO_2 each year generated from ethanol production at a nearby Archer Daniels Midland biofuels plant. The gas will be held 7,000 feet beneath the surface in the saline Mount Simon Sandstone formation that has the capacity to sequester all of the 250 million tons of CO_2 produced each year by industry in Illinois.

Some governments have begun carbon taxes to reduce carbon emissions into the atmosphere. A carbon tax is a form of pollution tax (C2ES, 2020). It levies a fee on how much carbon is emitted. Households and firms switching to renewable energy would pay no tax.

Sweden enacted a carbon tax in 1991 (Carbon Tax Center, 2020). However, the tax does not apply to electricity generation or biomass energy generation (widely used by Swedish households now) and industries pay only half of the tax. The government implemented the carbon tax gradually with the first taxes set at €23 per ton of CO_2 emissions, but went to €123 in 2019 (Schiebe, 2019). During the period from 1990 to 2017, the Swedish GDP increased 78 percent, while Sweden's greenhouse gas emissions declined 26 percent.

This suggests that imposing a carbon tax that is neutral (the proceeds from the tax reduce other taxes) will not impede economic growth for a country.

The World Bank estimates that less than five percent of emissions covered by carbon taxation is priced at a level that would achieve the goals of the Paris Agreement, such as at $40–80 per ton by 2020, or $50–90 per ton of CO_2 by 2030 (Schiebe, 2019). Australia's government set a low carbon tax of about $19.60 per ton of carbon between 2012 and 2014, and saw a drop in the country's carbon emissions. However, political winds shifted in 2014 and the Australian government repealed the tax.

Prospects for a Low-Carbon Future

In sum, government can entrepreneurially build demonstration projects to validate CCS technologies, but it seems more is needed or a tragedy of the commons will result as the atmosphere accumulates CO_2 and forecasted climate disruption accelerates in a non-linear manner (Shultz and Holbrook, 1999). Without the externality of greenhouse gas emissions being included in the price for energy, private firms do not find CCS to be financially viable with current technologies. Richard Jones, deputy executive director of the International Energy Agency (IEA), warned that with current polices, CCS will have a hard time being deployed.

British Columbia's Carbon Tax

Newer policies might focus on including the full cost of emitting carbon in market pricing with a carbon tax placed on CO_2 used in business operations. Despite the reluctance of national governments to raise any taxes in a time of economic uncertainty, the provincial government of British Columbia went ahead and imposed its own carbon tax of about C$10 per ton of CO_2 in 2008 that increased to C$30 per ton of CO_2 in 2012 (Marshall, 2011). (In 2020, one US dollar could buy 1.32 Canadian dollars and one Euro could buy 1.55 Canadian dollars.) The tax is revenue-neutral in that the government lowers the taxes of corporations and individuals at a rate comparable with the carbon tax they pay.

The carbon tax first required British Columbians to pay C$.18 more for a gallon of gasoline (Marshall, 2011). In July 2012, the next phase of the carbon tax required British Columbians to pay C$.27 more for a gallon of gasoline when the tax rises to C$30 a ton of CO_2-equivalent. Because 85 percent of British Columbia's electricity comes from hydropower, the tax has little effect on electricity users. Instead, most of tax is being paid by drivers and by businesses, as well as by individuals using natural gas, propane, or coal. The cost for other fuels, such as natural gas or coal, varies by their carbon content. Combustion accounts for three fourths of the province's CO_2 emissions, and the tax applies to these. The rest of the province's emissions have other sources, such as methane seeping from landfills.

As a result of the carbon tax, public institutions have sought to include more energy-efficient technologies (Marshall, 2011). For example, in the Resort Municipality of Whistler, community manager Ted Battiston says the tax played a role in changing from propane tanks to solar panels and geothermal pumps in the heating unit of the local swimming pool. Heavy emitters of greenhouse gases, such as cement manufacturers, complain loudly about how imported cement is now threatening the vitality of their businesses. Alternatively, businesses with a small carbon footprint are not complaining much about the tax. This brings the heavy emitters to call for a different way of recycling the carbon-tax revenue. According to these heavy emitters, instead of the tax proceeds going to every business, more of the cash should help carbon-intensive companies improve their energy efficiency.

Those monitoring the effect of the carbon tax in British Columbia agree that it reduced consumption of gasoline, as well as overall emissions (Harrison, 2019). It did this with a stronger adoption of fuel-efficient vehicles. Importantly, job loss or harm to low-income households did not occur to any significant degree. However, because emissions lowered and then levelled off, it appears that a more sizeable carbon tax and other complementary measures will be needed to attain the desired reductions in emissions in the future.

So what does British Columbia's example mean for national governments? Paul Bledsoe, a senior adviser at the Bipartisan Policy Center, believes that a tax on energy is one of the few ways that the US government could obtain new sources of revenue if tax reform is done to reduce the federal deficit. One goal of reform would be to reduce taxes for corporations and individuals – exactly what a carbon or energy tax could finance.

'The enormous political appeal of cutting corporate and individual tax rates as part of debt reduction has the potential to more than offset the political push back on a consumption tax, at the right moment,' Bledsoe said (Marshall, 2011, p. 6).

EPA and Emissions Regulation

In April 2007, the US Supreme Court declared that Massachusetts had standing to bring a legal suit against the EPA for not regulating greenhouse gases – specifically CO_2 – emitted from automobile tailpipes. Previously, CO_2 had not been considered a 'pollutant' under the Clean Air Act. In a 5–4 decision, the Supreme Court asserted that Massachusetts faced harm that was both actual and imminent because of the risk of harm from costly storms and the loss of coastal shore that would result from climate change (Yergin, 2011, p. 502).

Some called the ruling the most important environmental ruling of all time. In addition to classifying CO_2 as a pollutant, it termed the EPA's current stance of nonregulation as being not in accordance with the law. If Congress did not legislate the regulation of carbon, the EPA was supposed to.

The EPA's subsequent move to regulate emissions from stationary sources, such as coal-fired electricity-generating plants, drew a backlash from Congress and more than a dozen states, such as Texas (Galbraith, 2010). It seems that the battle over CO_2 regulation will depend on the composition of the Congress in the coming years. The stance of Congress will also be crucial in determining whether an international regime for climate change emerges.

In addition to the opportunities businesses now recognize as accompanying concern about environmental issues, such as global climate change and loss of biodiversity, businesses have begun to realize that sustainable business practices can contribute to their increased competitiveness. Walmart is a case in point. In 2005, CEO Lee Scott declared that climate change was at the top of his list of environmental challenges that had to be addressed (Humes, 2011, p. 103). Air and water pollution, water shortages, destruction of critical habitats, and the reduction of biodiversity rounded out his list of environmental challenges. Later, Scott would testify before Congress twice in 2009 advocating for reduction of greenhouse gas emissions. In these ways and in a myriad of operational changes, Walmart began turning away from a ruthless approach to business that disregarded the environment and communities. Other businesses could no longer say that sustainable business practices were too risky if Walmart had adopted them. How strange could environmentally friendly business leaders be if Walmart now wanted a low-carbon future?

Walmart Sets Sail to Harness Winds of Change for Sustainable Business Practices

Rather than continuing to view corporate social responsibility as an ethical veneer to shield the firm from criticism in society, Walmart realized that the most sustainable business, the cleanest, and the least wasteful would gain a competitive advantage (Humes, 2011, p. 3). Costs would be lowered (meaning profits would likely rise accordingly), and customers would be pleased with better products and services (and other stakeholders would be pleased, as well). This advantage would not accrue in some abstract future time, but now – during the watch of the company's current leaders. Accepting this premise, then, led to understanding that the pivotal question facing this era of business would be not if business will obey the laws of nature but when and how and on whose terms? Would Walmart be an innovator and lead sustainability – thereby obtaining the valuable knowledge acquisition first-movers can obtain – or would it wait for its competition, the courts, or Congress to bring compelling force for Walmart to do this?

Since 2005, Walmart has accepted that sustainable business practices represent a better way to do business (Humes, 2011). The firm turned away from ingrained thinking that such business practices meant extra costs, and instead, it saw these sustainable business practices as ways to eliminate waste and the costs that go with such waste. The firm had noticed the operational efficiencies obtained by Patagonia and Nike. Walmart had also struggled with persistent criticism of its operations.

Green Light for Sustainable Business Practices at Walmart

Although inspiring a movement among businesses to direct philanthropy toward organizations that defend or improve the natural environment is a major accomplishment by itself, Patagonia's most significant accomplishment to date might be winning over business leaders of firms that will never join 1 Percent for the Planet to recognize that industry and ecology are inherently connected. By working with one firm, Walmart, Chouinard might more favorably impact the marketplace than in any other way.

Chouinard has visited Walmart's headquarters in Bentonville, Arkansas, to explain the operating principles of Patagonia to Walmart's leaders, as well as to a gathering of 1,200 buyers for Walmart (Ridgeway, 2010). Chouinard told the audience to lead 'an examined life' so you know the consequences of your actions, and once you know them 'clean up your act' (Ridgeway, 2010, p. 44). Afterward, Walmart CEO Lee Scott went to the podium with his closing remarks:

'There's a third of you out there who know what we're doing and why we're doing it,' Scott said. 'There's another third who don't quite understand but you're getting there. And there's a final third telling yourselves this isn't the company that Sam Walton founded, and you don't understand and you may not be willing to learn. In the future, there may not be a place for you at Walmart' (Ridgeway, 2010, p. 44).

'The revolution really has started,' Chouinard later remarked about his work with Walmart. 'I'm blown away by Walmart. If Walmart does one-tenth of what they say they are going to do, it will be incredible' (Casey, 2007, p. 5).

By 2017, Walmart's efforts for adopting renewable energy, eliminating waste and selling products that sustain the environment had matured to the point where the financial return of these efforts became undeniable (Henderson, 2020). For example, Walmart had met its goal of doubling the transportation fleet's efficiency (which logs more than 700 million miles per year in North America) and was saving more than $1 billion a year – about four percent of its annual profit. Observers estimate that Walmart saves more than $250 million each year from the increased energy efficiency of its more than 11,000 stores in 28 countries.

In 2017, Walmart launched Project Gigaton to remove 1 billion metric tons of greenhouse gas emissions from the global value chain by 2030 (Stevens, 2019). That would be like taking 212 million cars off highways for one year (Fialka, 2019). More than 5,000 suppliers of Walmart joined the effort. Unlike government regulations which stop at national borders, the effects of Project Gigaton cascaded across international borders.

For example, Procter & Gamble reformulated the Tide detergent brand to clean well in cold water and then initiated a new ad campaign focused on consumers making the switch to cold water washing. InBev's Anheuser-Busch built a massive wind farm in Oklahoma that can provide enough electricity to produce all of the beer the firm brews in the US. Kellogg set a goal of training half a million US farmers in techniques to lower greenhouse gas emissions. Additionally, Unilever attained the milestone of having half of its plastic packaging derived from post-consumer recycled materials.

'The Index'

The first step in this project to develop 'The Index' was to notify Walmart's suppliers of its intentions (and what this would mean for them). Accordingly, the firm sent a letter to its suppliers in 2009 posing 15 questions to them about their own processes and operations (Walmart, 2011). These are depicted in Figure 9.5. Today, Walmart has named its program for evaluating suppliers on the Sustainability Index as the Sustainability Insight System (THESIS).

The second step in developing The Index was the formation of an independently governed Sustainability Consortium that would construct the product database – the essential ingredient to The Index. Duke intended this product database to be open, composed from many sources, reviewed by peers, and carrying no hype for brands included in the database (Humes, 2011, p. 192).

Today, the Sustainability Consortium (TSC) identifies the environmental and social issues that matter in meaningful ways to sustainability for Walmart (Walmart, 2020). TSC analyzes information across a product's life cycle (from sourcing, manufacturing, transporting, selling, customer usage, and end of use) and identifies 'hot spots' for improvement. Key performance indicators (KPIs) are developed in the form of survey questions used to measure sustainability performance for a product category. Suppliers respond to 15 questions on surveys about each product category they supply to Walmart. Walmart then shares opportunities for special attention by the supplier.

Founding members of this consortium included the green household cleaning products company Seventh Generation; agribusiness giants Monsanto, Cargill, and Tyson Foods; cleaning products company Clorox; Dairy Management, Inc.; Waste Management; Disney; SC Johnson; Procter & Gamble; PepsiCo; computer manufacturers Hewlett-Packard and

Dell; and a dozen others. Walmart competitors, Best Buy and Safeway, joined after a few months. Despite the lower rate for nonprofits ($10,000 compared to $100,000 for firms), only one joined – the environmental group World Wildlife Fund. By 2020, others had joined, such as Arizona State University, Cornell University, the University of Arkansas, the Nature Conservancy, and Green Seal which certifies products as having the highest standards for health and environmental leadership (Sustainability Consortium, 2020).

	Sustainability Supplier Assessment questions
Energy and climate Reduce energy costs and greenhouse emissions	1. Have you measured and taken steps to reduce your corporate greenhouse gas emissions? (Y/N)
	2. Have you opted to report your greenhouse gas emissions and climate change strategy to the Carbon Disclosure Project (CDP)? (Y/N)
	3. What are your total annual greenhouse gas emissions in the most recent year measured? (Enter total metric tons CO_2e, e.g. CDP 2009 Questionnaire, Questions 7–11 Scope 1 and 2 emissions)
	4. Have you set publicly available greenhouse gas reduction targets? If yes, what are those targets? (Enter total metric tons and target date, e.g. CDP 2009 Questionnaire, Question 23)
Material efficiency Reduce waste and enhance quality	Scores will be automatically calculated based on participation in the Packaging Scorecard in addition to the following:
	5. If measured, please report total amount of solid waste generated from the facilities that produce your products for Walmart for the most recent year measured. (Enter total lbs)
	6. Have you set publicly available solid waste reduction targets? If yes, what are those targets? (Enter total lbs and target date)
	7. If measured, please report total water use from the facilities that produce your product(s) for Walmart for the most recent year measured. (Enter total gallons)
	8. Have you set publically available water use reduction targets? If yes, what are those targets? (Enter total gallons and target date)
Nature and resources High-quality, responsibly sourced raw materials	9. Have you established publicly available sustainability purchasing guidelines for your direct suppliers that address issues such as environmental compliance, employment practices, and product/ingredient safety? (Y/N)
	10. Have you obtained third party certifications for any of the products that you sell to Walmart? If so, from the list of certifications below, please select those for which any of your products are, or utilize materials that are, currently certified.
People and community Vibrant, productive workplaces and communities	11. Do you know the location of 100% of the facilities that produce your product(s)? (Y/N)
	12. Before beginning a business relationship with a manufacturing facility, do you evaluate their quality of production and capacity for production? (Y/N)

	Sustainability Supplier Assessment questions
	13. Do you have a process for managing social compliance at the manufacturing level? (Y/N)
	14. Do you work with your supply base to resolve issues found during social compliance evaluations and also document specific corrections and improvements? (Y/N)
	15. Do you invest in community development activities in the markets you source from and/or operate within? (Y/N)

Figure 9.5   Fifteen questions Walmart proposed to its suppliers as part of its Supplier Sustainability Assessment

Source: Walmart. Supplier Sustainability Assessment. Page 4 of 32. www.walmartstores.com/download/4055.pdf

By 2019, the Sustainability Index included data from suppliers on important environmental, social, and other performance indicators (Walmart, 2019). The Index reflects responses from more than 1,500 suppliers across 115 product categories in Walmart and Sam's Club in the US. More than 80 percent of goods in Walmart stores come from participating suppliers (who have improved their Sustainability Index scores by 28 percent in 2018 compared to 2016 scores).

The third step for The Index would be the creation of the tags and apps that would allow The Index to be readily used by consumers in their shopping. Upon the formation of the consortium, not every firm in the consortium wanted a big red tag for nonsustainability attached to their products in stores, so the idea of a red (not sustainable) or green tag (sustainable) for products did not initially receive unanimous support within the consortium (Humes, 2011, p. 194). By comparison, other firms in the consortium felt confident that they would receive favorable ratings for sustainability and wanted to have their sustainability scores known by the public as soon as possible.

By 2020, this step remains undeveloped by Walmart and the Sustainability Consortium. No mention of such tags or a mobile app is made in Walmart's 2019 Environment, Social and Governance Report. Likewise, no mention of tags or such a mobile app is included on the Sustainability Consortium's website.

Consumer Product Guides to the Rescue?

Despite the challenges Walmart has encountered in developing The Index, a nonprofit GoodGuide made inroads on offering credible sustainability ratings for products on three dimensions: (a) health, (b) the environment, and (c) society (labor and human rights). The company founded in 2007 by Dara O'Rourke, a supply-chain expert and professor at the University of California – Berkeley, rated more than 500,000 consumer items on these three dimensions on a scale from 1 to 10. GoodGuide also offered a mobile app that allows the user to swipe a product's bar code at the store to receive GoodGuide's rating. Despite serving more than 10 million users in its history, GoodGuide paused its work in June 2020.

Time will tell if a consumer-oriented product rating service like GoodGuide will reappear. The enormity of tracking hundreds of thousands of stock keeping units (SKUs) and continually evaluating them on valid dimensions in a reliable way proves to be daunting. However, business solutions offered by new entrepreneurial firms offering trustworthy ratings of products on sustainability dimensions should not be ruled out in the future.

In the UK, Ethical Consumer is a leading consumer organization that has been researching and evaluating the social and environmental records of firms since 1989 (Ethical Consumer, 2020a). Consumers can search the ethical ratings of more than 40,000 firms and brands at www.ethicalconsumer.org.

One category covered by Ethical Consumer is fashion and clothing. Figure 9.6 depicts the final ratings of designer clothing brands. Consumers can read about what to buy (recycled clothing, organic, people before profits), as well as what not to buy (fur, leather, viscose), best buys (none recommended for designer clothing because of the poor scores) and what firms to avoid (such as Chanel, Louis Vuitton, and Prada among others). Consumers who pay a subscription fee can read more detail about how the firms faired on dimensions, such as (1) environment, (2) people, (3) animals, and (4) politics.

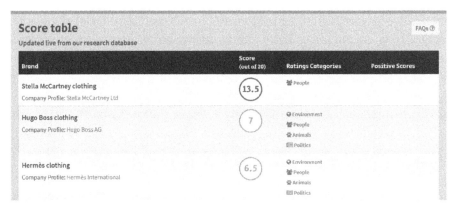

Figure 9.6   Ethical consumers' ratings of designer clothing brands

Source: Ethical Consumer (2020b).

Measuring a Product's Carbon Footprint

A product's carbon footprint represents the amount of carbon dioxide and other greenhouse gases that are emitted into the atmosphere when products are made, shipped, stored, and then used by consumers. According to Nic Marks, founder of the New Economic Foundation's Center for Well-Being based in London, the introduction of the carbon footprint concept has been the most important development in recent years for the environmental movement (Marks, 2007, personal communication). Calculators for business and individual carbon footprints are now easily accessible at websites such as www.carbonfoot-print.com. By using such calculators, citizens can understand their own possible contribution to global climate change. In this way, carbon emissions are no longer clear, odorless, and tasteless; instead they take on a more concrete form in the minds of individuals. With such measurement comes responsibility and accountability, where before there was none or very little.

However, it turns out that measuring a product's carbon footprint requires a standardized approach that still needs to be refined. For example, when carbon footprint measurement began, firms focused on the product ingredients. But this told little about upstream processing (before the manufacturer received the inputs used in manufacturing), as well as about downstream activities (such as shipping of the product and the use and disposal of the product by consumers). In sum, a product's carbon footprint often depends on the breadth of the lens used to compute the carbon footprint. For example, the biggest contributor to a laundry detergent's carbon footprint is the clothes dryer – a downstream process not directly related to the ingredients of the detergent (Ball, 2008). With this in mind, it is easier to understand that the simplest way to cut carbon emissions may be to use less of a product, or to use it in a way that is less convenient – such as washing one's clothes by hand. Drying laundry outside on a clothes line will result in 4.4 pounds less carbon dioxide per load being emitted into the atmosphere.

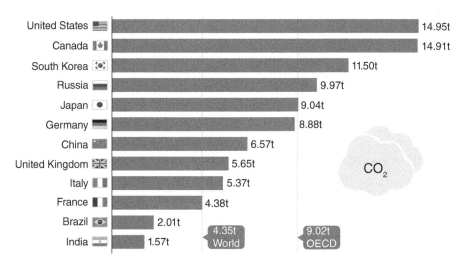

Figure 9.7 CO_2 emissions per capita among the world's largest economies in 2016

Source: Richter (2019). Shared under the CC BY-ND license by Statista.

As can be seen in Figure 9.7 the average person in the United States is responsible for the emission of 79.5 pounds of carbon dioxide each day (Richter, 2019). This is equal to 14.95 metric tons per year. This leads the world, but Canada is a close second. The simplest statistic about the carbon footprint is that for every mile a car drives, it emits about one pound of carbon dioxide. The average car in the United States emits five tons of carbon dioxide every year.

But as firms calculated the carbon footprints of their products, they discovered some amazing things. For example, Stonyfield Farm, the leading US producer of organic yogurt and a major supplier to Walmart, believed that energy used in making the yogurt was the biggest piece of the carbon footprint for its yogurt (Humes, 2011, p. 194). Stonyfield's leaders were stunned to learn that energy was a distant fourth in determining the size of its carbon footprint. The milk used to make the yogurt was first, followed by packaging and distribution. Stonyfield's leaders learned that cows burp regularly to digest their food (moving it across four stomachs). With these burps, the cows emit methane – a greenhouse gas. Methane gas is 25 times more harmful as a greenhouse gas than carbon dioxide. As a result, a cow's carbon footprint is 80 percent of a car's (Ball, 2008). This means that in terms of contribution to global climate change, a cattle herd represents a fleet of cars about 80 percent the size of the number of cows in the herd.

To bring firms to a common approach for measuring the carbon footprints of their products, the International Standards Organization (ISO) issued guidance in ISO 14064-1 in Spring 2006; companies around the world are now using it and the related GHG (greenhouse gas) Protocol to calculate emissions consistently (Carbon Clear, 2009). Firms announcing their carbon footprint should be following these guidelines or major pieces of their carbon footprint will be ignored.

CONCLUSION

This chapter began by posing the following question: 'Is it possible to use business for the benefit of the environment?' A review of Yvon Chouinard's outdoor clothing company Patagonia highlighted how the firm has not only directed millions of dollars to nonprofits supporting environmental conservation and activism, but also it has inspired legions of customers and other businesses to pursue more environmentally friendly ways to conduct their affairs.

For 'no-growth' proponents of macromarketing's critical school, the reality of operating a business remains unpalatable. Chouinard once told an audience of Walmart employees that if a company were going to make anything, it had to acknowledge that it would damage the world (Humes, 2011, p. 204). For those who focus on the environment as the prime source of value for human living, Chouinard's words mean that business in its current form and with its objective of growth is an enemy of the environment. In this view, the atmosphere would be regarded as a public good, that no one human or one business has the right to appropriate for its own purposes. Alternatively, for the 'some-growth' proponents of macromarketing's developmental school, managing the environment is acceptable. In this view, the atmosphere would be regarded as a common good – if humans could just agree on the rules for managing it as a common good.

In sum, it seems that although it is not possible to conduct business without changing the environment, it is possible to conduct business so that the environment benefits. In other words, business can be done not just in an eco-efficient way (doing less bad) but also in an eco-effective way (that replenishes, restores, and nourishes the rest of the world) (McDonough and Braungart, 2002). However, businesses are now developing more sustainable products and business practices that would be termed eco-effective – and some of these will be presented in the next chapter.

With the population of the world expected to grow from 7 billion today to 9 billion by 2050 (it is forecast to decline slowly after this), firms like Walmart will be poised to engage many more customers around the world. However, Walmart CEO Duke explains, '[I]f our environmental demands continue at the same rate, we will need the equivalent of two planets to maintain our standard of living in another 25 years' (Keegan, 2011, p. 134). With this in mind, the solution offered by the critical school of macromarketing that calls for less consumption seems to be an important element in future approaches to doing business in a way that benefits the environment. In short, demarketing consumption will likely be a social marketing effort that will take a broad and enduring effort to make it cool to consume less in the future.

QUESTIONS

- In what ways does Patagonia benefit the environment?
- To what extent can other firms benefit the environment like Patagonia?
- Is the atmosphere that surrounds the Earth a public good, a common good, or something else? What might it become in the future at some time?
- What role do you envision governments taking with regard to global climate change in the future? Explain. What would it take for government to take a different role than the one you envision?
- Compare and contrast the environmental stewardship of Patagonia and Walmart.
- What is the most surprising question to you that Walmart asks of its suppliers in its Sustainability Supplier Assessment Questions featured in Figure 9.6?
- Using a 1 to 10 scale with '1' representing 'enemy of the environment' and 10 representing 'replenishing and restoring the environment,' how would you rate Patagonia? Walmart? How would you expect to rate them in 10 years? What does this mean for society and societies?

Mavericks Who Made It

Jim Neiman

Source: Federal Reserve Bank of Kansas City (2020).

In 1906, President Theodore Roosevelt established Devils Tower – a flat-topped tower of gray, igneous rock rising more than 280 meters above the surrounding forest and grasslands of the Black Hills in far-northeastern Wyoming – as the first national monument protected area in the United States (National Park Service, 2011). About six miles from Devil's Tower, in the exposed-red clay hillsides of the Black Hills, lies Hulett, Wyoming (population 500) – headquarters for Neiman Enterprises, Inc. (NEI).

Jim Neiman's grandfather, A. C. Neiman, built a saw mill in the Black Hills to process Ponderosa pine timber. Today, NEI owns the last saw mill operating in Wyoming, three other mills 60 miles from Hulett in the South Dakota Black Hills, and Montrose Forest Products in western Colorado (Mimiaga, 2018).

In 2000, Neiman decided to integrate sustainable business practices into the operations of the firm he inherited from his father. Rather than force his firm to embrace these sustainable business practices rapidly and earn the Sustainable Forestry Initiative's (SFI) certification, Neiman chose to educate his employees and allow them to embrace the principles of sustainability over a ten-year period. He wanted a more sustainable approach to business baked into the culture of his firm. In 2010, Neiman Enterprises operations received SFI certification. Neiman commented:

> It took time so people could buy into it. It was about culture change. It was about bringing them along, rather than ruling by edict. We wanted to pass decision-making to the lowest level, so the new philosophy of the company would actually permeate the culture.
>
> (Neiman, 2011, personal communication)

The SFI promotes sustainable forest management, and certification indicates the firm sources its wood fiber legally from noncontroversial forests. Certification also indicates the firm employs sustainable forestry practices to protect water quality, biodiversity, wildlife habitat, species at risk, and Forests with Exceptional Conservation (SFI, 2011). The firm's employees, as well as independent contractors working for the firm, must be trained in sustainable forestry practices. In short, SFI-certified forest-products companies value the long-term productivity and health of forests. This includes soil productivity and protection from wildfire, insects, disease, and invasive plants and animals.

Neiman explains:

> Certification is expensive. I spend between $150,000 to $250,000 per year to accomplish all that certification requires and I don't get a penny back. Our employees ask 'why are you doing this when you don't get any financial incentive?' My answer is that you have to believe in it. I want to have the right thing done on the ground – not just doing what a customer might want.
>
> (Neiman, 2011, personal communication)

Rather than tightly focusing on delivering the grades of wood that a customer at Home Depot might want when they want it, Neiman wants his 600 employees and 300 contract workers to follow the firm's sustainability philosophy whose first principle is integrity.

'How do you really get the right thing done out there where our people work?' Neiman asked:

> It means convincing 28 logging crews who are independent, 75 logging truckers who are independent, that they have to follow our philosophy. For example, in the Spring the ground is wet, and we might be almost out of logs in the mill. Yet, somebody wants to pull out a truck and go out on the wet ground to retrieve some logs in the forest. But our philosophy would say it is of a higher importance to run out of logs in the mill, rather than risk our equipment and people in precarious situations in the forest, then. You'd be surprised how employees can be more forward-thinking before Spring and figure out how to put more logs down in retrievable places.
>
> (Neiman, 2011, personal communication)

Jim Neiman's story illustrates some of the complexity and controversy that comes with working in an industry so deeply involved with the environment. Integrating sustainable business practices into his firm took time and still requires hundreds of thousands of dollars each year to maintain. Neiman consults regularly with foresters, and he serves on four land-use planning boards at the local, Black Hills, regional, and national levels.

'Sustainability – it goes way deep,' Neiman said. 'How do you sustain the family business? How do you keep the community healthy?'

Questions

- Why did Neiman choose to take the slow approach in obtaining certification by the Sustainable Forest Initiative?
- What are the costs to Neiman for pursuing sustainability at Neiman Enterprises? In the community?
- How would those from macromarketing's critical school assess Neiman's performance in sustainability? How would those from macromarketing's developmental school make the same assessment?
- What does Neiman's story say about living one's life with an environmental-orientation in a rural community, as opposed to a suburban locale or a city?

REFERENCES

1 Percent for the Planet. (2011). *1 Percent for the Planet*. Retrieved from www.onepercentforth-eplanet.org

America's Pledge (2020). America's Pledge. Accessed at www.americaspledgeonclimate.com/

Ball, J. (2008). Six products, six carbon footprints. *The Wall Street Journal*. October 6, 2008. Retrieved from www.online.wsj.com

BBC News. (2017). Paris climate deal: Trump pulls out of 2015 accord. *BBC News*, June 1, 2017. Accessed at www.bbc.com/news/world-us-canada-40127326.

Beer, J. (2019). Uphill climb. *Fast Company*, November 2019, 53–8.

Black, R. (2011, July 5). Global warming lull down to China's coal growth. *BBC News*. Retrieved from www.bbc.co.uk

Bradsher, K. (2006, November 7). China to pass U.S. in 2009 in emissions. *The New York Times*. Retrieved from www.nytimes.com

Brand, S. (2009). *Whole earth discipline: An ecopragmatist manifesto*. New York, NY: Viking.

C2ES. (2020). Carbon tax basics. Center for Climate and Energy Solutions. Accessed at www.c2es.org/content/carbon-tax-basics/.

Carbon Clear. (2009, February 2). Dell, carbon footprints and boundaries. *Carbon Clear Blog*. Retrieved from http://carbonclear.blogspot.com

Carbon Tax Center. (2020). Where carbon is taxed. Carbon Tax Center. Accessed at www.carbontax.org/where-carbon-is-taxed/

Carrington, D. (2020). Covid-19 lockdown will have 'negligible' impact on climate crisis – study. *The Guardian*, August 7, 2020. Accessed at www.theguardian.com/environment/2020/aug/07/covid-19-lockdown-will-have-negligible-impact-on-climate-crisis-study#:~:text=Shine%20said%20a%20green%20recovery,to%20undetectable%20reductions%20in%20warming

Casey, S. (2007, May 29). Patagonia: Blueprint for green business. *Fortune*. Retrieved from http://cnnmoney.com

ChinaPower. (2020). How is China's energy footprint changing? ChinaPower. Accessed at https://chinapower.csis.org/energy-footprint/

Chouinard, Y. (2005). *Let my people go surfing: The education of a reluctant businessman*. New York, NY: Penguin Books.

Chouinard, Y. (2010). Leading the examined life is a pain in the ass. *Patagonia environmental initiatives 2010* (p. 5). Ventura, CA: Patagonia.

Cohen, B., and Winn, M.I. (2007). Market imperfections, opportunity and sustainable entrepreneurship. *Journal of Business Venturing*, 22, 29–49.

Conservation Alliance. (2020). *About us*. Retrieved from www.conservationalliance.com/who-we-are/

Corporate Knights. (2020). Green 50: Top business moves that helped the planet. *Corporate Knights*, April 20, 2020. Accessed at www.corporateknights.com/channels/leadership/green-50-15873659/

E360 Digest. (2019). China's Belt and Road Initiative could drive warming to 2.7 degrees. *YaleEnvironment360*, September 4, 2019. Accessed at https://e360.yale.edu/digest/chinas-belt-and-road-initiative-could-drive-warming-to-2-7-degrees#:~:text=China's%20Belt%20and%20Road%20Initiative%2C%20a%20multi%2Dtrillion%2Ddollar,projects%20being%20funded%2C%20according%20to

EDF. (2020). Why China is at the center of our climate strategy. Environmental Defense Fund. Accessed at www.edf.org/climate/why-china-center-our-climate-strategy

Energy.gov. (2020). DOE announces major milestone reached for Illinois industrial ccs project. Energy.gov, Office of fossil energy, April 7, 2017. Accessed at www.energy.gov/fe/articles/doe-announces-major-milestone-reached-illinois-industrial-ccs-project#:~:text=The%20U.S.%20Department%20of%20Energy,into%20a%20large%20saline%20reservoir.andtext=Simon%20Sandstone%20in%20the%20Illinois,saline%20aquifers%20in%20the%20world

EPA. (2005). *Everyday choices: Opportunities for environmental stewardship*. Report to Stephen L. Johnson, Administrator, US Environmental Protection Agency. EPA Innovation Action Council. Washington, DC.

Ethical Consumer. (2020a). Ethical Consumer. Accessed at www.ethicalconsumer.org/

Ethical Consumer. (2020b). Ethical designer clothing. Ethical Consumer. Accessed at www.ethicalconsumer.org/fashion-clothing/shopping-guide/ethical-designer-clothing

Eurostat. (2020). Energy production and imports. *Eurostat*, June 2020. Accessed at https://ec.europa.eu/eurostat/statistics-explained/pdfscache/1216.pdf

Federal Reserve Bank of Kansas City. (2020). Jim D. Nieman. Accessed at www.kansascityfed.org/people/eac/jneiman

Fialka, J. (2019). Walmart has thousands of suppliers. It's slashing their CO_2. *E&E News*, May 14, 2019. Accessed at www.eenews.net/stories/1060328353/

Friedman, L. (2019). Trump serves notice to quit Paris Climate Agreement. *New York Times*, November 4, 2019. Accessed at www.nytimes.com/2019/11/04/climate/trump-paris-agreement-climate.html

Friedman, T. (2008) The world is hot, flat, and crowded: Why we need a green revolution. New York, NY: Farrar, Straus & Giroux.

Galbraith, K. (2010, December 16). Politics at two levels in fight with the EPA. *The New York Times*. Retrieved from www.nytimes.com

Gingrich, N., and Maple, T.L. (2007). *A contract with the earth*. Baltimore, MD: Johns Hopkins Press.

Harrison, K. (2019). Lessons from British Columbia's carbon tax. *Policy Options*, July 11, 2019. Accessed at https://policyoptions.irpp.org/magazines/july-2019/lessons-from-british-columbias-carbon-tax/

Hawken, P. (Ed.). (2017). *Drawdown: The most comprehensive plan ever proposed to reverse global warming*. London: Penguin.

Henderson, R. (2020). *Reimagining capitalism in a world on fire*. London: Hachette UK.

Hook, L. (2019). Climate change: how China moved from leader to laggard. *Financial Times*, November 24, 2019. Accessed at www.ft.com/content/be1250c6-0c4d-11ea-b2d6-9bf4d1957a67

Humes, E. (2011). *Force of nature: The unlikely story of Walmart's green revolution*. New York, NY: Harper Business.

Jha, A. (2008, September 5). Explainer: How carbon is captured and stored. *The Guardian*. Retrieved from www.guardian.co.uk

Keegan, P. (2011, July 25). The trouble with green product ratings. *Fortune*, 130–4.

Lallanilla, M. (2011, May 21). Theodore Roosevelt and the environment: Was Teddy Roosevelt a true environmentalist? *About.com*. Retrieved from http://greenliving.about.com

Locker, M. (2019). China's air pollution is so bad that solar panels don't work anymore. *Fast Company*, September 12, 2019. Accessed at www.fastcompany.com/90375916/chinas-air-pollution-is-so-bad-solar-panels-no-longer-work

Lomborg, B. (2007). *Cool it: The skeptical environmentalist's guide to global warming*. New York, NY: Alfred A. Knopf.

Lovins, L.H. (2010). Foreword. In M. Russo (Ed.), *Companies on a mission: Entrepreneurial strategies for growing sustainability, responsibly, and profitably* (pp. x–xii). Stanford, CA: Stanford University Press.

Marks, N. (2007). Personal communication at International Society of Quality of Life Studies (ISQOLS) Conference, San Diego, CA.

Marshall, C. (2011, March 22). British Columbia survives 3 years and $848 million worth of carbon taxes. *The New York Times*. Retrieved from www.nytimes.com

McDonough, W., and Braungart, M. (2002). *Cradle to cradle*. New York, NY: North Point Press.

Mimiaga, J. (2018). Montrose mill eyes San Juan Forest for timber. *The Durango Herald*, February 4, 2018. Accessed at https://durangoherald.com/articles/207132#slide=0

Mittica, C.J. (2019). Patagonia shifts corporate sales strategy. *Advertising Specialty Institute*, April 3, 2019. Accessed at www.asicentral.com/news/newsletters/promogram/april-2019/patagonia-shifts-corporate-sales-strategy/#:~:text=According%20to%20Inc.,environmental%20stewardship%20and%20fair%20labor

Myers, L. (2011). Personal communication with the author during the author's visit to Patagonia's headquarters in Ventura, CA.

National Park Service. (2011). *Devil's tower*. Retrieved from www.nps.gov/deto/index.htm

Neiman, J. (2011). Personal communication with the author via telephone.

Otani, A. (2019). Patagonia triggers a market panic over new rules on its power vests. *The Wall Street Journal*, April 8, 2019. Accessed at www.wsj.com/articles/patagonia-triggers-a-market-panic-over-new-rules-on-its-power-vests-11554736920#:~:text=Patagonia's%20new%20rule%20surfaced%20when,fast%20as%20a%20market%20panic

Patagonia. (2011). Patagonia's Mission Statement. Retrieved from www.patagonia.com

Patagonia. (2018). Annual benefit corporation report: Fiscal year 2017. Accessed at www.patagonia.com/static/on/demandware.static/-/Library-Sites-PatagoniaShared/default/dw824fac0f/PDF-US/2017-BCORP-pages_022218.pdf

Pettway, J. (2019). Warming we want. *Bloomberg Businessweek*, December 16, 2019. Accessed at www.bloomberg.com/news/articles/2019-12-13/this-parka-stylishly-marries-social-impact-and-sustainability

Pew Center on Global Climate Change. (2011). Coal and climate change facts. Retrieved from www.pewclimate.org

REI (2020a). Who we are. Accessed at www.rei.com/about-rei

REI (2020b). What is the circular economy. Accessed at www.rei.com/blog/stewardship/what-is-the-circular-economy

Richter, F. (2019). The global disparity in carbon footprints. *Statista*, December 2, 2019. Accessed at www.statista.com/chart/16292/per-capita-co2-emissions-of-the-largest-economies/

Richter, F. (2020). These are the top 10 manufacturing countries in the world, World Economic Forum, February 25, 2020. Accessed at www.weforum.org/agenda/2020/02/countries-manufacturing-trade-exports-economics/

Ridgeway, R. (2010). Use business to inspire and implement solutions to the environmental crisis. *Patagonia environmental initiatives 2010* (p. 44). Ventura, CA: Patagonia.

Ritchie, H. and Roser, M. (2020). CO_2 and Greenhouse Gas Emissions, Our World in Data. Accessed at https://ourworldindata.org/co2-and-other-greenhouse-gas-emissions

Schiebe, T. (2019). Should every country on earth copy Sweden's carbon tax? *Carbon Pricing Leadership*, October 18, 2019. Accessed at www.carbonpricingleadership.org/blogs/2019/10/18/should-every-country-on-earth-copy-swedens-carbon-tax

SFI. (2011). Sustainable Forestry Initiative. Retrieved from www.sfiprogram.org

Shellenberger, M. (2020). *Apocalypse never: Why environmental alarmism hurts us all*. New York: HarperCollins.

Shultz, C.J., and Holbrook, M.B. (1999). Marketing and the tragedy of the commons: A synthesis, commentary, and analysis for action. *Journal of Public Policy and Marketing*, 18(2), 218–29.

Slav, I. (2019). China's renewable boom hits the wall. Oilprice.com. September 29, 2019. Accessed at https://oilprice.com/Energy/Energy-General/Chinas-Renewable-Boom-Hits-The-Wall.html

Standaert, M. (2019). Why China's renewable energy transition is losing momentum. *YaleEnvironment360*, September 26, 2019. Accessed at https://e360.yale.edu/features/why-chinas-renewable-energy-transition-is-losing-momentum

Stevens, P. (2019). Behind Walmart's push to eliminate 1 gigaton of greenhouse gases by 2030. *CNBC*, December 15, 2019. Accessed at www.cnbc.com/2019/12/15/walmarts-project-gigaton-is-its-most-ambitious-climate-goal-yet.html

Sustainability Consortium. (2020). The Sustainability Consortium. Accessed at www.sustainabilityconsortium.org/

Temple-West, P. (2020). China's carbon trading scheme struggles to take off. *Financial Times*, June 4, 2020. Accessed at www.ft.com/content/35a0a860-8eab-11ea-af59-5283fc4c0cb0

Thorne, D.M., Ferrell, O.C., and Ferrell, L. (2008). *Business and society: A strategic approach to social responsibility* (3rd edn.). Boston, MA: Houghton Mifflin.

UNFCC (2020). What is the Paris Agreement? Accessed at https://unfccc.int/process-and-meetings/the-paris-agreement/what-is-the-paris-agreement

US Climate Alliance. (2020). States united for climate action. Accessed at www.usclimatealliance.org/

Varian, H.R. (1992). *Microeconomic analysis* (3rd edn.). New York, NY: W.W. Norton.

Walljasper, J. (2010). *All that we share: A field guide to the commons.* New York, NY: The New Press.

Walmart. (2011). Sustainability Index. Retrieved from http://walmartstores.com/sustainability/9292.aspx

Walmart. (2019). 2019 Environmental, Social and Governance Report. Accessed at https://corporate.walmart.com/media-library/document/2019-environmental-social-governance-report/_proxyDocument?id=0000016c-20b5-d46a-afff-f5bdafd30000

Walmart. (2020). Walmart's THESIS index. Accessed at www.walmartsustainabilityhub.com/sustainability-index

Weyrich, P.M., and Lind, W.S. (2009). *The next conservatism.* South Bend, IN: St. Augustine's Press.

Yergin, D. (2011). *The quest: Energy, security, and the remaking of the modern world.* New York, NY: The Penguin Press.

10
SUSTAINABLE BUSINESS PRACTICES

Throwing Shade

Source: Photo by Micheile Henderson on Unsplash.

Bitcoin Energy Usage

Did you ever think someone – not a nation state – could create a new currency? This would be a private currency and these have existed in the past – usually created by a bank (Orcutt, 2019). In the 1830s in the US, 90 percent of the money took the form of private banknotes. Exchange rates fluctuated wildly for many of these banknotes because of the changing trust banknote holders had in the issuing bank's ability to buy back the banknotes.

Rumors would frequently fuel exchange-rate chaos. Not surprisingly, frustration came to many holding such banknotes. National currencies with a national banking system stabilized things because people imparted credibility to the issuing institution. (Although countries prone to

(Continued)

printing money, such as Venezuela, have experienced sudden declines in the exchange rate of the Venezuelan currency relative to the Euro of 30 percent in 2012 and 40 percent in 2016 (XE, 2020).)

Digital currency is alluring to some in the era of the internet. In the coming years, groups of countries might issue their own digital currency (Winck, 2020). In the meantime, a private currency has emerged in recent years called Bitcoin which is based on blockchain technology.

Blockchain is a distributed ledger system for use on the internet (Reiff, 2020). It allows all the parties to a transaction to verify that the transaction occurred as proposed by the parties. The cryptographic structure of blockchain ensures that tampering with the transaction history will be detected immediately by other network participants.

Bitcoin is an open system in which anyone in the network can participate without permission, so that payments can be sent, stored and received. Bitcoin serves as the universal unit of value within the Bitcoin peer-to-peer network. For Bitcoin, the blockchain acts as a complete record of every Bitcoin transaction ever made (Baraniuk, 2020).

Bitcoins are issued according to a predictable schedule on average every ten minutes through a process called mining. In such mining, computers are connected to the network to verify transactions. Such verification involves solving puzzles (similar to identifying a randomly selected number) (McCarthy, 2019). Some miners employ warehouses full of computers in pursuit of the Bitcoin rewards. Bitcoin is a volatile currency and has hit an all-time high of $20,000 per Bitcoin but went to half that value in a matter of weeks (Bambrough, 2020). One Bitcoin miner reports that the cost to mine 1 BTC is around $8,200 for his operation (Young, 2020). The primary costs for a Bitcoin miner comes from electricity used to run computers used in mining (CBECI, 2020).

Bitcoin consumes enormous amounts of energy because it involves thousands of miners around the world (with the majority currently in China) competing to solve the puzzles for verifying a transaction that results in receiving a reward of Bitcoin (de Vries, 2018). The more miners, the more difficult the cryptographic challenge – therefore, more energy would be used to mine Bitcoin.

Although Bitcoin mining remains a very private undertaking cloaked in secrecy, recent estimates of the amount of energy directed around the world to Bitcoin mining is around 64 TerraWattHours (TWh) of electricity (Vincent, 2019). This is more electrical energy than the entire country of Switzerland consumes in a year (58 TWh). Annualized Bitcoin electricity consumption grew by about 20 percent from 2018 to 2020 (CBECI, 2020).

Defenders of Bitcoin say that the carbon footprint is what should be the focus – not electricity consumption (implying that Bitcoin mining conducted in Iceland which has abundant geothermal power to generate electricity would result in little greenhouse gas emissions into the earth's atmosphere) (Baraniuk, 2019). Defenders also note that the always-on but inactive electronic devices in the US could power the Bitcoin network four times each year (Vincent, 2019).

Questions to Consider

- What are your thoughts about Bitcoin's intensive energy consumption?
- Would the world be better off without a currency that can be used outside of the banking and credit card system?
- Would you exchange an amount of currency from the US, Europe, Australia or China that is equal to your living expenses for the next year in order to invest it in Bitcoin?
- Currently, speculative investors are those buying Bitcoin. Is it better for society that their money goes into such speculation about a virtual currency?

CHAPTER OVERVIEW AND LEARNING OBJECTIVES

This chapter will highlight some of the most important topics in sustainable business practices – especially those related to new ventures led by entrepreneurs. Environmentally oriented businesses sometimes spark controversy because of (a) their involvement in political action and (b) the potential of other worthy social causes being eclipsed by the attention environmental issues might receive from the media and in public discourse.

A set of contributing factors to the recent turn by some firms toward sustainability can be understood by considering the context in which business is now conducted. Specifically, social, technological, and resource changes comprise the 'STaR' elements of the context for business and must now be considered (Werbach, 2009). A brief examination of what fuels environmentally oriented firms – consumers purchasing 'green' brands – will give insight into the possible future of such firms.

Firm responses to the environmental imperative are diverse. As sustainability consultant Darren Duber-Smith observes, no firm has ever attained 100 percent sustainable status (Duber-Smith, 2009). A 'cradle-to-cradle' approach to turn waste for firms into food for other entities is at the core of architect William McDonough's emphasis on reusing and recycling to be more environmentally effective. As a consultant, McDonough and his partner Michael Braungart have developed the McDonough-Braungart Protocol to assist firms such as the Ford Motor Company and furniture-maker Herman Miller to improve the environmental stewardship of their operations. The McDonough-Braungart Protocol represents one way for firms to self-regulate themselves. Voluntary compliance to internationally respected standards is one avenue for firms to pursue self-regulation. The International Standards Organization based in Switzerland offers an ISO 14001 certification program for environmental management similar to the quality standards in manufacturing, such as ISO 9000, or the most recently developed standards for social responsibility – ISO 26000 (see Chapter 4). Other approaches include CERES, and the Natural Step (Mager and Sibilia, 2010).

As part of self-regulation, metrics for environmental stewardship are important for environmentally oriented firms. The carbon footprint is one metric that enables firms to gauge their contribution to increasing the amount of carbon in the atmosphere – a key factor in global climate change. Such metrics often lead firms to realize that their supply chain accounts for a major portion of the carbon footprint for their products and services. The elusive pursuit of carbon neutrality raises questions about how carbon neutral a firm can become.

Any product, service, or process that delivers value using limited or zero nonrenewable resources and/or creates significantly less waste than conventional offerings can be classified as 'clean tech'. Three main sectors of clean tech include (a) transportation, (b) water, and (c) energy. Examples of ventures from each of these sectors will be featured in this chapter's Mavericks Who Made It. This chapter concludes with not one but four Mavericks in Markets to illustrate how four types of market imperfections hold opportunities for entrepreneurs to create profit-making solutions for environmental problems (Cohen and Winn, 2007, p. 31). These market imperfections to which ventures can be targeted follow: (a) inefficient systems, (b) externalities, (c) flawed pricing mechanisms, and (d) imperfectly distributed information.

After this chapter, you should be able to answer the following questions:

- What are the four stages of entrepreneurship?
- What is sustainable entrepreneurship?
- What is ISO 14001? CERES? The Natural Step?
- What is the LOHAS segment of consumers?
- What is 'cradle-to-cradle' design or the 'circular economy'?
- What is clean tech? What are the different types of clean tech?

Mia Birk – an innovator in city government and later in the private sector

Source: miabirk.com. Photo featured on *Joyride: Pedaling Toward a Healthier Planet*, first edition. 2010. Cadence Press. Photographer © Erin Janke.

UNDERSTANDING SUSTAINABLE ENTREPRENEURSHIP
From Intrapreneur to Entrepreneur

Entrepreneurs are those who provide a new product or service working for themselves in the private sector. Intrapreneurs work inside firms or governments and promote innovative product development and marketing through employee-entrepreneurial activity (Peterson, 2020). Both develop and use new ways to produce or deliver existing goods and services at a lower cost: 'Entrepreneurs innovate. Innovation is the specific instrument of entrepreneurship' (Drucker, 1985, p. 30). The effect of innovation is the creative destruction (old forms of business being made obsolete by new forms) cited by the twentieth-century economist Joseph Schumpeter who celebrated the entrepreneur. Sustainable entrepreneurship is the process through which individuals and teams create value by focusing on the well-being of the natural environment and communities in the pursuit of opportunities (Shepherd and Patzelt, 2011).

The bicycle and pedestrian movement gaining momentum now has developed over many years through the sometimes patient and sometimes daring efforts of bicycle activists, city planners, policy makers, and bicycle commuters in thousands of communities around the world. Mia Birk (pictured opposite) became one of the most high-profile leaders of this movement as manager of Portland, Oregon's bicycle program, and later as President and Co-Owner of Alta Planning + Design based in Portland, Oregon. She now heads Mia Birk Consulting, which does professional coaching and business consulting (Birk, 2020).

Birk obtained a bachelor's degree in government and French from the University of Texas at Austin. When she went from her suburban home in Dallas to continue her studies in Washington, DC, car parking loomed as a problem. Her brother gave her his ten-speed bicycle to use. Despite being a self-described 'couch potato' at the time, she used his bicycle and liked the by-products of bicycle commuting. She lost weight and felt better.

'Within a few weeks, I was in the best shape of my life, and a lifelong love affair had begun,' Birk said. 'Since then, I have been a dedicated bicyclist for recreation, touring, exercise, and daily utilitarian trips. I have two children – ages 13 and 9 and see bicycling as a win–win strategy for maintaining my family's health, safety, budget, and community connection' (Szczepanski, 2010, p. 1).

In 1988, Birk began as a grad student emphasizing international-environmental-studies at Johns Hopkins University. She studied transportation and 'how where we live affects how we get around' (Moon, 2010, p. 1).

She realized that the bicycle offered a win–win proposition to relieve congestion in cities of the world, reduce air pollution, and reduce obesity for individuals. Birk was in Washington, DC, in 1991 when a federal transportation bill first included funding for trails, bike lanes, and sidewalks. Because she was working with a coalition focused on energy conservation, she became aware that jobs would soon be available in the bicycle and pedestrian field (Moon, 2010).

Birk's credibility in the bicycle and pedestrian movement originated from her accomplishments as a public sector worker in Portland from 1993 to 1999 during the city's rise to become the top bicycling city in the United States (Moon, 2010). During this time, Birk served as Portland's bicycle program manager.

'People think Portlanders just drank some microbrew one night and started riding bikes in the morning,' Birk said. 'Not the case at all' (Dundas, 2011, p. 11). The truth is that, despite some forward-looking funding for beginning bike trails as a reaction to the 1973 Arab Oil Embargo, Birk often endured bitter public meetings and resistance in Portland. Portland's culture and transportation system, like many other US cities, focused on the automobile. But Birk proved skillful in creating change inside the system of city government, regional planning organizations, citizen groups, and businesses (Dundas, 2011, p. 11).

Early in her time as Portland's bike program manager, she mobilized citizen support that led to the city council adopting a bikeway-network plan. She later helped this plan come into reality by navigating endless challenges and problems. Along the way, she had to overcome antiquated traffic engineering standards, fight federal regulators, explain her actions to the skeptical journalists of *The Oregonian* newspaper, cajole reluctant city maintenance workers to sweep glass in bike lanes and fix dangerous drainage grates, and push along colored bike lanes, bike bridges, and a trail along the Willamette River (Birk and Kurmanskie, 2010). 'There are political battles behind every single piece of infrastructure that exists,' Birk said. 'To succeed in that arena, you have to build teams' (Dundas, 2011, p. 12). Since 2008, *Bicycling* magazine has rated Portland as one of the 'best cities for cycling' placing it in the top five cities (Maus, 2018).

Mia Birk's story highlights important aspects of taking an entrepreneurial orientation. First, entrepreneurship does not begin with a product or service but with an opportunity that is rooted in the external environment (Morris, 1998). From her work in promoting energy conservation policy in Washington, DC, she recognized that the federal transportation legislation's inclusion of funding for bicycle and pedestrian travel would create many opportunities for transforming urban landscapes into communities aggressive about including such travel in their transportation systems. She took the opportunity to go to Portland as the city's bicycle program manager recognizing that Oregon was forward-thinking in developing alternatives to automobile travel. Oregon was already using a portion of the state budget to enhance roadways for bicycle travel. This illustrates how the opportunity – public funding of bicycle and pedestrian transportation infrastructure – existed in the external environment outside of any one firm.

Then, over a period of six years in the 1990s, Birk provided community-wide leadership to change the culture of Portland to be more bicycle friendly (Mapes, 2009). Importantly, she learned what it took to win approval for infrastructure improvements for alternative means of transportation so that many constituencies were pleased with the outcome. This illustrates how entrepreneurs are not born, but they develop over time through learning.

When Michael Jones contacted her after she had left her position with the city government, she was ready to join him by opening the Portland office of his new firm. In this way, she would develop the opportunities for planning and designing bicycle and pedestrian transportation into the plans of cities across the United States and beyond. In 2009, Birk and Jones spun off Alta Bicycle share, Inc., which successfully launched and operated the bike-sharing systems in Melbourne, Washington, D.C., Boston, Chicago, and New York City, among others. She also co-founded a professional association (Association of Pedestrian and Bicycle Professionals), an academic program (Initiative for Bicycle and Pedestrian Innovation), and a coalition of cities that developed a fresh approach to urban bikeway design (NACTO Urban Bikeway Design Guide.)

Capital bikeshare has 500 docking stations in the Washington, DC area

Source: Image courtesy of Mr.TinDC via Flickr. Shared under the CC BY-ND 2.0 license.

In all of its bike-sharing programs, Alta Bicycle Share partnered with Public Bike Share Corporation (PBSC) of Montreal, which provided the bicycles and kiosks with solar-powered docking stations, theft-resistant locking devices, and credit-card processing technology (Coster, 2011). Lyft acquired Alta Bicycle Share in 2014 and Birk stepped away from Alta Planning + Design the next year (Maus, 2015).

Birk recalled that when she joined Alta it had about a dozen projects worth about $100,000. In 2015 when she left, Alta had about 400 active projects, 20 offices, and $25 million in annual revenue.

'At the beginning, people would ask me, "What is that you do again?"' Birk said. 'Portland had its bike plan, but that was about it. Nationwide, there wasn't even a field for bicycle transportation consulting services. I had to create the language around what I did.'

Stages of Entrepreneurship

Entrepreneurship does not only occur at a particular point in time. Rather, a dynamic process of entrepreneurship takes time to unfold (Morris, 1998). Across identifiable stages, the entrepreneurship process can be managed. Results of research suggest that the process of entrepreneurship can be characterized by four phases (see Table 10.1): (a) searching, (b) planning, (c) marshaling, and (d) implementing (McGee et al., 2009).

Table 10.1　Stages of entrepreneurship

Searching – developing a unique idea or identifying a special opportunity.
Planning – converting the idea/opportunity into a workable business plan.
Marshaling – assembling resources to bring the venture into existence.
Implementing – growing the business.

Source: McGee et al. (2009).

The *searching* phase involves the development by the entrepreneur of a unique idea and/or identification of a special opportunity. This phase draws on the entrepreneur's creative talents and the ability to innovate. Entrepreneurs, as compared with managers, are particularly adept at perceiving and exploiting opportunities before these opportunities are recognized by others (Hisrich and Peters, 1998). Birk and her colleagues were not the first company to field a bike-sharing program. In Washington, DC, Clear Channel Communications, provider of advertisements and signage at subway and bus stops, launched SmartBike in 2008 (Martinez, 2010). However, marketing problems plagued SmartBike. Without enough bikes and bike stations and too little promotion, SmartBike never fared well. Its pricing was only targeted to commuters with an annual $40 subscription fee. Tourists had no cheaper option. However, Capital Bikeshare, launched by Alta Bicycle Share, had more bikes and plenty of promotion.

The *planning* phase consists of activities by which the entrepreneur converts the idea into a workable business plan (McGee et al., 2009). Here, the entrepreneur may or may not actually write a formal business plan. However, he or she must evaluate the idea or business concept and give it meaning as a business. The plan addresses questions such as: What is the size of the market? Where will the business establishment be located? What are the product specifications? How and by whom will the product be manufactured? What are the start-up costs? What are the recurring operating costs of doing business? Will the venture be able to make a profit, and if so, how soon after founding? How rapidly will the business grow, and what resources are required to sustain its growth?

The *marshaling* phase involves assembling resources to bring the venture into existence (McGee et al., 2009). At the end of the planning phase, the business is only 'on paper' or in the mind of the entrepreneur. To bring the business into existence, the entrepreneur gathers (marshals) necessary resources such as capital, labor, customers, and suppliers without which the venture cannot exist or sustain itself.

Capital Bikeshare is based on a public–private partnership with capital expenditures for kiosks and bicycles provided by public funding, while user fees covering the operations run by private companies, such as Alta Bicycle Share (Martinez, 2010). The city retains any advertising revenue at the kiosks or on the bicycles. Additionally, the city controls the colors of the bicycles (Whitford, 2011).

The final phase is *implementing* (McGee et al., 2009). The entrepreneur is responsible for growing the business and sustaining the business past its infancy. To this end, the successful entrepreneur applies good management skills and principles. As an executive-level manager, the entrepreneur engages in strategic planning and manages a variety of business relationships with suppliers, customers, employees, and providers of capital. Growing an enterprise requires vision and the ability to solve problems quickly and efficiently. Not unique to entrepreneurship, these tasks are also required of effective managers. However, the entrepreneur is the primary risk-bearer of the enterprise with a financial stake in its long-term growth and success.

Operational risk for launching a bike-sharing program emerges from having the venture's property stolen or damaged. Alta Bicycle Share knows that the moment bikes and stations are established, they will be challenged by thieves or vandals. 'The first thing people do – mostly teenagers – is try to steal the bikes. They'll jerk them up and down and side to side,' Alta Bicycle Share CEO Alison Cohen said. 'In Montreal they have a picture of a Ford F-150 with a rope connected to a bike, but the truck couldn't get the bike out of the dock. With a system that's secure like that, theft and vandalism are very minimal. The only real theft we've seen in the US has been people using a stolen credit card to take a bike and not return it' (Whitford, 2011, p. 1).

Entrepreneurs are calculated risk-takers (Morris, 1998). They are not wild-eyed risk takers. Research suggests that their propensity to accept risk is not very different from society at large. They will thoroughly analyze and evaluate the prospects for ventures and deals based on the risks evident for financial returns, technical success, and sufficient numbers of customers paying for their products or services.

In addition to the risk-taking inherent in pursuing innovation, entrepreneurs must bring proactiveness to the implementation of the plan to bring their focal concept into a viable product or service and an ongoing business enterprise (Covin and Slevin, 1989). In other words, they must put their plan into action. This almost always requires perseverance, adaptability, and a willingness to accept some responsibility for failure of the venture (Morris, 1998).

GREEN OPPORTUNITIES FOR SUSTAINABLE ENTERPRISES
Concern for the Planet and Communities on the Rise

Opportunities always reside outside of the firm and not in product or service concepts themselves. For example, 'better mousetraps that nobody wants' can describe the largest category of new product failures (Morris, 1998, p. 26). In other words, a new product can be technologically sophisticated, but when it is introduced into the marketplace, its sales lag and it fails. Such failure could occur because (a) customers are already satisfied, (b) the concept is too difficult to comprehend, (c) the perceived switching costs are too painful, or (d) customers simply do not have a need for such a product or service.

Concern about climate change topped the list of issues across respondents in 14 countries (US, Canada, Australia, Japan, South Korea, and EU Countries) surveyed in Spring of 2020 (Poushter and Huang, 2020). The median percentage across these countries was 70 percent for those saying they perceived global climate change as a major threat to their countries. Such concerns set the stage for firms doing more for reducing greenhouse gas emissions. Efforts such as RE100 have emerged in recent years to transition firms to 100 percent renewable energy (RE100, 2020). Hundreds of major corporations have joined RE100 and have committed to use renewable energy for all of their needs in the coming few years. Some of these firms are Allianz Group (German-based insurance firm), Apple, Tesco (UK-based grocery retailer), and Tata Motors (India).

Second, institutions have proposed goals, standards, and approaches to better the environment and communities. For example, the Sustainable Development Goals (SDGs) serve as a blueprint to achieve a better and more sustainable future for all (United Nations, 2020), and the UN Global Compact asks companies to support a set of core values in the areas of human rights, labor standards, the environment, and anti-corruption (these were discussed in Chapter 4). British environmentalist and social commentator John Elkington estimates that the SDGs (a set of 17 goals with 169 related targets) offers an unprecedented opportunity for businesses worth up to $12 trillion a year in just four of 60 sectors (food and agriculture, cities, energy and materials, and health and well-being) (Elkington, 2017).

Other institutions and NGOs have made contributions to raising awareness of issues related to sustainability. For example, in 2000, the US Green Building Council developed an internationally recognized certification system for the design, construction, and operation of environmentally friendly buildings called the Leadership in Energy and Environmental Design (LEED) Green Building Rating Systems™ (USGBC, 2011). Receiving one of the top LEED certifications, such as Silver, Gold, or Platinum, translates into understandable advantages for owning and maintaining these certified buildings – if for no other reasons than the reduced expense of operating them.

NGOs such as the International Standards Organization based in Geneva, Switzerland, developed a suite of standards for environmental quality management – ISO 14000 – which today is the most widely implemented environmental management system (Mager and Sibilia, 2010). ISO 14000 first asks a business to create an environmental policy. The next step is to determine the environmental impacts of all the products, services, and activities done by the firm. Then, the firm plans its environmental objectives and measurable targets. Finally, the firm implements its plan, checks it in an ongoing way, makes corrections, and engages in management review of its progress.

Similar sets of principles for environmental management include the CERES principles, which mandate that results of reports on the environmental impact of the firm be made public, and the Natural Step Framework, developed by Swedish oncologist and karate-champion Dr. Karl-Henrik Robèrt (Mager and Sibilia, 2010). The Natural Step was adopted and made popular by Interface, Inc.'s founder and CEO Ray Anderson (see Chapter 1).

The principles of the Natural Step to become a sustainable society are reducing (a) the progressive buildup of substances extracted from the Earth's crust (such as heavy metals and fossil fuels), (b) the chemicals and compounds produced by industrial processes (dioxins, DDT, PVC), (c) the progressive physical degradation of nature and natural processes (over-harvesting of forests), and (d) conditions that undermine individuals' capacities to their basic human needs (such as unsafe working conditions and meager wages).

In working with hundreds of companies, municipalities, academic institutions, and not-for-profit organizations all over the world, the nonprofit The Natural Step has found that sustainable decision-making does not lead to negative outcomes for firms. But, rather, adopting sustainable business practices leads to new opportunities, reduced costs, and dramatically reduced ecological and social impacts.

Businesses Make Changes for the Natural Environment

Consumers have watched businesses become more environmentally oriented in recent years. Walmart's transition is still in progress, but it typifies some of the most earnest efforts to adopt sustainable business practices that will not be missed by consumers over the world.

NASCAR

A very visible business in the United States, NASCAR, the automobile racing organization owned by the France family, has now embraced an environmental orientation (NASCAR, 2020). NASCAR is similar to many for-profit businesses today in that it is focused on cutting costs by recycling, conserving, and generating its own energy. Accordingly, NASCAR's teams, track operators, and sponsors have adopted an ambitious set of green initiatives that includes planting trees to offset carbon emissions and deploying sheep to keep the infield grass short.

Drawing on the imagery of the green flag waved above the track under which the cars pass when beginning a NASCAR race, NASCAR Green is the program which NASCAR runs throughout the year with more than 15 green partners. Some of the activities for NASCAR Green include: (1) racing on a blended biofuel called Sunoco Green E15, (2) pursuing large-scale recycling efforts at race tracks that include racing oils and tires, (3) diverting food from waste and to productive uses, (4) using solar power at tracks, (5) sourcing from organic farms for the menu in hospitality suites, and (6) employing more energy-efficient track sweepers. The NASCAR Tree Planting Program planted more than 500,000 trees across the country by 2020 as a carbon offset for the fuel consumed by NASCAR race vehicles.

NASCAR has also supported other projects like the installation in 2010 of 40,000 solar panels over 25 acres at Pocono Raceway in Long Pond, Pennsylvania. After spending about $15 million to build the three-megawatt solar farm, the track now saves about $500,000 a year in energy costs and has produced electricity equal to 324,000 gallons of gasoline.

'We gained a lot of fans because of it,' said Brandon Igdalsky, Pocono Raceway's president. 'Our generation is trying to clean up the things that our grandparents and great-grandparents did' (Belson, 2011, para. 15).

The Roush Fenway team, a joint venture between Roush Racing and Fenway Sports Group (owners of the Boston Red Sox), builds race cars and fields race teams. It recycles 96 percent of each car it produces. It has also eliminated Styrofoam cups from its operations and has bought bicycles for workers to get around its facility in North Carolina. All of these steps for NASCAR are only the beginning of a long process to clean up the sport.

'We're realists and we race cars that burn a fossil fuel that get four to five miles per gallon, and we can't change that,' said Ian Prince, the chief sustainability officer at Roush Fenway. 'But we can change the other 99 percent of it' (Belson, 2011, para. 23).

McDonald's

Businesses and environmentalists have increasingly been working together. For example, McDonald's and Greenpeace have combined efforts to avoid further destruction of the Amazon Rainforest (Langert, 2019). After initially criticizing McDonald's in 2006 for buying chickens raised on soybeans grown on illegal farms carved out of the Amazon Rainforest in Brazil, the following year Greenpeace joined forces with McDonald's to pressure the major soy traders in Brazil into placing an unprecedented two-year moratorium on the purchase of any soy from newly deforested areas (Butler, 2009).

Bob Langert, McDonald's vice president of sustainability at the time, reported that the Greenpeace soy campaign initially discombobulated McDonald's leadership. Greenpeace protesters in chicken costumes entered McDonald's restaurants in the UK and Germany with big signs reading 'Every bite you take out of a Chicken McNugget is a bite out of the rainforest' (Langert, 2019, p. 172).

McDonald's supply chain represented less than half of a percent of soy purchasing due to Brazilian soy being used in chicken feed in Europe and Asia (hence, the connection to Chicken McNuggets). At first, McDonald's leaders wanted to reply in defense that their part of a deforestation problem in the Amazon was miniscule. 'Internally, I countered the "small" concern head on,' Langert said (Langert, 2016). 'Small does not mean you sit back. Everyone's impact is small. I was raised in a McDonald's culture that believed we could use our convening and collaborative power to bring diverse stakeholders together.'

Greenpeace's major target was not McDonald's, but Cargill – a privately owned global food corporation based in Minnesota in the US that was heavily involved in soy bean production in Brazil. However, Greenpeace saw that such a private firm (although large enough to be ranked as the 15th largest corporation in the US) was invisible to consumers. Without a marketing budget the size of McDonald's to send their message about soy farms encroaching on the Amazon forest, Greenpeace targeted McDonald's – a global brand with close connection to consumers.

Greenpeace only expected McDonald's to change its behavior and that other firms would eventually follow. Instead, McDonald's supply-chain executives called together representatives of their top 15 suppliers (accounting for 80 percent of materials used by McDonald's) and told them that McDonald's expected them to monitor and manage their upstream suppliers. Previously, the only expectation of a McDonald's supplier was to be responsible for their own processing facility. This marked a pivotal sea change.

By 2016, Paolo Adario, who headed the Amazon campaign for Greenpeace of Brazil in 2006, reported the moratorium (that still is in place) proved to be a monumental success. 'After 10 years, overall Amazon deforestation has dropped 80 percent,' Adario said (Langert, 2016). 'And everyone continued to make money in soy (and in beef), because they improved their profile image.'

Tom's of Maine

New brands have entered the marketplace positioned as delivering sustainable benefits. For example, Tom's of Maine entered as a manufacturer of natural-ingredients-only personal care products in 1970 (Tom's of Maine, 2020). Tom and Kate Chappell moved from

Philadelphia where Tom worked for an insurance company to Kennebunk, Maine, in 1968. Because of their goal to simplify their lives, they sought out natural, unprocessed foods, as well as unadulterated products. As they were unable to find natural personal care products for themselves and their children, Tom and Kate decided to create and sell their own. They launched their venture with a $5,000 loan from a friend and the philosophy that their products would not harm the environment.

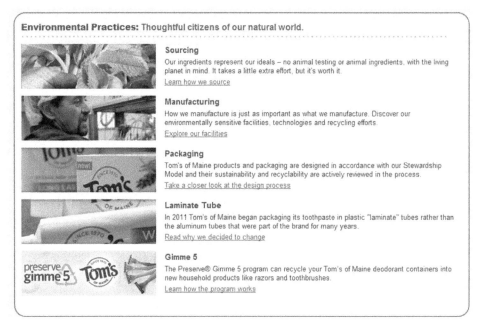

Figure 10.1   Good business at Tom's of Maine focuses on environmental stewardship

Source: www.tomsofmaine.com

Over the years, the product line of Tom's of Maine moved from nonphosphate laundry detergent to natural personal care products, such as the first natural toothpaste (1975) and deodorant (1976). Recognizing the future value of an established brand with an authentic commitment to sustainable business practices in the fast-growing natural, personal-care-products category, Colgate-Palmolive purchased 84 percent of Tom's of Maine in 2006 for $100 million (Wohl, 2006). The Chappells hold the remaining stock in their business that now boasts 90 products that are distributed in more than 40,000 retail outlets where millions of consumers encounter them in their shopping.

'When we first started out, this brand-new idea of natural products and sustainable companies seemed a little crazy to some,' Tom Chappell said. 'In the years since, though, more and more people have begun to believe, like we do, that nature can provide many of the health benefits we need – and that companies should minimize their environmental impact while working towards positive change in our communities. Together, we've really started to make a difference' (Tom's of Maine, 2020, para. 1).

Consumers Turn toward Green

Segmentation studies on US consumers in recent years have identified a Lifestyles of Health and Sustainability (LOHAS) segment that is the most interested in green products and services (Ottman, 2011). Researchers estimate that one in four consumers in the US are LOHAS consumers (41 million) who spend more than $290 billion annually in their shopping (Sung and Woo, 2019). Demographically, these consumers tend to be married, educated, middle-aged, and female. LOHAS consumers have the second highest income level, so they have the means needed to buy a variety of products and services – and perhaps paying a premium for some of these.

LOHAS consumers are active in their communities and support environmental and social causes. They are conscious stewards of the environment as evidenced by their energy and water conservation, their use of cloth shopping bags, and their advocacy for environmental causes. They will use the internet to investigate new green brands, and 71 percent of them report a willingness to boycott brands that offend their values (this is twice as high as any other segment).

Importantly, they are early adopters of green technologies, and they are vocal in recommending green products and services to friends. This means that they have an impact (positive or negative) in the diffusion of innovations for any green product of which they form an opinion. In other words, they would play the role of a valued expert on green products and services in their social network. Considering that the growing market in the United States for goods and services focused on sustainability-oriented products and services, the role of LOHAS consumers is a crucial one for brands positioning themselves as promoting sustainable living. In research conducted by the Natural Marketing Institute, other segments express varying degrees of interest in sustainable living (Ottman, 2011). However, no segment is as committed to green purchasing as the LOHAS segment.

Another set of studies found evidence that altruism – in the form of buying green products that cost more – signals one's willingness and ability to incur costs for others' benefit (Griskevicius, Tybur, and Van den Bergh, 2010). These results suggest that such altruism is a 'costly signal' associated with status. In other words, in addition to signaling that a person is prosocial (doing things for others), altruism can demonstrate that one has the resources (time, energy, money, relationships, or other) and the ability to incur the costs of self-sacrifice for public welfare. Interestingly, eliciting status motives for respondents increased the desire for green products when shopping in public (but not private) and when green products cost more (but not less) than nongreen products.

It seems that the key question about green consumption is 'how rapidly is it being adopted by consumers around the world?' Studies have now identified LOHAS consumer segments of substantial size in many countries of the world (LOHAS, 2020). With Walmart's decision to promote green products, green consumption will likely become part of mainstream consumption in the future. With the accountability mechanisms of the Web and social media in the twenty-first century, which firms want to be known for providing products and services that are more harmful to the natural environment and communities?

Businesses Turn toward Green

Using Nature's Principles

Naturalists define sustainability as the capacity of healthy ecosystems to continue functioning indefinitely (Unruh, 2008). One can perceive the idea of ecosystem sustainability in the United Nations' Bruntland Commission report as the commission defined sustainable development as meeting 'the needs of the present without compromising the ability of future generations to meet their own needs' (World Commission on Environment and Development, 1987). Because of the usefulness of the sustainability framework for improving the efficiency and effectiveness of businesses and society, further consideration of how nature can inform approaches to human activities is warranted.

In recent years, researchers and thinkers have investigated how the principles of nature and Earth's complex and self-regulating biosphere can be applied to the operations of businesses (Unruh, 2008). In nature, cycles characterize living organisms and ecosystems. Dead animals and plants become food for other animals and plants. Using a life-cycle approach, firms have analyzed their operations using a 'cradle-to-grave' approach of all steps from material extraction to disposal to understand the energy, resources, and emissions associated with the production and marketing of their brands (Ottman, 2011). An outcome of such an approach was that firms pursuing sustainable business practices emphasized 'reduce, reuse, and recycle' (Unruh, 2008, p. 113). However, if firms still included synthetically derived materials in their products, such as polyvinylchloride (PVC), their efforts to reduce, reuse, and recycle would remain problem-ridden for the environment. Synthetic compounds, such as PVC, are 'monstrous hybrids' in which biological and technical ingredients are combined in a way that makes it infeasible to separate them at the end of the product's life (Lee and Bony, 2008).

Going beyond this 'cradle-to-grave' approach in which products (made of monstrous hybrids) go to a landfill after their useful life, architect William McDonough and his chemist business-partner Michael Braungart have become leading advocates for a 'cradle-to-cradle' approach for firms (MBDC, 2020). Such an approach illustrates the concept of a circular economy (CE) with closed material loops (Unruh, 2018). Using the McDonough Braungart Design Chemistry (MBDC) consulting firm's cradle-to-cradle (C2C) design protocol, the concept of waste goes away. Using C2C, firms design products, packaging, and systems from the very beginning to be fully recyclable (McDonough and Braungart, 2002a). The C2C concept also designs monstrous hybrids out of products. McDonough and Braungart compared the C2C approach to traditional practice in the following way:

> The characteristic design approach of the last century was 'cradle to grave' It involved digging up, cutting down, or burning natural resources – releasing toxic material into the environment in the process – to make products that became useless waste at the end of their useful lives. By contrast, [the] cradle-to-cradle approach mirrors nature's regenerative cycles so that at the end of its useful life, a product and its component materials are used to make equally valuable products. C2C thinking does not just focus on minimizing toxic pollution and reducing natural resources waste. It goes one step further, demanding that companies redesign industrial processes so that they don't generate pollution and waste in the first place.
>
> (Lee and Bony, 2008, p. 5)

Using as few raw materials as possible in the design of products mimics nature's ways. This makes recycling easier than using many or making a common mistake of the industrial age by including many synthetic materials in the manufacture of modern products. For example, MBDC collaborated with L'Oreal USA in the development of Goddess Strength Shampoo and Conditioner for its Carol's Daughter brand (MBDC, 2020). This brand achieved the Silver level of MBDC's program due to its (1) material health (no harmful chemicals as ingredients), (2) material reutilization (renewable and biodegradable ingredients), (3) renewable energy use (100 percent during production), (4) water stewardship (during production), and (5) social fairness (for workers and communities).

MBDC examined the composition of the Aeron desk chair made by furniture manufacturer Herman Miller based in Zeeland, Michigan, and operating in more than 40 countries (Miller, 2020). MBDC found that more than 200 components made from more than 800 chemical compounds were used in the manufacture of the Aeron. Herman Miller used the analysis conducted by MBDC to design its award-winning Mirra desk chair whose dramatically simplified set of materials allows the Mirra to be 96 percent recyclable (Unruh, 2008, p. 115). Herman Miller has more than twenty Cradle to Cradle Certified Products and each of the Herman Miller facilities around the world are powered totally by renewable energy.

Benefits from Using Nature's Principles in Business

Architects and building developers striving to obtain LEED certification for the environmental sustainability of their buildings would use inputs such as the Cradle to Cradle Certified Product Scorecard as depicted in Figure 10.2 in choosing the materials and office furniture for their buildings. Points toward LEED certification would be gained by using environmentally certified products in a building being considered for LEED certification. Products with high ratings not only contribute to the sustainability of the building, but also make such buildings less costly to maintain. Importantly, such green buildings are more productive places for employees as a result of better indoor air quality, lighting, and toxin-free furniture. Such products can qualify for the US EPA Environmentally Preferable Purchase Program (www.epa.gov/greenerproducts/about-environmentally-preferable-purchasing-program). In these ways, environmental certification can give access to buyers and marketplaces where green has added value.

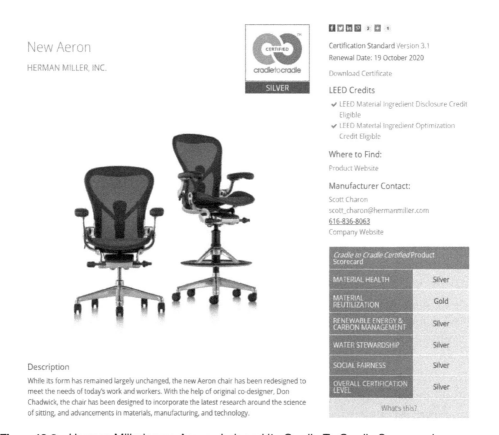

Figure 10.2   Herman Miller's new Aeron chair and its Cradle To Cradle Scorecard

Source: www.c2ccertified.org/products/scorecard/new-aeron-herman-miller-inc

Firms such as office-furniture manufacturer Herman Miller have gained numerous advantages from adopting closed-loop recycling principles of nature's ways in pursuing sustainability for their products. For example, Herman Miller has become a more flexible market player because its procurement process seeks materials that will not be regulated or restricted in the future (MBDC, 2020). Herman Miller stopped producing the paneled exterior of its iconic Eames chairs out of rosewood because it recognized rosewood was an endangered species (Michler and Fehrenbacher, 2011). By switching to walnut for the Eames chair, Herman Miller avoided a more expensive material (and one likely to be regulated or restricted in the future).

In the manufacturing process, Herman Miller gained financial benefits by avoiding employee exposure to harmful chemicals and reducing regulatory costs. In the design process, Herman Miller created a source of more readily accessible raw materials by designing products for end-of-life material recovery. It seems now that this ability to forecast the return of materials to the industry for future use will be the most significant economic gain from intelligent product design imparted by a C2C approach (McDonough and Braungart, 2002b). Finally, Herman Miller won a more defensible position in the marketplace with its products characterized by strong environmental performance. This means that Herman Miller products have higher quality because they were better designed by using the healthiest materials for users that can later be recycled into products of equal or greater value in the next cycle (upcycling).

Using recycled materials drastically reduces costs. For example, Patagonia's Common Threads Recycling program turns last season's Patagonia's Capilene brand performance underwear into this season's second-generation polyester fibers used in the manufacture of Patagonia clothing. It has also extended this recycling to fleece. Energy costs for making such second-generation polyester are 76 percent below those for virgin sourcing (Unruh, 2008).

Taking a cradle-to-cradle perspective for Patagonia means that the Patagonia website prominently profiles how to (a) buy and sell used Patagonia gear on eBay, (b) send in Patagonia gear for repair at a modest cost, and (c) send in gear for donation to the recycling program (Patagonia, 2020). In this way, Patagonia reinforces the idea of the durability of its products in the mind of consumers – an important reason to choose Patagonia. It also positions itself as not only a manufacturer, but also a collaborator with customers interested in reducing consumption. By taking back used products for recycling, Patagonia also assumes a role in reverse logistics – getting the product back from the user for reprocessing. This is accomplished through the mail for underwear (that it hopes is clean) and through drop-off bins at retail outlets (Unruh, 2008). In this way, Patagonia nurtures relationships with customers important to its future.

The Pathway to a More Sustainable Business

Sustainability-oriented products are increasingly part of the mainstream in marketplaces. Although many firms have not taken the leadership roles in the movement of sustainable business practices, such as Herman Miller and Patagonia, increasingly the good sense of seeking virtuous closed-loop cycles is being adopted by businesses around the world.

Among respondents who say ESG programs create value, the share seeing short- and long-term value has grown.

Share of respondents who say given program creates value, %[1]

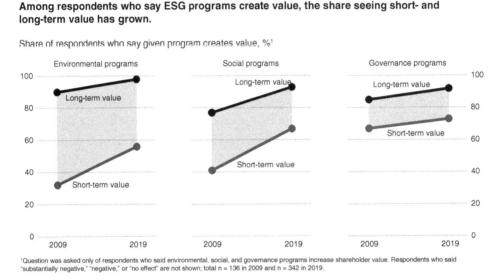

[1]Question was asked only of respondents who said environmental, social, and governance programs increase shareholder value. Respondents who said "substantially negative," "negative," or "no effect" are not shown; total n = 136 in 2009 and n = 342 in 2019.

Figure 10.3   Comparison of survey results (2009 and 2019) of senior leaders of firms around the globe about the value of environmental, social, and governance programs

Source: Exhibit from 'Is apparel manufacturing coming home?', October 2018, McKinsey & Company, www.mckinsey.com. (c) 2020 McKinsey & Company. All rights reserved. Reprinted by permission.

Figure 10.3 depicts the comparison of survey results from 2009 and 2019 of senior leaders of firms around the globe about the value of environmental, social, and governance programs. As can be seen, in the most recent survey from 2019, the clear majority of these senior leaders see these sustainability-related ESG programs as creating value in both the short term and the long term. In the long term, more than 90 percent see such value. This suggests that sustainability is not a 'minority opinion' across firms of the world – but a majority view among business leaders. Clearly, businesses have moved a long way toward sustainability since McDonough and Braungart first introduced cradle-to-cradle principles in the 1990s. These results also suggest that many more firms will likely intensify their move to integrate sustainability concepts into their operations in the coming years.

Clean tech refers to any product, service, or process that delivers its value by using limited or zero nonrenewable resources and/or creates much less waste than conventional offerings (Pernick and Wilder, 2007, p. 2). Opportunities for clean tech breakthroughs currently appear fruitful in (a) solar energy, (b) wind power, (c) biofuels and biomaterials, (d) green buildings, (e) personal transportation, (f) batteries for mobile power, (g) the smart grid, and (h) water filtration.

Encouragingly, clean tech energy increasingly is more affordable (Winston, 2019). With the cost of building new wind and solar facilities falling in recent years, three-quarters of coal-fired electricity-generation plants in the US are more expensive to run than new ones run by renewable energy. In April 2020, the US obtained more energy from renewables than from coal for the first time in what is being called 'the coal crossover'. Likewise, low-carbon energy has similarly overtaken coal in countries such as the UK, Sweden, Denmark, Portugal, Nicaragua, and Costa Rica.

Additionally, electric transportation is expanding. Electric vehicles (EVs) are still a small part of the car fleet, but Tesla's Model 3 became the top-selling car in California in the first quarter of 2020 (Schmidt, 2020). China now has more than 400,000 electric buses on the road (Winston, 2019). More than 30 million in India ride on electric rickshaws every day. Daimler, manufacturer of Mercedes-Benz, announced it will now direct all research and development to electric vehicles, rather than internal-combustion engines.

CONCLUSION

This chapter examined sustainable entrepreneurship. Researchers have identified a process for entrepreneurship that features four stages: (a) searching, (b) planning, (c) marshaling, and (d) implementation. Entrepreneurs come in many forms, but most are motivated by achievement – accomplishing what they set out to do (Morris, 1998). Money, while necessary to fund the venture and help grow it, often becomes more of a scorecard for intrinsically motivated entrepreneurs. Sustainable entrepreneurs create value by focusing on the well-being of the natural environment and communities in the pursuit of opportunities (Shepherd and Patzelt, 2011).

Sustainable entrepreneurs, like all entrepreneurs, are agents of change. Not surprisingly, sustainable entrepreneurs find themselves embroiled in controversy because (a) opponents of growth see them as bringing more consumption and material depletion of the Earth's resources, (b) political action is part of what some of them do, and (c) their successes with their own causes sometimes move other causes lower in priority in public discourse.

Macromarketing scholars have noted that more consumers are changing their attitudes and lifestyles to reflect more concern for the planet and communities today (McDonagh and Prothero, 2014). This is likely a result of (a) global disruptions such as the economic meltdown of 2008 and the COVID-19 pandemic of 2020 that brought many consumers to rethink the promises of endless economic growth, (b) the emergence of environmentally oriented media programming that reinforced nurturing attitudes toward care of the Earth, and (c) institutions that developed frameworks for activities to better the environment and communities, such as the UN's Sustainable Development Goals, the UN Global Compact for businesses, LEED certification for buildings, ISO 14000, CERES, and the Natural Step.

To what degree consumers and businesses go 'green' remains to be seen. Consumers in the segment Lifestyles of Health and Sustainability (LOHAS) already represent millions who will prioritize what firms, their products, and services contribute to sustainability in their purchase decisions. Other research suggests that making green purchases can win status for consumers (Griskevicius et al., 2010). Despite such an advance for green purchasing, some consumers still interpret sustainable positioning of brands as indicative that the brands will not get the job done as well as conventional brands (Luchs et al., 2010).

Cradle-to-cradle design pursues biomimicry in applying nature's principles to the operation of business (Unruh, 2018). Here, recycling takes a central role with the 'waste' of one process becoming the 'food' for another. Research suggests that firms typically go through five stages in integrating sustainable business practices into their operations: (a) complying with the law, (b) driving toward efficiencies, (c) designing eco-friendly products, (d) developing new business models, and (e) creating next-practice platforms that change existing ways of doing things (Nidumolu et al., 2009).

This chapter also considered clean tech, which refers to delivering value by using limited or zero nonrenewable resources and/or creating much less waste than conventional offerings (Pernick and Wilder, 2007, p. 2). The chapter concludes with a look at four Mavericks Who Made It. The stories of these mavericks illustrate how each addressed a market imperfection to help solve an environmental problem that became the opportunity to earn rewards in the marketplace.

QUESTIONS

- How would you compare your assessment of the viability of sustainable ventures before you read the chapter with your assessment now? What is one thing you learned that puts into perspective how a business could help solve environmental problems?
- Thinking about the sustainable entrepreneurs you encountered in the chapter, what is a theme that unifies many of the elements of their stories? Elaborate why you see this theme.
- What makes sustainable entrepreneurs distinct from conventional entrepreneurs?
- To what degree do you think sustainability is a fad? What does NASCAR's adoption of sustainable business practices say about sustainable business practices being a fad?
- What aspect of sustainable entrepreneurship in the chapter encourages you to consider joining a sustainable venture or starting your own?
- What are some ways society could encourage and reinforce sustainable entrepreneurship?

Mavericks Who Made It

Clean-Tech Opportunities Emerge from Four Market Imperfections

Market imperfections have contributed to environmental degradation (Cohen and Winn, 2007, p. 35). However, these same imperfections offer rich opportunities for entrepreneurially oriented firms to develop new technologies and business models that can not only reduce environmental harm but also actually reverse the effects of environmental degradation.

Four types of market imperfections can be identified that offer sustainable entrepreneurs the chance to create profit-making solutions (Cohen and Winn, 2007, p. 31). These are (a) inefficient systems, (b) externalities, (c) flawed pricing mechanisms, and (d) imperfectly distributed information. If entrepreneurs can successfully introduce environmental innovations into the marketplace, a more sustainable future will likely develop for all.

Market Imperfection 1: Inefficient Systems – David Tse of NovoNutrients

Given the problems created by excessive carbon emissions of CO_2, what could be the impact of a new product that consumes CO_2? NovoNutrients (a venture based in Silicon Valley, California) develops protein meal through carbon capture and uses it in the rapidly growing fish and shrimp feed markets (Byrne, 2020). By changing one part of the food system into a circular economy for food, NovoNutrients minimizes waste by using it as a feedstock (NovoNutrients, 2021).

NovoNutrients' gas fermentation process uses two inputs on a massive scale: CO_2 and hydrogen (Wright, 2020). The firm's process uses CO_2 sourced from the untreated waste emissions from cement plants, ethanol factories, pulp and paper refineries and other industrial sources. The two gases speed the growth of the bacteria strains, which the firm calls a 'microbial consortium.' After fermentation, the result is a product 70 percent protein that can feed fish, pets and even people.

The key ingredient in the commercial feed used in fish farming is fishmeal, a powder made from the ground-up bodies of tiny fish such as anchovies. By comparison, Novo Nutrients makes Novomeal (a nutritionally complete substitute for fishmeal) from the proteins of bacteria incubated in giant steel vessels similar to beer vats, called bioreactors.

Using its microbial process, NovoNutrients takes untreated industrial emissions of CO_2 and can turn them into protein flour. Such protein flour can form the amino acids found in meat. However, initially, the firm will target fish farming.

'Made from specialty microbes that grow on CO_2, our product is a natural, non-GMO, complete protein with all the amino acids and without mercury or other contaminants that are found in fish flour, which is made by grinding up little, wild-caught fish,' NovoNutrients CEO David Tse said.

(Continued)

Figure 10.4   NovoNutrients Uses Microbes Feeding on CO_2 to Create Protein Powder Used in Fish Farming.

Source: Photo by David Gabrielyan on Unsplash.

Feed is the biggest cost of fish farming, a \$232 billion global industry and it is likely to become more expensive and is subject to price volatility that can eliminate profits for fish-farming operations (Bercovici, 2019). By comparison, the supply of bacteria is unlimited for practical purposes – as long as nutrients exist to feed them.

There is no shortage of free CO_2 pouring out of factories, power plants, and automobiles. 'The annual CO_2 emissions from a large cement plant would create 3 billion dollars of our protein flour, worth the same as the entire annual soy production of the state of Nebraska – 330 million bushels a year,' Tse said (NovoNutrients, 2021).

With the increasing popularity of alternative proteins, such as almond milk to plant-based burgers, NovoNutrients looks forward to a day when the firm will supply the processed-food industry, too. 'It's more of a question of consumer preferences,' Tse said. 'Today, it'd be very hard to run a Super Bowl ad that convinces people that they should be eating bacterial protein.'

What firms like NovoNutrients might be constructing is nothing less than the infrastructure for an entirely new economy. This new economy will be based on producing food, energy, and material goods by sequestering harmful chemicals rather than by emitting them. In such a new economy, landfill content will result in jet fuel, and mushrooms will serve to create wood-type products using primarily renewable power. 'What we're doing has the potential to change not only the food system,' Tse says, 'but also the way other goods are manufactured.'

Market Imperfection 2: Externalities – Bruce Kania of Floating Island International

For the past two centuries, industrialization and population growth have served as the focus of progress in many societies (BioHaven Solutions, 2020). A cost for such progress has been the widespread contamination and destruction of wetlands and waterways. Such costs represent negative externalities because a downstream third party incurs these costs without receiving equivalent benefits as those in the original set of exchanges (Cohen and Winn, 2007). In addition to the environment and future generations experiencing degraded ecosystems, those depending on waterways for safe drinking water and for recreational opportunities in the current generation also experience this externality of development.

In 2000, inventor and outdoorsman Bruce Kania bought a farm east of Billings, Montana, near the Yellowstone River. Roaming his farmland with his dog, he experienced an externality related to water contamination resulting from modern methods of farming and ranching. Every time his black dog Rufus jumped into a pond, the dog came out red and reeked of a foul odor (Stark, 2006).

Kania soon realized that his farm was at the end of a 60-mile irrigation ditch that carried nitrogen and phosphorous from fertilizers that had run off into the ditch and been carried downstream by the water in the irrigation ditch (Stark, 2006). Too many nutrients like these in water led to too much algae. Such an overabundance of algae restricted other tiny species upon which insects, birds, and fish depended. The result was foul water and a damaged ecosystem.

Concerned for his dog, Kania instinctively felt 'we could do better' and sensed a genuine opportunity for invention (Floating Island International, 2011a). Kania had become intrigued with biomimicry as a way of solving human problems using solutions modeled on nature. He asked himself whether a new and natural stewardship tool could be developed that could clean water and, in the process, improve life for all the creatures who live in it. (Floating Island International, 2011b).

To answer this question, Kania brought together a team of engineers and plant specialists who turned to the floating peat bogs of Northern Wisconsin for inspiration (Floating Island International, 2011b). Kania had grown up among these floating islands, where world-record fish are to be found within crystal-clear waters. The team set about 'biomimicking' these floating riparian structures. By 2020, the firm has launched more than 8,000 islands around the world (BioHaven Solutions, 2020).

They created an island capable of supporting the weight of plants and soil. Layers of a flexible, matrix material made from postconsumer materials (recycled plastic drink bottles) form the floating island. Plants are then inserted into precut pockets. The matrix material serves as a cushiony batting that is porous and allows the plants' roots to reach the water.

Figure 10.5 depicts how the floating islands clean water. Circulation carries particulates including nitrates, phosphates, and ammonia across the roots of the plants on the underside of the floating

(Continued)

water. As the plants grow, tiny microbes begin clinging to the island. These microbes take excess nutrients out of the water.

Microbes are responsible for breaking down nutrients and other water-borne pollutants, but to be effective, they need a surface to stick to. The floating island matrix, with its dense fibers and porous texture, is the perfect surface area for growing large amounts of microbes (in the form of biofilm) in a short time. Nutrients circulating in the water come into contact with these biofilms and are consumed by them, while a smaller fraction is taken up by plant roots. The team called the breakthrough technology BioHaven floating islands.

Figure 10.5   Floating island wetlands (FTW) process for cleaning water

Source: https://www.floatingislandinternational.com/products/biohaven-technology/

The unique design of these floating islands means that 250 square feet of island can clean and restore an acre's worth of wetland surface area. In testing, 22 persons crammed onto a 250-square-foot island and stayed afloat (Stark, 2006, p. 2). These floating islands can be launched in either shallow or deep water, and they can be securely anchored or tethered to ensure that they remain in a specific location. They are almost infinitely customizable, and they can be configured in a variety of ways. Wildlife, such as waterfowl and turtles, are attracted to the floating islands.

By 2010, more than 4,000 islands had been launched by Floating Island International for cleaning not only lakes and streams but also for wastewater lagoons, farm effluent ponds, and any other waterway impacted by sewage or landfill effluent (Floating Island International, 2011b).

Floating islands are being deployed along the steel bulkheads that line the final one mile of the shipping channel of Cleveland, Ohio's Cuyahoga River (the same one that caught fire in 1969) that runs into Lake Erie (Scott, 2011). The floating islands replicate the once green-leafy banks of the river that hosted insects upon which fish fed (Scott, 2011).

Floating Island International's successes help one understand how externalities can become opportunities for eco-entrepreneurs oriented to solving problems in the natural environment. In the case of Floating Island International, an entrepreneurial achievement in solving smaller environmental problems can make enormous environmental challenges now seem like opportunities for the ambitious entrepreneur.

Kania envisions floating islands restoring 'dead zones' such as the pollution-laden mouth of the Mississippi River, or the Chesapeake Bay near Washington, DC. 'How do you cure a dead zone?' Kania asked. 'One island at a time' (Stark, 2006, p. 2). Kania also envisions floating islands that would buffer the effects of hurricanes in coastal areas, and take in excess carbon dioxide contributing to global climate change.

Market Imperfection 3: Flawed Pricing Mechanisms – Karl Ulrich and TerraPass

Conventional theories of economics assume natural resources are plentiful and that their market value accurately reflects supply and demand. Many ecosystem services (such as clean air and water, renewable energy, and a regulated climate) are undervalued or not priced at all (Cohen and Winn, 2007). A more sustainable economic system would price natural capital appropriately. Research published in *Nature* that was conducted by a team comprising ecologists, economists, and geologists from a variety of universities estimated the current value of ecological services that allow the Earth to be inhabited would be $33 trillion each year (Costanza et al., 1997). This was nearly double the combined output of the world's nations when the study was conducted.

Renewable energy resources (solar, wind, wave, tidal, geothermal, landfill gas, and biomass sources, such as wood, fiber, ethanol, butanol, and biodiesel) are now emerging, but they struggle to be economically competitive with nonrenewable energy with its established infrastructure for extraction, processing, and distribution (and all of the cost efficiencies related to these).

Renewables have done well in states and countries (such as California and Germany) where the government has mandated quotas for renewable energy in the portfolio of energy sources. In California, the renewable portfolio standard (RPS) is set to be 60 percent by the end of 2030 (CPUC, 2020). Renewables have also thrived where the resource exists in abundance and prices for rival uses of the renewable have declined. This happened with ethanol made from sugar cane in Brazil in the first part of the twenty-first century (Orsato, 2009, p. 131). Nevertheless, about $100 billion is still needed to overhaul the distribution system as well as to improve the efficiency of the sugar mills in Brazil for global export.

(Continued)

To help renewable energy projects obtain funding, inventor and Wharton Business School Professor Karl Ulrich and his class of 41 MBA students launched a venture called TerraPass in 2004 that sells carbon offsets (TerraPass, 2020a). A carbon offset is a certificate representing the reduction of one metric ton (2,205 lbs) of carbon dioxide emissions, the principal cause of global warming (TerraPass, 2020b). Although complex in practice, carbon offsets represent a fairly simple idea. Consumers and businesses can determine how much carbon dioxide their activities generate and then pay TerraPass money to counterbalance the environmental damage they have caused. Figure 10.6 depicts this process.

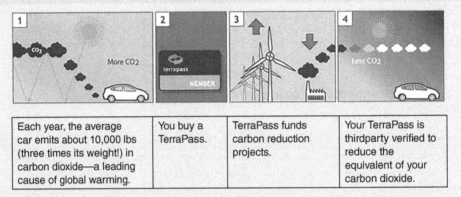

1	2	3	4
Each year, the average car emits about 10,000 lbs (three times its weight!) in carbon dioxide—a leading cause of global warming.	You buy a TerraPass.	TerraPass funds carbon reduction projects.	Your TerraPass is thirdparty verified to reduce the equivalent of your carbon dioxide.

Figure 10.6   How carbon offsets work

Source: TerraPass (2020b), www.terrapass.com/about/how-carbon-offsets-work.html

For every ton of carbon emissions reduced through renewable energy projects, one carbon offset would be created. Renewable energy project developers can then sell these offsets to finance their projects. For example, a wind farm generates clean energy, which reduces carbon emissions from coal-burning power plants. To finance its operations, a wind farm can sell these reductions in the form of carbon offsets. TerraPass, which is a for-profit company, invests in things like wind power, landfill gas reclamation, and biomass energy production.

The *New York Times* named TerraPass one of 2005's most noteworthy ideas. Today, the company is not alone in its field with dozens of competitors – but it has excelled by packaging its product well. For example, the average individual in the US consumes in a way that 18 tons of carbon enters the atmosphere (TerraPass, 2020b). Such an individual can offset such carbon consumption for $180.

Within its first year, TerraPass registered over 2,400 members, reduced 36 million pounds of CO_2, and earned countless national press and blog articles. TerraPass has grown steadily (Terrapass, 2020a). The firm has a small staff in an office near the Bay Bridge in downtown San Francisco. The firm works directly with carbon reduction projects, providing revenue to dairy farms, landfill gas installations, and other projects that yield carbon credits. Importantly, TerraPass has helped individuals and businesses to reduce over 1 billion pounds of carbon dioxide.

In concrete terms, the enduring value of the work of TerraPass will likely be operating as a major player in the funding of the infrastructure for renewable energy resources that otherwise would have not made the grade as a result of conventional market pricing. Not bad for what was once an MBA course project.

'I look around and I think we've had an impact,' Ulrich said (Pompilio, 2008, para. 40).

Market Imperfection 4: Imperfectly Distributed Information – Yoan Nussbaumer of Chargemap

Western Europe is now the largest market for electric vehicles (EV) in the world, with sales of hybrid and plug-in vehicles exceeding China's by 90,000 units in 2020, for a total of 1.33 million of these autos sold (Powell, 2021). In 2020, overall market share in the EU for EVs increased to 12.4 per cent. In addition to Tesla's EV models, Volkswagen has introduced the ID3, while Renault has introduced the Zoe and Kia has launched the Niro. A major factor in this adoption of EVs was the EU's legislation requiring the dramatic reduction of carbon dioxide emission across a manufacturer's fleet by the end of 2020. By December, one in four cars sold across the EU was a plug-in EV.

The infrastructure to support the charging of these EVs has proliferated in recent years. In 2020, the EU had 224,538 public charging points (Reuters, 2021). But how does someone traveling by car in the EU find available charging stations?

Figure 10.7   Chargemap helps owners of electric vehicles find charging stations

Source: Photo by Ralph Hutter on Unsplash.

(Continued)

Chargemap offers a solution to the problem of imperfectly distributed information about charging stations across Europe (Chargemap, 2021). In 2009, Chargemap founder Yoann Nussbaumer was living in his hometown of Strasbourg, France and looked into buying an electric car. He could not find any.

Nussbaumer then thought of Chargemap: a tool that brings electric car drivers together in order to share information about charging points, which would help them charge their car everywhere. In 2011, with a few enthusiasts, he began to look for charging terminals and started to document them. The small team took photos of these terminals and tested the working processes.

Gradually, electric car drivers took over, thanks to the Chargemap mobile app. Chargemap now checks the information sent to them by community members before publishing this information in its map of charging stations. In effect, Chargemap is like a wiki endeavor in which users contribute to the content of the information resource – mapped locations of charging stations for EVs.

By 2021, the Chargemap community boasted more than 650,000 members who had uploaded more than 300,000 photos of different charging stations. The members share information with each other about charging experiences in order to boost the efficient use of the disaggregated network of charging stations across Europe.

A nagging problem for EV owners is being able to make payment at these charging stations. Accordingly, Chargemap developed an access and payment RFID card called the Chargemap Pass for use at charging stations. The Chargemap app identifies charging stations that accept the Chargemap Pass. There is no subscription required for the Chargemap Pass – only a reasonable commission that is taken by Chargemap on each charging session. In the future, the Chargemap app itself will allow charging itself.

'Our goal is to offer to electric car drivers the best charging experience in order to promote the development of these vehicles, which are less damaging to air quality,' Nussbaumer said. 'It's our reason to wake up every morning, and we're proud of it!'

Questions

- Into which of the four Mavericks in Markets ventures would you *most* like to make a $50,000 stock investment, if this were possible? Explain.
- Into which venture would you *least* like to make a $50,000 stock investment, if this were possible? Explain.
- Which venture do you believe will result in having the most positive impact on the natural environment? The least? Explain.
- Considering all the sustainable entrepreneurs featured in this chapter from Mia Birk to Yoan Nussbaumer, what role did higher education play in identifying the venture idea for these sustainable entrepreneurs? Do environmental problems targeted by sustainable entrepreneurs require more technical or intellectual skills as part of the entrepreneurs' tool kit?

REFERENCES

Bambrough, B. (2020). Bitcoin just suddenly surged toward $12,000 but now might not be the time to buy – Here's why. *Forbes*, July 27, 2020. Accessed at www.forbes.com/sites/billybambrough/2020/07/27/bitcoin-just-suddenly-surged-toward-12000-but-now-might-not-be-the-time-to-buy-heres-why/#6da52ecd7bec

Baraniuk, C. (2019). Bitcoin's energy consumption 'equals that of Switzerland'. *BBC News*, July 3, 2019. Accessed at www.bbc.com/news/technology-48853230

Baraniuk, C. (2020). Blockchain: The revolution that has not quite happened. *BBC News*, February 11, 2020. Accessed at www.bbc.com/news/business-51281233

Belson, K. (2011, September 13). Gentlemen, start conserving. *The New York Times*. Retrieved from www.nytimes.com

Bercovici, J. (2019). How sea-monkeys, NovoNutrients, and synthetic biology will save the world. *Inc.*, May, 2019. Accessed at www.inc.com/magazine/201905/jeff-bercovici/syn-bio-novonutrients-bioeconomy-sustainable-food-industry-carbon-bioengineering.html.

BioHaven Solutions. (2020). BioHaven Solutions. Accessed at www.floatingislandinternational.com/solutions/

Birk, M. (2020). Mia Birk: Career and business consulting. Accessed at www.miabirk.com/

Birk, M., and Kurmanskie, J. (2010). *Joyride: Pedaling toward a healthier planet*. Portland, OR: Cadence Press.

Brett, C. (2019). Koin Rewards and TrueLayer to use open banking for ethical loyalty rewards. *Enterprise Times*, July 26, 2019. Accessed at www.enterprisetimes.co.uk/2019/07/26/koin-rewards-and-truelayer-to-use-open-banking-for-ethical-loyalty-rewards/

Butler, K. (2009, August 18). Greenpeace: Lovin' McDonald's. *Mother Jones*. Retrieved from http://motherjones.com

Byrne, J. (2020). NovoNutrients: Skretting cooperation helps accelerate large-scale bacterial meal scale-up. *FeedNavigator*, September 16, 2020. Accessed at www.feednavigator.com/Article/2020/09/16/NovoNutrients-Skretting-cooperation-helps-accelerate-large-scale-bacterial-meal-scale-up.

CBECI. (2020). Electricity consumption. Cambridge Bitcoin Electricity Consumption Index. Accessed at https://cbeci.org/faq/

Chargemap. (2021). About Chargemap. Accessed at https://chargemap.com/about.

Cohen, B., and Winn, M.I. (2007). Market imperfections, opportunity and sustainable entrepreneurship. *Journal of Business Venturing*, 22(1), 29–49.

Costanza, R., d'Arge, R. de Groot, R., Farber, S., Grasso, M., Hannon, B., Limburg, K., Naeem, S., O'Neil, R.V., Raruelo, J., Raskin, R.G., Sutton, R., and van den Belt, M. (1997). The value of the world's ecosystem services and natural capital. *Nature*, 237, 253–60.

Coster, H. (2011, June 27). Beating a new path for commuters. *Forbes*. Retrieved from www.forbes.com

Covin, J.G., and Slevin, D.P. (1989, January). Strategic management of small firms in hostile and benign environments. *Strategic Management Journal*, 10(1), 75–87.

CPUC. (2020). Renewables portfolio standard (rps) program. California Public Utilities Commission. Accessed at www.cpuc.ca.gov/Renewables/

de Vries, A. (2018). Bitcoin's growing energy problem. *Joule*, 2(5), 801–5.

Drucker, P. (1985). *Innovation and entrepreneurship*. New York, NY: Harper Business.

Duber-Smith, D. (2009, March–April). Sustainability: The green imperative. *ICOSA*, 92–4.

Dundas, Z. (2011, October). Brainstorm: Explore the genesis of innovation: 12 Oregonians changing our world. *Portland Monthly*. Retrieved from www.portlandmonthlymag.com

Elkington, J. (2017). Saving the planet from ecological disaster is a $12 trillion opportunity. *Harvard Business Review*, May, 4.

Floating Island International. (2011a). Our vision. Retrieved from www.floatingislandinternational.com

Floating Island International. (2011b). Company profile. Retrieved from www.floatingisland international.com

Friedman, T.L. (2008). Hot, flat and crowded: Why we need a green revolution – and how it can renew America. New York, NY: Farrar, Straus and Giroux.

Griskevicius, V., Tybur, J.M., and Van den Bergh, B. (2010). Going green to be seen: Status, reputation, and conspicuous conservation. *Journal of Personality and Social Psychology*, 98(3), 392–404.

Hisrich, R.D., and Peters, M.P. (1998). *Entrepreneurship*. Boston, MA: Irwin McGraw-Hill.

Langert, B. (2016). Greenpeace, McDonald's and the power of collaboration. *GreenBiz*, April 18, 2016. Accessed at www.greenbiz.com/article/greenpeace-mcdonalds-and-power-collaboration

Langert, B. (2019). *The battle to do good: Inside McDonald's sustainability journey*. Bingley, UK: Emerald Publishing Limited.

Lee, D., and Bony, L. (2008). *Cradle-to-Cradle design at Herman Miller: Moving toward environmental sustainability*. Case number 9-607-003. Boston, MA: Harvard Business School Press.

LOHAS. (2020). LOHAS online. Retrieved from www.lohas.com.au

Luchs, M.G., Naylor, R.W., Irwin, J.R., and Raghunathan, R. (2010, September).The sustainability liability: Potential negative effects of ethicality on product preference. *Journal of Marketing*, 74(5), 18–31.

Mager, D., and Sibilia, J. (2010). *Street smart sustainability: The entrepreneur's guide to profitably greening your organization's DNA*. San Francisco, CA: Berrett-Koehler.

Mapes, J. (2009). *Pedaling revolution: How cyclists are changing American cities*. Corvallis: Oregon State University Press.

Martinez, M. (2010, September 20). Washington, D.C., launches the nation's largest bike share program. *Grist*. Retrieved from www.grist.org

Maus, J. (2015). Bicycle planning icon Mia Birk is leaving Alta Planning after 16 year career. BikePortland.org. Accessed at https://bikeportland.org/2015/11/05/bicycle-planning-icon-mia-birk-is-leaving-alta-planning-after-16-year-career-167619

Maus, J. (2018). Portland slips to 5th in Bicycling Magazine 'Best Bike City' rankings. *BikePortland.org*, October 10, 2018. Accessed at https://bikeportland.org/2018/10/10/portland-slips-to-5th-in-bicycling-magazine-best-bike-city-rankings-290806

MBDC. (2020). Creators of the cradle to cradle design framework. Accessed at https://mbdc.com/

McCarthy, N. (2019). Bitcoin devours more electricity than Switzerland. *Forbes*, July 8, 2019. Accessed at www.forbes.com/sites/niallmccarthy/2019/07/08/bitcoin-devours-more-electricity-than-switzerland-infographic/#2dd721bb21c0

McDonagh, P., and Prothero, A. (2014). Sustainability marketing research: Past, present and future. *Journal of Marketing Management*, 30(11–12), 1186–1219.

McDonough, W., and Braungart, M. (2002a). *Cradle to cradle*. New York, NY: North Point Press.

McDonough, W., and Braungart, M. (2002b). The anatomy of transformation: Herman Miller's journey to sustainability. Retrieved from www.mcdonough.com/writings/anatomy_transformation.htm

McGee, J., Peterson, M., Mueller, S., and Sequiera, J. (2009). Entrepreneurial self-efficacy: Refining the measure. *Entrepreneurship Theory and Practice*, 33(4), 965–88.

Michler, A., and Fehrenbacher, J. (2011, April 24). Inhabit interview: Green Architect and Cradle to Cradle Founder William McDonough. *Inhabit*. Retrieved from http://inhabitat.com/inhabitat-interview-green-architect-cradle-to-cradle-founder-william-mcdonough/

Miller, H. (2020). Our vision and policy. Retrieved from www.hermanmiller.com/our-values/environmental-advocacy/our-vision-and-policy/

Moon, D. (2010, October 8). Bicycle guru shares passion in new book. *The Jewish Review*. Retrieved from www.jewishreview.org

Morris, M.H. (1998). *Entrepreneurial intensity: Sustainable advantages for individuals, organizations, and societies*. Westport, CT: Quorum Books.

NASCAR. (2020). NASCAR Green – an industry effort. Accessed at https://green.nascar.com/nascar-green-an-industry-effort/

Nidumolu, R., Prahalad, C.K., and Rangaswami, M.R. (2009). Why sustainability is now the key driver of innovation. *Harvard Business Review*, 87(9), 56–64.

NovoNutrients. (2021). Too little protein, too much carbon. NovoNutrients. Accessed at www.novonutrients.com/novonutrients-at-indiebio-demo-day

Orcutt, M. (2019). We've had private currencies like Libra before. It was chaos. *MIT Technology Review*, July 25, 2019. Accessed at www.technologyreview.com/2019/07/25/134042/weve-had-private-currencies-like-libra-before-it-was-chaos/

Orsato, R.J. (2009). *Sustainable strategies: When does it pay to be green?* New York, NY: Palgrave Macmillan.

Ottman, J.A. (2011). *The new rules of green marketing: Strategies, tools, and inspiration for sustainable branding.* London, UK: Berrett Koehler.

Patagonia. (2020). Patagonia's mission statement. Retrieved from www.patagonia.com

Pernick, R., and Wilder, C. (2007). *The clean tech revolution: The next big growth and investment opportunity.* New York, NY: Collins.

Peterson, M. (2020). Modeling country entrepreneurial activity to inform entrepreneurial-marketing research. *Journal of Business Research*, 113, 105–16.

Pompilio, N. (2008, November). Practicing what he preaches. *Wharton Alumni Magazine*. Retrieved from http://whartonmagazine.com/issues/summer-2008/practicing-what-he-preaches/

Poushter, J., and Huang, C. (2020). Despite pandemic, many Europeans still see climate change as greatest threat to their countries, Pew Center Research, September 9, 2020. Accessed at www.pewresearch.org/global/2020/09/09/despite-pandemic-many-europeans-still-see-climate-change-as-greatest-threat-to-their-countries/

Powell, J. (2021). The European electric vehicle landscape. *Financial Times*, January 27, 2021. Accessed at www.ft.com/content/4cbf843e-2503-462c-a9cf-1fdc502ffddc.

RE100. (2020). RE100 members. Accessed at www.there100.org/

Reiff, N. (2020). Blockchain explained. *Investopedia*, February 1, 2020. Accessed at www.investopedia.com/terms/b/blockchain.asp#what-is-blockchain

Reuters. (2021). EU told 1 million public EV charging stations needed by 2024. Reuters, February 11, 2021. Accessed at www.reuters.com/article/us-europe-autos-electric/eu-told-1-million-public-ev-charging-stations-needed-by-2024-idUSKBN2AB0UG.

Schmidt, B. (2020). Tesla beats Toyota and Honda as model 3 becomes top selling car in California. *The Driven*, June 4, 2020. Accessed at https://thedriven.io/2020/06/04/tesla-beats-toyota-and-honda-as-model-3-becomes-top-selling-car-in-california/#:~:text=The%20Tesla%20Model%203%20has%20become%20the%20best,Camry%20and%20Corolla%20and%20Honda%E2%80%99s%20Civic%20and%20Accord

Scott, M. (2011, September 3). Greening the Cuyahoga River: Man-made floating plant islands the latest scheme in recovery efforts. *The Plain Dealer*. Retrieved from http://blog.cleveland.com/metro/2011/09/greening_the_cuyahoga_river_ma.html

Shepherd, D.A., and Patzelt, H. (2011, January). The new field of sustainable entrepreneurship: Studying entrepreneurial action linking 'what is to be sustained' with 'what is to be developed'. *Entrepreneurship Theory and Practice*, 35(1), 137–63.

Stark, M. (2006, July 9). Man claims his floating island invention can clean pollution. *Napa Valley Register*. Retrieved from http://napavalleyregister.com/business

Sung, J., and Woo, H. (2019). Investigating male consumers' lifestyle of health and sustainability (LOHAS) and perception toward slow fashion. *Journal of Retailing and Consumer Services*, 49, 120–8.

Szczepanski, C. (2010, November 3). Up close and personal with Mia Birk. *Momentum*. Retrieved from http://momentumplanet.com

TerraPass. (2020a). About TerraPass. www.terrapass.com/

TerraPass. (2020b). Carbon offsets explained. Retrieved from www.terrapass.com/climate-change/carbon-offsets-explained

Tom's of Maine. (2020). From our family to yours. Accessed at www.tomsofmaine.com/the-backstory

United Nations. (2020). Sustainable Development Goals. Accessed at www.un.org/sustainabledevelopment/sustainable-development-goals/

Unruh, G.C. (2008, February). The biosphere rules. *Harvard Business Review*. Retrieved from http://hbr.org/2008/02/the-biosphere-rules/ar/1

Unruh, G. (2018). Circular economy, 3D printing, and the biosphere rules. *California Management Review*, 60(3), 95–111.

USGBC. (2011). An introduction to LEED. Retrieved from www.usgbc.org

Vincent, J. (2019). Bitcoin consumes more energy than Switzerland, according to new estimate. *The Verge*, July 4, 2019. Accessed at www.theverge.com/2019/7/4/20682109/bitcoin-energy-consumption-annual-calculation-cambridge-index-cbeci-country-comparison

Werbach, A. (2009). *Strategy of sustainability: A business manifesto*. Boston, MA: Harvard Business Press.

Whitford, D. (2011, May 17). The technology behind bike sharing systems. *Fortune Tech*. Retrieved from http://tech.fortune.cnn.com

Winck, B. (2020). Central banks band together to consider issuing their own digital currencies. *Markets Insider*, January 21, 2020. Accessed at https://markets.businessinsider.com/currencies/news/central-banks-join-study-issuing-digital-currencies-ecb-boe-japan-2020-1-1028832417#

Winston, A. (2019). The top sustainability stories of 2019. *Harvard Business Review*, December 30, 2019. Accessed at https://hbr.org/2019/12/the-top-sustainability-stories-of-2019#:~:text=%20The%20Top%20Sustainability%20Stories%20of%202019%20,and%20sustainability%20grow.%20The%20year%20was...%20More%20

Wohl, J. (2006, March 22). Colgate to buy majority stake in Tom's of Maine. *Environmental News Network*. Retrieved from www.enn.com

World Commission on Environment and Development. (1987). *Our common future*. New York, NY: Oxford University Press USA.

Wright, J. (2020). NovoNutrients partners up on its pathway to commercialization. *Global Aquaculture Alliance*, November 16, 2020. Accessed at www.aquaculturealliance.org/advocate/ novonutrients-partners-up-on-its-pathway-to-commercialization/

XE. (2020). XE currency charts: VEF to EUR. Accessed at www.xe.com/currencycharts/?from =VEFandto=EUR andview=10Y

Young, J. (2020) Why the actual cost of mining Bitcoin can leave it vulnerable to a deep correction. *Forbes*, June 7, 2020. Accessed at www.forbes.com/sites/youngjoseph/2020/06/07/ why-the-actual-cost-of-mining-bitcoin-can-leave-it-vulnerable-to-a-deep-correction/#b4ff 81e60670

PART IV

Sustainable Marketing for Equity

11
DEVELOPING MARKETS

Throwing Shade

Source: Photo by Matthew Lakeland on Unsplash.

Golden Rice

In villages across Sub-Saharan Africa and Asia, some of the kids recently seen outdoors and playing with their friends at twilight will head directly home while others tarry and linger in the darkness outdoors. The reason some of the kids broke from their friends and went indoors was that they can't see at night. They have night blindness caused by vitamin A deficiency (Price, 2015, p. 91).

(Continued)

But night blindness is not the only result of not having enough vitamin A in one's diet. Vitamin A deficiency is the leading cause of preventable blindness in children and about half of children who go blind this way die within a year of becoming blind (Regis, 2019, p. 2). In 2010, UNICEF reported that providing enough vitamin A to undernourished children would prevent from 1.9 million to 2.7 million deaths annually – more than HIV/AIDS, tuberculosis or malaria. Such kids would only need 600 micrograms per day of vitamin A – about the weight of one grain of sugar.

In 1999, after a six-year effort, two European researchers, Peter Beyer and Ingo Potrykus succeeded in developing a strain of rice with an increased level of beta carotene. The human body converts beta carotene to vitamin A after being ingested. As biologists, the two initially called their new rice 'yellow endosperm rice'. When marketing savvy Mechai Viravaidya (the head of the NGO Population and Community Development Association in Thailand) heard about the breakthrough at a dinner in Bangkok with Peter Toenniessen of the Rockefeller Foundation which had sponsored the research of Beyer and Potrykus, Viravaidya suggested the name 'Golden Rice'. In Viraviadya's view, consumers needed to know this new rice was better than white rice which consists of carbohydrates and little else.

Golden Rice contained enough beta carotene to trigger the body's conversion of it to vitamin A because Beyer and Potrykus had borrowed snippets of DNA from bacteria and daffodils through genetic engineering (Nash, 2000). Since the mid-1990s, European environmentalists and consumer-advocacy groups had waged protests against genetically modified organisms (GMOs). While the target of opposition for GMO protesters typically was Roundup Ready beans or corn (where the plant becomes resistant to being sprayed by the weed-killer Roundup), Golden Rice was the first product of bioengineering designed to help the consumer – rather than the farmer. Despite this, the environmental NGO Greenpeace chose to oppose Golden Rice.

In 2004, Syngenta renounced all commercial interest in Golden Rice. The rice would benefit the poor and disadvantaged – not multinational enterprises (Regis, 2019). Still, governments in most countries following the Cartagena Protocol of Biosafety (adopted by more than 100 nations in 2000) focused on unknown risks. In practice, it was not clear whether these risks would ever be known. As a result, the rollout of Golden Rice around the world has been slow. And each year, one million children in poor countries in Africa and Southeast Asia die grim deaths.

For Europeans who might believe that all GMOs are banned in the EU, this is not really the case. In 2001, the EU imposed a de facto moratorium on new GMO approvals. By 2015, 17 of the 27 EU countries had banned GMOs (Regis, 2019, p. 93). Ten have not, including Spain which steadfastly continues raising its own genetically modified corn which it had done before 2001. Further, every European nation imports GMO crops for use as livestock feed. Each year, EU countries import more than 30 million tons of GMO corn and soy – making the EU one of the world's largest regional consumers of genetically engineered crops.

Questions to Consider

- What are your thoughts about Golden Rice?
- Would the world be better off without genetically modified food, such as Golden Rice?
- What do you think of developed countries delaying and obstructing the distribution of Golden Rice in poor countries of the world while using GMO crops to feed livestock on a large scale – which means that consumers in these developed countries ingest food derived from GMOs every day?
- What do you think disadvantaged consumers in developing countries fighting malnutrition might think about people in developed countries keeping Golden Rice away from them after 20 years without any reported problems?

CHAPTER OVERVIEW AND LEARNING OBJECTIVES

This chapter will focus on the nature of developing markets and will give a special examination of the poor in developing countries. The World Bank (2020) classifies 210 countries as low-, middle-, or high-income countries based on gross national income (GNI) per capita. The low-income (GNI/capita of $1,025 or less) and middle-income countries (GNI/capita from $1,026–$12,375) are sometimes referred to as developing countries.

Once considered like a foreboding swamp for modern multinational enterprises (MNEs), developing markets now seem to offer some of the best prospects for economic growth in the coming years. Led by China and India, developing markets accounted for almost two-thirds of the world's GDP growth and more than half the consumption since 2004 (Woetzel, 2019).

Global management-consulting firm McKinsey and Company has identified 18 developing markets that have outperformed others over time. Long-term growth in these 18 countries has lifted more than one billion people out of extreme poverty since 1990. Seven of these have averaged GDP growth of at least 3.5 percent since 1970 (China, Hong Kong, Indonesia, Malaysia, Singapore, South Korea, and Thailand). Eleven of these have achieved average growth of at least five percent since 2000 (Azerbaijan, Belarus, Cambodia, Ethiopia, India, Kazakhstan, Laos, Myanmar, Turkmenistan, Uzbekistan, and Vietnam). Looking to the future, countries adopting similar pro-growth agendas as these 18 countries are positioning themselves for rapid growth (Bangladesh, Bolivia, the Philippines, Rwanda, and Sri Lanka).

After summarizing current perspectives about the success and failure of economic development across countries, this chapter will review macro factors for developing markets (Shultz et al., 2012). Six important dimensions of developing countries will be explained, including (a) culture, (b) population, (c) geography and climate, (d) economy, (e) political system, and (f) infrastructure. Institutions of society will also be featured in the final dimension of developing countries as they are proposed to be 'soft' infrastructure (Khanna and Palepu, 2011).

The poor in developing countries deserve special attention for marketers and leaders of business because of the larger share of the population they comprise in developing countries. Before his death in 2010, University of Michigan business professor C.K. Prahalad called the developed world's businesses to wake up to the fortune they could obtain by marketing to the very poorest consumers in countries, such as India (Prahalad, 2005). Among many, the MNEs that have responded to Prahalad's justifications for pursuing the 'fortune at the bottom of the pyramid' (BOP) have been consumer packaged goods companies like Unilever and Procter & Gamble. However, skeptics assert that this fortune resulting from BOP marketing is a mirage (Karnani, 2007).

After this chapter, you should be able to answer the following questions:

- Is global development succeeding? Explain.
- What does the rise of 'emerging giants' say about business in developing countries today?
- What are six important macro factors for understanding developing market contexts?
- Why might there be a fortune at the bottom of the pyramid by marketing to poor consumers in developing countries?
- Why might a fortune at the bottom of the pyramid be a mirage?

WHAT WE KNOW ABOUT COUNTRY DEVELOPMENT
Challenges in Explaining Economic Development

When considering developing countries, it is encouraging to remember that some of these countries actually become developed countries. The 'Four Asian Tigers' – Singapore, Hong Kong, Taiwan, and South Korea – began serious economic growth in the 1960s and became developed countries as a result of rapid economic growth in the 1980s and the 1990s (The Economist, 2019). Notably, each of these countries has earned rankings in the top 30 for quality of life (Economist Intelligence Unit, 2005).

This rise is remarkable when remembering that South Korea and Taiwan were no larger economically than sub-Saharan African countries in the 1950s (Rodrik, 2011, p. 146). Each of these 'tigers' really did not have natural resources of which to speak, so this forced them to emphasize human development – primarily education and entrepreneurship – in their rise (Friedman, 2012). Governments in these countries also improved their investment climate by (a) keeping taxes low, (b) controlling inflation, (c) bringing discipline to the operation of their bureaucracies, and (d) investing in infrastructure development (Rodrik, 2011, p. 147). In sum, a variety of factors contributed to the development success of these countries.

Despite the remarkable stories of the Four Asian Tigers, few other developing countries have had similar records of growth and prosperity. Accordingly, understanding why some countries grow and generally improve people's living standards and why others do not remains a perplexing question for macromarketers and developmental economists (Dapice, 2008). The transnational entity charged with assisting long-term development of countries, the World Bank, acknowledges that it still does not know the sufficient conditions for growth. 'We can characterize the successful economies of the postwar period, but we cannot name with certainty the factors that sealed their success, or the factors they could have succeeded without. It would be preferable if it were otherwise,' the World Bank Commission on Growth and Development said (World Bank, 2008, p. 33).

Using the narrow view of development as growth in GDP per capita, macromarketing research suggests that rich countries grow about 2 percent per year (Dapice, 2008, p. 414). For poor nations to catch up over a long period spanning decades would require at least a 3 percent growth rate each year. Since 1975, only 11 countries that are not rich have grown this fast. Most of these are Asian: China, India, Indonesia, Laos, Sri Lanka, Thailand Vietnam, Botswana, Chile, Lebanon, and Poland.

Importantly, it is not easy to identify a 'silver bullet' – a seemingly magical solution to a complicated problem – for development across these countries. For example, a closer examination of this set of countries shows that the government's ability to deliver services and create a stable environment for investment is not the only explanation for growth. India receives good ratings for its governance, but it has grown more slowly than China or Vietnam, which receive less favorable ratings for governance (Dapice, 2008, p. 414).

For those who encourage an unleashing of the market with minimum interference by government as the avenue for economic growth, evidence suggests some sobering findings. For example, the Heritage Foundation's Index of Economic Freedom (that focuses on the economic policies and laws of countries) ranks the fastest growing 18 nations (discussed above) as 'mostly unfree' (at the bottom half of their list of countries based on economic freedom (Heritage Foundation, 2020). The exceptions include Singapore (the top-ranked country) along with Azerbaijan, Belarus, Indonesia, and Kazakhstan (in the category 'moderately free').

It seems that nations with restrictions on economic freedom can grow fast – at least for a decade or two (Dapice, 2008, pp. 414–15). A question remains about how long such growth can be sustained because growth rates can be very volatile over two decades or more (Kenny, 2011, p. 33).

The Complexity, Heterogeneity, and Unintended Consequences of Aggregate Marketing Systems

Complex

As discussed in Chapter 2, the aggregate marketing system is the collection of all marketing systems in society (Wilkie and Moore, 1999). Macromarketing scholarship offers three primary generalizations about aggregate marketing systems that offer some insight into the difficulty researchers have in explaining economic growth for countries. First, aggregate marketing systems are highly complex (Mittelstaedt, Kilbourne, and Mittelstaedt, 2006, p. 133). They are made up of thousands of firms, nongovernmental organizations (NGOs), and regulators, along with millions of households. As a result, it is not surprising that one variable cannot explain economic growth or lack of it.

Heterogeneous

Second, aggregate marketing systems are heterogeneous (Mittelstaedt et al., 2006, p. 134). In other words, they are different. Countries have different geographies (including climates) and natural resource endowments. These starting conditions for countries affect the types of markets and the resulting economic system that develops. For example, snow plows are not needed in Saudi Arabia, which is uniquely endowed with oil reserves on the eastern side of the country. Not surprisingly, marketing systems have developed in Saudi Arabia that are focused on the export of oil and the importation of food and manufactured goods.

In addition to country geographies contributing to the heterogeneity of aggregate marketing systems, macromarketing researchers have identified five preconditions for markets that make markets heterogeneous (Klein and Nason, 2000, p. 270). These are (a) a legal system to establish and protect property rights, contract rights, and choice; (b) adequate information systems; (c) physical infrastructure to facilitate transportation and communication; (d) regard for social aspects of marketing (such as environmental protection, food safety, and cultural enhancement); and (e) a reliable financial system.

A country's history influences these preconditions. For example, Namibia (northwest of South Africa) and Java (an island, part of Indonesia) have differences in their aggregate marketing systems because each had a different colonizer (Shultz et al., 2012). Germany colonized Namibia, while Holland colonized Java. Each colonizer brought different ideas, administrative practices, and technologies. Additionally, each colonizer built on a different cultural foundation. Tribal groups lived at subsistence levels in Namibia prior to the Germans colonizing in 1884. For this reason, German colonizers strongly influenced the market preconditions of Namibia. In contrast, Java was a center of Hindu/Buddhist Empires and then Islamic Sultanates prior to the arrival of the Dutch. Accordingly, Java's aggregate marketing system carries the imprint of multiple cultures from Asia that traded extensively throughout the region, as well as Dutch influence.

Unintended Consequences

Third, macromarketing scholarship recognizes that choices of marketplace actors have consequences far beyond themselves, for better or worse (Mittelstaedt et al., 2006, p. 135). These can be in the form of externalities (uncalculated costs or benefits of exchange) or social consequences (any unforeseen effect to those involved in a transaction or to those not involved in a transaction). For example, Vietnamese environmental police had to disguise themselves as night fishermen on the Thi Vai River to investigate allegations that the Taiwanese food-additive and chemical manufacturer Vedan had constructed an elaborate underground system from one of its factories (Nguyen and Pham, 2011). During this 2009 investigation, the environmental police discovered an 800-meter pipe of Vedan's that had been discharging untreated wastewater directly into the river for 14 years. The Vietnamese government responded slowly over the next two years as a result of conflicting purposes of government agencies, as well as of delays engendered by a vast bureaucracy. Distrust for foreign direct investment increased among farmers, consumers, and government officials as a result of the Vedan scandal.

Yet, in April 2016, Formosa Ha Tinh Steel, a sprawling $10.6 billion, Taiwanese-owned steel-plant caused a massive fish kill along a 200 km stretch of coastline off the coast of Ha Tinh, Vietnam in a very similar way – a secretly-dug pipe was used for sending toxic chemicals from steel production out into the East Sea (Nguyen, 2016). The Vietnamese government gave a muted response to protect a generous investor and bolster its reputation as being friendly to foreign investment, but street protests (an unusual occurrence in the police state of Vietnam) flared up across Vietnam in the coming months. Formosa Ha Tinh Steel's leaders apologized and paid a $500 million fine. Such externalities and social consequences may bedevil attempts to boost economic development in the future.

A social consequence of marketing in developing countries can be discerned in Macromarketing founder Charles C. Slater's framing of the developing country problem in this way:

> The trend in most underdeveloped societies is for the expanding population in traditional sectors to gradually drift into urban slums and create a proletariat. Meanwhile, the upper income elite continue to consume imported luxuries so that the nation has a high requirement for foreign exchange and limited demand for internal production. Foreign exchange can usually be most easily earned by maintaining labor intensive plantations for export commodities which delay the education and industrialization changes need for takeoff.

> (Slater, 1977, p. 120)

Here, elites want luxuries unavailable in the home country. Cheap labor is used to export agricultural commodities. With this cash, the elites buy the imported luxuries or invest overseas – and the cycle repeats itself year after year. By purchasing imported luxuries or investing overseas, a social consequence results from these transactions. Development lags and the only opportunities remain low-paying jobs on the farms of the elite. As a result, farm laborers and their children have few prospects for developing themselves as wage earners over the course of their lives.

For the country to break out of this cycle, growth must be a serious priority for those who govern the country (Dapice, 2008, p. 416). In the end, economic growth is a political choice and often a difficult one to make and sustain over time. Most elites and interest groups are more concerned about their relative share of power and/or wealth than they are about the rate of overall economic growth for their country. Those who would be hurt by new policies resist the adoption and implementation of such policies – at least at first, but possibly longer.

In sum, economic development results from many factors. The first 40 years of macromarketing scholarship offers three primary generalizations that help understand the challenge of explaining economic development. First, aggregate marketing systems are highly complex. Second, aggregate marketing systems are heterogeneous. Third, market transactions frequently have consequences for those not involved in them.

Gains for Developing Countries

Although discussions about developing countries often turn to the poverty in these countries (poor consumers will be given treatment later in this chapter, too), there actually is much development to report: 'Despite counterclaims and hand wringing, things are getting better, everywhere,' senior fellow at the Center for Global Development Charles Kenny said (Kenny, 2011, p. x).

'It is simply impossible to explain the last one hundred years of global progress – a decline in extreme poverty from about three-quarters of the world's population to less than one in ten since 1900, a decline in global child mortality from nearly a quarter to below one in twenty newborns dying before their fifth birthday since 1950 – without a central part of the story being the increased movement of goods, people, and ideas,' Kenny said (Kenny, 2020). Figure 11.1 depicts the economic improvement for humans this century as the share of those living in low-income countries has dropped precipitously.

In sum, globalization has reshaped the developing world for good since 1950. Progress in developing countries has resulted from the spread of technologies (such as vaccinations), as well as from the spread of ideas (such as sending one's daughter to school). Regarding the

Population by income group, 1993–2019 (% of total)

Low Income   Lower-Middle Income   Upper-Middle Income   High Income

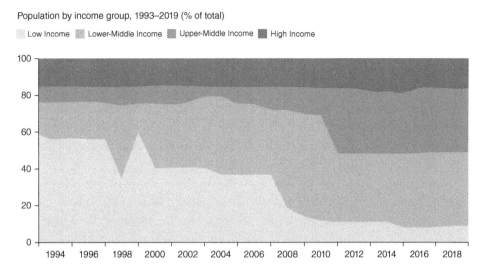

Figure 11.1   Since 1993, the share of the world population living in low-income countries has dropped from almost 60 percent to less than 10 percent

Source: World Bank (2019a). Shared under the CC BY-4.0 license.

movement of people, emigrants from Nigeria going to a place like the US earn 10 times as much income. But even for those who do not emigrate, there is a benefit from many who do emigrate. The annual value of global remittances to developing countries is $66 billion – three times the amount of flows in foreign aid.

Although Africa and many other parts of the world have lagged in income growth, they have made marked improvement in health, education, gender equality, security, and human rights (Kenny, 2011, p. 4). By broadening one's view of developing countries from income growth to quality of life or well-being, many of the gains for developing countries become evident. In education, the best measure of a country's human capital – the average number of years of schooling for adults – increased from around two years to seven years from 1900 to 2000. In health, global average infant mortality has declined by more than half since 1960. In literacy, 86 percent of the global population of adults can read in 2019 (in 1950, only half could read) (Kiprop, 2019).

Looking only at developing countries, it is hard to believe the gains in quality of life that can be seen. In the Middle East and North Africa, life expectancy has increased from 46 to 74 years from 1960 to 2018 (World Bank, 2019b). Much of this can be attributed to a reduction in infant mortality.

Macro Factors for Understanding the Context of Developing Markets

Developing market researchers have identified six important dimensions of developing country contexts for business practitioners, public policy makers, NGOs, and scholars (Shultz et al., 2012). These are (a) culture, (b) population, (c) geography and climate, (d) economy, (e) political system, and (f) infrastructure. Institutions of society are included in the final dimension of developing countries because they are proposed to be 'soft' infrastructure (Khanna and Palepu, 2011).

When comparing the lowest income countries in the world with the highest income countries in the world, marked differences become evident. Figure 11.2 depicts such differences in eight social indicators. The inner ring represents the low-income countries, while the outer ring signifies the high-income countries on these indicators using a 0–10 scale with 10 signifying the most favorable rating on these indicators and 0 representing the worst rating. The culture macro factor is represented by the gender development index at the nine o'clock position. This index covers demography, education, health, labor force and employment, and political participation for women.

The variables at the top (human development index of income, health, and education) and the bottom (average years of schooling for adults) represent the population macro factor. The geography and climate macro factor is not represented because these are natural endowments and not the result of man-made efforts as the other social indicators are. Employment in services (lower left part of graph) is an indicator of the economy macro-factor. Regulatory quality (three o'clock position on the graph) and days to start a business (upper right part of the graph) represent the political system macro factor. Finally, internet users per 1,000 people (upper left of graph) and total expenditure for research and development expenditures as a percentage of GDP (lower right of graph) represent the infrastructure macro factor. As can be seen by comparing the two rings of the graph, the low-income and high-income countries are very different on these social indicators. Some of the poorest of poor consumers are in these low-income countries. (These will be discussed later in this chapter.)

Culture

Culture is the learned meaning system of a people group that provides a guide for those in the group about how to think and behave (Cateora, Gilly, and Graham, 2011, p. 102). Values, beliefs, and attitudes are commonly shared by members of a cultural group (Harrison, 2006, p. 6). These can support and promote prosperity because they strongly affect perceptions of individuals and organizations about the way to win (Porter, 2000).

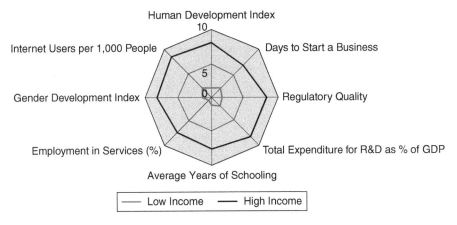

Figure 11.2 Comparison of low- and high-income countries on eight social indicators

Source: World Bank (2011). Data provided by World Bank under CC BY 4.0 license.

Table 11.1 presents the framework proposed by Argentine lawyer and political essayist Mariano Grondona to explain the differences between what he terms progress-prone cultures and progress-resistant cultures (Grondona, 2000). A worldview of progress-prone cultures includes personal agency for the individual, as compared with fatalism for the progress-resistant culture. The expandability of wealth characterizes progress-prone cultures, as opposed to a peasant mentality that wealth is finite. (If someone gains, someone else must lose.) In terms of values and virtues, progress-prone cultures reinforce trust in public or commercial activities with lesser values like punctuality being important. By comparison, progress-resistant cultures reinforce mistrust and give little emphasis to lesser values, such as punctuality.

Economic behavior in progress-prone cultures is influenced by regard given to entrepreneurial effort in competitive markets. Progress-resistant cultures see rent-seeking (taking advantage of what their position allows for self-gain) by cultural elites in government as the privilege granted to those who attain power.

Social behavior in progress-prone cultures can be characterized by a self-governing citizenry in which half the population (women) are able to function as the equals of the other half (men). Progress-resistant cultures tend to carry patriarchal hierarchy in which male chiefs or strong men dominate others because of their place in the tribe or kinship group. Women might run the home but usually not business, government, or civic organizations.

Table 11.1   Condensed typology of progress-prone and progress-resistant cultures

Dimension	Progress-prone culture	Progress-resistant culture
World view		
Destiny	I can influence my destiny for the better	Fatalism, resignation, sorcery
Wealth	Product of human creativity is wealth expandable (positive sum)	What exists (zero-sum) is wealth; not expandable
Values, virtues		
Ethical code	Rigorous within realistic norms; feeds trust	Elastic, wide gap twixt utopian norms and behavior. Mistrust reinforced
The lesser values	A job well done, tidiness, and punctuality matter	Lesser virtues unimportant
Economic behavior		
Entrepreneurship	Investment and creativity	Rent seeking: income derives from government connections
Competition	Leads to excellence	Is a sign of aggression, and a threat to equality and privilege
Advancement	Based on merit, connections	Based on family and/or patron connections
Social behavior		
Rule of law/corruption	Reasonably law abiding; corruption is prosecuted	Money, connections matter; corruption is tolerated
Family	The idea of 'family' extends to the broader society	The family is a fortress against the broader society
Gender relationships	If gender equality not a reality, at least not inconsistent with value system	Women subordinate to men in most dimensions of life

Source: Grondona (2000).

Population

Population characteristics contribute much to country development. Important aspects of a population for country are (a) urbanization, (b) health, and (c) education. As shown in Figure 11.3, urbanization has risen steadily since 1960 and exceeded the number living in rural areas in 2006 (Ritchie and Roser, 2019). The UN estimates that 55 percent of the world's population lived in urban areas in 2018. Researchers forecast this urbanization trend to continue through 2050 when two-thirds of the world's population will live in cities – about 7 billion of the world's population then.

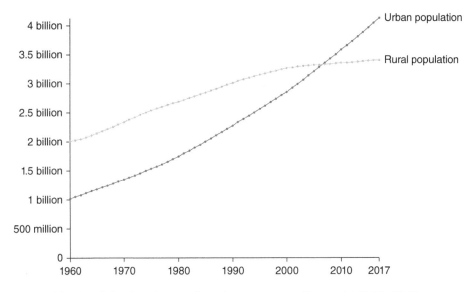

Figure 11.3   Number living in urban and rural areas across the world, 1960–2017

Source: Ritchie and Roser (2019). Hannah Ritchie (2018) - *Urbanization*. Published online at OurWorldInData.org. Retrieved from: https://ourworldindata.org/urbanization

Although the concentration of people living in cities makes industrialization more of a possibility, in many countries, the move to the cities exacerbates housing shortages resulting in expansive slums. At the same time, towns and villages in rural areas have emptied leaving mostly the elderly in some (Batson, 2008). Those who remain rely economically on cash sent back from those who left. Currently in China, the largest migration in human history is under way. One hundred and fifty million people have already migrated internally in China in pursuit of jobs in the cities, and there are predictions that 300 million more people will eventually migrate to the Chinese cities from 2010 to 2040 (The Economist, 2010). China's urbanization matches the world's urbanization for the year 2000 in Figure 11.3. It will likely soon catch up with the world's urbanization percentage and continue along with it to 2050.

The health and education of a country's population contribute much to country development because they represent important elements of human capital (Baumol, Litan, and Schramm, 2007, p. 159). Figure 11.4 depicts life expectancies for the world's regions since 1770. As can be seen, life expectancies have dramatically increased since 1950. Africa still lags here, but it has almost doubled its average life expectancies during this time.

Figure 11.5 depicts educational outcomes for countries by GDP in 2015, respectively (Roser and Ortiz-Ospina, 2016; Roser, Ortiz-Ospina, and Ritchie, 2019). The vertical axis of the figure represents average scores across standardized achievement tests. To maximize coverage by country, researchers harmonized and pooled across subjects, (such as math, reading, science) and levels (primary and secondary education). Figure 11.5 captures a linear relationship between average learning outcomes and GDP. Countries with higher (lower) GDPs tend to have higher (lower) learning outcomes.

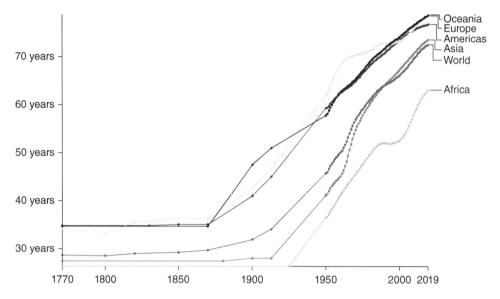

Figure 11.4   Life expectancies for world's regions, 1770–2019

Source: Roser, Ortiz-Ospina, and Ritchie (2019). Max Roser, Esteban Ortiz-Ospina and Hannah Ritchie (2013) - *Life Expectancy*. Published online at OurWorldInData.org. Retrieved from: https://ourworldindata.org/life-expectancy

In sum, health and education indicators are important in development because they represent important aspects of human capital – the wellness and knowledge of a society.

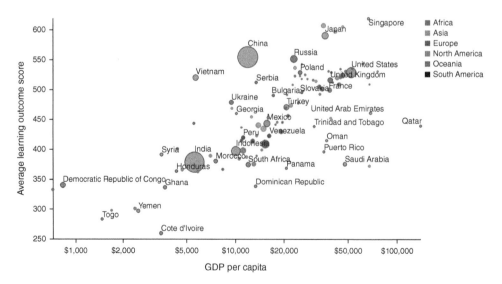

Figure 11.5   Average learning outcomes vs GDP per capita, 2015

Source: Roser and Ortiz-Ospina (2016). Altinok, N., N. Angrist and H.A. Patrinos. 2018. *Global data set on education quality (1965-2015)*. World Bank Policy Research Working Paper No. 8314. Washington, DC. Shared under the CC BY license.

Geography and Climate

Temperate regions of the world are undeniably more developed than the tropical countries. Of the 24 countries classified as 'industrial,' not one lies between the tropics of Cancer and Capricorn (about 23 degrees north and south of the Equator), except a bit of Australia and the Hawaiian Islands (Hausmann, 2001). Figure 11.6 depicts this benefit of a higher latitude.

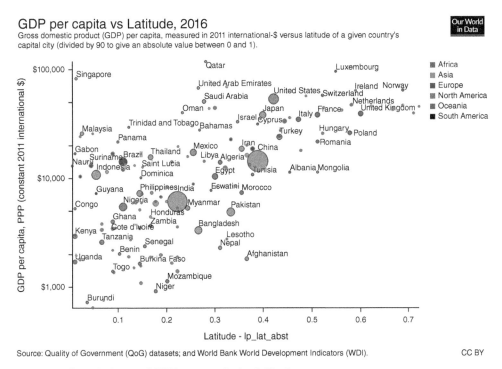

Source: Quality of Government (QoG) datasets; and World Bank World Development Indicators (WDI).   CC BY

Figure 11.6   Population and GDP per capita by latitude

Source: Our World in Data https://ourworldindata.org/grapher/gdp-per-capita-vs-latitude Quality of Government (QoG) datasets; and World Bank World Development Indicators (WD). Shared under the CC BY license.

Figure 11.6 depicts population (size of the circle), GDP per capita (left axis), and latitude (bottom axis) (Our World in Data, 2020). As can be seen, there are no countries below $10,000 GDP per capita above the latitude of 0.4 in 2016. One can also imagine a line bisecting the cloud of points that would be sloping upward. Such an upward slope represents a linear relationship between GDP per capita and latitude. A way of expressing this linear relationship would be that as latitude increases there is a rise in GDP per capita. In other words, wealthier countries tend to be in northern latitudes.

Philosophers and social scientists from previous centuries proposed simplistic explanations for such latitude differences. For example, Montesquieu believed climate might have a direct effect on human temperament, work effort, and social harmony (Mellinger, Sachs, and Gallup, 2000). During times of colonial rule, ideas such as Montesquieu's implied racial superiority for the ruling empires. Not surprisingly, these ideas became popular among imperialists.

Although rejecting notions from past eras regarding climate's links with race, work effort, or culture, new economic geographers view climate as one of many important influences on development. Some social scientists have argued that climate helps determine the means of production (small farming in the temperate regions and plantation farming in the tropics). With such a profound effect on production, climate would thereby indirectly affect the organization of society and the possibilities for development.

Coastal location (which results in lower transportation costs and increased access to markets and new technological approaches and ideas) would be another dimension of geography critical to development. Being a landlocked country is a disadvantage because of the complications (risks) this adds to foreign trade (Wolf, 2004, p. 147). Although a landlocked country like Switzerland successfully oriented its economy to serve the markets of its neighbors in Europe, countries such as Uganda have neighbors that are economically troubled or burdened with civil strife, such as Kenya, Sudan, Rwanda, Somalia, the Democratic Republic of the Congo, and Tanzania (Collier, 2007, p. 55). With poor transport links to the coast, and economically depressed neighbors, its ability to integrate itself in global markets through manufacturing (to date the most reliable driver of rapid development) has proved difficult.

Scholars have developed three reasons why tropical countries are consistently poorer than temperate ones. These include agricultural factors, health factors, and factors related to the mobilization of scientific resources (Sachs, 2000). Eurasia's east–west geographical layout and the north–south layout in Africa and the Americas have influenced historical patterns of agricultural innovation and, thus, economic growth (Diamond, 1997). Because climate changes little with longitude, but markedly with latitude, the countries of Eurasia happily had fairly common climatic conditions. Such uniformity allowed agricultural innovations developed in one region to travel long distances and be shared by many regions. On the contrary, new agricultural varieties developed in the tropics of Africa or the Americas could not travel very far before the climate changed dramatically.

Agriculture in the tropics faces reduced productivity of perennial crops and staple foods. This is true because of (a) weak soils, high soil erosion, and depletion of nutrients from tropical rainforest conditions; (b) water control difficulties and risk of drought in wet-dry tropics; (c) high incidence of pests; and (d) high rate of spoilage for food in storage (Sachs, 2000).

The incidence of infectious disease is also higher in the tropics. Flies and mosquitoes that flourish in the warm climate carry major vector-borne diseases, such as malaria, hookworm, schistosomiasis (a parasitic worm that feeds on red blood cells in its victims contracted through exposure to contaminated water), river blindness, and yellow fever. Because the afflicted countries tend to be poor and underdeveloped with respect to the temperate countries, tropical diseases do not receive research-and-development (R&D) investments that instead might be directed to cures for baldness in Western markets (Hausmann, 2001). In sum, changes in latitude have a profound inhibiting effect on the diffusion of technological innovations to the tropics in crucial sectors for development, such as agriculture, health, and construction (Sachs, 2000). Overcoming distance to developed markets through increased globalization in these economic sectors could help overcome what has been called 'the tyranny of geography' in the tropics.

Economy

Economies of countries can be described in several ways, such as level of development, or percentage of the labor force working in the agricultural, manufacturing, or service sectors. For example, 41 percent of the labor force in the United States worked on farms in 1900 (Dimitri, Effland, and Conklin, 2005). However, by 2019, only 1.3 percent of the labor force worked on farms (Lepley, 2019). In the early part of the twentieth century, the United States industrialized. But after 1950, it entered a postindustrialization phase in which the service sector (such as healthcare, education, financial services, government, media, entertainment, hospitality, and tourism) became dominant (Lee and Mather, 2008, p. 7).

Figure 11.7 presents a comparison of a postindustrial economy (the United Kingdom), an economy transitioning from industry to more service (China), an industrializing economy

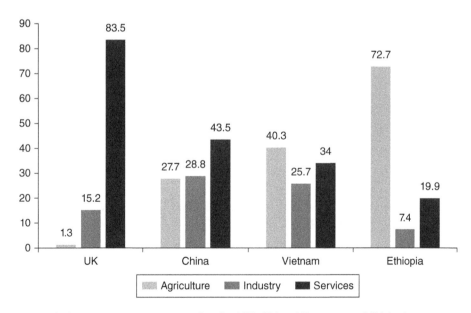

Figure 11.7 Labor sector percentages for the UK, China, Vietnam, and Ethiopia

Source: CIA (2020).

(Vietnam) and an agricultural economy (Ethiopia) based on the percentage of the labor force in each country working in service, industry, and agriculture (CIA, 2020). As shown, the most workers in the United Kingdom are in the services sector (83.5 percent), while the least in China are in agriculture (27.7 percent), but the most are in agriculture for Vietnam (40.3 percent) and for Ethiopia (72.7 percent).

Political Stability

Civil War

Working political systems are often taken for granted in developed countries. For example, when Al Gore lost to George W. Bush in the 2000 presidential election, the election was very close. It was so close that it took three weeks of recounting votes in Florida and a trip to the US Supreme Court to resolve the issue with a 5–4 vote by the Supreme Court justices favoring the case put forward by Bush's attorneys that recounting in Florida should stop. Although many in the United States grimaced at the arcane workings of the Electoral College (Gore polled more votes in the popular vote, but fewer in the Electoral College), both men were on the podium at the inauguration of Bush in January 2001. The important point here is that power changed hands peacefully – as expected by the citizens of the United States.

By comparison, 1,200 people died and more than 500,000 Kenyans fled their homes in violence that took on an ethnic dimension after the 2007 elections in Kenya (BBC, 2011). Although calm eventually returned to Kenya, the eruption of violence after the 2007 elections suggests that societies often have enormous pent-up tensions that can be triggered by such events as an election.

It must be remembered that when the United States was a developing country in 1860, the election of Abraham Lincoln (who did not advocate the termination of slavery – just its restriction to states where slavery currently existed) was so disagreeable to many living in the southern United States, they took up arms as rebels and initiated a civil war that lasted four years. Three percent of the entire population died as soldiers in the US Civil War – 620,000 (however, a new study asserts that 750,000 actually died as soldiers (Glover, 2011)). This was by far the bloodiest war in human history up to that time. These numbers put the violence in Kenya in better perspective, but they also highlight the cost a society pays when its political system ruptures into civil war.

Slow growth, stagnation, or economic depression makes a country prone to civil war (Collier, 2007, p. 20). When looking toward the countries where the poorest billion people on the planet dwell, 73 percent of these countries have recently had a civil war or are currently in one (Collier, 2007). Half of these civil wars are resumptions of earlier civil wars.

The costs of civil war are many. It is like development in reverse – shrinking economic output by 2.3 percent each year on average (Collier, 2007). A country enduring a seven-year civil war will have an economy 15 percent smaller than when it began. Surprisingly, most who die in civil wars are not victims of bullets or shrapnel but of disease. This is, in part, a result of the sudden migrations of refugees to safer areas. Refugees are exposed to disease vectors during their treks when they are weakened. They later infect humans in the safer areas.

Sadly, the economic losses and disease do not stop at the end of the civil war. Governments of postconflict countries typically double military spending over what it was before conflict began (Collier, 2007, p. 27). Kalashnikov rifles (the weapon of choice for developing country rebels) flood countries during times of conflict. After conflicts, such weapons remain cheap. Not surprisingly, homicide rates spike as the culture of violence and extortion cannot be suddenly terminated after formal cessation of hostilities.

The problems of civil war spill over to neighboring countries. Weapons smuggled from Libya at the end of the Libyan civil war apparently flowed into the surrounding region. 'Arms were stolen in Libya and are being disseminated all over the region,' President Mahamadou Issoufou of Niger (Libya's neighbor to the south) said. 'Saharan countries are facing terrorist threats, arms and criminal trafficking. The Libya crisis is amplifying those crises' (Maylie and Hinshaw, 2011, p. 1).

Neighboring countries must also endure (a) lost trading opportunities with the country experiencing civil war, (b) an influx of refugees that strain social services and infrastructure, and (c) the rise of criminal activities emanating from the civil war. All of this tends to destabilize neighboring countries. For example, 95 percent of the global production of hard drugs comes from conflict countries (Collier, 2007, p. 31). In this way, conflict creates territory beyond the control of a recognized government – a good match for illegal activities. Osama Bin Laden chose to set up Al Qaeda operations in Afghanistan for this reason.

Coups

Another violent challenge to government can take the form of a coup d'état. Usually, leadership in the military forces takes over the country in such a coup. A script for a coup might include capturing the current leader and cabinet members, securing communication centers (television, radio, newspapers) to broadcast programming favorable to the coup, and declaring martial law because of the national emergency that the deposed leaders thrust the country into because of their incompetence or illegal activities. Under martial law, the army is now responsible for governmental activities. The new military rulers usually suspend most civil rights (such as giving reasons for jailing citizens) and impose curfews to restrict public activity. Later, a new constitution might be introduced and martial law rescinded.

As a 27-year-old army captain, Libya's Muammar al-Qaddafi led a bloodless coup that deposed King Idris I of Libya on September 1, 1969 (History.com, 2011) (the king had left the country to seek medical treatment at a Turkish spa). Qaddafi ruled with an iron hand for 42 years. However, as unrest spread through much of the Arab world during February 2011, massive street protests against the Qaddafi regime initiated a civil war between revolutionaries and loyalists. In March, an international coalition began conducting airstrikes against Qaddafi strongholds under the authority of a UN Security Council resolution. On October 20, Qaddafi died at the hands of a mob who administered vigilante street justice after capturing him near his hometown of Sirte. In 2020, military fighting continues as well as economic and social chaos for many in Libya (Pack, 2020).

Marsh is a global firm with offices around the world focused on insurance broking and risk management. The firm provides research on political risk – the likelihood that government action or inaction would affect business operations in a country. Figure 11.8 depicts its 2019 political risk map. As shown, countries with high or severe levels of political risk include most of Africa, Syria eastward to Pakistan, Bosnia, Ukraine, as well as other countries of Central America, South America, Asia.

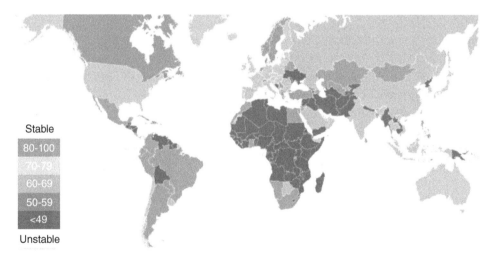

Figure 11.8   Political risk map

Source: Marsh (2020).

Infrastructure

Physical and Institutional Infrastructure

In developed markets, a range of intermediaries provide the information and contract enforcement needed to make commercial transactions (Khanna and Palepu, 2011, p. 14).

Most developing countries lack the infrastructure – both physical and institutional – needed for the smooth running of markets. Physical infrastructure includes publicly owned goods, such as ports, harbors, airports, miles of railroads and highways, bridges, ferries, and water and sewer systems. In some countries, private companies operate other physical infrastructure, such as electrical utilities, communication systems (telephone, cell phone, internet service providers, television, and radio), warehouses, refrigerated warehouses, and banks. Institutional infrastructure includes government-run courts and judicial systems, advertising agencies, media outlets, marketing research companies, logistics consultants, credit-rating agencies, and online clearinghouses for goods and services (for example, eBay and Orbitz).

Legal systems are of utmost importance to countries and the conduct of business. The legal system can take four forms: (a) common law evolving over time based on judicial rulings – in the United Kingdom and its former colonies, (b) civil law made by legislative action or official edict – in most of the rest of the world, (c) Islamic law where Sharia law is in effect, or (d) Marxist-Socialist tenets in communist countries, such as North Korea, Cuba, and China (Cateora et al., 2011, pp. 187–90). Although common law proves to be the most flexible for businesses, what is important is that the legal system is viewed widely by residents and foreign investors as trustworthy, stable, and effective (Baumol et al., 2007, p. 155). In this way, all parties to exchanges can reasonably expect to know what the rules are when they conduct business or lead their private lives.

Because of thin budgeting for governmental services in many developing countries, judicial systems can become ineffective. For example, because of a huge backlog of cases, resolving disputes in Indian courts can take 5 to 15 years (Khanna and Palepu, 2011, p. 14). Family or clan patriarchs might be used if the dispute is between two parties from the developing country, but this typically strikes foreign businesses as disadvantageous. The end result frequently is that deals are not initiated as a result of such institutional voids that increase the risk to intolerable levels for MNEs.

Researchers of productive entrepreneurship propose that governmental institutions can create conditions that will promote the kind of entrepreneurial activity leading to economic growth for a society (Sobel, 2008). Governments can facilitate the operation of markets through an effective legal system (Forbes and Ames, 2009, pp. 313–16). First, the rule of law must be established and respected within a country. This means that government leaders, government agencies, and any other individuals (mafia chieftains) cannot act arbitrarily toward businesses and private individuals. This implies that government limits itself in its ability to tax and regulate businesses. Additionally, the judicial system must be fair and balanced, so that contracts can be enforced without bias. Second, property rights must be respected (Carman, 1982). When this happens, land, buildings, and equipment can be used as collateral for growing a business. Without this ability, stagnation occurs (de Soto, 2003). When ownership of property is respected in a society, entrepreneurs will take the necessary risks to conceive, launch, and implement their business plans. This includes intellectual property, such as inventions, new software, new music, and creative works.

Corruption

Corruption is the abuse of public power or authority for private benefit (Anokhin and Schulze, 2009). It comes in two forms: (a) petty corruption (low-level government officials seeking relatively small amounts of money), and (b) grand corruption (high-ranking government officials seeking huge sums of money).

Petty Corruption. Petty corruption contributes to the delays in distributing products in the marketing system of a country (The Economist, 2002). In a 500 km trip from the capital city of Douala to Bertoua, a small town in Cameroon's southeastern rainforest, a Guinness beer truck encountered 47 roadblocks manned by off-duty policemen set up for the seeking of bribes to allow motorists to continue their journeys. That is one roadblock every 8 km. Instead of a 20-hour journey, the trip took four days.

Bridges and roads had washed out in the heavy seasonal rains and these added to delays. The impact on any business is that just-in-time inventory management is out of the question. Consequently, Guinness Cameroon has to keep 40 days of inventory in the factory along with the crates, drums of malt, hops, and bottle caps to continue operations. Inventory, along with its storage, security, and insurance, costs money. Out in distant corners of Cameroon, wholesalers have to carry as much as five months of inventory at the beginning of the rainy season when roads become most subject to flooding and damage from hard rains.

Figure 11.9 depicts the results of Transparency International's Global Corruption Barometer interviews with tens of thousands of interviews across 119 countries from March 2014 to January 2017 (Transparency International, 2017).

Typically, those in the lowest 20 percent income bracket reported a higher incidence of bribing eight of the nine institutions when compared with those in the highest 20 percent income bracket. Given that any bribe would represent a larger chunk of the poor's income, the burden of bribery is relatively heavier for the poor. Many respondents reported that the last bribe was paid 'to avoid a problem with the authorities'. In these regions with developing countries, the police are the service provider with the highest frequency of receiving bribes. Almost one-quarter of respondents cited 'speeding things up' as the reason for the bribe, followed by 'to receive a service they were entitled to' (Transparency International, 2017).

Grand Corruption. Grand corruption is perpetrated by those in high-ranking leadership positions for a country. After the end of the Libyan civil war, Libya's National Transitional Council estimated former Libyan leader Muammar al-Qaddafi had hidden more than $220 billion in bank accounts and investments around the world – an amount representing $30,000 for every Libyan (Richter, 2011). About one-third of Libyans live in poverty (Faulkner, 2017).

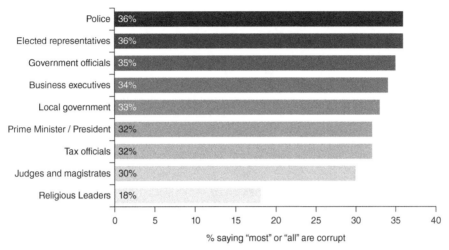

HOW CORRUPT ARE DIFFERENT INSTITUTIONS
AND GROUPS IN SOCIETY?

- GLOBAL AVERAGE

Q. How many of the following people do you think are involved in corruption, or haven't you heard enough about them to say?
Base: all respondents, excluding missing responses. Chart shows percentage of respondents who answered that either "Most" or
"All" of them are corrupt. "None", "Some" and "Don't know" responses are not shown for ease of comparison

Figure 11.9   Global average of institutional corruption in society

Source: Transparency International (2017). This work from Transparency International (2017) is licensed under CC BY-ND license.

Most of the money was under the name of government institutions such as the Central Bank of Libya, the Libyan Investment Authority, the Libyan Foreign Bank, the Libyan National Oil Corp, and the Libya Africa Investment Portfolio. Qaddafi and his family members had access to these accounts.

Researchers estimate that, on average, dictators take about 3 percent of their nations' incomes in the form of excessive taxation (Mulligan, 2011). Judging from Qaddafi's share of Libya's national wealth it appears that Qaddafi stole this percentage. However, other costs accrued to the Libyan people because the Qaddafi regime's security services included torturing and executing political enemies, making exiles living overseas disappear, as well as blocking unfavorable websites outside of the country (MacFarquhar, 2009, p. 32).

No Institutions and Weak Institutions

Under Qaddafi's rule, Libya had no parliament, political parties, unions, NGOs, or independent newspapers or media outlets (MacFarquhar, 2009, p. 25). Because he had led a coup as an army officer, Qadaffi never trusted the military and frequently moved around its commanders and would not allow coordination across Libya's military units. This later proved fateful to Qaddafi himself, as his military forces could not unify their actions to stop the uprising against him that began in February 2011 and ended with his lynching in October of the same year.

During the last years of his 42 years of despotic rule, the official Libyan television news ended each night with dated video clips of rioting and civil unrest in cities of the West with the announcer intoning that it was only a matter of time before the decaying West came to adopt Libya's Popular Committees as the way of societal organization. Government-run newspapers typically filled themselves with songs, poems, and salutes to Qaddafi penned by Africans from the many countries where he directed foreign aid.

For writing about the Popular Committee meetings and how they showed Libyans as being discouraged with the incompetence of their rulers and their low quality of life, *New York Times* Cairo bureau chief Neil MacFarquhar never again received a visa to visit the country under Qaddafi's rule after his two-week visa expired in 2001. Keep in mind that MacFarquhar's writings were never published inside Libya but outside of it in the West.

A free press is an important ingredient in checking corruption in a society. In developed countries, the press is regarded as the 'fourth estate', meaning it is the unofficial fourth branch of government that exposes government corruption, bad business practices, and the criminal activity of individuals (Quelch and Jocz, 2007, p. 208). The journalistic press enables freedom of speech. It consists of newspapers and magazines, television and radio broadcasters, book publishers, cable operators, and the blogosphere. An informed citizenry results from strong and active journalism. This enables democratic processes to be more effective.

Chapter 6 related the story of Peter Eigen and the NGO he founded, Transparency International (TI). An examination of Figure 6.5 in Chapter 6 (depicting TI's Corruption Perceptions Index) suggests how developing countries in particular carry a burden of corruption. Researchers have found that increasing the corruption level in a country from that of Singapore (9.5 on a 10-point scale for lack of corruption) to Mexico's (3.1 on the same scale) is equivalent to raising the tax rate by more than 20 percentage points (Eigen, 2002). Not surprisingly, global investors tend to stay away from countries with high levels of corruption.

Companies may bribe employees in other firms to secure business and facilitate the functioning of hidden cartels seeking to control supplies of products. Employees from large firms can exploit their influence by demanding bribes or kickbacks from potential suppliers. Bribery can also be disguised through offering clients gifts and corporate hospitality that are inappropriate in value.

The effects of this particular form of bribery can be felt through the entire supply chain, distorting markets and competition, increasing costs to firms, harming smaller companies that cannot afford to compete on these terms, and firms with high integrity that refuse to do so. This not only prevents a fair and efficient private sector but also reduces the quality of products and services to the consumer.

Summary of Macro Factors for Developing Country Contexts

In sum, the physical and institutional infrastructure for a country matters much to a society and its proper functioning. To repair or overhaul such infrastructure can be costly in terms of time and financial resources.

After reviewing the six macro factors for countries, one should gain an appreciation for the challenges confronting many developing countries across these six dimensions. Some countries might have (a) cultures characterized as progress-resistant, (b) low levels of health and education, (c) poor natural resources and a harsh climate, (d) an economy based on agriculture or extractive industries (such as mining or oil production), (e) civil war in recent years, and (f) weak institutions afflicted by corruption. Most of the countries with high or severe levels of terrorism and political violence face such disadvantages in development. Despite similar challenges across these six dimensions, some developing countries have managed to show promise for developing themselves in recent years. These countries have been described as 'emerging markets' (Khanna and Palepu, 2011).

Emerging Markets

Although a variety of lists have appeared in recent years to label the most promising developing countries as 'emerging markets', there is no consensus definition of emerging markets.

In general, emerging markets can be characterized by (a) poverty (low-middle income and not industrialized), (b) capital markets (low market capitalization relative to GDP and low sovereign debt ratings), and (c) growth potential (economic liberalization, openness to foreign direct investment, and recent economic growth) (Khanna and Palepu, 2011, p. 4). In short, emerging markets offer attractive investment opportunities for MNEs to acquire firms in these markets or to introduce their own brands there. MNEs expect to find 70 percent of their future growth in emerging markets – 40 percent in China and India, alone (Eyring, Johnson, and Nair, 2011). Table 11.2 presents investment-analysis firm MSCI's list of 23 developed and 26 emerging market countries.

Not surprisingly, MNEs have taken an increased interest in emerging markets in recent years. For example, consumer packaged goods manufacturer H.J. Heinz gave focus to emerging markets and the share of revenues coming from emerging markets climbed to 20 percent in 2011 (Johnson, 2011).

In evaluating possible acquisitions in emerging markets, Heinz looks at several of the same aspects of businesses as in developed countries, such as operating metrics of the business, recent and forecasted growth, as well as how the business fits with Heinz's core business. But Heinz also uses an entire set of biggest M issues when evaluating acquisitions in emerging markets. 'We look at how the company goes to market, the tax system, the regulatory environment, currency trends, and the political climate, comparing them with what exists in the United States,' Johnson, Heinz's CEO, said. He continued:

Table 11.2   A listing of developed and emerging markets

DEVELOPED MARKETS			EMERGING MARKETS		
Americas	Europe and Middle East	Pacific	Americas	Europe and Middle East and Africa	Asia
Canada	Austria	Australia	Argentina	Czech Republic	China
Unites States	Belgium	Hong Kong	Brazil	Egypt	India
	Denmark	Japan	Chile	Greece	Indonesia
	Finland	New Zealand	Colombia	Hungary	Korea
	France	Singapore	Mexico	Poland	Malaysia
	Germany		Peru	Qatar	Pakistan
	Ireland			Russia	Philippines
	Israel			Saudi Arabia	Taiwan
	Italy			South Africa	Thailand
	Netherlands			Turkey	
	Norway			United Arab Emirates	
	Portugal				
	Spain				
	Sweden				
	Switzerland				
	United Kingdom				

Source: MSCI (2020).

We take these things for granted in developed economies, but they're a big consideration in emerging markets, where governments are often much more active. This process may take a lot of time, and the companies we're considering as acquisitions are sometimes frustrated by that, but these issues are very important. We have walked away from deals in Ukraine, Vietnam and other markets because our due diligence told us there were considerable risks involved in trying to generate acceptable returns on the businesses.

(Johnson, 2011, p. 49)

Firms from developed countries like Heinz's have learned that they need to make adaptations to their marketing mixture of product, place, price, and promotion when they go to the emerging markets. Products frequently need to be adapted to the tastes of the host culture if consumers have intimate involvement with them. For example, ketchup in the Philippines is made from bananas and tastes differently from ketchup in the West. Places of distribution also have to be relevant for host cultures.

Supermarket chains only cover about 15 percent of the market in India, whereas in the United States, they cover virtually 100 percent of the market. In emerging markets, corner stores and open-air markets comprise a majority of food retailing. Prices need to be kept relevant for consumers in emerging markets. Often, this is done by offering different sizes, such as packets of soy sauce, instead of bottles of soy sauce. Finally, the promotion of brands must be done with an understanding of how host-country consumers live. If they are not likely to have refrigerators, then it is useless to sell them quantities that must be stored in refrigerated places. Having local managers in place addresses many of these issues in better ways than having expatriate staff members of the MNE there to run the business in the host country.

'We have learned that to succeed in emerging markets, you need to be risk aware but not risk averse,' Johnson said. He continued:

> Indonesia provides a great example of that. We bought a big business there in 1999. The country was just starting to democratize and have elections: it wasn't especially stable. Frankly, some people wondered if it was a good place for an American company. Today that's a $400 million business for us, versus $80 million when we bought it. Generally, we focus on the long term. Our Indian business took seven or eight years to get right. You have to be patient, flexible, and open to ideas from local management.

> (Johnson, 2011, p. 50).

H.J. Heinz lost Johnson's acumen regarding emerging markets when Berkshire Hathaway bought the firm in 2013 and gave Johnson one of the largest payouts ever at more than $200 million (Strauss, 2013). Without Johnson's leadership, H.J. Heinz's effectiveness in emerging markets slipped after 2011. After merging H.J. Heinz with Kraft, Berkshire Hathaway saw the revenues attributable to emerging markets for Kraft Heinz going to 10 percent in 2016 (Menker, 2017).

In an effort to repair its underperformance in emerging markets, H.J. Heinz's parent company Berkshire Hathaway led by investor Warren Buffet tried to buy Unilever in 2015. (Unilever does more than half of its business in emerging markets.) The offer was quickly rebuffed by Unilever's board of directors. In 2019, Unilever reported 2.9 percent growth in sales led by its emerging-market business which grew 5.3 percent (Unilever, 2020).

CONCLUSION

This chapter examined country development. Undeniably, quality of life has improved for millions all over the world during the last 50 years. Health and education have improved markedly in many regions. Today, several firms from developing countries now challenge MNEs from developed countries in markets around the world. Such emerging giants include India's Tata Motors, China's PC-maker Lenovo, and Kuwait's rising telecommunications company Zain. Despite these successes, researchers estimate that 700 million people exist on $2 a day (Gates, 2019). The World Bank's international poverty line is $1.90 a day.

A review of six important dimensions of developing countries suggests some of the complexities in country development. These six macro factors of developing country contexts include (a) culture, (b) population, (c) geography and climate, (d) economy, (e) political system, and (f) infrastructure. Institutions of society were included in this final dimension of developing countries as they represent 'soft' infrastructure (Khanna and Palepu, 2011).

Emerging markets such as those listed in Table 11.2 have captured the imagination of MNE leaders around the world. The opportunities to win millions of new customers are now proving to be very attractive when compared with the forecasted sluggish growth in developed markets.

BOP marketing has caught the attention of leaders of MNEs and transnational organizations in recent years. Before his death in 2010, University of Michigan business professor C.K. Prahalad called the developed world's businesses to find their fortune by marketing to the very poorest consumers in countries, such as India (Prahalad, 2005). At this time, few firms have had an easy time in figuring out how to market to the poorest of the poor. It seems that some firms might be having success with the emerging middle-class consumers in developing markets. Nevertheless, many MNEs see their future in developing markets and succeeding with poor consumers there.

QUESTIONS

- How can macromarketing's three primary generalizations help explain country development?
- What are the six macro factors of developing country contexts?
- Which of these six macro factors do you believe is the most critical to achieving an improved quality of life for citizens of developing countries?
- Compare and contrast progress-prone cultures and progress-resistant cultures.
- What can be said about what is happening in the world today regarding the three important population dimensions presented in this chapter?
- What are the advantages and disadvantages of each of the four types of capitalism?
- What are the types of costs civil war imposes on a country and its neighbors?
- What are the two types of infrastructure presented in the chapter?
- Name emerging market countries you were surprised to see included in Table 11.2.
- In your view, will MNEs find a fortune at the bottom of the pyramid?

Mavericks Who Made It

Myriam Sidibe

Source: https://twitter.com/myriam_sidibe

Myriam Sidibe was born in Mali – a large, land-locked country in western Africa (Sidibe, 2020). From an early age, she wanted to work with the most vulnerable people. She received a bachelor's degree in engineering from Montréal's McGill University and a master's degree in water and waste engineering from Loughborough University in the UK.

Sidibe joined International Rescue Committee, a US-based NGO targeting emergency contexts. She was sent to Burundi, a small country in central Africa (northwest of Tanzania) torn by ethnic conflict. Her NGO focused on building toilets – but not how many used the toilets. Sibide's work increasingly became writing grant applications for funding. Over time, Sibide realized that her life's work might become writing grants for toilets that local people in poor contexts did not use. This did not seem right to Sidibe, so she eventually left to pursue a doctorate in public health in London graduating from the London School of Hygiene and Tropical Medicine.

After receiving her doctorate, Sidibe joined Unilever, an Anglo-Dutch global company selling fast-moving consumer goods. Unilever assigned her to the Lifebuoy soap brand.

> After a few months there (at Unilever), I fell in love, not with a fancy marketer but with a word. Crazy as this sounds, the word was 'consumer'. I realized that Unilever didn't treat its audiences as beneficiaries (as NGOs patronizingly tend to do), but as consumers. Instead of offering hand-me-downs and pity, Unilever treated consumers, however vulnerable they might be, with respect and dignity. That's because consumers have a choice: they choose with their wallet what to do with their money.
>
> (Sidibe, 2020, p. 7)

(Continued)

Sidibe found the private-sector approach an exciting one. It was the polar opposite of what made her uneasy working for an NGO in Burundi. Instead of giving resources to beneficiaries who had no choice, she was making solutions attractive to consumers who did have a choice – regardless of their humble circumstances.

Sidibe spent the next ten years with Lifebuoy's marketing team, attending daily meetings on topics such as packaging, fragrances, product design, ad copy, pricing and profit margins. Her work focused on developing the world's most far-reaching antibacterial soap. She never felt her public-health-values had to be compromised working for a for-profit firm, such as Unilever. With Unilever, she co-founded Global Handwashing Day in 2008 – a celebration recognized by the UN which occurs every October 15 in more than 100 countries. She also developed a handwashing program for schools that has been translated into 19 languages. Lifebuoy's behavior-change programs have reached one billion consumers from 2010 to 2020.

In 2020, Sidibe was a fellow at the Harvard Kennedy School (Lin and Shirley, 2020). She will likely continue addressing the third of the UN's Sustainable Development Goals: Good Health and Wellbeing. Her life experience (living in more than 20 countries in her life) and working in both the private sector and the civil sector with NGOs will likely allow her to be effective in bringing social change across many sectors in the future (Responsible Business, 2020). In an era of pandemic response, her insights about motivating handwashing are timely. In 2020, her book *Brands on a Mission: How to Achieve Social Impact and Business Growth through Purpose* came out (Sidibe, 2020).

'The situation in developing and emerging markets is still very fragile and ad hoc,' Sidibe said. So many diseases there are preventable. Marketing can be planned in a way that enables companies to grow while helping people to become healthier and more empowered' (Aziz, 2020).

Questions

- Were you surprised that someone with a background working with NGOs in developing countries and a PhD in public health would find the work for a global firm like Unilever so personally rewarding?
- How much greater was the scale of impact for Sidibe's work with an NGO in Burundi than with Unilever's Lifebuoy?
- What was it about a market approach to handwashing that made Unilever more successful in Sidibe's view than what Sidibe had experienced with an NGO approach?
- What does Sidibe's story say about the importance of evaluating the actual impact of one's work? Explain.

REFERENCES

Anokhin, S., and Schulze, W.S. (2009). Entrepreneurship, innovation, and corruption. *Journal of Business Venturing*, 24(5), 465–76.

Aziz, A. (2020). Brands on a mission: Dr. Myriam Sidibe's new book challenges companies to take action in public health as the foundation for social justice. *Forbes*, July 13, 2020. Accessed at www.forbes.com/sites/afdhelaziz/2020/07/13/brands-on-a-mission-dr-myriam-sidibes-new-book-challenges-companies-to-take-action-in-public-health-as-the-foundation-for-social-justice/#375b46a06f69

Batson, A. (2008, April 12). On the move. *The Wall Street Journal*. Retrieved from http://online.wsj.com

Baumol, W.J., Litan, R.E., and Schramm, C.J. (2007). *Good capitalism, bad capitalism and the economics of growth and prosperity*. New Haven, CT: Yale University Press.

BBC. (2011, September 21). Kenya election violence: Uhuru Kenyatta at The Hague. *BBC News Africa*. Retrieved from www.bbc.co.uk

Carman, J. (1982, Spring). Private property and the regulation of vertical channel systems. *Journal of Macromarketing*, 2(1), 20–6.

Cateora, P.R., Gilly, M.C., and Graham, J.L. (2011). *International marketing* (15th edn.). New York, NY: McGraw-Hill Irwin.

CIA. (2020). CIA factbook. *Guide to country comparisons*. Retrieved from www.cia.gov/library/publications/the-world-factbook/

Collier, P. (2007). *The bottom billion: Why the poorest countries are failing and what can be done about it*. New York, NY: Oxford University Press.

Dapice, D. (2008). What do we know about economic development? *Journal of Macromarketing*, 28(4), 413–17.

de Soto, H. (2003). *The mystery of capital: Why capitalism triumphs in the West and fails everywhere else*. New York, NY: Basic Books.

Diamond, J. (1997). *Guns, germs, and steel: The fates of human societies*. New York, NY: W.W. Norton.

Dimitri, C., Effland, A., and Conklin, N. (2005, June). *The 20th century transformation of U.S. agriculture and farm policy*. USDA Electronic Information Bulletin Number 3. Retrieved from www.ers.usda.gov/publications/eib3/eib3.htm

The Economist. (2002, December 21). The road to hell is unpaved. *The Economist*. Retrieved from www.economist.com/node/1487583

The Economist. (2010, May 6). Migration in China: Invisible and heavy shackles. *The Economist*. Retrieved from www.economist.com

The Economist. (2019). After half a century of success, the Asian tigers must reinvent themselves. *The Economist*, December 5, 2019. Accessed at www.economist.com/

special-report/2019/12/05/after-half-a-century-of-success-the-asian-tigers-must-reinvent-themselves

Economist Intelligence Unit. (2005). The Economist Intelligence Unit's quality of life index. *The Economist*. Retrieved from www.economist.com/media/pdf/quality_of_life.pdf

Eigen, P. (2002). Controlling corruption: A key to development-oriented trade. *Trade, Equity and Development*, 4, 1–8. Retrieved from www.ceip.org

Eyring, M.J., Johnson, M.W., and Nair, H. (2011, January–February). New business models in emerging markets. *Harvard Business Review*, 89–95.

Faulkner, J. (2017). Causes of poverty in Libya. The Borgen Project. Accessed at https://borgenproject.org/causes-of-poverty-in-libya/

Forbes, S., and Ames, E. (2009). *How capitalism will save us: Why free people and free markets are the best answer in today's economy*. New York, NY: Crown Business.

Friedman, T.L. (2012, March 10). Pass the books. Hold the oil. *The New York Times*. Retrieved from www.nytimes.com

Gates, B. (2019). What's it like to live on less than $2 a day? *GatesNotes*, September 6, 2019. Accessed at www.gatesnotes.com/Development/Life-on-less-than-2-dollars-a-day.

Glover, G. (2011, September 21). New analysis suggests Civil War took bigger toll than previously estimated. *Binghamton University Press Release*. Retrieved from www.eurekalert.org/pub_releases/2011-09/bu-nas092111.php

Grondona, M. (2000). A cultural typology of economic development. In L.E. Harrison and S.P. Huntington (Eds.), *Culture matters: How values shape human progress* (pp. 44–55). New York, NY: Basic Books.

Harrison, L.E. (2006). *The central liberal truth: How politics can change a culture and save it from itself*. New York, NY: Oxford University Press.

Hausmann, R. (2001, January–February). Prisoners of geography. *Foreign Policy*. Retrieved from www.jstor.org/stable/3183225

Heritage Foundation. (2020). 2020 index of economic freedom. Accessed at www.heritage.org/index/ranking

History.com. (2011). Qaddafi leads coup in Libya: September 1, 1969. *This day in history*. Retrieved from www.history.com/this-day-in-history/qaddafi-leads-coup-in-libya

Johnson, B. (2011, October). The CEO of Heinz on powering growth in emerging markets. *Harvard Business Review*, 89(10), 47–50.

Karnani, A. (2007). The mirage of marketing to the bottom of the pyramid: How the private sector can help alleviate poverty. *California Management Review*, 49(4), 90–111.

Kenny, C. (2011). *Getting better: Why global development is succeeding – and how we can improve the world even more*. New York, NY: Basic Books.

Kenny, C. (2020). A manifesto for globalization. *Center for Global Development*, July 22, 2020. Accessed at www.cgdev.org/publication/manifesto-globalization

Khanna, T., and Palepu, K.G. (2011). *Winning in emerging markets: A road map for strategy and execution*. Boston, MA: Harvard Business Press.

Kiprop, V. (2019). What percentage of the global population is literate? *World Atlas*, November 21, 2019. Accessed at www.worldatlas.com/articles/what-percentage-of-the-global-population-is-literate.html

Klein, T.A., and Nason, R.W. (2000). Marketing and development: Macromarketing perspectives. In P.N. Bloom and G.T. Gundlach (Eds.), *Handbook of marketing and society* (pp. 263–97). Thousand Oaks, CA: Sage.

Lee, M.A., and Mather, M. (2008, June). U.S. labor force trends. *Population Bulletin*, 63(2), 3–16.

Lepley, S. (2019). 9 mind-blowing facts about the US farming industry. *Markets Insider*, May 30, 2019. Accessed at https://markets.businessinsider.com/news/stocks/farming-industry-facts-us-2019-5-1028242678#

Lin, K., and Shirley, S.M. (2020). A Harvard handwashing expert weighs in on corporate responsibility amid the COVID-19 pandemic. *The Crimson*, April 9, 2020. Accessed at www.thecrimson.com/article/2020/4/9/handwashing-phd/

MacFarquhar, N. (2009). *The media relations department of Hizbollah wishes you a happy birthday: Unexpected encounters in the changing Middle East*. New York, NY: PublicAffairs.

Marsh. (2020). Political risk map 2019. Accessed at www.marsh.com/us/campaigns/political-risk-map-2019.html

Maylie, D., and Hinshaw, D. (2011, November 12). Alarm over smuggled Libyan arms. *The Wall Street Journal*. Retrieved from http://online.wsj.com

Mellinger, A.D., Sachs, J.D., and Gallup, J.L. (2000). Climate, coastal proximity, and development. In G.L. Clark, M.P. Feldman, and M.S. Gertler (Eds.), *The Oxford handbook of economic geography* (pp. 169–194). Oxford, UK: Oxford University Press.

Menker, S. (2017). Kraft Heinz pivots to emerging markets. *LinkedIn*, March 2, 2017. Accessed at www.linkedin.com/pulse/kraft-heinz-pivots-emerging-markets-sara-menker/

Mittelstaedt, J.D., Kilbourne, W.E., and Mittelstaedt, R.A. (2006). Macromarketing as agorology: Macromarketing theory and the study of the agora. *Journal of Macromarketing*, 26(2), 131–42.

MSCI (2020). MSCI ACWI Index. Accessed at www.msci.com/acwi

Mulligan, C.B. (2011, October 26). Was Qaddafi overpaid? *The New York Times*. Retrieved from http://economix.blogs.nytimes.com/2011/10/26/was-qaddafi-overpaid/

Nash, M. (2000). Grains of hope. *Time*, August 7, 2000. Accessed at http://content.time.com/time/world/article/0,8599,2047898,00.html

Nguyen, H.P., and Pham, H.T. (2011). The dark side of development in Vietnam: Lessons from the killing of the Thi Vai River. *Journal of Macromarketing*, 32(1), 74–86.

Nguyen, M. (2016). Formosa unit offers $500 million for causing toxic disaster in Vietnam. *Reuters*, June 30, 2016. Accessed at www.reuters.com/article/us-vietnam-environment-idUKKCN0ZG1F5

Our World in Data. (2020). GDP per capita vs. Latitude, 2016. *Our World in Data*. Accessed at https://ourworldindata.org/grapher/gdp-per-capita-vs-latitude

Pack, J. (2020). Economic transparency and structural reform remain Libya's last hope. *Middle East Institute*, September 14, 2020. Accessed at www.mei.edu/publications/economic-transparency-and-structural-reform-remain-libyas-last-hope

Porter, M. (2000). Attitudes, values, beliefs, and the microeconomics of prosperity. In L.E. Harrison and S.P. Huntington (Eds.), *Culture matters: How values shape human progress* (pp. 14–28). New York, NY: Basic Books.

Prahalad, C.K. (2005). *The fortune at the bottom of the pyramid: Eradicating poverty through profits*. Upper Saddle River, NJ: Wharton School.

Price. C. (2015). *Vitamania: How vitamins revolutionized the way we think about food*. New York: Penguin Books.

Quelch, J.A., and Jocz, K.E. (2007). *Greater good: How good marketing makes for better democracy*. Boston, MA: Harvard Business Press.

Regis, E. (2019). *Golden rice: The imperiled birth of a gmo superfood*. Baltimore, MD: Johns Hopkins University Press.

Responsible Business. (2020). Myriam Sidibe. Accessed at www.responsiblebusiness.com/speakers/myriam-sidebe/

Richter, P. (2011, October 22). Gaddafi salted away about $200 billion. *The Age*. Retrieved from www.theage.com.au

Ritchie, H., and Roser, M. (2019). Urbanization. *Our World in Data*, November 2019. Accessed at https://ourworldindata.org/urbanization

Rodrik, D. (2011). *The globalization paradox: Democracy and the future of the world economy*. New York, NY: W.W. Norton.

Roser, M., and Ortiz-Ospina, E. (2016). Global education. Our World in Data. Accessed at https://ourworldindata.org/global-education

Roser, M., Ortiz-Ospina, E., and Ritchie, H. (2019). Life expectancy. *Our World in Data*, October 2019. Accessed at https://ourworldindata.org/life-expectancy

Sachs, J. (2000). Notes on a new sociology of economic development. In L.E. Harrison and S.P. Huntington (Eds.), *Culture matters: How values shape human progress* (pp. 29–43). New York, NY: Basic Books.

Shultz, C.J. II, Deshpande, R., Cornwell, T.B., Ekici, A., Kothandaraman, P., Peterson, M., Shapiro, S., Taulkdar, D., and Veeck, A. (2012). Marketing and public policy: Transformative research in developing markets. *Journal of Public Policy and Marketing*, 31(2), 178–184.

Sidibe. M. (2020). *Brands on a mission: How to achieve social impact and business growth through purpose*. London: Routledge

Slater, C.C. (1977). A theory of market process. In C.C. Slater (Ed.), *Macro-Marketing: Distributive processes from a societal perspective* (pp. 117–40). Boulder, CO: Graduate School of Business, University of Colorado.

Sobel, R.S. (2008). Testing Baumol: Institutional quality and the productivity of entrepreneurship. *Journal of Business Venturing*, 23(6), 641–55.

Strauss, G. (2013). Heinz CEO William Johnson: $212 million man. *USA Today*, March 4, 2013. Accessed at www.usatoday.com/story/money/business/2013/03/04/heinz-ceo-johnson-212-million/1963253/

Transparency International. (2017). People and corruption: Citizens' voices from around the world, Global Corruption Barometer: Transparency International, November 14, 2017. Accessed at www.transparency.org/news/feature/global_corruption_barometer_citizens_voices_from_around_the_world

Unilever. (2020). Full-year growth led by emerging markets and home care. Accessed at www.unilever.com/news/press-releases/2020/full-year-growth-led-by-emerging-markets-and-home-care.html

Wilkie, W.L., and Moore, E.S. (1999). Marketing's contributions to society. *Journal of Marketing*, 63, 198–218.

Woetzel, J. (2019). Form third world to first in class. *Milken Institute Review*, April 26, 2019. Accessed at www.milkenreview.org/articles/from-third-world-to-first-in-class

Wolf, M. (2004). *Why globalization works*. New Haven, CT: Yale University Press.

World Bank. (2008). The growth report: Strategies for sustained growth and inclusive development. Commission on Growth and Development. Retrieved from www.growthcommission.org

World Bank. (2011). Data. Retrieved from http://data.worldbank.org

World Bank. (2019a). Classifying countries by income. *The World Bank*, September 9, 2019. Accessed at https://datatopics.worldbank.org/world-development-indicators/stories/the-classification-of-countries-by-income.html

World Bank. (2019b). Life expectancy at birth, total (years) – Middle East and North Africa. Accessed at https://data.worldbank.org/indicator/SP.DYN.LE00.IN?locations=ZQ

World Bank (2020). Data. World Bank Country and Lending Groups. Accessed at https://datahelpdesk.worldbank.org/knowledgebase/articles/906519-world-bank-country-and-lending-groups

12
POVERTY ALLEVIATION

Throwing Shade

Source: Photo by Annie Spratt on Unsplash.

Market Dynamics for Vanilla Beans

Madagascar is an island larger than France about 700 kilometers off the southeast coast of Africa – opposite of Mozambique. While a bit less than 16 million people lived there in 2000, about 27 million people lived there in 2019 (World Bank, 2020a). That is an increase in population of 71 percent over this period – a 2.8 percent annual growth rate.

(Continued)

Most of the population lives in the countryside in Madagascar and earning a living is precarious for many. The poverty headcount ratio at $1.90 a day in 2012 showed that 77.6 percent of those in Madagascar could be classified as living on less than $1.90 per day.

The lack of economic opportunity for many living in Madagascar explains the dedication farmers show for growing vanilla beans in the northeast part of the island (Reel, 2019).

Numbering about 80,000, these smallholder farmers pursue an agricultural undertaking like few others on the planet. In places where vanilla orchids are cultivated outside of Mexico, each vanilla orchid must be pollinated by hand in order to produce one 20 cm pod of vanilla beans because only the Mexican insects move on the orchids to successfully pollinate them.

The farmers live outside in the forested vanilla-fields and monitor their plants continually during the blooming season because the blooms remain fertile only a matter of hours. Once the vanilla beans begin to grow, these farmers sleep near their plants with a machete in order to run off thieves. The entire cycle of planting to harvesting vanilla beans for the market takes about one year.

About 80 percent of the world's natural vanilla comes from smallholder farms in Madagascar (Bomgardner, 2016). Because of the remoteness of the farms and the difficulty of travel over streams with no bridges and deeply rutted muddy roads, many of the farmers carry their sack of vanilla beans (weighing 40 kilograms) on their heads as they walk in flip-flops to a regional vanilla market for a seasonal auction (Reel, 2019).

Once at the market, the farmers have their sacks inspected by a government agent. The farmers then band together, determine a price for their vanilla crop and put it on a chalkboard. The handful of buyers there consider the chalked price, mutter among themselves and then later put their aggregated counteroffer on the chalkboard after erasing the farmers offer. This goes on for a day, but could go on for a week.

The oddity of having collective bargaining for buyers and sellers in this market comes from the inability of the farmers or buyers to easily move to other markets. Despite being the far end of a global supply chain, world market forces influence what happens in these remote regional vanilla auctions.

For example, in 2015, Nestlé, the world's largest food and beverage company, responded to mounting pressure and announced it would eliminate artificial additives used for vanilla flavoring (much used in chocolate to make cocoa taste less bitter) (Bomgardner, 2016). General Mills, Hershey's and Kellogg's followed Nestlé. Because of a cyclone damaging crop in Madagascar and the move by global firms, average prices for vanilla coming from the hinterlands of Madagascar went to $600 per kilogram in 2017 (more than the price of silver).

Unfortunately, the farmers in Madagascar receive about a tenth of such a world price for cured and ready-to-use vanilla beans. Because of the remoteness of farms in Madagascar with farmers living off the grid without access to passable roads and because of farmers speaking only their local, indigenous dialect, efforts to have 'fair trade' programs buy directly from farmers guaranteeing quality have been less effective than such fair-trade programs in coffee and cocoa (Rain, 2017).

Ominously, the high price for vanilla – while bringing a boon to those in the vanilla trade in Madagascar – might portent the demise of the vanilla industry because global firms might identify other natural (rather than artificial) substitutes for vanilla or change the formulations of their products to exclude vanilla. (Baker/Sahabevava, 2018).

Questions to Consider

- Are things getting better for vanilla farmers?
- Could things become too good for vanilla farmers?
- Who do you think would be more likely to change its recipes or formulations for products currently using vanilla, a multinational corporation or an individual ice-cream shop?
- What does the story of vanilla say about the limits of fair trade programs?

CHAPTER OVERVIEW AND LEARNING OBJECTIVES

This chapter will highlight social innovation in poverty alleviation. Paul Polak's story highlights how an NGO can use a simple approach when applying business principles to produce meaningful gains for the poor. Polak's immersion approach to understanding poverty in field settings sets him apart from most others in government, transnational organizations (such as the UN), nonprofits, and business. 'In 1981, I said, "I'm going to interview 100 $1-a-day families every year, come rain or shine, and learn from them first,"' Polak said (McNeill, 2011, p. D4). Because of his rich experiences with the poor and where they live and work, his ideas about poverty alleviation will frame much of this chapter.

Surprising to some, interventions on behalf of the poor or disadvantaged might sometimes do more harm than good. This chapter will review controversies regarding aid to alleviate poverty. The chapter will also provide an overview of interventions by governments, development agencies, and NGOs.

Social entrepreneurship occurs when an entrepreneur with a social vision creates a venture intending to result in social consequences (Yunus and Weber, 2010, p. 4). New forms of social entrepreneurship manifesting themselves in philanthropy, in hybrid organizational structures combining for-profit and nonprofit structures, and in for-profit businesses seeking to earn profits by serving poor consumers will be presented in this chapter.

After this chapter, you should be able to answer the following questions:

- How can charitable actions actually hurt recipients of charity?
- How effective have government and transnational organizations' poverty alleviation efforts been over the years?

- What is social entrepreneurship?
- What are four possible structures for social enterprises today?
- What is a B Corporation?

PUTTING POVERTY ALLEVIATION INTO PERSPECTIVE
Wisdom from a Longtime Poverty Alleviator

As an outsider to government, development agencies, and corporate business, Paul Polak achieved what few have done – helping millions of the rural poor earn more money (McNeill, 2019). The nongovernmental organization (NGO) he founded, International Development Enterprises (IDE), claims to have helped more than 34 million – mostly rural farmers – increase their incomes (IDE, 2020). This is especially noteworthy as the United Nations (UN), governments, aid agencies, NGOs, and corporate philanthropy programs have difficulty measuring the impact of their poverty alleviation programs or sustaining results of these programs for more than a few years.

Paul Polak came to poverty alleviation as a result of his desire to help the clients of his psychiatry practice in Denver, Colorado. As a skilled interviewer and listener, Polak inductively developed his own views on poverty from the hundreds of interviews he conducted with the poor on their small farms in countries like Nepal, India, Ethiopia, and Zambia. You can read more about Polak as the Maverick Who Made It at the end of this chapter.

Although he did not present his thoughts on addressing social problems with a business approach, Polak's steps to practical problem solving for any social problem all related to business. First, Polak believed that field interviewing of poor people is a must. This is in the finest traditions of social science and contemporary business. Importantly, Polak noted that the knowledge from interviewing accumulates over time. Simply put, the more interviewing, the more knowledge one will have to draw on when attempting to solve social problems. Second, the process of innovation matters. Just as successful innovators in business, social innovators also must use their research to address the needs of a targeted group of customers. Polak's targeted group comprises small-acreage farmers in Asia and Africa.

Third, the marketing mixture (the 4 Ps of product, price, place of distribution, and promotion) must be composed correctly. A worthy invention to assist poor farmers must be combined with effective distribution and promotion of the invention at an affordable price for rural farmers. Fourth, planning and the implementation of plans must be done in a vigorous manner. Polak recommended three-year plans. 'If you can't come up with a specific plan for the next three-year period, you'll never get anywhere,' Polak said (Polak, 2008, p. 22). He also recommended adapting any plan to the specific demands of the local environment when the plan does not play out as expected. The final ingredient is tenacity, which all entrepreneurs must bring to any venture. It will likely look hopeless at several points during the journey of any venture. Hanging on until success is achieved cannot be understated.

Three Poverty Eradication Myths

Polak found that poor people valued and cared for things they had bought (Hagerty, 2019). He also asserted that three great poverty eradication myths exist today (Polak, 2008, p. 27). The first myth is that we can donate people out of poverty. Polak says:

> 'It's exactly the multinational corporations that use the business approach you advocate who have caused the problem of poverty in the first place,' they would say. 'Poor people simply can't afford to buy the things they need, and they need these things very badly. The only way to make a real difference is to donate these things to them.' And the development organizations continued to donate mountains of food, free village hand pumps that broke down with a year and were never fixed, and thousands of free tractors that continue to rust under the African sun. Most importantly, more and more people are beginning to realize that making it possible for very poor people to invest their own time and money in attractive, affordable opportunities to increase their income is the only realistic path out of poverty for most of them.

> (Polak, 2008, p. 34)

According to Polak, the second myth is that national economic growth will end poverty (Polak, 2008, p. 40). From 1950 to 2001, the world's per capita GDP increased by a factor of 2.87 (Maddison, 2007, p. 234). However, bottom-of-the-pyramid approaches to poverty alleviation propose that 4 billion people still live on less than $2 per day (Prahalad, 2005, p. 4).

Although countries such as China and India have posted sustained economic growth of 8 percent and 6 percent, respectively, for many years, hundreds of millions across these two countries live in extreme poverty on less than $1 per day (Polak, 2008, p. 40). Most of the poor in the world live in remote rural areas, so urban-centered growth continues to bypass them. Accordingly, growth in remote rural areas is needed to impact most of the poor.

Table 12.1   Polak's three myths of poverty alleviation

1.   We can donate people out of poverty.
2.   National economic growth will end poverty.
3.   Big business will end poverty.

Source: Polak (2008). *Out of poverty: What works when traditional approaches fail*. San Francisco, CA: Berrett-Koehler. Used with permission.

The third myth of poverty alleviation concerns big business ending poverty (Polak, 2008, p. 41). Although the move of multinational enterprises (MNEs) to develop their operations in developing countries will likely continue, Polak viewed most MNEs as currently not knowing how to make a profit serving illiterate customers living in remote areas with no mass media. A challenge for MNEs will be fielding products and services designed to reach price points affordable to those who earn less than one or two dollars a day when sold at an unsubsidized fair market price.

Even in a developed country like the United States with all the MNEs operating, the US Census Bureau reports that 11.8 percent of the population (38.1 million citizens) lived below the poverty line in 2018 (Semega et al., 2019). The poverty line for a family of four was $26,200 in 2020 (HHS, 2020). This was the highest poverty line since the Census Bureau began tracking poverty statistics since 1959.

The Role of Aid

Macromarketing researchers have categorized 50 solutions to poverty, which can be seen in Table 12.2 (Kotler, Roberto, and Leisner, 2006). In the 1980s, international aid agencies introduced interventions or safety nets in developing countries hit by natural disasters. The first five solutions to poverty represent these relief interventions to protect the poor – especially the extremely poor living on $1 per day or less. As shown, these solutions focus on cash, food, or public works. The sixth through the eighth poverty solutions in Table 12.2 represent the 'triple R framework' of relief, rehabilitation, and reconciliation in postconflict situations. The 9th through the 15th solutions focus on social safety net programs intended to provide protection from deteriorated conditions of life the poor often experience. Healthcare for vulnerable populations complete the set of solutions that became popular in the 1980s.

Table 12.2 Fifty solutions to poverty

1980s – Interventions	1990s – Social protection services	2000s – Empowerment solutions
Postdisaster relief	**Social assistance (old-style social welfare)**	**Social equity services**
1. cash transfers	21. disability benefits	32. victims of domestic violence or sexual abuse
2. direct feeding programs	22. single-parent allowances	33. marginalized minorities
3. free food distribution	23. social pensions for the elderly poor	34. stigmatized groups
4. price subsidies	**Social insurance schemes**	**Material-asset building assistance**
5. public works programs	24. pensions	35. expanding financial assets: working capital

1980s – Interventions	1990s – Social protection services	2000s – Empowerment solutions
Post-conflict rehabilitation	25. health insurance	36. expanding physical assets, for example, land, housing, or livestock
6. relief institutions and services	26. maternity benefits	**Human capability-building assistance**
7. rehabilitation assistance	27. unemployment benefits	37. education
8. reconciliation and peace-building	28. funeral societies	38. good health
Social safety net programs	**Social service for the poor – special care**	39. production
9. social security for informal workers	29. orphanages for abandoned kids	40. other life-enhancing skills
10. services for school dropouts and street kids	30. care for those unable to provide	**Social capability-building assistance**
11. workfare (emergency work relief)	31. refugee and displaced-person camps	41. collective problem solving
12. microfinance and self-employment		42. collective action
13. maternal and child health services		43. creating 'bridging' to other groups
Postdisaster relief		
14. psychosocial care for affected families		**Empowerment support services**
15. assistance for the elderly and disabled		44. boosting community-driven development
Healthcare for vulnerable populations		45. citizen report cards on gov't services
16. ambulatory care		46. promoting pro-poor regulatory change
17. hospital emergency room and inpatient care		47. new linkages with mkts and banks
18. drug abuse, disability and mental illness		48. increasing access to IT for market access
19. assistive care for daily living		49. strengthening networks of the poor
20. medication assistance and health support		50. supporting reforms for access to justice

Source: Kotler et al. (2006).

In the 1990s, social protection services became popular as poverty solutions. These included social safety net measures but also covered longer term solutions. Toward the end of the last century and in the first decade of the current century, empowerment solutions rose in prominence. These sought to expand individual freedom of choice for the poor in their lives. The World Bank made empowerment its primary strategy in 'attacking poverty.' Many of these empowerment solutions focused on improving the poor's ability to interact with institutions (such as business and government) that affect their lives and to hold these institutions accountable.

Overall, these 50 solutions (and hundreds more) have posted a spotty record of success around the world since 1980 (Kotler et al., 2006, pp. 237–8; Karlan and Appel, 2011, p. 5). Some have worked in some places but not in others. The ones that have worked have not always sustained success.

Macromarketing researchers have offered several reasons for the uneven outcomes of these 50 poverty solutions. First, the poor are a heterogeneous group. This implies that segments characterize the population of the poor, and that field research where the poor live and work is needed to understand these subgroups of the poor effectively. For example, those living on $4 to $5 a day might belong to the middle-class in some countries (Polak, 2008, p. 42). By comparison, extreme poverty would characterize those living on $1 a day or less who would likely regularly suffer hunger and malnutrition. Second, poverty alleviation encounters a surprising degree of complexity. For example, poverty can come and go. Natural disasters and civil unrest can disrupt conditions where one lives, or alternatively, poor decisions, sickness or injury can degrade a person's ability to earn a living. Third, rising from poverty might require accessing many institutions that function with varying degrees of effectiveness or corruption, such as governments, schools, international development agencies, and businesses.

Complexities of Aid

Almost all of the 50 solutions to poverty presented in Table 12.2 invariably structure an unbalanced power arrangement between donors (the helpers) and receivers of aid (the helped). However, this power imbalance often creates problems if sustained over time for relief and rehabilitation (humanitarian aid) to development situations (Corbett and Fikkert, 2014). Following natural disasters or societal trauma, the provision of material assistance constitutes relief to reduce immediate suffering. Poverty solutions 1 through 5 in Table 12.2 represent such relief intended to 'stop the bleeding'. Such solutions end after days or weeks. Rehabilitation begins after 'the bleeding stops' with the goal of restoring people and their communities to positive aspects of their pre-crisis conditions. Poverty solutions 6 through 8 in Table 12.2 often involve working *with* those afflicted (rather than doing things *for* or *to* the poor). Such solutions end after months or a few years. However, there are exceptions. The Canadian government estimated that returning Haiti to its pre-crisis conditions prior to its devastating January 2010 earthquake in which 200,000 died (including one third of all senior civil servants) would take ten years (Chung, 2010, p. 1; Wroughton, 2010, p. 1). In 2020, life for most Haitians remains difficult, despite the more than $10 billion donated to Haiti's relief (Eschenbacher, 2020). Sixty percent of Haitians survive on less than $2.40 per day. Protests occur regularly against fuel hikes, corruption, unemployment, inflation, and killings linked to government officials (Danticat, 2020).

Development between helpers and the helped represents longer term projects extending for years. Here, the power imbalance between the helper and the helped can create serious problems. A 'Samaritan's dilemma' emerges where the help offered by the helper results in a reduced effort of the helped activity participating in their own development (Gibson et al., 2005). Although helpers receive a 'warm glow' from helping, the helped receive more perceived value when they expend less effort to receive the aid they know will be forthcoming.

Paternalism characterizes such imbalanced relationships, as the helpers do for the helped what the helped could do for themselves (Corbett and Fikkert, 2014). The helpers have their feelings of goodness and superiority reinforced, while the helped have their feelings of inferiority underlined to them and to those in their communities. 'NGOs flatter themselves into thinking that they save lives,' former Zambian Agriculture Minister Guy Scott said. 'It is arrogant of the West to think that without whites, without pop stars, Africans would all be dead' (Astier, 2006, p. 2).

The helped may actually lose skills and motivation over time (Gibson et al., 2005, p. 39). In the remote, central-Sudanese region of the Nuba Mountains, Yousif Kowa led an insurrection against the Sudanese government that began in the 1980s and lasted until a tenuous peace agreement in 2005. Kowa made it clear that unchecked humanitarianism was a threat to the self-reliant spirit of the Nuba tribe numbering more than one million (Fisher, 2011). According to Kowa, food relief – when continued – distorted farmer incentives and created dependence. Kowa recalled a trip he made in 1993 to an area in southern Sudan that had received much food aid from the United Nations. 'The people of the area are great farmers,' Kowa said. 'But because there is this relief food, they did not farm for three years. I could see the difficulty. It was spoiling people. They just sleep and have food. It is very bad' (Fisher, 2011, p. 3).

'It is axiomatic that flooding the market with food drives down the price for local farmers,' economist William Easterly said (Astier, 2006, p. 2).

Because of the problems that develop in long-term development, the poverty solutions on the right side of Table 12.2 emphasize the empowerment of the poor. Despite this new emphasis, aid agencies – not the poor themselves – still decide how aid is given and in what form (goods, services, information, awareness-raising, and skills training). 'Today, only a tiny amount of aid (almost certainly less than 10 percent) is given directly to poor people and poor communities for them to choose how to use it,' foreign-aid expert Roger C. Riddell said. 'Even recipients who are committed to using aid effectively are not equal partners. They remain junior partners who have to struggle to make use of funds over which they have and retain limited control' (Riddell, 2007, p. 387).

Aid in the Context of Total Overseas Economic Engagement

Since 1950, support for aid has gone up and down. But since 9/11, support for aid has surged as governments of developed countries became keen to stabilize the development of poor countries during the fight against global terrorism (Riddell, 2007, p. 5). In inflation-adjusted 2015 dollars, the total aid given by developed country governments to developing countries doubled from $80 billion in 2001 to $160 billion in 2018 (World Bank, 2020b).

But government aid is just one part of the total economic engagement of developed countries with developing countries. Figure 12.1 depicts private investment, official flows, and remittances sent home from overseas workers (Barne and Pirlea, 2019). As can be seen, remittances now are the leading source of external funding for low- and middle-income countries (excluding China). In five countries, these remittance surpass 25 percent of the country GDP. These countries are Tonga, Kyrgyz Republic, Tajikistan, Haiti, and Nepal. In absolute amounts of remittances sent home, India ($78.6 billion) and China ($67.4 billion) lead the countries of the world.

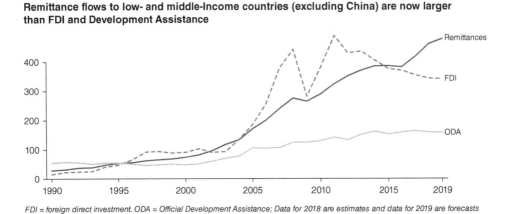

Remittance flows to low- and middle-Income countries (excluding China) are now larger than FDI and Development Assistance

FDI = foreign direct investment. ODA = Official Development Assistance; Data for 2018 are estimates and data for 2019 are forecasts

Figure 12.1   Money sent home by overseas workers now leads sources of external funds

Source: Barne and Pirlea (2019). Shared under the CC BY-4.0 license.

The Organization of Economic Development (OECD) represents the industrialized countries of the world. Figure 12.2 depicts the OECD's Development Assistance Committee's data regarding foreign aid as a percent of donor country GDP while 12.3 depicts foreign aid in absolute terms ($US billion). As can be seen in Figure 12.2, Sweden gives the most foreign aid as a percentage of country GDP, followed by Luxembourg, Norway, and Denmark. The UN offers the target for developed countries of having 0.7 percent of country GDP directed to foreign aid. Only four countries match or exceed this target.

In Figure 12.3, the US can be seen to give the most foreign aid in absolute terms, followed by Germany and the UK. Excluding funds spent on processing and hosting refugees, foreign aid was stable from 2017 to 2018. With less being spent on hosting refugees (because arrivals slowed) 2018 foreign aid declined in real terms from 2017 to $149.3 billion for the OECD countries.

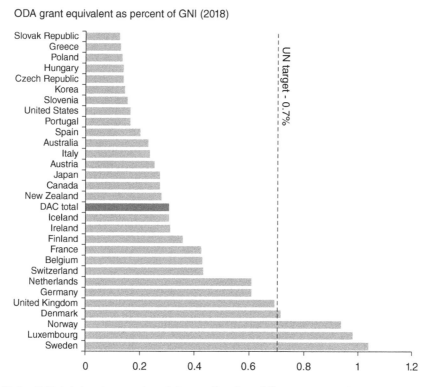

Figure 12.2 Official development assistance (foreign aid) as percent of country GDP (OECD, 2019)

ODA grant equivalent - USD billion (2018)

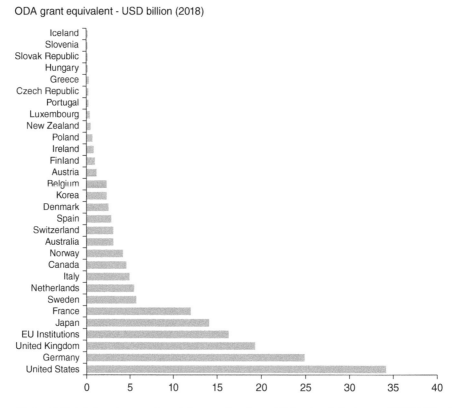

Figure 12.3   Official development assistance (foreign aid) in absolute terms ($US billion)

Source: OECD (2019), The Heavy Burden of Obesity: The Economics of Prevention, OECD Health Policy Studies, OECD Publishing, Paris, https://doi.org/10.1787/67450d67-en. Accessed in 2020.

Innovation in Aid

'I couldn't defend a lot of foreign aid over the past years, much of which disappeared into the pockets of corrupt foreign leaders,' former US Secretary of State Condoleezza Rice said. 'But foreign aid is one of the most important parts of diplomacy. We need countries that are responsible. A stable society is not going to become a failed state. But every taxpayer ought to be asking is it working?' (Easton, 2011, p. 164).

A critic of 'big push' plans to alleviate poverty is economist William Easterly who dared to criticize the effectiveness of World Bank programs when he worked there. He lost his job for speaking out against the World Bank programs and agreeing with Rice's assertion that aid should be scrutinized by those funding it (Postrel, 2006). 'This is the tragedy in which the West spent $2.3 trillion on foreign aid over the last five decades and still had not managed to get 12-cent medicines to children to prevent half of all malaria deaths,' Easterly said.

'The West spent $2.3 trillion and still had not managed to get $4 bed nets to poor families. The West spent $2.3 trillion and still had not managed to get $3 to each new mother to prevent five million child deaths' (Easterly, 2006, p. 4).

Before 1982, USAID sent less than 15 percent of its annual spending through local and international NGOs and universities (Natsios, 2009). Facing the reality that sending aid during the Cold War to foreign governments, such as Zaire's anti-communist regime led by Mobutu Sese Seko, resulted in no public services or reform, USAID's leaders decided to pursue different ways to send aid to foreign countries. USAID began directing grants and contracts to NGOs, universities, and businesses. As a result, transparency, accountability, and performance of aid programs increased. Today, donor government aid agencies increasingly work with corporations and NGOs to encourage development in poor countries.

One different kind of government aid program is the Millennium Challenge Corporation (MCC), which US President George W. Bush jointly announced at the White House with U2 star Bono in 2002 (Easton, 2011, p. 158). The focus of the MCC is funding private enterprises in developing countries that must have a democratic government, economic freedom, and lack of corruption. The MCC evaluates countries on 24 criteria using third-party social indicators to qualify them for large grants that would go to private business ventures or social enterprises in these countries (MCC, 2011). Table 12.3 presents these criteria that come under the headings of (a) ruling justly, (b) economic freedom, and (c) investing in people. With such criteria for society's performance in the public, private, and social sectors, the MCC approach resonates with research suggesting donors and international NGOs move 'toward thinking about how they can support progressive forces of change, so that local NGOs can call their own governments to account', the Institute of Development Studies' Andy Sumner said (Ruvinsky, 2011, p. 9).

Table 12.3 The Millennium Challenge Corporation's criteria for country eligibility

Ruling justly	Economic freedom	Investing in people
1. Civil liberties	1. Inflation	1. Public expenditure – health
2. Political rights	2. Fiscal policy	2. Public expenditure – primary education
3. Freedom of information	3. Business start-up	3. Immunization rates
4. Government effectiveness	4. Trade policy	4. Girls' education
	5. Regulatory quality	5. Primary education completion
5. Rule of law	6. Land rights and access	6. Secondary education enrollment (lower middle-income countries)
6. Control of corruption	7. Access to credit	7. Child health
	8. Gender in the economy	8. Natural resource protection

Source: Millennium Challenge Corporation (MCC, 2011).

Developing countries have to compete for MCC funding of projects, so government leaders gain the impetus for curbing their anti-democratic impulses, as well as for fighting corruption. More than $8 billion in MCC aid has gone to countries such as the Philippines, Georgia, and El Salvador. When Nicaragua suppressed the political opposition in local elections in 2008, it lost a $62 million MCC grant. Likewise, when Malawi in southern Africa used violence to quell demonstrations there, it lost a $350 million MCC grant.

The MCC takes a different approach than other aid agencies such as USAID or the World Bank that establish sizable staffs of expatriates in countries receiving aid. By comparison, MCC posts only two expatriates in a country, but these are backed by a team of engineers and auditors in Washington, DC. Projects are designed and administered by a coalition of host-country government officials, business and labor leaders, along with environmentalists. The coalition engages in hot debates about projects and funding in its own exercise of democracy.

In 2020, the NGO Publish What You Fund (PWYF) ranked the MCC as top among US agencies and seventh in the world for aid transparency (MCC, 2020). Unlike other aid, the funding is designed to end. 'My goal is to replace our money with private sector money,' MCC Director Daniel Yohannes said (Easton, 2011, p. 156).

In Ghana, located in western Africa, more than half a billion dollars has funded the training of 65,000 farmers, the construction of storage facilities, and the paving of gutted dirt roads to enable fresh produce to arrive in distant markets in a timely way (Easton, 2011, p. 156). Such accomplishments have enabled Ghanaian farmer Tony Botchway to develop a pineapple and mango processing plant in the central town of Nsorbi that pays 750 workers more than the minimum wage. Botchway's firm, called Bomarts, is profitable, exports to Spain and Switzerland, and now serves as a supplier for MNE Dole. 'We're ready to compete with Costa Rican producers,' Botchway said (Easton, 2011, p. 156).

SOCIAL ENTREPRENEURSHIP
Creating Social Value

Social entrepreneurship is a process in which citizens launch ventures or transform existing institutions to advance solutions for social or environmental problems (Bornstein and Davis, 2010, p. 1). 'Social entrepreneurship is really a democratization of capitalism,' said Nicky Santos, who is both a marketing professor at Creighton University in Omaha, Nebraska and a Jesuit priest. 'It's having local people take agency. It's much more in line with recognizing human dignity' (Harper, 2018).

Although many think of nonprofit ventures as comprising the domain of social entrepreneurship, for-profit ventures fall in this domain as well (Yunus and Weber, 2010, p. 4).

Chapter 1 introduced Fábio Rosa and his Project Light in Brazil as a prototypical social entrepreneur. Rosa's mission of bringing electrification to the rural poor of Brazil's southernmost state of Rio Grande do Sul using steel wire brought enormous social value to hundreds of poor families (Bornstein, 2004). Chapter 1 also introduced Tom Szaky and his privately owned TerraCycle that manufactures fashion accessories, such as over-the-shoulder handbags and backpacks made from juice packs that are stitched together (Szaky, 2009). With more than 14 million people in 11 countries collecting waste for TerraCycle, TerraCycle's recycling has created more than 280 different products sold at major retailers, such as Walmart and Whole Foods Market.

Like traditional entrepreneurs, Rosa and Szaky pursue the accumulation of physical and financial capital. However, by explicitly addressing social or environmental problems in the missions of their ventures, they can be considered social entrepreneurs. The biggest advantage social entrepreneurs have is an authentic voice that is their own, as well as the authentic voices from user testimonials of their products and services (McGee, 2007). In other words, their persistence and effectiveness in addressing social problems makes their words about the solution to these problems persuasive and compelling to others.

Social entrepreneurs play the role of change agents (Dees, 1998). They adopt a mission of achieving an enduring solution to problems affecting society, rather than achieving an enduring advantage for their organization (Hamby, Pierce, and Brinberg, 2017).

They often are intrepid in this pursuit, overcoming formidable obstacles and the initial lack of interest of others. They frequently must act boldly without being limited by the resources they currently control.

Some of the most exciting accomplishments of social entrepreneurs in recent years have come from enabling poor people to function more effectively in the marketplace. Finding buyers for high-quality produce or artisan crafts characterize some of the ways the poor have earned more income in markets. For example, Paul Polak and his International Development Enterprises have worked with more than 6.9 million households in eleven countries (in Africa, Asia and Central America) to provide low-cost access to water and effective markets. The work of IDE has helped increase the average family's annual income by $269 within the first year (IDE, 2020).

Another example of social entrepreneurship can be seen in the story of alternative trade organizations (known as fair trade). Fairtrade International has led a movement whose objective is to ensure the ethical treatment of workers (Clark, 2011). By bringing together retailers and other marketers in wealthy countries with small-scale producers of foods, such as tea, coffee, fruits, flowers, and vegetables, these small-scale producers receive a larger portion of the final sale price to the customer. For example, Fairtrade only certifies coffee if it does not come from estate farms or agribusiness and is grown in sustainable ways, ensuring that coffee will not be bought at lower than a fair-trade price, which prevents price fluctuations in the market from working against a small-farmer cooperative's farm (Haight, 2011; see Figure 12.3). Additionally, a fair-trade premium (about $.20 per pound of coffee) will be paid into a communal fund at the cooperative so that workers and farmers can improve their social, economic, and environmental conditions. In 2017, more than 1.7 million farmers and workers participated in Fairtrade (Fairtrade International, 2020).

Reports have surfaced about a recurring unevenness in the receipt of benefits for buyers (not always obtaining the top-grade coffee for the fair market price when the market price for top-grade coffee is higher) or for sellers (the fair-trade premium goes to the farmers' democratically governed farmers' cooperative and not to the farmers themselves). However, macromarketing researchers have found evidence suggesting that Latin American coffee producers supplying one alternative trade organization, Fair Trade USA, reported a greater overall sense of well-being and a more positive outlook for their future when compared with nonmembers of such an alternative trade organization (Geiger-Oneto and Arnould, 2011).

Figure 12.4   Fair Trade certified logo

Source: Fair Trade USA, www.fairtradeusa.org

Fair trade is an example of a social innovation that is distinct from commercial innovations. Social innovations provide novel solutions to a social problem (that are more effective, efficient, and sustainable than existing solutions) in which the value created accrues primarily to society as a whole rather than to private individuals, such as entrepreneurs, investors, or ordinary consumers (Phills, Deiglmeier, and Miller, 2008).

Structures for Social Enterprises

Social entrepreneurship (focused on entrepreneurs) and social enterprise (focused on organizations) have their roots in the nonprofit sector where the creation of social value – benefit to the public or society as a whole – is the underlying objective of NGOs (Phills et al., 2008). Toward the end of creating social value, NGOs have applied marketing principles in their social marketing campaigns.

Social marketing involves the marketing of behaviors that benefit society, as well as the target audience (Kotler and Lee, 2009, p. 53). Society can benefit through improved public health, development, safety, environment, and communities. For example, if an anti-smoking campaign is effective, then public health will improve as a result of fewer respiratory illnesses and smoking-related cancer cases. In development, NGOs such as IDE have used social marketing to impart better farming practices to the rural poor.

As some social problems have proved difficult to eliminate and have actually increased in size and scope in many countries (such as poverty, malnutrition, energy resource depletion, environmental degradation, the trafficking of contraband, and HIV/AIDS and flu pandemics), the limits of the nonprofit – or citizen sector – to complement government fully in stemming these social problems have become evident. Business leaders have begun to realize that their businesses can have a role to play in addressing social problems. With the rise of corporate social responsibility in the late 1980s, founders of firms such as Patagonia, the Body Shop, and Ben & Jerry's have viewed their businesses both as a vehicle to make money and as a means to improve society (Vogel, 2005).

Today, the boundaries between the nonprofit, government, and business sectors have become diffused and semipermeable as ideas, values, roles, relationships, and capital flow more freely across these sectors (Phills et al., 2008). In recent years, nonprofit and government leaders have looked to businesses to learn about management, entrepreneurship, and performance measurement. Government and business leaders increasingly turn to nonprofit leaders to understand social and environmental issues better, and how to succeed in bottom-of-the-pyramid settings of developing countries.

As a result of the increased interplay among nonprofits, government, and business, a variety of structures have emerged in recent years for social enterprises (Kelly, 2009). Current US law does not currently recognize any single legal entity that would allow receiving (a) charitable contributions that would be tax-deductible for donors, (b) invested equity capital that would produce capital gains to be taken by investors, or (c) quasi-invested capital such as loans from foundations that do not expect a market rate of return (Bromberger, 2011). Some social entrepreneurs have found ways to integrate aspects of the for-profit and nonprofit models for structuring their enterprises. Figure 12.5 depicts a matrix for these structures based on the upside potential for profit or social benefit, as well as the legal aspect of being a for-profit or a nonprofit entity.

| | | Social enterprise structure | |
		For-profit structure	*Nonprofit structure*
Upside potential for	Profits	**For-profit** ex: Bharat Financial Inclusion (formerly SKS Microfinance and now wholly owned by IndusInd Bank) ex: Salesforce.com (business philanthropy)	**Nonprofit with a mission-related enterprise** ex: Essential Eldercare (surplus revenues) ex: Fair Trade USA (revenue shortage)
	Social value	**For-profit with a social overlay** ex: Equal Exchange (worker co-op) ex: Organic Valley (producer co-op) ex: Grameen Bank (customer co-op)	**Nonprofit** ex: Acumen Fund Kiva Ashoka

Figure 12.5 Profit/social value potential for social enterprise structures

For-Profit

In the upper-left quadrant is the traditional for-profit model. Advantages of the for-profit model include the relative ease of raising money as equity or debt, and the ease of selling or shutting down (as long as creditors receive their due) (Fruchterman, 2011). Disadvantages for the for-profit model include being required by law to put the interests of the shareholders first, meaning making money for them. Taxes on income and property must also be paid to governments, and for-profit companies cannot accept foundation grants or nontaxable contributions.

An example of a for-profit corporation focused on alleviating poverty is Bharat Financial Inclusion (BFI) Ltd. of India – formerly known as SKS Microfinance of India. BFI distributes small loans that begin at Rs. 2,000 to Rs. 12,000 (about $44–$260) to poor women so they can start and expand simple businesses and increase their incomes (SKS Microfinance, 2011). The microenterprises of these poor women range from raising cows and goats (in order to sell their milk) to opening a village tea stall. A major challenge for social enterprises is scaling up their operations to influence more than just a locale or a region. SKS switched from a nonprofit model to a for-profit model early in its existence in order to access the financial resources that could come from being listed on the Bombay Stock Exchange, as well as on the New York Stock Exchange.

Although this move in 2010 resulted in millions more dollars as a base from which to lend to poor consumers, the idea of profiting from poor people poses an ethical dilemma in the view of macromarketers (Laczniak and Santos, 2011). The move to a for-profit orientation for SKS brought strident opposition from Muhammad Yunus among others – especially in India.

The move became politically controversial and in 2011, Akula left his CEO position with the firm as the Andrha Pradesh state government in India clamped down on microfinance firms (Associated Press, 2011).

The firm changed its name to Bharat Financial Inclusion (BFI) in 2016 and in 2019 became a wholly owned subsidiary of IndusInd Bank Ltd to end India's first for-profit enterprise focused solely on microlending (Malik, 2019). With its acquisition of BFI, IndusInd Bank (the best performing lender in India since 2008) gained a presence in more than 115,000 villages in India where BFI operates. Through BFI, IndusInd Bank increased its cross-selling, lending and low-cost deposit-mobilization efforts in these villages (Ghosh and Antony, 2019).

Creative business persons have tweaked the for-profit model to pursue different forms of philanthropy. For example, sales-support-software firm Salesforce.com's founder and CEO Marc Benioff developed a '1-1-1 rule' in which 1 percent of the firm's equity, 1 percent of its profit, and 1 percent of employees' time went into a nonprofit (a 501(c)(3) public charity) (Rose, 2011). Benioff said:

> We run 10,000 non-profits for free. We do not charge universities for our services. We will deliver hundreds of thousands of hours of community service. Google copied our 1-1-1 model, and others have, too. That's been probably our most successful part of our business, far more than our business success – our ability to inspire others to do philanthropy. It's been a huge missing part of Silicon Valley.
>
> (Rose, 2011, p. 52)

Giving back remains part of Salesforce's corporate DNA today. The firm has given more than $1.3 billion in technology, volunteer time and grants to communities through the Salesforce Foundation and a nonprofit (Salesforce.org) created in 2009 to be the agent of impact for Salesforce.com employees (Salesforce.org, 2020).

Unfortunately, Salesforce's philanthropy is tainted by paying no federal income taxes (ITEP, 2019). In effect, it looks like Salesforce might fund all of its philanthropy from avoiding all federal income taxes. On its $800 million profits in 2018, Salesforce avoided $168 million in federal corporate taxes (using a corporate tax rate of 21 percent).

Google's philanthropy is not structured as a charitable foundation but as a division of the firm itself. In this way, Google declines a tax-exempt status for its 'for-profit philanthropy' but gains full access to Google's staff, technology, and products in the process (Kelly, 2009).

Large publicly traded companies have integrated a social priority with their imperative for generating ongoing profits in several ways worth noting (Kelly, 2009). A dual-class governance structure at carpet-tile manufacturer Interface, Inc. (featured in Chapter 1) put supervoting shares in the hands of Chairman Ray Anderson and a few other top executives, giving them control of 72 percent of votes for the board – although they own far less than a majority of publicly traded shares. As a result, Interface has stayed focused on its drive toward sustainability. Google also adopted a similar dual-class stock configuration when it went public in 2004 that vested power with its founders. The New York Times Company is controlled by the Sulzberger family, which has allowed *The New York Times* to stay focused on its mission of serving an informed electorate. A foundation controls Novo Nordisk, a Danish pharmaceutical company. This has enabled the firm to remain committed to its mission of defeating diabetes. Companies like these are termed mission-controlled companies.

For-Profit With a Social Overlay

The lower-left quadrant of Figure 12.5 represents the hybrid forms that have a for-profit legal structure with upside potential for social value rather than profits (Bromberger, 2011). These are for-profits with a social overlay (Fruchterman, 2011). Some of these structures have existed for decades. These include stakeholder-owned firms in the form of cooperatives. Such cooperatives might be formed by workers as in the case of Equal Exchange – a fair-trade food company based in West Bridgewater, Massachusetts (www.equalexchange.coop). Alternatively, a cooperative might be formed by producers as in the case of Cooperative Regions of Organic Producers Pool (CROPP), better known by its brand name in grocery stores – Organic Valley – based in La Farge, Wisconsin. CROPP is owned by the 1,800 organic family farms that produce the dairy, eggs, and meat it distributes. 'We don't have any need for profits much over 2 percent,' CROPP CEO George Siemon said. 'We'd just pay taxes on it. We'd rather give it to the farmers' (Kelly, 2009, p. 6). Finally, a cooperative can be owned by customers as in the case of Bangladesh's Grameen Bank that is owned by the poor people who are its depositors and customers (Yunus and Weber, 2010, p. 2).

For-profits with a social overlay now include new structures approved in some states that are being adopted elsewhere. Instead of being either for-profit or nonprofit, these new structures allow an enterprise to be 'for-benefit' (Sabeti, 2011).

In 2020, 37 states (such as California, Illinois, Virginia, Utah, and Vermont) have enacted statutes allowing for the creation of for-profit corporations with a primary charitable purpose called benefit corporations. A branded form of a benefit corporation is the beneficial corporation – 'B Corporation, or B Corp' – a new type of corporation that uses a business structure to solve social and environmental problems.

B Lab, a nonprofit organization, certifies B Corporations the same way TransFair certifies Fair Trade coffee or USGBC certifies LEED buildings. Annual scores on the legal structure of firms for the more than 3,500 B Corps (in 70 countries and 150 industries) expands corporate accountability so they are required to make decisions that are good for society, not just their shareholders (B Lab, 2020). States such as Vermont, Maryland, New Jersey, and Virginia have passed laws backing B Corps. Seventh Generation is the nation's most recognized brand of natural household and personal care products. It became a founding B Corporation in 1991 because the firm believes there must be a standard for corporate responsibility in the United States.

Figure 12.6 depicts Patagonia's B Corp rating page. As shown, five dimensions comprise the B Corp score card: (a) accountability, (b) employees, (c) consumers, (d) community, and (e) environment. Firms become certified as a B Corp when they achieve 80 points or more. Agora Management earned 151.4 points in 2019. It attained levels of excellence in environment and community. Such ratings can be useful in demonstrating to employees, clients, and investors the firm's success in creating social value.

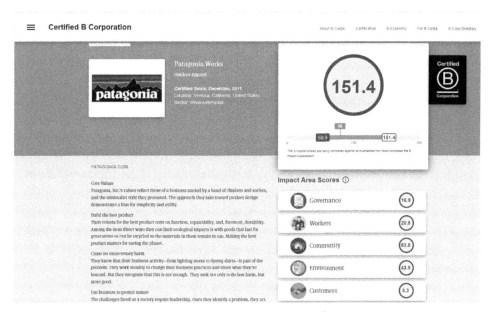

Figure 12.6   Patagonia's B Corp rating page

Source: B Lab, https://bcorporation.net/directory/patagonia-inc.

In October 2011, California added the Social Purpose Corporation (SPC) – a new corporate form similar to a benefit corporation that allows a corporation to integrate the for-profit philosophy of the traditional corporation with a *special purpose* mission that is similar to a charitable purpose (NEO Law Group, 2015). This special purpose might be promoting or minimizing short- or long-term effects on (a) the FPC's employees, suppliers, customers, and creditors; (b) the environment; or (c) the community and society. While a benefit corporation must consider a number of stakeholders (such as shareholders, employees, partners, customers, community, as well as the local and global environment), an SPC must only take into account its shareholders and its special purpose (such as protecting wildlife in a designated area or increasing awareness about climate change).

A low-profit limited liability company (L3C) is another version of the for-profit with a social overlay. For example, the *Chicago Reader*, an alternative weekly newspaper founded in 1971 that is distributed for free, became an L3C (Field, 2019). The L3C status allows the *Chicago Reader* (www.chicagoreader.com) to focus on its mission to provide 'a more curated and critical look at what's going on in the Chicago area', rather than compiling editorial content that would ensure the maximum amount of profit. The L3C structure also allows for foundations to make program-related investments (PRIs) in L3Cs in order to meet the Internal Revenue Service's requirement that foundations distribute 5 percent of assets each year. In other words, foundations can receive credit for financially boosting the *Chicago Reader*. Today, L3Cs are recognized in Illinois, Michigan, Louisiana, Maine, Rhode Island, Utah, Vermont, and Wyoming (Marcum and Blair, 2019). There are more than 1,650 registered L3Cs now.

In settings outside the United States, an analog to the L3C would be what Nobel Peace Prize winner Muhammad Yunus calls a social business – a nonloss, nondividend company with an owner and social objectives (Yunus and Weber, 2010, p. 4). 'The existing company law in most countries is enough to create a social business,' Yunus said. 'That's the beauty of the concept. The only thing is, it must be specified in the charter that the owners cannot take dividends. They only get back their investment' (Wimmer, 2012, p. 194).

Yunus sees social businesses as allowing owners to express their selflessness, and to attract investors – a feature unavailable to nonprofits. In sum, the social business is run like a business with long-term planning. It generates income from business activities and focuses on long-term impact – rather than on chasing donations year to year (Wimmer, 2012, p. 195).

Yunus' Grameen Danone is an example of a social business. It is a joint venture with French MNE Groupe Danone that attacks the problem of malnutrition by selling affordable yogurt fortified with micronutrients in rural areas of Bangladesh (Yunus and Weber, 2010, p. 1). The joint venture, founded in 2006, produces a yogurt enriched with crucial nutrients priced at 6 BDT (= 0.06 EUR), which even the poorest can afford. Grameen Danone Foods improves the lives of poor people not only by improving their health, but also benefits accrue to those manning the whole value chain. For example, the milk for the yogurt is purchased from small farmers. The production is designed in such a way as to give as many people as possible a job. Finally, sales ladies distribute the yogurt door-to-door and receive a 10 percent commission.

In sum, for-profits with a social overlay have the same advantages as a standard for-profit. However, they have additional options for raising capital as it is easier for foundations to invest in an L3C. A disadvantage of for-profits with a social overlay is that investors may not want to invest in such a form without strong social motivations. In other words, investment financing may be limited.

Nonprofits with a Mission-Related Enterprise

The upper-right quadrant of Figure 12.5 depicts nonprofits with a mission-related enterprise. Tax-exempt nonprofits that have earned income that is clearly related to their social mission are nonprofits with a mission-related enterprise (Fruchterman, 2011). Although many types of nonprofits earn income from selling goods and services (theaters, museums, colleges, and used-goods stores), income cannot be distributed to investors or shareholders (but it can be used to repay loans for the nonprofit).

Fair Trade USA is a nonprofit, but it obtains most of its revenues from service fees charged to retailers when they buy shipments of Fair Trade goods such as coffee, chocolate, and fruits. Fair Trade USA was launched in 1998 to help coffee farmers around the world, but now includes 40 other categories, such as tomatoes (Corkery, 2019). In 2018, Fair Trade USA generated about $105 million in premiums for smallholder farmers. Fair Trade USA earns about $15 million in fees that brands pay for the certification process and their right to use the label of Fair Trade USA.

IONA Senior Services launched a mission-related social-enterprise Essential Eldercare that sells premier eldercare in the Washington, DC Metro area (4 Lenses, 2020). The income from selling these service are then used to support IONA's nonprofit activities focused on providing fee or subsidized eldercare services to low-income elderly residents in the Metro area. Such services to the poor include adult day-care, fitness, computer classes, recreational activities, counselling, and meals. By meeting the needs of an affluent target market, Essential Eldercare generates surplus income to serve disadvantaged seniors.

Nonprofits with mission-related enterprises face no taxation on mission-related income (Fruchterman, 2011, p. 47). They can also raise philanthropic funds for any of their programs. Because of the charitable nature of the enterprise, the products and services offered by the mission-related enterprise usually have a selling advantage. However, nonprofits with mission-related enterprises cannot raise capital in financial markets because of their status as a nonprofit. Philanthropists and debt stand as the only sources for funding.

Nonprofits

The lower right quadrant of Figure 12.5 depicts nonprofits. The social mission of nonprofits is their most distinguishing characteristic. All resources for nonprofits come from donations of money, products, or time (Fruchterman, 2011, p. 47). Nonprofits do not have any earned-income enterprises. In the United States, traditional nonprofits carry the tax classification of a 501(c)(3) charity or a 501(c)(3) foundation.

The Red Cross and the Red Crescent are nonprofits that provide relief after natural disasters (ICRC, 2020). Habitat for Humanity is a faith-based nonprofit that seeks to eliminate poverty housing and homelessness from the world (Habitat for Humanity, 2020). Habitat for Humanity has helped build more than 500,000 decent, affordable houses around the world that now house more than two million people.

Jacqueline Novogratz founded the nonprofit Acumen Fund as a venture capital fund for the poor in developing countries (Novogratz, 2011). Investors in developed countries avoid placing long-term bets in troubled regions of the world. They seek a quicker payback and less risk. By comparison, the Acumen Fund scours the world to identify worthy ventures that would benefit the poor in developing countries using 'patient capital' that will allow up to 15 years for payback (Acumen Fund, 2020). Investments have included International Development Enterprises India (a subsidiary of Paul Polak's IDE) and its water-saving drip irrigation system, WaterHealth International of Irvine, California's water purification system, as well as d.light Design, a privately held, San Francisco-based company that sells affordable solar-powered LED lights in the developing world. Since 2001, the Acumen Fund has invested $128 million in 128 businesses across 14 countries. Of this funding, $29 million has been returned and reinvested.

Figure 12.7   Kiva's website helps lenders identify worthy targets for microfinance loans

Source: www.kiva.org

Kiva is a nonprofit organization that connects people through crowdfunding of micro-finance lending to alleviate poverty (Kiva, 2020; see Figure 12.7). Using the internet and a worldwide network of microfinance institutions, Kiva lets individuals lend as little as $25 to help create opportunity around the world. Since its founding in 2005, Kiva has helped 1.9 million lenders make $1.4 billion in loans to 3.5 million borrowers. In 2019, 81 percent of Kiva loans went to women around the world. The repayment rate for these loans is 98 per-cent (Wall Street Journal, 2015).

Some of the most exciting social innovations in recent years have resulted from social entrepreneurs sponsored early in their ventures by the educational foundation Ashoka, which was founded by Bill Drayton. Ashoka searches the world for social entrepreneurs gear-ing up to launch a social venture and then sponsors them for three years with a salary as Ashoka Fellows (Ashoka, 2020). Ashoka Fellows receive coaching to boost the success of their ventures. Being an Ashoka Fellow helped Rakhee Choudhury launch her venture to teach women in India's far-northeastern Assam Valley the traditional weaving skills they need to earn income at the same time they deepen their pride in the Assamese culture.

Nonprofits do not have a conflict between the venture and the social objectives like a for-profit enterprise might. Importantly, donors to nonprofits receive a tax deduction for their donations in the United States. A drawback to the nonprofit model is that traditional fundraising is the only way to raise financial resources. Social business advocate Muhammad Yunus said:

> Relying on charitable donations is not a sustainable way of running an organization. It forces NGO leaders to spend a lot of time, energy, and money on fund-raising efforts. Even when these are successful, most NGOs are perennially strapped for cash and unable to sustain, let alone expand, their most effective programs.
>
> (Yunus and Weber, 2010, p. 6)

CONCLUSION

This chapter considered poverty alleviation and its related issues. Poverty makes itself pre-sent in almost all countries today. In 1990, 93 percent of poor people lived in poor countries (Ruvinksy, 2011). In 2019, 62 percent of the world's poor lived in middle-income countries with gross national income per capita between $1,036 and $4,045, such as India and Nigeria (World Bank, 2020c). The implication is that ameliorating poverty used to be more straight-forward with aid and resource transfers. Today, a more comprehensive approach is needed to impact poverty that would include government, NGOs, and businesses.

Macromarketing researchers have listed 50 solutions to poverty that have been pursued since the end of World War II, but the record of success for these solutions is weak overall when these are applied outside of relief situations (after natural disaster or war) to development projects. Part of this is a result of the contextual factors that have to be considered to understand poverty in each locale.

Social entrepreneurs such as Paul Polak have done extensive field research in the contexts of the poor in many Asian and African countries. He perceives commonality across the rural poor he has interviewed – poor farmers need more income. Toward this end, his International Development Enterprises have sought to boost the marketing effectiveness of poor farmers. Importantly, his market-based approach avoids the trap of paternalism (doing for others what they could do for themselves), as well as side-stepping corrupt government officials. Polak's wisdom about poverty alleviation approaches should encourage those taking the 'biggest M' approach to marketing and to poverty alleviation. In light of business' leading role in cross-border financial flows from developed to developing countries, it seems that market-based approaches to poverty alleviation will grow in importance in the coming years. Evidence for this can be seen in the US-based Millennium Challenge Corporation's new version of foreign aid that directs aid to private enterprises in qualifying countries rather than to foreign governments.

Social entrepreneurs offer many reasons to be hopeful about poverty alleviation efforts in the future. Because of the increasing interplay among governments, NGOs, and businesses in poverty alleviation, new hybrid forms combining aspects of for-profit and nonprofit have become more important in recent years. For-profits with a social overlay include cooperatives, benefit corporations (B corps), flexible purpose corporations, and low-profit limited-liability companies (L3C). Nonprofits with mission-related enterprises have businesses as subsidiaries that contribute to the budget of the nonprofit or, in some cases, provide surplus funds that are then reinvested in the programs of the nonprofits.

QUESTIONS

- Why do you think poverty alleviation has become a concern for business in recent years?
- What are the three poverty eradication myths proposed by Paul Polak?
- After examining the empowerment solutions on the right side of Table 12.2's Fifty Solutions to Poverty, which one do you think would have the most potential for poverty alleviation in the city or region in which you live? The least potential?
- What is the most surprising aspect of foreign aid that you learned in this chapter? Explain. What are the implications of this for business in the future? For NGOs? For governments?
- What are three aspects of the Millennium Challenge Corporation's approach to awarding and administering foreign aid that distinguish it from traditional approaches to foreign aid?
- Reviewing Figure 12.5, what is the most intriguing version of structure for social enterprises to you? If you started a venture with a social dimension, which one would you choose? Explain.

Mavericks Who Made It

Paul Polak

Source: ideglobal.org

Although he looked like someone's retired grandfather (he was), Paul Polak (who died at 86 in 2019) might have been one of the most effective alleviators of poverty to have ever lived (Hagerty, 2019). As an outsider, Polak has avoided many biases and flawed thinking about poverty swirling in the subculture of those desiring to alleviate poverty. For example, in the 1980s when Polak began working with poor people, many in development agencies considered business or solutions to poverty that included business as tainted or undesirable. Polak said:

> In the first twenty years of my work with IDE, development leaders were outraged by my notion that you can and should sell things to poor people at a fair market price instead of giving things to them for nothing. 'Business' was a dirty word to development organizations. I'm happy to say that all this is now changing. With the abject failure of central planning in socialist countries, there is a new awareness in development circles that unleashing the energy of the marketplace is the best help we can give to poor people in their efforts to escape poverty permanently.

> (Polak, 2008, pp. 39–40)

When he began his work with the poor, Polak did not bring any predetermined model of poverty alleviation. Instead, he dared to bring much of himself and his previous life experiences to his work with the poor. In his life, Polak had been a refugee (escaping from the Holocaust from what is now the Czech Republic), farmer, psychiatrist, businessperson (in real-estate rehabilitation), inventor (in the oil and gas industry), and entrepreneur. Polak would draw on learning in each of these realms of his life as he moved ahead as a social entrepreneur set to alleviate poverty.

(Continued)

Pursuing Opportunity

Polak inherited an entrepreneur's instincts for starting ventures from his father. As a 15-year-old living near Hamilton, Ontario, Polak enlisted the assistance of two local farmers who provided seven acres on which the three of them planted, fertilized, and harvested strawberries. Polak made an agreement with a large grocery and food distributor Loblaw's and became the principal supplier of strawberries for half of the 195,000 living in Hamilton at the time. At the end of two summers, Polak had earned $700 – equivalent to $7,000 now – and it seemed like a lot of money to him.

Polak's success as a teenage farmer gave him a deep appreciation for what it takes to run a small farm and make money. 'The challenges, opportunities, and hard work I experienced in the strawberry business mirror the challenges one-acre farmers face every day as they try to make a living from their scattered quarter-acre plots,' Polak said (Polak, 2008, p. 4).

Despite the advantages Polak had as a farmer, the lessons he learned about himself proved to be invaluable to him. 'I learned that learning new things every day brought me more pleasure and happiness than anything else I could do with my life,' Polak said (Polak, 2008, p. 4).

Polak followed his interest in learning new things all the way to medical school, where he earned a degree in psychiatry (McNeill, 2011). He moved to Denver, Colorado, and obtained a job working at the Fort Logan Mental Health Center.

In his work as a psychiatrist, Polak learned that he could be more influential in the lives of his patients if he understood the context in which they lived. 'I was one of the pioneers in treating people more effectively in real-life settings,' Polak said. He continued:

> The conventional assumption is that patients are admitted to psychiatric institutions because a therapist or family member says they're mentally ill. But I talked to a lot of our patients as if they were customers, and they defined something going on in their family or workplace as the primary reason they were there. So I started going into patients' homes or workplaces.

> (McNeill, 2011, p. D4)

Polak's instincts to consider his patients holistically and to treat them as a businessperson would – as customers with important perspectives – led him to recognize that many of his patients were very poor. This led to his interest in poverty and his first overseas trip to investigate poverty in 1981.

'My wife's a Mennonite, and they had programs in Bangladesh,' Polak said. 'It had hit me between the eyes that homeless people in Denver were living on $500 a month, but there were people overseas living on $30 a month. So I took a trip to Bangladesh' (McNeill, 2011, p. D4).

Doing What He Knows – Overseas

'I learned quickly that the best way to satisfy my curiosity about poverty is to have long conversations with poor people in the places where they live and work and dream, and to listen to what they have to say,' Polak said (Polak, 2008, p. 27). He continued:

Over 28 years, I've interviewed over 3,000 families. I spend about six hours with each one – walking with them through their fields, asking what they had for breakfast, how far their kids walk to school, what they feed their dog, what all their sources of income are. This is not rocket science. Any businessman knows this: You've got to talk to your customers.

(Polak, 2008, p. 27)

Polak distilled four simple points from his interviews with poor people (Polak, 2008, p. 10). First, the biggest reason people are poor is because they do not have enough money. Second, most of the extremely poor people in the world earn their current income from one-acre farms. Third, these one-acre farmers can earn much more if they find a way to grow and sell high-value, labor-intensive crops, such as off-season fruits and vegetables. Fourth, to do this, they need access to cheap, small-farm irrigation, good seeds and fertilizer, and markets (buyers) where they can sell these crops at a profit. Notably, each of these four points deals with business.

Each year since 1981, Polak interviewed at least 100 of IDE's small-acreage customers. 'All my ideas for projects that worked, and even some that didn't work, came from what I learned from these small-acreage farmers, and now all the people who work for IDE talk to and learn from these farmers every day,' Polak said (Polak, 2008, p. 23).

Over the years, Polak and his IDE team invented devices to help small-acreage farmers, such as drip-irrigation systems (a hose with small holes that leaks water slowly across an area) and a treadle pump (similar to a stair-climber apparatus for exercise, but one that pumps water from a well for irrigation). Polak and his team not only emphasize invention to assist in farming but also distribution and promotion. In the case of treadle pumps in Bangladesh, IDE created a private sector supply chain by energizing 75 small-scale manufacturers, more than 2,000 village dealers, and 3,000 well-drillers, all earning a living by making, selling, and installing treadle pumps at an unsubsidized, fair-market price of $25 each. Although told by development experts in 1985 that treadle pumps could never make a significant impact (because they irrigate only half an acre of land), more than 1.5 million treadle pumps now irrigate 750,000 acres at a fraction of the cost a dam/canal system would require to do the same thing.

Today, IDE is a global effort across 14 countries and employing more than 1,000 persons directly (IDE, 2020). IDE indirectly helps many more through its market-based approaches in agriculture, water, sanitation, hygiene, and finance. Since its beginning in 1982, IDE and its donors have directed $78 million to end rural poverty (Polak, 2008, p. 47). During the same time period, dollar-a-day/small-acreage farmers have invested $139 million in income-generating tools, such as the treadle pumps and drip-irrigation systems promoted by IDE. On these combined investments of $217 million, these small-acreage farmers have realized $288 million per year in permanent new net income.

'This is only a drop in the bucket in the context of 1.1 billion dollar-a-day people in the world,' Polak said. 'The good news is that potentially this approach can be scaled up to move 500 million or more rural dollar-a-day people out of poverty (Polak, 2008, p. 47).

(Continued)

Questions

- What elements in Polak's life have contributed to his success in poverty alleviation? Be specific. Explain how each of these might influence his entrepreneur's story.
- Why do you think Polak and IDE have had success in poverty alleviation in Asia and Africa when others with more resources have failed?
- How important is learning for Polak? How do you see evidence of this across his life?
- If you could ask Polak one question, what would it be?

REFERENCES

4 Lenses. (2020). The four lenses strategic framework. Accessed at www.4lenses.org/node/111

Acumen Fund. (2020). About Acumen. Accessed at https://acumen.org/about/

Ashoka. (2020). About us. Retrieved from http://ashoka.org/about

Associated Press. (2011). SKS founder and chairman Vikram Akula steps down as micro-lender struggles to revive itself. *The Washington Post*. Retrieved from www.washingtonpost.com

Astier, H. (2006, February 1). Can aid do more harm than good? *BBC News*. Retrieved from http://newsvote.bbc.co.uk

B Lab. (2020). About B Corps. Retrieved from https://bcorporation.net/about-b-corps

Baker/Sahabevava, A. (2018). Vanilla is nearly as expensive as sliver. That spells trouble for Madagascar. *Time*, June 13, 2018. Accessed at https://time.com/5308143/vanilla-price-climate-change-madagascar/

Barne, D. and Pirlea, F. (2019). Money sent home by workers now largest source of external financing in low- and middle-income countries (excluding China), World Bank Blogs, July 2, 2019. Accessed at https://blogs.worldbank.org/opendata/money-sent-home-workers-now-largest-source-external-financing-low-and-middle-income

Bomgardner, M.M. (2016). The problem with vanilla. *Chemical and Engineering News*, 94(36), September 12, 2016. Accessed at https://cen.acs.org/articles/94/i36/problem-vanilla.html

Bornstein, D. (2004). *How to change the world: Social entrepreneurs and the power of new ideas*. New York, NY: Oxford University Press.

Bornstein, D., and Davis, S. (2010). *Social entrepreneurship: What everyone needs to know*. New York, NY: Oxford University Press.

Bromberger, A.R. (2011, Spring). A new type of hybrid. *Stanford Social Innovation Review*, 9(3), 49–53.

Chung, A. (2010, January 26). Haiti: 10 years and $10 billion in aid? *The Toronto Star*. Retrieved from www.thestar.com/news/world/article/755860--haiti-10-years-and-10-billion-in-aid

Clark, S. (2011, November 7–13). An American rebel roils ethical commerce. *Bloomberg BusinessWeek*, 15.

Corbett, S., and Fikkert, B. (2014). *When helping hurts: How to alleviate poverty without hurting the poor... and yourself*. Chicago, IL: Moody Publishers.

Corkery, M. (2019). Chobani turns to fair-trade program to help struggling dairy industry. *The New York Times*, July 2, 2019. Accessed at www.nytimes.com/2019/07/02/business/chobani-fair-trade-yogurt-dairy.html

Danticat, E. (2020). Haiti faces difficult questions ten years after a devastating earthquake. *The New Yorker*, January 11, 2020. Accessed at www.newyorker.com/news/daily-comment/haiti-faces-difficult-questions-ten-years-after-a-devastating-earthquake

Dees, J.G. (1998). The meaning of social entrepreneurship. Retrieved from www.caseatduke.org/ documents/dees_SE.pdf

Easterly, W. (2006). *The white man's burden: Why the West's efforts to aid the rest have done so much ill and so little good*. New York, NY: Penguin Books.

Easton, N. (2011, November 21). Foreign aid, capitalist style. *Fortune*, 154–64.

Eschenbacher, S. (2020). Ten years after devastating quake, Haitians struggle to survive. *Reuters*, January 12, 2020. Accessed at www.reuters.com/article/us-haiti-quake-life/ten-years-after-devastating-quake-haitians-struggle-to-survive-idUSKBN1ZB0N0

Fairtrade International. (2020). 2019–2020 Annual Report, December 8, 2020. Accessed at www.fairtrade.net/library/2019-2020-annual-report

Field, A. (2019). The Chicago Reader, now an L3C, looks to combine social impact and expansion, *Forbes*, February 27, 2019. Accessed at www.forbes.com/sites/annefield/2019/02/27/the-chicago-reader-now-an-l3c-looks-to-combine-social-impact-and-expansion/#7a7c36f6328d

Fisher, I. (2011, February 11). Can international aid do more good than harm? *The New York Times*. Retrieved from www.nytimes.com

Fruchterman, J. (2011, Spring). For love or lucre. *Stanford Social Innovation Review*, 42–7.

Geiger-Oneto, S., and Arnould, E.J. (2011). Alternative trade organization and subjective quality of life: The case of Latin American coffee producers. *Journal of Macromarketing*, 31(3), 276–90.

Ghosh, S., and Antony, A. (2019). After rising 1,500%, IndusInd bets on microfinance firm buy to extend gains. *Business Standard*, July 24, 2019. Accessed at www.business-standard.com/article/finance/after-rising-1-500-indusind-bets-on-microfinance-firm-buy-to-extend-gains-119072400126_1.html

Gibson, C.C., Andersson, K., Ostrom, E., and Shivakumar, S. (2005). *The Samaritan's dilemma: The political economy of development aid*. New York, NY: Oxford University Press.

Habitat for Humanity. (2020). Habitat for Humanity fact sheet. Retrieved from www.habitat.org/how/factsheet.aspx

Hagerty, J.R. (2019). Paul Polak built better tools for farmers in poor countries. *The Wall Street Journal*, October 25, 2019. Accessed at www.wsj.com/articles/paul-polak-built-better-tools-for-farmers-in-poor-countries-11572013800

Haight, C. (2011, Summer). The problem with fair trade coffee. *Stanford Social Innovation Review*, 74–9.

Hamby, A., Pierce, M., and Brinberg, D. (2017). Solving complex problems: Enduring solutions through social entrepreneurship, community action, and social marketing. *Journal of Macromarketing*, 37(4), 369–80.

Harper, B. (2018). The Jesuit business network is fighting poverty in Africa and beyond. *America*, September 21, 2018. Accessed at www.americamagazine.org/politics-society/2018/09/21/jesuit-business-network-fighting-poverty-africa-and-beyond

HHS. (2020). HHS Poverty Guidelines for 2020. *U.S. federal poverty guidelines used to determine financial eligibility for certain federal programs*. Accessed at https://aspe.hhs.gov/poverty-guidelines

ICRC. (2020). The International Red Cross and Red Crescent Movement. Retrieved from www.icrc.org/en/who-we-are/movement

IDE. (2020). The bottom line. International Development Enterprises. Accessed at www.ide-global.org/story/measurement-and-evaluation

ITEP. (2019). 60 profitable Fortune 500 companies avoided all federal income taxes in 2018. Institute on Taxation and Economic Policy, April 11, 2019. Accessed at https://itep.org/notadime/

Karlan, D., and Appel, J. (2011). *More than good intentions: How a new economics is helping to solve global poverty*. New York, NY: Dutton.

Kelly, M. (2009). Not just for profit. *strategy+business*, 54, 1–10.

Kiva. (2020). Kiva website. Retrieved from www.Kiva.org/

Kotler, P., and Lee, N. R. (2009). *Up and out of poverty: The social marketing solution*. Upper Saddle River, NJ: Wharton School.

Kotler, P., Roberto, N., and Leisner, T. (2006). Alleviating poverty: A macro/micro marketing perspective. *Journal of Macromarketing*, 26(2), 233–9.

Laczniak, G.R., and Santos, J.N.C. (2011). The integrative justice model for marketing to the poor: An extension of S-D logic to distributive justice and macromarketing. *Journal of Macromarketing*, 31(2), 135–47.

Maddison, A. (2007). *The world economy: Historical statistics*. Paris, France: OECD. Retrieved from www.ggdc.net/maddison/other_books/new_HS-7.pdf

Malik, S. (2019). What the IndusInd-Bharat financial combine looks like. *Bloomberg Quint.* July 3, 2019. Accessed at www.bloombergquint.com/business/how-the-indusind-bharat-financial-merger-entity-looks-like

Marcum, T.M., and Blair, E.S. (2019). The value of values: An update on the L3C entity, its uses and possibilities. *UMKC Law Review*, 88, 927.

MCC. (2011). Millennium Challenge Corporation. Retrieved from www.mcc.gov.

MCC. (2020). MCC ranks first among U.S. agencies in the 2020 aid transparency index. *Millennium Challenge Corporation*, June 24, 2020. Accessed at www.mcc.gov/news-and-events/release/062420-2020-aid-transparency-index

McGee, L. (2007, June). Social entrepreneurship and macromarketing. Paper presented by Senior Marketing Officer – Ashoka. Macromarketing Society Conference, Washington, DC.

McNeill, D.G., Jr. (2011, September 27). An entrepreneur creating chances at a better life. *The New York Times*, D4.

McNeill, D.G., Jr. (2019). Paul Polak, entrepreneur for those living on $2 a day, dies at 86. *The New York Times*, October 20, 2019. Accessed at www.nytimes.com/2019/10/20/health/paul-polak-dies.html

Natsios, A.S. (2009, Fall). Public/private alliances transform aid. *Stanford Social Innovation Review*, 42–7.

NEO Law Group. (2015). California social purpose corporation: An overview. *Nonprofit Law Blog*, November 10, 2015. Accessed at https://nonprofitlawblog.com/california-social-purpose-corporation-an-overview/

Novogratz, J. (2011, October 24–30). Making a case for patient capital. *Bloomberg BusinessWeek*, 62.

OECD. (2019). Official development assistance (ODA). Accessed at www.oecd.org/dac/financing-sustainable-development/development-finance-standards/official-development-assistance.htm

Phills, J.A., Jr., Deiglmeier, K., and Miller, T.D. (2008, Fall). Rediscovering social innovation. *Stanford Social Innovation Review*, 34–43.

Polak, P. (2008). *Out of poverty: What works when traditional approaches fail.* San Francisco, CA: Berrett-Koehler.

Postrel, V. (2006, March 19). The poverty puzzle. *The New York Times*. Retrieved from www.nytimes.com

Prahalad, C.K. (2005). *The fortune at the bottom of the pyramid: Eradicating poverty through profits.* Upper Saddle River, NJ: Wharton School.

Rain, P. (2017). Is fair trade vanilla really fair? *The Vanilla Company*, January 21, 2017. Accessed at https://vanillaqueen.com/fair-trade-vanilla/

Reel, M. (2019). The wild economics of plain vanilla. *Bloomberg Businessweek*, December 23, 2019, 60–9.

Riddell, R.C. (2007). *Does foreign aid really work?* New York, NY: Oxford University Press.

Rose, C. (2011, December 5–11). Charlie Rose talks to Marc Benioff. *Bloomberg Business Week*, 52.

Ruvinsky, J. (2011, Summer). The new bottom billion. *Stanford Social Innovation Review*, 9.

Sabeti, H. (2011, November). The for-benefit enterprise. *Harvard Business Review*, 98–104.

Salesforce.org. (2020). Salesforce.org. About us. Accessed at www.salesforce.org/about-us/

Semega, J. Kollar, M., Creamer, J., and Mohanty, A. (2019). Income and poverty in the United States: 2018. United States Census Bureau, September 10, 2019. Accessed at www.census.gov/library/publications/2019/demo/p60-266.html#:~:text=The%20official%20poverty%20rate%20in,consecutive%20annual%20decline%20in%20povertyandtext=In%20 2018%2C%20there%20were%2038.1,million%20fewer%20people%20than%202017

SKS Microfinance. (2011). Know SKS. Retrieved from www.sksindia.com/know_sks.php

Szaky, T. (2009). *Revolution in a bottle*. New York, NY: Penguin Group.

Vogel, D. (2005). The market for virtue: The potential and limits of corporate social responsibility. Washington, DC: Brookings Institution Press.

Wall Street Journal. (2015). Financial inclusion challenge finalist: Kiva. June 15, 2015. Accessed at www.wsj.com/video/financial-inclusion-challenge-finalist-kiva/D7440226-C296-427E-A449-8F849D3D4D06.html

Wimmer, N. (2012). *Green energy for a billion poor: How Grameen Shakti created a winning model for social business*. Vaterstetten, Germany: MCRE Verlag.

World Bank. (2020a). Madagascar. Accessed at https://data.worldbank.org/country/madagascar

World Bank. (2020b). Net official development assistance and official aid received (constant 2015 US$). *World Bank*. Accessed at https://data.worldbank.org/indicator/DT.ODA. ALLD.KD

World Bank. (2020c). The World Bank in middle income countries. Accessed at www.world bank.org/en/country/mic/overview

Wroughton, L. (2010, February 10). World Bank maps out Haiti recovery plan. *The Vancouver Sun*. Retrieved from www.vancouversun.com

Yunus, M., and Weber, K. (2010). *Building a social business: The new kind of capitalism that serves humanity's most pressing needs*. New York, NY: PublicAffairs.

Index

Page numbers in *italics* refer to Figures and Tables.